5/06

LAPPING AMERICA

LAPPING AMERICA

Claude Clayton Smith

BURFORD BOOKS

Printed in the United States of America.

10 9 8 7 6 5 4 3 2 1

Library of Congress Cataloging-in-Publication Data
Smith, Claude Clayton, 1944–
        Lapping America / Claude Clayton Smith.
                p.   cm.
        ISBN 1-58080-139-0
        1. United States—Description and travel.   2. Smith,
Claude Clayton, 1944—Travel—United States.   3. United States—
History, Local.   4. Automobile driving on highways.   I. Title.

E169.Z82S625   2006
917.304'931—dc22   2005034449

In memory of my mother,
Jane Dorothy Kriss Smith,
whom I saw for the last time
while lapping America

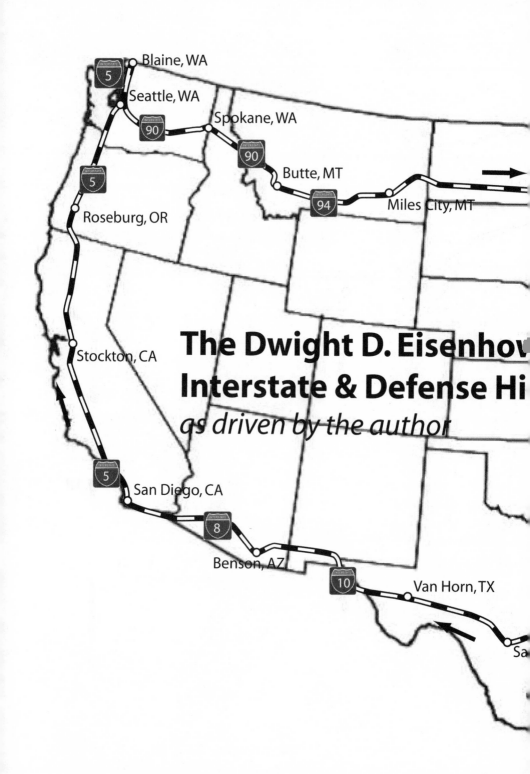

The Dwight D. Eisenhower
Interstate & Defense Highway
as driven by the author

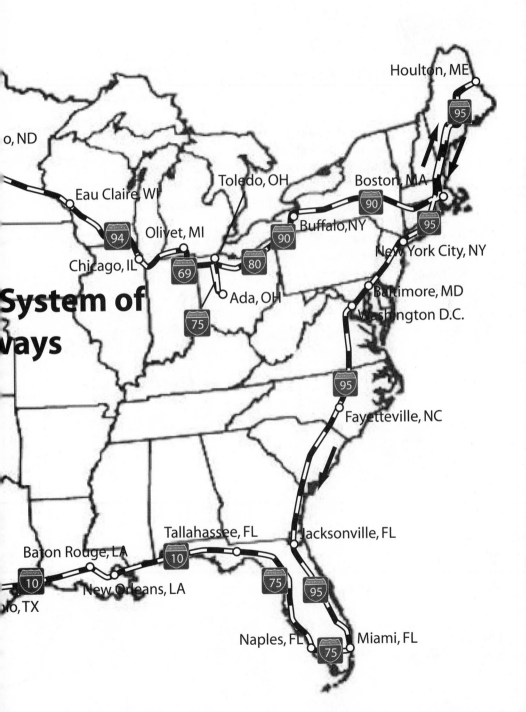

System of
ways

Houlton, ME

95

Boston, MA
90

Eau Claire, WI

Toledo, OH

94

Olivet, MI

Buffalo, NY
90

95

Chicago, IL
69

80

New York City, NY

Ada, OH

Baltimore, MD

75

Washington D.C.

95

Fayetteville, NC

Tallahassee, FL

Jacksonville, FL

Baton Rouge, LA

10

75

95

10

New Orleans, LA

o, TX

Naples, FL
75

Miami, FL

o, ND

Map by Robert Grannan

Acknowledgments

I am grateful to Ohio Northern University for granting me a sabbatical leave to pursue this project, and to The Anderson Center for Interdisciplinary Studies for a residency in which to complete the manuscript. I wish to thank, too, the people en route who offered their opinions of the Interstate System, and those relatives and friends whose warm hospitality provided a welcome alternative to anonymous motels. I am indebted, especially, to my wife Elaine for maintaining our "empty nest" while I was away, and for editing this manuscript, page by page, when I returned. Finally, I owe a big thank-you to Peter Burford, who made this book happen.

Brief sections of *Lapping America*, in slightly altered form, have appeared in *Full Circle, Delirium,* and the *Great River Review.*

—Claude Clayton Smith
Ada, Ohio

1

I THOUGHT I HAD COME UP WITH THE PERFECT VANITY PLATES FOR MY BIG trip—*LAP USA*. After all, that's exactly what I was doing, making a grand lap of America, one turn on the Interstates around the perimeter of the forty-eight states. But not everybody read those plates the same way. One college student at an Ohio rest area wanted to know what kind of laptop I was using. *He* had an Apple Powerbook G3/300 with third-generation power PC chips and he was going to speed-bump that puppy to 400 megahertz. What did I think of *that*? I told him I thought Megahertz was a giant car rental company and he shook his head in disgust. Then there was the woman of a certain profession at a Mississippi welcome center who offered to use my lap in any way I wanted. I respectfully declined. So much for vanity plates. *LAP USA*. I think next time I'll go incognito. But it's hard to do in a red Corvette.

* * *

U.S. Route 1, based on old Indian trails, runs the length of the eastern seaboard from Maine to Florida. In Stratford, Connecticut, it's known as the Boston Post Road and intersects Main Street near the center of town. As a kid I saw that intersection as the crossroads to the world. The arrow-shaped wooden signs said it all—*New York* to the right (55 miles), *Boston* to the left (160). Whenever I rode my bike to the dentist at the south end of town I'd have to negotiate that intersection, waiting for the red light to halt the world's traffic. I was never in a hurry. This was in the years before toothpaste with fluoride, when the candy readily available at my grandmother's house sent me to the dentist all too often. But crossing the Boston Post Road made it worthwhile. That intersection thrilled me—the cars, the trucks, the horns, the sigh of air brakes, the throaty rumbling of mufflers, the hot gritty exhaust—all careening into the madcap future. I would imagine myself one day pulling up to that red light in a vehicle of my own, turning left or right (the direction didn't matter) and striking out for exotic destinations.

And that day would come. Eventually. But my very first journey along U.S. Route 1 was courtesy of the Stratford Knot Hole Club, a summer excursion to New York City to see the invincible Yankees of yesteryear—Mantle and Berra, Bauer and Ford, Noren (off whose bat I once snagged a souvenir ball) and McDougald (whose daughter my cousin would one day marry). Casey Stengel led them and the boys of

Stratford loved them. But the annual pilgrimage, made by chartered bus along the Boston Post Road, was sheer agony—more than four hours of red light after red light, right through the business districts of Stratford, Bridgeport, Fairfield, Westport, Norwalk, Darien, Stamford, Greenwich, and finally the Bronx. One year we left right after breakfast and still missed the first inning, although game time was 2:00 p.m. The Yankee Stadium bleachers and relentless summer sun were as unbearable as that bus ride, making the trip home, which always ended in darkness, excruciatingly tedious, the game over, all expectation gone.

Then one day during dinner my father casually mentioned that in a few years we'd be able to drive to New York in less than an hour. We'd be able to drive from Stratford to *California* without a single red light. He'd been reading something in the newspaper about the Federal-Aid Highway Act. It was 1956, and President Eisenhower had just assured funding for the Interstate System. More than a decade earlier the Federal-Aid Highway Act of 1944—the year of my birth—had called for forty thousand miles of highways to serve the national defense. And now, finally, the system was going to be built. "Coast to coast without a red light," my father repeated. I didn't believe it. I didn't care about Eisenhower or California or the National Defense. But Yankee Stadium in an hour—*Wow!*

"The new highways," my father added, "will be *up in the sky.*" Incredible! I pictured roads crisscrossing the nation like the Golden Gate Bridge. Anything as prosaic and practical as ramps and over-passes was simply too dull to imagine. Through Connecticut the new road would be called *I-95*, and like U.S. Route 1 it would run from Maine to Florida, linking with similar roads all over America. "I-95," my father said, "will make Route 1 *obsolete.*" But I didn't know that big word. It'd be enough to take the Golden Gate Bridge to New York City. It'd be enough not to miss the first inning.

Construction began but, as with all construction, after a few days you get used to it, so I began to ignore the heavy equipment rumbling about Stratford—the dump trucks, road graders, bulldozers, cement mixers, the pickups with their noisy, tanned crews. A few years passed, my older brother got his driver's license, and a section of I-95 opened in Connecticut. I'll never forget my first ride. A friend had stopped by on his way to the local beach on Long Island Sound, beyond the den-tist's at the very end of Main Street. My brother said we'd meet him there shortly. Then he gave me a wink. What he really meant was that we'd *beat* him there.

We took the old family Chevy, but instead of wading through traffic lights along Main Street we got on I-95, flying up the entrance ramp as if blasting into outer space, suddenly finding ourselves on a wide, white expanse of newly minted concrete—two lanes east and two lanes west—divided by a ribbon of bright green grass. We hit sixty in no time, then coasted off the exit ramp a mile or so later, exhilarated by the thrill of the open road. It was just up and down, like Alan Shepard's first space flight—Exit 32 (West Broad Street) to Exit 30 (Surf Avenue)—but I felt like a full-fledged astronaut.

We beat that friend to the beach by fifteen minutes.

I have been in love with the Interstates ever since.

* * *

The Dwight D. Eisenhower System of Interstate and Defense Highways is the largest public works project in history, more extensive than the pyramids and the Great Wall of China. Eisenhower (I remember the *I LIKE IKE* buttons from my grammar school days) got the idea when he captured the Autobahn from the Germans during World War II, an idea he brought with him to the White House in 1952. As a young man he had driven across America—from Washington, DC, to California—in sixty-two days. As president, he envisioned forty thousand miles of high-speed divided highways, linking major cities all across the country, which would cut the trip to seventy-two hours.

The Department of Transportation's forty-year report issued in 1996 calls the Interstate System "the best investment a nation ever made." Without the Interstates, which touch all states except Alaska, "life in America would be far different—more risky, less prosperous, and lacking in efficiency and comfort." Although the Interstate System comprises only 1 percent of the existing roads in America, it carries 23 percent of all traffic, including nearly half of all tractor-trailer traffic. As for individual travel, the Interstates annually carry one trillion "person miles," the equivalent of around-the-world trips for thirty-seven million people, with a 70 percent lower injury rate than the rest of our roads. This makes the Interstates the safest component of our national transportation network.

In 1958 it was estimated that it would take $41 billion to complete the Interstate System. Through 1995 the project had cost $329 billion, or $58 billion in 1957 dollars. Adjusting for inflation, system revisions and additions, new environmental safety laws, relocation, and other requirements, the 1996 report finds the original estimate "amazingly accurate." And the impact on the economy has been dramatic. Each dollar spent on the Interstate System reduces product cost by more than twenty-three cents. As Alexis de Tocqueville prophetically observed in *Democracy in America*, the classic account of his 1831 visit to the United States, the roads ". . . play a prodigious part in the pros-

3

perity of the Union." Quality of life has also improved, as the Interstates give us more time, expanded mobility, and three times less pollution than stop-and-go traffic.

As for the National Defense, STAHNET—the U.S. military's Strategic Highway Corridor Network—relies primarily on the Interstates. The U.S. Army cited the Interstate System as critical to the success of operations Desert Shield and Desert Storm, and I presume it played a similar role during the wars in Kosovo, Afghanistan, and yet again in Iraq. As the 40-year report notes, "No constituent nation of the late Soviet Union has begun to develop such a comprehensive transportation system." I know that for a fact. On three occasions during the 1990's I traveled in Russia on roads that defy description, the very best of which are inferior to our worst Interstates.

In 1890, the year of Ike's birth, a "good roads movement" began in America, to free the country from the muck, mire, and potholes of dirt roads. At the turn of the century there were only 8,000 vehicles on the national landscape, but by 1929 the number had increased to 40 million. Today, more than 200 million vehicles vie for space on our highways. What's so exciting about the Interstates is the standards they engendered. As Eisenhower imagined the system, all roads would be four lanes, divided, with no intersections. There would be sweeping curves with adequate sight distances, and gentle grades so trucks would not have to lumber along and hold up traffic. Where needed, there would be extra lanes for slow vehicles. There would be no blind hills. Any rise in the distance that might block a driver's view would be leveled. Adjoining roadways of opposing traffic would be divided by a median, usually an unpaved center section. Lanes would be twelve feet wide, with ten-foot shoulders on both the median and outer edges. The roads would allow for scenic natural features and be designed for seventy miles per hour. Bridge clearance, originally set for thirteen feet, was raised to fourteen to accommodate vehicles carrying rockets. And one mile in every five would be a straight stretch to serve as a runway if necessary.

As my father used to say, "If you're going to do something, *do it right.*"

But it has been fashionable for American travel writers to denigrate the Interstate System. "From the beginning of my journey," John Steinbeck wrote in *Travels with Charley*, "I had avoided the great high-speed slashes of concrete and tar called 'throughways' and 'superhighways' [where the] nature of the road describes the nature of the travel. The straightness of the way, the swish of traffic, the unbroken speed are hypnotic, and while the miles peel off, an imperceptible exhaustion sets in." Although William Least Heat-Moon began his spiritual tour of

America's back roads on I-70 in Columbia, Missouri—"the fastest route east out of the homeland"—after that, as he wrote in *Blue Highways*, "the 42,500 miles of straight and wide could lead to hell for all I cared." The late Charles Kuralt, who based his journalistic career on America's blue highways, was equally blunt: "The interstate highway system is a wonderful thing. It makes it possible to go from coast to coast without seeing anything and meeting anybody. If the United States interests you, stay off the Interstates." Recent foreign travelers have been negative as well. "I disliked I-75 on sight," wrote Jonathan Raban in *Hunting Mister Heartbreak*. "It was flat, straight, crowded with trucks powering down from the big cities of Ohio and Indiana to Atlanta and Mobile. After less than an hour on this thundering racetrack, I was sleepwalking through the driving."

But Raban relied on the Interstates when it suited him, as did Steinbeck, Least Heat-Moon, and Kuralt before him, writers who didn't always put their motors where their mouths were. Raban had picked up I-75 in Tennessee, heading south to Chattanooga. His aim was to get there fast, which he did. Steinbeck used what is now I-90 to bypass Buffalo and Erie on his way to Ohio. Least Heat-Moon took I-64 through southern Illinois and Indiana, then looped Cincinnati "fast on the Interstate." Later, in New England, he actually fled to I-95 because he found U.S. Route 1—the dear old Boston Post Road—"too ugly." Kuralt depended on the Interstates each weekend to get to the nearest airport for a New York flight in time for his *Sunday Morning* TV program. He even did a story from I-90, stopping during a winter storm in Wyoming to film the blowing snow and record the sound of the wind. During that particular adventure a bloody woman emerged from the whiteout in a battered car—one of seventeen vehicles in a chain-reaction crash—and the CBS crew took care of her and helped rescue her dog. Good thing they had taken the Interstate.

Complain as you may, the Interstates aren't all flat, monotonous, and bumper to bumper nationwide. Not all 42,787 (at last count) miles. And you could only go without seeing *anything*, as Kuralt argued, by going blindfolded. As for meeting people, if you're so inclined, there are thousands of people to be met at the rest areas and service plazas, a more representative sample of the American population than you'll find on the blue highways. The idea that you can only meet *real* people—authentic, interesting people—"off the beaten path" is sheer hyperbole, a romantic and rhetorical ploy. Travel too far down America's back roads and you'll find the likes of David Koresh or the Unabomber. As somebody once said, local color can be black and blue. And red in the neck.

According to the Federal Highway Administration of the U.S. Department of Transportation, the Interstate System is "essentially complete," a phrase reflecting the fact that 99.98 percent of the planned highways is open to traffic. Officials are not, however, close to identifying where "the final mile" will be, although there is speculation that it could be the I-93 connector in the Boston area known as "the Big Dig," or an I-95 connector outside Philadelphia. At any rate, officials hope that the final section will be finished in time for the system's golden anniversary in 2006—"too far ahead," says Dwight A. Horne, chief of the Federal-Aid and Design Division, "to predict when or where to plan a ceremony, if one is desired."

It was Horne's last four words, written to me early in 1998, that spurred me to prepare for a 10,000-mile odyssey I had been dreaming about for twenty years, a grand lap of America—one turn on the Interstates around the perimeter of the contiguous forty-eight states—the America that existed in the backyard of my boyhood when the Interstate System was conceived. The millennium was approaching, and certainly the greatest public works project in the history of the world deserved special recognition, if not outright celebration. But in the face of twentieth-century tributes and reassessments of all kinds—the hundred best books, the hundred best films, the hundred best sports stars, etc.—where were the paeans to the Interstates?

I decided to take matters into my own hands, to get behind the wheel and make a dramatic 10,000-mile journey that would serve as a symbolic thank-you to those responsible for the Dwight D. Eisenhower System of Interstate and Defense Highways. Beginning south of Toledo, Ohio, on I-75, I would travel east via I-80 and I-90 and take I-95 from the Canadian border in Maine to its end in Miami. Then I would take I-75 out of Florida and head for San Diego via I-10 and I-8. From the Mexican border at Tijuana I would drive I-5 to the Canadian border north of Seattle, finally returning to Ohio—"the heart of it all"—via I-90 and I-94. In each corner of the country I would plant a small flag in honor of the Interstate System. My very route, were I to toss bread crumbs out the window, would create a map of America.

My choice of vehicle was symbolic as well—a 1996 torch-red six-speed LT4 Corvette coupe, with a black removable sunroof, an automobile I could ill afford. But I wanted to cruise the Interstates in the country's best car, one that represented—for better or worse—the speed, power, wealth, style, and mobility of millennial America itself. Purchased two months before departure, the 'Vette was virtually virginal—only 5,000 miles on the odometer—its black leather interior heady with new-car perfume.

But there were other reasons for my odyssey. I wanted to interview people all around the country about their opinions of the Interstate System, to see if the general public was as cynical about the Interstates as our travel writers. In the process I hoped to experience that ultimate Interstate pleasure—the perfect ride—those moments when the road is smooth, the traffic light, the weather gorgeous, and the scenery stunning, when time is transcended and the soul takes flight. I had experienced such moments before, on I-90 through the Mohawk River Valley in upstate New York and on I-81 through Virginia's Shenandoah Valley. Surely many more were waiting to be savored in the 10,000 miles I planned to travel. And I wanted to stop in Lowell, Massachusetts, to plant a flag at the grave of Jack Kerouac, author of *On the Road*, whose headlong drives across America before the Interstates even existed had inspired generations of road warriors, myself included. Finally, if I was going to fulfill my fantasy and lap America in a Corvette, I wanted to see how fast that Corvette could go. I had heard of places in our vast open states where speed limits don't exist, or if they *do* you can simply ignore them. I wanted to find such places and let the 'Vette do its thing. For the sheer hell of it. I wanted to open it up and blow some doors in.

Crazy? Some of my friends thought so, while others begged to come along. But I was committed to traveling alone—a lone dog without his Charley—as so many others had done before me. When I explained the project to John Updike, with whom I have corresponded intermittently for more than three decades, his response was less than sanguine. "As to the Dwight D. Eisenhower System of Interstate and Defense Highways," he wrote to me in 1999, "what a strange thing to love. It killed the railroads and turned the entire country into one big pinball game. Or rather it made it all as monotonous as Dwight's native Kansas. Still, good luck on your travels."

Undaunted, I was granted sabbatical leave for the fall of 1999 and made plans to take off soon after Labor Day, the traditional departure time for Steinbeck, Raban, *et al.*, when America "gets back to normal." Steinbeck, especially, irked me. He had claimed that superhighways *"promote the self* [my emphasis] by fostering daydreams." But that's precisely the point. They give you time to think. Not to promote but analyze. To clarify. To come to terms. And what better subject than one's self? What are our daydreams but a form of Zen reverie? Since my fall-quarter leave was for ten weeks only, I planned to circumnavigate the country in five, leaving time to process my notes and tape recordings. As it turned out, I completed the grand lap in thirty-three days. With world enough and time for introspection.

As Steinbeck concluded from his travels with Charley, "we know so little of our own geography." That was reason enough to go. To get the lay of the land. I wanted to see the USA in my Chevrolet and let the Interstates determine what I saw. But I was through rationalizing. It was time to hit the road. To lap up the landscape. To lap up America.

* * *

I left on a Monday—September 13, 1999—toward the end of a summer filled with disasters both natural and man-made. The East Coast was burning up, the West Coast was burning down, and the hurricane season was brewing in the Atlantic like a manic coffeepot. We had endured the loss of John-John, a string of mass murders, and were in the throes of the Y2K countdown. Hurricane Dennis had lingered through Labor Day, confounding the economy along the eastern seaboard, ending vacations prematurely, and sending children back to school in a sour mood. But in Ohio all was green and quiet. Our little village of Ada had somehow escaped the droughts that were ravaging the nation. The weather had been beautiful for days—blue skies and low humidity with temperatures no more than eighty—absolutely perfect for my departure. Until the very last minute.

Sunday night I woke to what sounded like rain on the roof. Then my big day dawned dark and drizzly, foggy and cold—Charles Lindbergh weather. An Internet check revealed that Hurricane Floyd was on the way, a Category 4 storm threatening to become a "Cat 5." Weather-watchers were unanimous in their warnings: "Keep a very, very close eye on the progress of this major hurricane!" But there was more. The season's ninth tropical depression had been upgraded to a tropical storm—*Gert*. I'd have to deal with both her and her big brother a week or so down the road. "No teeth for the present," I mused stoically, as Macbeth had said of Banquo's son.

Backing the 'Vette from the garage at eight-fifteen, I hit a switch and the headlights somersaulted out of the sleek hood to reveal the slanting rain. It was the first time I had used the headlights, the first time the car had ever been rained on. Not good vibes. In the headlights' full glare my wife and older son, who had not yet returned to college (our younger son was already on campus, beginning his freshman year), stood silhouetted in the garage like criminals, their shadows large on the wall. But there was only one criminal in our rural neighborhood that morning—*me*. I was abandoning home, job, and family (with everyone's blessing!) to pursue a long-standing personal dream. With a toot of the horn I slipped into the fog like a thief, then headed up Main Street to I-75, passing a colleague on her way in to work. She glanced at the 'Vette but didn't see me, the day dark enough without my tinted windows. I could imagine the classes she'd be teaching, the meetings she'd attend, and suddenly I was buoyant, gripped by a giddy sense of release. The brief encounter helped me focus on the task ahead. This woman's husband had argued that Interstate medians should be used for rail service, and as I reached the entrance ramp it seemed like an idea worth exploring.

I-75 to Toledo cuts through the wide-open outback of northwest Ohio. The terrain—mostly farmland planted with corn, wheat, and soybeans—is flat, but not oppressively so. In some places it might be said to *roll*, but I have a friend in Maryland who says I'm deceived by this, that I've been living in Ohio for too long. Still, the I-75 landscape has two distinct features I would see nowhere else in America. The first is an abundance of farm ponds. You see a farm pond every few minutes. At every entrance, exit, and overpass farm ponds hug the highway to either side. Some are fringed with cattails, others have sandy beaches, and a few are protected from the west wind by rows of white pine. The shorelines are ringed with *riprap*, chunky gray quarry stone that prevents the banks from eroding. Almost all are rectangular—some long and thin, others nearly square—but very few are round, the more natural shape you'd expect.

Why all the ponds? The answer is simple. When I-75 was constructed in the late '50s and early '60s, fill dirt was needed for access ramps and inclines. Rather than truck the dirt in, engineers dug it on the spot. The result was a host of "borrow pits," precise excavations several acres in size. Then nature took over. Rain and run-off turned the pits into farm ponds, and state officials worked with local farmers to stock them. If the farmers didn't want fish, the birds stocked them anyway. Migrating ducks and geese and other waterfowl encounter a good deal of fish eggs. When they take off, the fish go with them, populating the next pond down the road. At least that's what the biologists tell me.

The second feature—totally annoying compared with the pastoral farm ponds—is the woodlots. Having grown up back east, I'm used to forests that run on and on. You can't tell where they begin and you can't tell where they end. Eastern forests are continuous, but not so in northwest Ohio, where *forest* is entirely the wrong word. Trees occur across the horizon in scattered *woodlots* ranging in size from a few acres to several hundred. Ohio was once totally forested, but pioneers developed special methods of clear-cutting, notching trunks across a wide area so that the crash of a single tree would tumble many more like matchsticks. Once the land was cleared and the stumps had been exhumed, subsequent growths returned—where allowed—in neurotic units.

9

Hence the regular blocks of elm, oak, swamp maple, thorny locust, and tall cottonwoods that fill the air in summer with a pillowy fluff.

A landscape of woodlots takes some getting used to. Treed stretches end as abruptly as they begin—*end and begin, end and begin*. The discontinuity is irritating, offending some sensibility deep within the self in the way that small children are disturbed by disembodied figures. And the woodlots cause a more practical problem—they bring the deer out of hiding, in search of vegetation at the very next woodlot. In the early morning you can see the deer bounding from block to block, leaping above the corn, wheat, and soybeans. I used to mistake them for large dogs, but they're faster and more nimble. The Ohio Division of Wildlife estimates that there are half a million deer in the state right now. Everybody knows someone who's hit one with a car, if they haven't hit one themselves. Diamond-shaped yellow signs with the silhouette of a leaping buck warn you where they cross I-75.

But not this morning. In the rain and fog and spray of mist from the trucks I couldn't see those yellow signs, let alone the farm ponds and woodlots. Traffic was heavier than I had expected—as many trucks as cars—and construction areas demanded careful attention. Thanks to President Clinton's record $203 billion highway bill, summer motorists had been warned to expect construction on an average of every forty miles. It was still summer and the predictions proved correct. I encountered two such areas before I had gone fifty miles.

At nine-thirty I pulled into a rest area just south of Bowling Green. The outside temperature, according to my dashboard monitor, had risen to a damp sixty-five degrees. I-75 rest areas are welcome oases—entirely green, entirely clean. This one was no exception. Trucks to the left, cars to the right. Then an attractive brick comfort station, with picnic tables and charcoal grills along winding sidewalks through a grove of tall trees. I parked among a host of empty spaces at the far end of the lot, just beyond a green Corvette the same year as mine. Its driver, returning from the brick building, waved briefly and the unexpected gesture thrilled me, my first ever from a fellow 'Vette owner, confirming my membership in some sort of club. In the weeks to come I would count fifty-eight Corvettes around the nation—mostly in Texas and Florida—exchanging salutes with many of the drivers. But that initial nod of recognition seemed to validate my mission, a moment of Corvette karma that dispelled the uncertainty I was beginning to feel about getting out of my own 'Vette to ask total strangers about the Interstates.

I had begun my interviews at home, surprised by my wife's negative response. But the fault was my own. In my enthusiasm for the Interstates, I had completely forgotten Elaine's Interstate traumas. But they were twenty years ago!

"How could you forget?" she said in disbelief. "I was pregnant with Owen when I hit that icy bridge on I-270."

We were living in Rockville, Maryland, at the time, and she was on her way to work. It had begun to snow. The long curving bridge that connects I-270 to the I-495 D.C. Beltway had glazed over, and its tooth-like expansion joints sent our old Impala into a spin. The car struck the left abutment while a tractor trailer slipped by on the right, then hit the right abutment as another trailer past on the left. Elaine escaped with a concussion, Owen safe in her womb, but the Impala was demolished.

"And then there was that guy on I-81," she continued. "Remember? Right after we moved to Virginia? I was going up to Roanoke in the Monza. Owen was strapped into his car seat beside me, when that creep in a Jeep-like vehicle pulled alongside."

The creep was masturbating, keeping pace with the Monza so Elaine couldn't miss the show. It did nothing for her appreciation of Interstate highways.

I turned to Owen for help. "You were along for the ride on both those occasions," I said. "What do *you* think?"

"Of the Interstates?"

"Yes."

"Well—" Owen thought for a moment. "I guess my stance is more philosophical than Mom's." He'd been commuting two hundred miles round trip down I-75 to an internship in Dayton. "I see the Interstates as *the Great Inbetween*. I'm sort of mystified by the contrast between their impersonal nature and the aesthetic appeal of the symmetry of moving vehicles."

I turned to Elaine, who laughed and shook her head. "Men!"

"Why don't you ask Adrian?" Owen suggested.

So I asked his brother Adrian, who had just got his driver's license. "For me," he said, "the Interstates are simply fast and exciting. They turn a routine run up I-75 to the Findlay Mall into a big adventure."

In contrast to my family, one of my colleagues dismissed my query outright. "The trucks have ruined the Interstates," he barked. "You'll see!"

Out of the rain in the brick building, I approached an attractive young woman by the water fountain. "The Interstates?" she said. "I don't know. I slept most of the way. *He* drove." She nodded at her husband, who was exiting the men's room, staring at me as if I was trying to pick up his wife. Remembering my own wife's trauma, I suddenly became self-conscious. The last thing I wanted was to become an Interstate intimidator.

"We drove all night from Florida," the husband said bluntly, reclaiming his wife by putting an arm around her shoulder. "We're heading home to Michigan. The Interstates are less crowded at night because the trucks pull off to sleep. There are no towns, no stops, so it's an easy roll. A straight shot home. Ready, honey?" He turned his back on me and they walked away.

An elderly Canadian gentleman, waiting for his wife, was less threatened by me. "The Interstates are the only roads we ever take for any distance," he said. "They're clean, well serviced, and in good shape. We're just returning from Branson, Missouri."

Outside again—the rain had let up—I explained to a lanky trucker and his shorter driving partner what my colleague had said about trucks ruining the Interstates.

"You tell that guy," the tall one said, "that everything in his home is delivered by trucks. The railroads can't do it as fast. The economy would fold without trucks on the Interstates."

His partner tugged on the bill of his cap, anxious to get back on the road. "The main problem for us is the damn construction. It's dangerous 'cause it takes so long to get done. They's always draggin' their feet. Meanwhile, people's gettin' killed."

On my way back to the 'Vette I took note of two signs. One said *Welcome To Ohio . . . The Heart Of It All*, a message repeated in German, Spanish, Japanese, French, and Italian—the only Interstate sign I would see in all of America in more than two languages. The second, which I'd see more frequently, said *The Dwight D. Eisenhower System of Interstate Highways*, its words surrounded by five white stars for the five-star general. Having never served in the military, I gave it my best Corvette salute.

It started raining again—hard—as I continued north to Toledo, where I picked up I-80 and my grand lap officially began. Until then I had felt like Sal Paradise in Jack Kerouac's *On the Road*: "All the way up I'd been worried about the fact that on this, my big opening day, I was only moving north." It was the late '40s and Sal was headed west. But I was heading east. Why? Why not lap America counterclockwise? Except for a few hundred miles between Albany and Boston and again between Orono, Maine, and the Canadian border, I was familiar with the Interstates on the first leg of my journey as far as Savannah, Georgia. By heading east I was saving the best for last. Beyond Savannah—if anything was left down there after Floyd and Gert had done their dirt—the thousands of miles remaining would be new for me all the way around to Chicago, just five hours from home.

Stopping for a ticket at the tollbooth, I was overwhelmed by a sense of occasion. I imagined myself in one of those toy Hot Wheels Corvettes on a huge relief map of America—large enough to cover an entire basketball court—with its raised mountain ranges, color-coded elevations, and long blue rivers. My little car was pointing east from Toledo and I had ten thousand miles ahead of me, the entire circumference of the forty-eight states. As I plucked the ticket from the automatic metal mouth, I was struck by the enormity of what I was undertaking. Then the ticket was in my shirt pocket and I flew from the gate.

I-80—the Ohio Turnpike—is a toll road that doubles as I-90 until Cleveland. It was undergoing major construction. A third lane was being added, service plazas were being renovated, and interchanges were being renumbered to conform to Federal Highway Administration standards. The most disturbing result of these improvements was the absence of a median strip. The shallow V-shaped grassy divider I had taken for granted on I-75 had been sacrificed for extra lanes, paved over and replaced by a low concrete wall. This put the opposing traffic at what seemed like arm's length, and with nothing but mudguards and mist surrounding me for miles, I sought relief shortly before noon at the Commodore Perry Travel Center.

I was glad I stopped. The place was brand new. The former service plaza, with room for dozens of trucks and hundreds of cars, had shut you in like a prisoner, its sprawling ugly buildings devoid of windows. The new facility looks like a community college, its main redbrick building centered on a bright rotunda-like dome that opens to the sky like an observation deck. Three porte cocheres extend from the dome toward ample parking areas, each offering a separate entrance, skylights, and protection from the weather. Inside, the smoke-free environment requires proper dress, and the concept of a travel center is more than a euphemism. There are sparkling restrooms, telephones, a business area, ATM machines, copy machines, Internet access, postal services, a game room, a vending area, and an information desk. But the main attraction is the domed "food court," with all the glassy high-ceilinged ambience of a swanky mall in a modern airport terminal. Businesses include Starbucks Coffee, Burger King, Jodi Maroni's (home of the *haut dog*), Cinnabon, Sbarro's, and Max & Irma's. Tables and chairs extend outside for patio dining. Gasoline pumps and service bays, equally open and accessible, lie beyond. Farthest off is the pet "exercise area," and there's even a kennel. New trees and shrubs had been planted, but the grass seed had not yet germinated. Above the main entrance stood a tall white concrete sculpture—three narrow obelisks each taller than the next—like X-Acto knives or the tail fins of jets. I couldn't quite figure it out. It seemed to reflect the Wright Brothers more than Commodore Perry, local hero of the War of 1812. Still, any effort at art in public places must be applauded. Inside, I stopped to inquire about the sculpture, but the information desk was unattended. Drop me a note if you know what that thing is.

By the time I returned to the 'Vette the rain had stopped, the sun was threatening to break through, and the temperature had risen to seventy. A flock of seagulls was scavenging in the freshly paved parking lot, an incongruous presence. But Lake Erie, never seen from I-80, is just a few miles north.

At one o'clock I paid a $2.95 toll and left I-80 on I-90 for Cleveland. In clear weather you can glimpse Cleveland from twenty miles out—a nondescript brown skyline—but today's overcast made it impossible. Like many Rust Belt cities Cleveland comes at you with a bleak median divider, dirty brick factories, smokestacks, cranes, and rows and rows of Archie Bunker houses. Then a high bridge over the Cuyahoga River gorge dumps you downtown in a maze of viaducts and overpasses. Buildings fly by—a tall structure like New York's Chrysler Building, a more attractive stair-step affair, and some glassy modern fronts that have not yet lost their shine. Below and left sit Jacobs Field and Gund Arena. But I had little time for rubbernecking. The road surface was horrendous—beat-up and bone-jarring—the worst I would see until New Orleans. The *Places Rated Almanac* had just named Cleveland the No. 2 recreation area in the nation, second only to (no surprise here) New Orleans. All those visitors must account for the battered roads, which local drivers seem to ignore. Meanwhile, my back was taking a severe pounding.

The Corvette, because it rides so low, is notorious for its rough ride, although late-model engineering has addressed that problem. My 'Vette had sports seats, which inflate in crucial places—at the base of the spine, midback, and between the shoulder blades. They also push up at the waist, as if you're being hugged by someone standing in front of you. Having twice had back surgery for a herniated disk, the latest operation coming—according to plan—just six weeks before departure, I could never have driven a 'Vette without sports seats. But the Interstate through Cleveland put me in such pain I had visions of having to abandon my grand lap on the very first day—like those round-the-world balloonists who abort their flight after lift-off due to some colossal mechanical failure. Or error in judgment.

Ignoring the potholes and slick pavement, the midday traffic whizzed by. A woman in a white car cut in front of me, gesticulating wildly, cigarette in one hand, cell phone in the other. *So who's driving?* I wondered. It's impossible to signal with a cell phone in your hand. That's one reason that death by cell phone has increased more rapidly than death by road rage. The Cleveland suburb of Brooklyn had recently passed a law prohibiting driving with handheld phones, the first such legislation in the nation. Obviously this woman wasn't from Brooklyn. I had a notion to send her the article about the new law that I'd clipped from the paper, but she swerved—once again without signaling—cutting off the guy on my right. Then she was gone before I could get her license number.

Leaving Cleveland brings an Interstate surprise. The road cuts sharply to the right and suddenly Lake Erie's on your left not a hundred yards away—a wall of dark water all the way to the horizon, a quivering meniscus on the beaker of Ohio. I thought of the little Dutch boy with his finger in the dike. Remove that finger and I-90 would wash away! Then Lake Erie plays peek-a-boo with the trees and waterfront homes—brimming along rock jetties, beaches, and boats—before it disappears for good behind a long tan wall. That wall runs for miles, ragged trees rising above its stucco surface. Built for privacy, or as a sound barrier, or to block pollution and headlights, it's the type of urban Interstate wall I would see all too frequently. This one varies in height from about six feet to sixteen. But the variety does nothing for the aesthetics.

Fortunately, the pavement smoothed out beyond the Cleveland city limits and I dismissed my back pain as opening-day tension. At two o'clock I stopped at a rest area to stretch and recover, in the process learning something about the Interstates without having to ask. A bespectacled teenager approached me, wanting to know if he was on the road to Chagrin Falls. I took out my atlas, placed it on the roof of the 'Vette, and opened it to Ohio. "You are *here*," I said, stabbing a finger at the page, "and you want to be *there*. You missed your turn. You have to go a little farther and turn around." He looked at me quizzically, disconcerted.

"I know all that," he said finally. "I have a map and directions in the car. I'm looking for someone I can follow to get back on route."

I tossed the atlas into the car. "Sorry," I said. "I need the men's room."

He was gone when I came out, but a second young man approached me, looking like a college freshman late for his first class. I know that look, because I teach a lot of freshmen who are late for their first class. Incredibly, he too was lost. He needed to turn around and go back to the Mentor exit.

"You just missed your ride," I said, explaining about the other guy to make him feel better.

The obvious lesson is that, for some people, the Interstates can be totally disorienting. And ironically amusing. One traveler was chagrined on his way to Chagrin Falls. The other needed a mentor. And the latter wouldn't let me go, lapsing into a discourse about his laptop computer when he saw the vanity plates on the 'Vette. It took a facetious pun to get rid of him.

Back on the highway I learned from National Public Radio that Gert was now officially the fifth hurricane of the season. But Floyd was coming first, with winds of a hundred fifty-five miles per hour. And just when it looked like the weather at least might clear up in Ohio, all vehicles streaming at me from Erie had their headlights on. It was raining to the east, the sky gray overhead but much darker in the distance. Good old dreary Erie, more than an hour away but already living up to its reputation. Some definite confluence of weather elements, moving west to east across America, funnels all bad weather through the Great Lakes to Erie. You can actually watch it happening from the Interstate, where the meteorology is more reliable than on the six o'clock news.

* * *

Before we leave Ohio here's an Interstate Item, from an article by Mark Williams of the Associated Press, regarding the completion of I-670 through downtown Columbus, the state capital:

Finishing the half-mile stretch will mark the end of nearly 50 years of construction of Ohio's Interstate System, and Clark Street, president of the Ohio Contractors Association and a former transportation executive, didn't think he'd live to see the day.

As was the case across the nation, most of Ohio's 1,300 miles of Interstate were built in the 1950s, '60s and '70s.

Interstate 670 was designed through Columbus with economic development in mind, to make it easier to reach the northwest side of town, a major growth area. The connector runs from Interstate 70 on the city's west side to Interstate 270 on the northeast side near Port Columbus International Airport.

Planning for the final segment began in 1965, with construction to begin in 1976, but a variety of problems, from funding to environmental concerns, postponed the start until 1993. According to Street, completion of the Interstate System in Ohio is a tribute to the people who planned it, the contractors who built it, and the public who paid for it.

Street concluded with a fascinating thought: An entire generation of Americans has grown up thinking that the Interstates have always existed.

Through the northwest corner of Pennsylvania and up the east coast of Lake Erie, I-90 traverses some lovely stretches of rolling country. The traffic finally thins out, the median is wide and grassy, and tall trees flank the highway—forests, not woodlots. The only annoyance is a recurring billboard—Niagara Falls Information. *EXIT NOW!* You never see Erie, but you know you've passed it when the weather improves. In this case, the rain gave way to gray mist. Visibility was limited, nearly obscuring the lush acres of waist-high vineyards that appear as if on cue across the New York line, where I-90 becomes the New York State Thruway. Green and leafy, the orderly rows of grapes looked like soybeans. But this was a new crop, a new agricultural zone, and a bumper sticker ahead of me confirmed it—*Vineyarders*, nickname of local sports teams. A refreshing change from all the *Bulldogs* of Ohio.

Stopping for coffee at a McDonald's about four in the afternoon I encountered a tour bus of elderly people. In early August the Midwest coach lines begin booking autumn Interstate excursions, but it was too early for colorful foliage. This group was going gambling at one of the Indian reservations, and the two teenage boys behind the counter—just reporting for work—were overwhelmed by the onslaught. "I'm on from four to eleven and I got a ton of homework," one complained. "Me too!" the other retorted. I could imagine them up past midnight, asleep in class the next day—destined for a future in the vineyards instead of college—and I had to remind myself that, for the next few weeks at least, I was exempt from worrying about anyone's education. Except my own.

By five-fifteen I had reached my goal for the day, an exit just east of Buffalo—three hundred seventy miles from Ada and out of range of tomorrow morning's rush hour. But to get there I had to endure the evening crunch. It was dark and drab and raining again. Police cars, fire engines, and ambulances clogged traffic in the southbound lanes, their flashing lights softly flaring in the slick pavement. As with Erie, I-90 skirts Buffalo, so you never see the city. The posted speed drops from sixty-five to fifty-five and a single concrete barrier divides the traffic. Overhead power lines and suburban bungalows set a blue-collar tone. There's another wall, only shorter than Cleveland's—light bronze, at a constant height, with segmented columns. I paid a toll of $2.10 and dropped my change in the rain, letting it roll where it might. A motorcycle had skidded off the highway, its leather-jacketed rider sitting under a bridge out of the weather, helmet in hand, beside his battered bike. A mile or so later I paid another toll of just fifteen cents and left I-90.

17

The problem with getting *on* the Interstates is that you have to get *off* them. This results in what I call an *Interstate ambush*, especially in urban areas in the late afternoon. The exit dumps you on a four-lane highway lined with every gas station, motel, and fast-food chain known to mankind. Moments earlier you were cruising at top speed but now you're stuck in a local gridlock, you don't know your way, and you're searching for Motel Find-Me-Not. The name of the chain doesn't matter (in lapping America I would deal with them all) because even if you *could* see its sign above all the other garish signs, you simply can't get there from here. The Motel Find-Me-Not directory says only this: *Exit I-90 at State Route So-and-So.* But there's a red light at the exit and you must turn left or right. Rain is drumming on the roof and there's a tractor-trailer on your rear. The light turns green, you hang a left on a whim, and the traffic sweeps you away in the wrong direction. Ten minutes later you stop at a gas station to phone Motel Find-Me-Not, where the local teenager at the desk is amused by your plight. *"We're right at the exit,"* she says brightly. *"You went the wrong way!"* It takes you another ten minutes to get turned around, waiting for the lights to let you re-cross two lanes of opposing traffic plus the perilous center turning lane. But when you reach the Interstate exit, Motel Find-Me-Not's still not there. So you stop at a fast-food place across from the traffic light. Fortunately there's a teenager out front with a squeegee, washing the large plate-glass windows despite all the rain. So you power down your own window and yell, *"Where the hell is Motel Find-Me-Not!"* And the teenager laughs, *"Right behind us!"* So you circle the parking lot and see the sign for Motel Find-Me-Not high in the trees. But the parking lot's fenced in. You can't get there from here either. So you circle out front again where the teenager's still washing windows in the rain. *"How do you get there?"* you scream. *"I don't know!"* he screams back. *"I only work here!"* And then you see it—the skinny access road catty-corner to the exit, between the fast-food parking lot and westbound Interstate entrance. You'll be certain to see it next time.

That's how I arrived in Buffalo. And too many other destinations en route. For which there wouldn't *be* a next time.

2

THE EASIEST PART OF ANY LENGTHY ADVENTURE IS THE FIRST DAY OUT. AFTER years OF planning and months of final preparation, it brings its own excitement and adrenaline. The toughest day is the second—when you wake up exhausted and realize you have to do it all over again.

I got out of bed at five-thirty and turned on the Weather Channel. Floyd was coming out of the Caribbean like a runaway weedeater, just shy of "Cat 5." Gert too was gaining force, five to six days behind. Outside, it was damp and chilly. To loosen up, I took a half-hour "power walk" around the motel, weird snippets of restless dreams revolving in my head. I had felt the 'Vette moving beneath me all night long.

Cars, vans, and small trucks filled every space in the parking lot, and a host of truckers and businessmen were already up and about, departing before dawn. I-90 thrummed with activity too, headlights glaring in the darkness on the embankment high above me. Splashing through puddles from yesterday's rain, I made an unscientific study as I walked. Of the first fifty vehicles that swished by overhead, thirty were trucks.

Back inside, sipping free coffee at the desk, I asked the portly clerk what he thought about the Interstates. He scratched his head, then laughed.

"Between Chicago and St. Louis, I-55 is pure water torture. It's so flat it looks like they ironed it. On the other hand, I-70 through Colorado is miraculous, how they cut it through the Rockies. In 1954, when I was just a kid, we drove out to Colorado. It took forever. Just think of the pioneers out there in their covered wagons. They must have been overwhelmed! Today you can cross those mountains in a few hours. But you can't relax on the Interstates. Not at seventy-five miles per hour. If you're in a car, you're a minority. We always get off to relax."

A man in a blue suit approached the desk, ready to check out, so I left the office and hopped the fence to catch breakfast at the fast-food place. By eight o'clock I was on the road, the sun breaking through to glisten on the dew-laden hills. Mists rose like ghosts from charming farms in the valleys, and for a pristine moment, with the rising sun in my eyes, the world before me resembled a nineteenth-century painting. Broad shafts of sunlight flooded the countryside. But the effect waned as the sun rose higher, and I could tell it would be another drab day. Traffic was heavy in both directions, buzzing with the inexhaustible energy of workaday America.

On his U.S.-Canadian lecture series in 1883, the British poet Matthew Arnold remarked on the many places with classical names across upstate New York, places I would pass as I continued east— *Corfu, Troy, Syracuse, Ithaca, Attica, Verona, Rome.* "The folly," Arnold claimed, "is due to a surveyor who, when the country was laid out, happened to possess a classical dictionary." But Arnold preferred that surveyor's approach to the American penchant for naming everything with a *ville* on the end, including my New York favorites, *Buggsville* and *Shortsville.* The latter, perhaps, had been founded by dwarfs. Or underwear manufacturers.

One bonus of Interstate travel is the historical information many states offer. New York puts up large square plaques titled *Historic New York,* all in easy-to-read raised bronze letters. The one at the Clifton Springs Service Center waxes poetic, discussing *the narrow and sparkling Finger Lakes* that run north to south through the valleys of central New York, *bordered by beautiful sloping shorelines cut by picturesque glens and gorges.* They include Lake Seneca, one of the deepest bodies of water in America. The plaque also explains how, in the eighteenth century, the Iroquois nation was devastated in retaliation for raids along the American frontier. And how, a century later, construction of feeder canals linked the Finger Lakes to the Erie Canal, spurring agricultural and industrial development. The local soil and climate made the region ideal for growing grapes. Hence the vineyards that grace the rolling landscape for miles.

In the Clifton Springs men's room I overheard a young man excitedly addressing his friend:

"So we're leaving the game and we just won by two touchdowns and Ray goes up to this old lady—she's about sixty-five or more—and plants this big kiss *smack in the middle* of her face! She's stunned for a minute, then she puts her arm around him and asks if he's married. It was the kind of thing where he was either gonna get arrested or she'd play along. Then she really got friendly and he couldn't get rid of her!"

Outside at the gas pumps a young male attendant was equally excited about I-90.

"The New York State Thruway," he told me, "is one of the better roads. It's well paved and well maintained, especially in winter. At the first drop of snow the plows and salt trucks are out. They don't joke around. Some people complain about the tolls, but I can't see why. You get service areas every twenty-five miles or so, and they meet all your needs. If you break down, they get you right off the highway. What more could you ask?"

"You like working here?"

"Love it."

"Why?"

"You wouldn't believe what goes on around here, in places like this."

"Such as?"

"Like last summer, for instance. I was on the night shift. It was hot as hell, and sometime after midnight these three chicks pull in, buck naked, in a convertible. With the top down."

"And their tops *off*."

The attendant grinned. "The driver pulls a tee shirt over her head, wiggles into a pair of cut-off jeans, and hops out barefoot to fill the tank. The other two—one in the front and one in the back—hit the floor. The chick at the pump sees me gawking and says, 'Take a picture. It'll last longer.'" He grinned again, talking rapidly as I turned to leave. "Always somethin' happenin'—and some of it's sad."

"Such as?"

"Like people abandoning their old folks."

"On purpose?"

"They just drive in here and leave 'em. It's a bigger problem than people think, all over the Interstates. A lot of the folks have that *whatchamacallit*—that don't-remember-nuthin' disease."

"Alzheimer's?"

"That's it."

"They always get left when the place's busy as hell. And once it quiets down they start wanderin' around. The people who leave 'em are sharp—they cut the labels off their clothes, so there's no way to identify 'em. And those old folks, they don't know who the hell they are."

The attendant was in his late teens, a high school dropout. Getting an Interstate education.

"One last thing," he said. "A scary thing. A friend of mine told me about it. He works at a place like this, outside Albany. He helped me find this job. He was on duty one night when a big old Cadillac comes roarin' up to the pumps, and this big old O.C.N. gets out and—"

"O.C.N.?"

"Never heard of that?"

I shook my head.

"*Order of the Crimson Nape.* What we call a *redneck*."

"Gotcha."

"This guy's in a big hurry, and when he runs inside to take a leak, my friend runs over by the car. There was a black woman in the back seat, bound and gagged. My friend got the hell out of there just before the O.C.N. came out again. He called the police as soon as they left, and the woman was rescued."

"Did your friend get a reward?"

"No such luck. She never even said thank you."

After a short walk I continued toward Syracuse, the traffic light to moderate, the day still gray. An inspiring glimpse of history lay just off the highway—an actual lock of the old Erie Canal, a wall of gray stone exposed like an archaeological dig. Farther along, I-90 crosses the Erie Canal itself, a narrow dark river, and in the vicinity I encountered one of the strangest vehicles I've ever seen, an old Greyhound bus in a blue paisley pattern. Painted across the rear was a child's sad face pressed against a chain-link fence, a young boy with haunting dark eyes. Above the fence, black letters said *Siloam*.

It was a vehicle right out of the '60s, like the bus of Ken Kesey and his Merry Pranksters. But this one was on a more serious mission. *Siloam* is a pool in Jerusalem where Jesus sent a blind man to wash himself in order to regain his sight. The message seemed clear: *Wake up, world! Don't be blind to oppression, for it's always the children who suffer!* Across the front of the bus a marquee specified a destination, but I couldn't decipher it backwards in my rearview mirror as I sped by.

Siloam. Shalom. Shanti, shanti.

By the time I stopped at the Oneida Service Center, the gray day had given way to mist and drizzle. It was after eleven and everyone in the coffee shop was intent on the television. The weatherman was adamant: "Keep an eye on Hurricane Floyd if you're traveling anywhere from Maine to Florida!" And I was traveling *everywhere* from Maine to Florida. I had thought I might outrun Floyd in the distant Northeast, but now I wasn't so sure. The present wet weather, much needed due to widespread droughts, was unrelated to the storm. Which meant it could only get worse.

I distracted myself by asking folks about the Interstates.

"I really enjoy the life," a pot-bellied trucker told me. "I been on the road for twenty-one years. It's only the construction that gets me. But the scenery's great. I seen all forty-eight states on the Interstates and always enjoy the different people I meet. Worst thing I ever seen was an accident in Arizona where three semi's piled up and all three drivers got killed. They was doin' over a hunnert. You goin' through Arizona? You'll love it."

Two young women on their way to Boston from California agreed about the construction. As soon as I saw them I thought of the Lady Godiva trio back down the highway. But they had their clothes on.

"The construction's a bummer," one said. "It slows you down for miles and miles for only a quarter mile of work! They can't get their efforts coordinated."

"But the scenery's terrific," the other chimed in. "I've been absolutely blown away by the scenery! I get mad when it gets dark and I can't see any more! We've been driving straight through, you know? But Montana's boring. You won't like Montana. And Chicago—Chicago's definitely messy. It's nothing to look forward to."

What I *had* been looking forward to was the Mohawk Valley, the most scenic stretch of I-90 through upstate New York, where the central plateau region gives way to rolling mountains and the highway follows the Mohawk River for miles, crossing and re-crossing it, traversing high gorges and funneling through rock ledges. Blasted from the hillsides, the vertical ledges have a beauty all their own—sharp edges and angles, striated colors, light and shadow on dripping water and moss. In July 1804, writing to his mother from America, the Irish lyrist and author Thomas Moore was ecstatic about his journey along the Mohawk: *Never did I feel my heart in a better tone of sensibility than that which is derived from the scenery on this river. There is a holy magnificence in the immense bank of woods that overhang it, which carries the heart to that satisfactory source of all these exquisite wonders, a Divinity!*

I had hoped for such reverie along the Mohawk myself. But all I saw was drizzle and mist. And a bumper sticker stating the obvious. *Mean People Suck.*

Then, like a miracle, the sun came out west of Albany. I seemed to have outrun the bad weather. The traffic thinned to a handful of cars, the afternoon temperature rose to seventy-six, and blue sky replaced the gray with fluffy white clouds. As if to bask in the warmth, hundreds of starlings suddenly alighted on a tall power station. Classical names now yielded to the Dutch—*Amsterdam, Guilderland, Rotterdam, Schuyler*—an Old World influence of a different sort. I paid a toll of eight-forty on the outskirts of Albany and darted from the booth. This was more like it. From here to Boston, the next hundred and sixty miles would be entirely new to me. And the weather, finally, was cooperating.

Albany is situated on a hill on the west bank of the Hudson River. A fifth the size of Cleveland, it's much older, more charming, and the Interstate is smooth, although the skyline is better seen from the east and south. The hill, rising amid sharp peaks and long ridges of the Adirondacks, is crowned by the capitol with its pointy towers and Dutch gingerbread façade. Nearby stands the thirty-four-story tower of

23

the Alfred E. Smith Office Building, then the colonnaded State Education Building.

Traffic picked up considerably downtown, growing even heavier east of the city where a series of *chicanes*—switchback S-curves—wind their way down to the Hudson. It was my first real chance to see what the 'Vette could do on its sixteen-inch racing tires. Pushed by the traffic, I hugged the corners like Richard Petty, leading the way to the river, where the final descent on I-90 is exciting. Three flat bridges span the broad Hudson side by side, with long views both upstream and down. As I crossed the river my mind fled to Sleepy Hollow, fabled green vale of American folklore nestled somewhere up the tree-lined shore. Built like Ichabod Crane and a pedagogue as well, I lost myself in dreams of the Headless Horseman—until a horn blared on my right. I had drifted from my lane.

* * *

Before we leave New York State, here's an Interstate Item: I-90, which begins in Seattle and ends in Boston, is the longest Interstate highway in America, measuring nearly three thousand miles. At $7.5 billion, it is second in expense only to I-95, which cost $8 billion to construct from Miami, Florida, to Houlton, Maine. Across New York State, I-90 covers 391 miles.

According to the Federal Highway Administration of the U.S. Department of Transportation, back in 1941, although the Defense Highway Act had provided ten million dollars for postwar planning of the Interstate System, the actual planning went slowly because all the engineers were devoted to the war effort. Some states, however, took matters into their own hands. When Thomas E. Dewey, who retired from his third term as New York's governor in 1955, despaired of ever completing the New York Thruway System—the revenues on hand were constantly diverted—he ordered a study of highway financing based on tolls. When the study showed that tolls alone wouldn't support the project, the state legislature created the New York Thruway Authority, with the power to issue $500 million in bonds, to be supplemented by tolls, a model of financing that other states soon followed.

Traveling west to east across I-90, you will find the following attractions just a short distance from the Interstate exits (specified here in parentheses): the Buffalo Zoological Gardens (51); Niagara Falls (50); the Victorian Doll Museum and Doll Hospital (47); the International Museum of Photography in the 50-room mansion of George Eastman, founder of the Eastman Kodak Company (45); the Sonnenberg Gardens (44), which the Smithsonian Institution calls "one of the most magnificent late-Victorian gardens ever created in America"; the Women's Rights National Historical Park (41), where Cady Stanton and friends convened the first women's rights convention; Emerson Park (40), with its Edwardian garden pavilion, summer theatre, and twelfth-century Owasco Indian village; and the Van Rensselaer Home, Ten Broeck Mansion, and Schuyler Mansion (4).

If you're lapping America at seventy-five miles per hour, you can traverse upstate New York in five hours and twenty minutes. To enjoy the above attractions at a leisurely pace, at least a week is recommended.

* * *

Twenty minutes beyond the Hudson, I-90 becomes the Massachusetts Turnpike. The change is announced by quaint signs bearing black Pilgrim hats. The Berkshires come next, rolling mountains the texture of green wool, their steep slopes and long grades punctuated by long chicanes hewn right through granite. More than anything, that gray granite means New England—along with the pines that dominate the hills, including the scraggly kind that cling to rock ledges.

The sign for Amherst meant Emily Dickinson. *I like to see it lap the miles/And lick the valleys up.* In that poem she's describing a train, of course, but as an undergraduate—like my own students—I thought it was a horse. No matter. Today, "it" was my torch-red Corvette lapping the miles, thundering *like Boanerges* through western Massachusetts, where the pretty highway is much like Connecticut's Merritt Parkway, the road I traveled frequently as an undergraduate between Stratford and Middletown.

The similarity brought John Updike to mind. In his short story "Packed Dirt, Churchgoing, A Dying Cat, A Traded Car," the speaker, who happens to be a writer, is making a final journey along the Merritt Parkway in a '55 Ford he's about to trade in. He picks up a hitchhiker—a sailor—who is puzzled by the writer. "What's the point?" the sailor asks finally. And the question is answered in the story's last line: *We in America need ceremonies.* . . . Such as paying our respects to an old family car.

Or paying our respects to the Interstate System.

Traffic was heavy through Springfield, the sun disappeared, and the clouds began spitting rain. I reached my cousin's home in Southborough at four o'clock, my driving done for the day, four hundred and twenty miles from Buffalo. Located just fifteen minutes west of Boston, Southborough is an upscale community off I-90, just inside the I-495 beltway.

"One of the main reasons we chose this place," my cousin Dennis explained that evening, "is because of immediate access to I-90 and 495."

"On the Interstates we can be anywhere," his wife Michele added. "In Boston, at our businesses, or with family in Connecticut."

"Both Michele and I grew up with I-95 in our backyards," Dennis said. "*Literally*. But my favorite is I-81 in Virginia. It's as if God unrolled the asphalt through the Appalachian Mountains and Civil War battle-fields. Then, of course, there's the Big Dig right here in Boston."

He meant I-93. The outdated elevated Interstate through the heart of the city was coming down, to be replaced by a massive tunnel under Boston Harbor, a three-mile stretch linking central Boston with the South Boston neighborhoods at the eastern end of the Massachusetts Turnpike.

Officially called the Central Artery Project, the "Big Dig" is one of the most challenging Interstate projects ever. Planned for completion in 2001, it was then five years behind schedule and costing three mil-lion dollars per day. To pay for the overruns, state officials were plan-ning to double the tolls, cut funding for other road projects, and renege on a promise to eliminate regular driver's license renewals in favor of lifetime licenses, measures that would not even make up half the deficit.

"It'll be great," Dennis concluded. "If they ever get it done."

Joining us later, cousin Patricia put a realistic end to the conversation.

"I work for Colonial Trucking," she said. "I manage their traffic throughout New England. Without the Interstates I wouldn't have a job."

* * *

According to the Associated Press, Boston ranks fifth in the nation in terms of the total number of hours the average driver spends each year in congested traffic. Sixty-six hours in all—nearly three full days—stuck in traffic.

Hoping to avoid contributing to that statistic, I left South-borough at a tardy nine Wednesday morning, headed for the Canadian border in Maine to plant my first ceremonial flag. But my intentional delay proved futile. Almost immediately I was swallowed up by the first traffic jam of my grand lap, cars screeching to a halt one after another to join a five-mile queue for the toll at the end of I-90. It took me an hour to negotiate the fifteen miles between Southborough and I-95 North, creeping along in first gear, clutch in, clutch out.

The country landscapes were behind me now, replaced in Framingham by large glass-and-steel corporate office buildings on both sides of the highway, then a drought-ridden brown and weedy median, then a rusty guardrail and an intimidating wire fence. The gray day—a cool sixty-five degrees—did nothing to help, and the resigned faces of the Boston commuters saddened me deeply.

How could anyone face such humiliation on a daily basis? It was inhuman, three lanes of traffic spreading into half a dozen toll booths, then immediately converging again, competing for every inch of space, jockeying into position for I-95 North or I-95 South. Earlier that summer, when I-90 was clogged with vacationers heading to New Hampshire and the coast of Maine, toll collectors had simply waved the traffic on through. That was not the case today. Today was part of the daily grind. And the toll would be taken.

According to the International Bridge, Tunnel and Turnpike Association, only fifty-five toll roads existed in the United States in 1992. But twenty-seven new pay-as-you-go expressways are currently underway in fourteen states. Designed to alleviate congestion, toll roads actually create their own congestion when cars and trucks stack up at the tollgates. But the slow disbursement of federal funds makes them necessary. Electronic payment lanes equipped with scanners are on the drawing board, but until they become widespread, Interstate snarls will remain a way of life. With at least one serious consequence. More babies are being born on the Interstates these days than ever before, as traffic jams prevent pregnant women from getting to the hospital on time.

Low to the ground in the 'Vette, I feared the big trucks wouldn't see me, that I'd get wedged beneath their bumpers and dragged away. The few trees, drought-dry and brittle, mirrored the commuters' despair. The frustrating hour made me realize how lucky I am in Ohio, living half a mile from campus, just a brief walk to work. But at the moment I was stuck in Massachusetts, my little Hot Wheels Corvette trying to turn north on that great relief map in my mind. With nothing to do but stare at mudguards. And read the Interstates signs.

Caution. Reduced Salt Area. I'd never seen that one before. New England winters being what they are, the Environmental Protection Agency monitors the spreading of rock salt to avoid contaminating local water supplies. Low salt can mean an unhealthy diet of slick roads, and in Boston the traveler is duly warned.

Sometime after ten, as soon as the traffic began to pick up, I stopped for coffee at the first available spot along the western edge of the city, where the woman behind the counter promptly wished me good *mawnin'* and told me all about her *dawta*. Her delightful accent revived my spirits. I was in Boston—cradle of the American Revolution—and I began to wonder if Paul Revere had ever sounded like that. *To ahms! To ahms! The British ah coming!*

Outside, I struck up a conversation with an elderly man who resembled Groucho Marx.

"The Interstates," he growled, "is all politics. That's all there is to it. Politics.

"Take Boston, this Big Dig. It's going to be a nice improvement, but who's paying for it? I'm a member of the National Republican Committee, and I know for a fact there's a surplus in Washington." He began digging through his wallet, as fat as a coupon caddy. "I got my membership card in here somewhere. I'd rather vote for a dead Republican than a live Democrat. The *government* should pay for the Interstates. There's a surplus in Washington. I'm a member of the National Republican Committee. I got proof."

He was still digging for that proof when I excused myself to get back on the road.

Half an hour north of Boston a long entrance ramp curves through tall ledges of brown granite, and an overhead sign announces *Maine, I-95 North*. New Hampshire isn't even mentioned, although it comes first, a twenty-mile stretch beyond the Merrimack, the tranquil river Thoreau once traveled for a week, alternately rowing and drifting, recording his thoughts. Old twin bridges shaped like protractors span the Merrimack, and soon a similar bridge, shaped like a protractor and seemingly made from an Erector Set, rises high above the Piscataqua with a wide aerial view of the New Hampshire countryside. Then you're dropped into Maine—*God's Country*, as the sign proclaims.

The sign was right on target, for Maine looks newly created by a glacier. Colorful outcroppings of rock dot the rolling terrain for miles. Huge boulders lie by the roadside. The trees get taller and more sturdy, especially the pines, their ragged sawtooth tops ringing the horizon. Some are spindly, their branches several feet apart, thinning to mere tufts higher up, as if gasping for air. Others, with their severely sloping branches, look like folded beach umbrellas, the kind of pines you find in illustrated fables. Among the deciduous trees the white birches stood out starkly.

In Portland, Maine, there's a Home Depot, a Toys "R" Us, and the type of strip-mall stuff you see everywhere. But then civilization begins to dwindle for good, with much less traffic and far fewer trucks. Portland is a cutoff of sorts, a welcome point-of-no-return as you head north. Coastal inlets follow, lined with sailboats and homes that look like lighthouses. A pickup truck ahead of me was towing a sleek cabin cruiser named *Oyster Bay*. Another hauled a yacht called *The Pequod*. Which made me think of Ahab. Then *The Perfect Storm*. Then Hurricane Floyd.

Heading north into Maine you pass rest stops touting *Lobster Available.* A billboard says *Ayeh,* a trademark expression I never heard. Then an Interstate sign announces *Downeast,* an actual location. As in Boston there are Reduced Salt Areas, then an entirely new warning— diamond-shaped yellow signs with the silhouette of an antlered moose, topped by a red border with white letters. *Attention!* Apparently these Maine moose were something to reckon with.

Rivers and streams made the long drive intriguing. Again and again dark waterways cleaved the forests, opening the deep terrain to tantalizing glimpses. To my left, water wound into the interior, to my right it ran for the sea. At the York River a low bridge crossed tidal mudflats, then came a host of rivers bearing Indian names—*Saco, Kennebec, Mattawampkeag, Penobscot.* Some were narrow and shallow, others wide and deep, tree branches overhanging every shore. The streams were smaller than the rivers and much prettier, like brooks, rocky and rippled or sandy and smooth. Several bore Indian names as well—*Soutapoustock* and *Cobbevescontee.* Others names were charmingly literal—*Birch Stream, Salmon Stream, Fish Stream,* then one identified by just a letter, *"B" Stream.* I wanted to explore them by canoe, wade them for trout, or simply float them lazily like Thoreau. But I was barreling north, the Canadian border on my mind.

* * *

The day continued overcast, the early-afternoon sun bouncing in and out, the temperature up to seventy-two. The farther north I went, the greener the wide median became, the brown grass giving way to grass that needed cutting. In one stretch a lone worker on a tractor was mowing the median, flooding the 'Vette with the pungent odor of damp clippings. In some medians willows grew in thick groves, with tall marsh grass in standing water. Then a birch forest divided the highway, dense enough to obscure the southbound lanes.

From Augusta to Bangor the ride was peaceful, marred only by the inconsistent sun. And in Orono I reached a personal milestone—the farthest north I had ever been on I-95. Scouting colleges when I-95 was in its infancy, I had taken a Greyhound from Stratford to Orono to visit a boyhood friend at the University of Maine. The state of Maine had overwhelmed me then—too wild, too far north, too far from home—and I had traveled with a lump in my throat, unable to imagine myself studying in such lonely territory. Now I was facing that lonely territory once again, en route to the Canadian border to stick a flag in the ground.

To gather my courage I stopped at a rustic rest area, half an acre of ground at the base of an eroded hillside, beneath a canopy of tall trees.

Large gray boulders, green with moss, lay among the exposed roots of pines and oaks. There was no grass—just dirt, leaves, and pine needles—and a small brick comfort station with a roof of wooden shingles. Two pavilions, also shingled, held mottled picnic tables.

Occasional trucks whined by on the highway, followed by total silence. Squirrels and chipmunks rattled in the underbrush. Only three or four cars were in the parking lot. One man stared at my license plate, didn't know what to make of it, and headed for the men's room. Another told me he liked the 'Vette's color. But he seemed too tight-lipped for further conversation.

North of the rest area I had the road to myself, except for occasional trucks hauling logs on flatbed trailers. Whenever I passed one, the air filled with pine perfume. Piled high in a triangle, the logs were held fast by thick chains, their sawed ends like pink slabs of prime rib.

Suddenly something flashed in the median several miles ahead—a small blaze of light that kept reflecting with varied intensity. Mesmerized, I studied it for minutes, then slowed down as I drew near. A bouquet of flowers was snagged high in the foliage, a variety of white and yellow flowers from which long blue ribbons fluttered. It was as if a couple had just been married on the shoulder and the bride had tossed her bouquet too exuberantly. Around the nation I would see many wreaths marking the site of fatal crashes, but here the median was unmarred, the trees and bushes intact—no indication that a car might have been blown off the road by one of those big logging trucks. I preferred the over-excited bride launching her bouquet (before embarking on an Interstate honeymoon, perhaps), an image I held in my head until the flashing disappeared in the rearview mirror.

In mid-afternoon, choosing an exit at random, I discovered an old general store with clapboard siding and a loosely shingled roof. Out front, a large, bearded biker stood in jeans and a black leather jacket, munching a Hershey bar and cleaning the windshield of his Harley. A fireman from southern California, he had ridden north to Washington, then across to Maine. He was on his way south to Florida, participating in a long-distance road rally. And like me, he was worried about Floyd, which he had heard was now battering the Carolinas. Still headed north, I tried to laugh it off.

"You doin' the four corners too?" he said. "I thought *I* was the only nut on the road!"

I asked him what it was like to ride a motorcycle on the Interstates.

"Trucks are a headache," he said. "I'll be doin' eighty and suddenly a truck'll pass me and I'll wonder what the hell's goin' on. Otherwise, I just do a lot of daydreamin'. I sing songs and think about everythin' but work. When I get back home, there'll be a banquet for everyone who makes it all the way 'round. They give you a certificate, and one of these." He rapped his thick knuckles on the windshield. It was covered with cartoon stickers like merit badges. Then he popped the rest of the Hershey bar into his mouth. "But the four corners is nuthin'. I've done the iron butt Interstate tour—a thousand miles a day for eleven days. That's why they call it the *iron butt.*"

The Hershey bar had made me hungry, so I went inside to get one for myself, and when I came out again the biking fireman was gone.

From the general store it was only eighty-five miles to the Canadian border, just beyond Houlton at the very end of I-95. The road was ascending now up a long inclined plane, and for the final half-hour I didn't see another car. Parallel to the highway and far to the west, a massive mountain upreared a pointed head, falling away to a range of smoother mountains that seemed to be going exactly where I was— into the sky and beyond.

A town called New Limerick got me thinking. *There once was a man from New Limerick, who.* . . . But the available rhymes were too naughty. I thought of the bearded biker instead, then checked NPR. President Clinton had declared the Carolinas a disaster area. Floyd was predicted to make landfall that evening, coming ashore as a Category 3 storm. Gert was now a "Cat 4."

But I-95 was beautiful, rising and falling with scenic vistas—like that big blue lake on my left, where the pines come steeply to the water's edge and the sky rides the smooth hills piggyback.

By four-fifteen I was five miles from Houlton (pop. 5267), the terrain rugged and gorgeous, wildflowers lacing the way. One mile out I had to chuckle—*Houlton International Airport.* Probably for Canada geese. But I had seen no geese, only crows. I had seen seagulls in Ohio and a flock of starlings in New York, and nothing but crows in Maine— enormous rooks hopping about their roadkill, ruffling their feathers whenever I whizzed by. *The caw of the open road.* I was getting punchy. I had come four hundred miles from Southborough, Massachusetts, and was about to plant my first Interstate flag.

At the Houlton exit came a sign for Route 1, the dear old Boston Post Road. I'd be taking it later to spend the night with a friend in Presque Isle. John Steinbeck had passed through Presque Isle with his dog Charley, and an old friend of mine had just moved there several weeks earlier. It somehow seemed fated. More Corvette karma. But first I had a ceremony to perform.

For months I had been trying to imagine what it would look like at the very end of I-95, the initial site of my symbolic Interstate thank-you. Well, I-95 comes to an end in a bleak and lonely stretch of high ragged pines. You know it ends because there's a blue-and-white chevron-shaped sign on the shoulder, atop a tall metal pole. *END 95.*

The end of I-95 at the U.S.-Canada border in Houlton, Maine.

Laughter is a funny thing. It sounds hollow when you're alone. You might *chuckle* to yourself, as I had done at the oxymoron of *Houlton* and *International,* but how often do you really crack up when you're by yourself? Yet there's a first time for everything and mine was at hand.

End 95. At the sight of that sign I howled, pulled onto the shoulder, and jumped from the 'Vette. The road had just been paved and smelled freshly of asphalt. There was no one around. Several hundred yards away, across the median in the southbound lanes, sat a Customs house not much bigger than a tollbooth. Excited, I popped the hatchback and rummaged among my things.

The millennial banners I was carrying were eighteen by eleven on a thirty-inch stick. They sported crisscrossed American flags on a solid blue background. And right in the center, in a star-spangled burst, they said *Millennium 2000.* Fearing hard ground because of widespread drought, I had brought a hammer and a foot-long star drill—a kind of

Phillips-head screwdriver without a handle. Kneeling at the base of the sign pole, I pounded the drill into the ground, wrestled it out again, and inserted the flag. Then I saluted and the ceremony was over.

It occurred to me that I ought to take a photo, but I wanted to be in the photo myself, and there was no one to help. After a few minutes one of those logging trucks rolled by, but I would have felt foolish waving it down. It was getting late—already after five—and I was expected in Presque Isle within the hour. Then another truck rolled through, and another. Just as I was about to give up, a northbound Bronco pulled off the shoulder about a hundred yards away, and out popped a winsome teenage lass. I waved, she hesitated, then came on over.

It was just like in the movies.

"What's a nice girl like you doing in a place like *this*?" I said.

She laughed, pointing across the way. "I work at the duty-free shop. It's not much of a job, but it gives me time do to my homework."

I explained what I was up to, handed her the camera, and she snapped my picture beneath *End 95*. Then I made a U-turn in Canada and took off for Presque Isle, much to the amusement of the elderly official who waved me through the Customs gate.

As Updike has written, *We in America need ceremonies.*

No matter how small or informal.

* * *

"I have mixed feelings about the Interstates," Eleanor said over dinner. "I hate the traffic jams at the tollbooths. Last summer I was stuck at the Baltimore Harbor Tunnel. Cars were backed up for miles. It was very hot and I needed the air conditioner, but I had to keep the heater on to vent the engine. It was maddening. On the other hand, I just love the scenery on the Interstates, especially here in Maine. It gets me thinking, and when I'm working on a project I'll often go right by my exit—on purpose—so as not to lose my train of thought."

I asked her about the strident moose warnings.

"Up here," she said, "you've got to take them seriously. It's not like hitting a deer. Eight people have been killed already this year."

In the morning I woke to raucous crows, which Eleanor had warned me about too.

"They're a really big problem," she had said over dinner, "especially where they roost."

On my six-thirty walk I saw one as big as an owl. The temperature was fifty-nine, it had begun to drizzle, and I had to duck into a local handi-food store to keep dry. Behind the counter stood a man of about thirty, with shoulder-length hair. He was dressed in blue jeans and a plain white T-shirt.

"How's Floyd doing?" I asked.

"Floyd *who?*"

"Floyd the Hurricane."

The clerk looked at me strangely. "Is there a hurricane? I don't have a TV. No radio neither. No TV, no radio, no movies, no car. I like it that way."

"Ever been on the Interstates?" I said.

"Been down to Bangor once," he said flatly. "But it was boring. Nothing but trees. It put me to sleep."

Eleanor, then Dean of Arts and Sciences at the University of Maine's Presque Isle campus, was off to work by the time I got back. When I stopped at her office to say goodbye, she said that Floyd was expected in Maine by nightfall. With high winds and rain. I hoped to make it to Bangor before it hit. But first I had another stop to make—to pay my respects to a descendant of America's first roadbuilders.

"Good luck with the Chief," Eleanor said. Then we hugged and I headed for the 'Vette, shifting gears literally and psychologically, with Chief Big Eagle in mind.

Stopping in Houlton for coffee before getting back on I-95, I learned from a waitress that the Interstates down south had been restricted to westbound traffic only—I-40 from Wilmington, I-26 from Charleston, I-16 and I-95 from Savannah. The idea was to speed up the evacuation of residents from coastal areas. But officials were being criticized for not ordering the move sooner.

"The good news," the waitress said, "is that Gert might be heading out to sea."

There was a large mural on the wall in the little coffee shop—men, women, and children happily harvesting rows of potatoes in wide fields set against the mountains, a pastoral scene in stark contrast with the turmoil down south.

"A few weeks from now," the waitress said, "all the leaf peepers will be coming up the Interstate. That's what we call 'em. *Leaf peepers.*" She was as down-home as the folks in the mural, and minutes later, as I pointed my little Hot Wheels Corvette toward Florida on that great relief map in my mind, a local sign summed up what I was feeling.

Maine. The way life should be.

* * *

Later that morning, as the rain steadily increased, I stopped in Springfield for a few hours to visit eighty-five-year-old Chief Big Eagle, former head of Connecticut's Paugussett Indians. I wanted to talk with him about the Interstates.

A retired trucker, the Chief had owned his own hauling company in the fifties and sixties, traversing America before the Interstates even existed. He had watched the system being built and then used it. But he had warned me in advance to avoid the subject, including in his letter a newspaper article about a variety of problems facing current truckers. It had been more than two decades since he had been on the road, but his loyalty was steadfast. Any reminder of things that irked him would make him testy. So I promised myself not to ask about the Interstates, so many of which, like the Pennsylvania Turnpike, follow the route of ancient Indian trails. My visit alone would have to stand in silent acknowledgment of our Native American pathfinders.

I hadn't seen the Chief since our last trip to Russia together in 1991, when we had met with the Indianists, citizens of the former Soviet Union who have devoted their lives to preserving Native American traditions. Irina, one of those Indianists who had since moved to the States, was visiting the Chief when I stopped in. The Paugussetts were currently embroiled in a controversial claim for federal recognition, and if the Bureau of Indian Affairs ruled in their favor, they intended to build the world's largest casino on the site of original reservation land in Bridgeport, Connecticut. But the Chief had retired to a cabin on a wooded mountaintop in Maine, leaving the business of the tribe in the hands of his son.

My only problem was getting to the cabin, several miles down a dirt-and-gravel road that had eroded to potholes and was slick from the rain. Worse still, the terrain was a roller coaster. Large rocks scraped the undercarriage of the 'Vette as I ascended, then descended, in first gear. A quarter mile from the cabin the road was washed out, so I retreated to the main highway, phoned the Chief from a general store, and he came down the mountain a back way to fetch me in his own car. Caked with mud, the 'Vette was left behind. And it was a good thing. The rain wasn't letting up. Had I made it to the cabin in the 'Vette, I would have never made it out.

Irina busied herself preparing stew in the kitchen while the Chief showed me his deer—half a dozen does and a fourteen-point buck penned up in the woods behind the cabin. He called them softly to the chickenwire fence, kissing them one by one on the nose. The does came first, shyly, and then the buck, watching me suspiciously with large glassy brown eyes. Then I made some slight movement—shook my head in disbelief or raised a hand—and the big animal bolted.

It was embarrassing. The Chief was at peace on his Maine mountain, with the rain splatting on the trees. But I was lapping America, unable to stand still, worrying about my mud-splattered 'Vette. And the big buck could sense it.

Turning from the fence, I asked the Chief about the claim for federal recognition.

"What'll you do if it's denied?" I said. Irina was waving from the window, calling us out of the rain for lunch.

"We'll do what we always do," the Chief said. "Appeal. Meanwhile, we wait."

When I arrived in Bangor in the late afternoon, the rain began in earnest, pounding hard and bouncing inches high. It was the rush hour, time for another Interstate ambush, and the Motel Find-Me-Not directory was no help at all. *I-95 Exit So and So. Use Route So and So to Bangor to junction of So and So Road and I-395. Turn left.*

And *good luck*, it should have added, because the directory was overbaked. All it needed to say was *Exit So and So*. Because the motel was right there off the exit. But I turned right, as instructed, on *Route So and So to Bangor*, looking for the very junction that intersects the exit. Twenty minutes later, chasing signs for I-395, I stopped to ask for directions, wedging the handle of my umbrella in the window as I hastily slammed the door, soaking myself and the interior of the 'Vette, damaging the window so it would leak for the rest of my grand lap.

Worse still, the directions I was given proved wrong. I was soon back on I-95, heading north, doubling back to the original exit, where I turned *left* and so arrived. As I had learned in Buffalo, you can find *anything* the second time around.

* * *

The storm continued outside.

In my room, having showered and settled down, I found a TV interview with Richard F. Weingroff, an Interstate historian with whom I had corresponded. He was saying nothing that was new to me—*Eisenhower, the Cold War, the national defense*—but it was good to hear anyway. It seemed fated, a moment of Corvette karma intended to cheer me up. The program, however, was no millennial tribute to the Interstates. That, I had come to believe, was *my* job.

I slipped a pair of rubbers over my walking shoes and braved the downpour with my umbrella to cross *Route So and So* for dinner at the nearest restaurant. It was sixty degrees and the wind had increased to gale force, driving the rain into my jeans right up to my thighs. I must have looked funny because the young waitress was laughing as I entered. But that was OK. I wanted to ask her about the Interstates.

"Well," she began, handing me a menu, "we definitely need more lanes down south near Boston. I go to Boston a lot on the weekends, but it's boring on the way down because I'm thinking about my weekend, and it's boring on the way back because it's dark."

I wanted to tell her about the guy I had met in Presque Isle—who knows, they might have hit it off—but she kept on talking.

"I used to work at a truck stop where the buses pull in. You know, all those foliage trips with the leaf peepers? I got good tips. So I guess that's what the Interstates mean to me. Good tips." She took a pencil from her hair. "Ready to order?"

I had the meat loaf—with a double order of mashed potatoes, in honor of the potato farmers in the mural at the coffee shop in Houlton. Then I got soaked all over again returning to the motel, where I fell asleep watching the evening news. Hurricane Floyd had finally caught me, slamming Bangor with wind, rain, and thunder, dropping trees and power lines and flooding area roads. But I slept right through it. And in the morning it was the phone, not the crows, that woke me—a call from a public affairs officer back at the campus in Ohio. The *Connecticut Post* wanted to interview me on the weekend. But that would be Sunday and today was only Friday, the day I had reserved for visiting Jack Kerouac's grave.

Meanwhile, the TV replayed horrendous scenes of Interstate traffic down south as the Floyd evacuations continued. But in Maine, between Bangor and Augusta, traffic was light, not really picking up until Portland, where the I-95 East Coast megalopolis begins. From here on—as I knew all too well—there'd be no relief until south of Richmond, Virginia. An unsettling thought in the *best* of weather.

The brunt of the storm had passed in the night, leaving the morning cool and misty, the constant highway spray out of sync with the delayed timing of the 'Vette's wipers. Out the side window it looked like a damp day for golf. Straight ahead it seemed to be raining like hell. Rivers and streams I had passed yesterday were now roiling—some muddy, some sudsy—and at one rest area a scribbled warning had been posted above the fountain. *Do not drink the water.* I had stopped for a candy bar, but the vending machine ate my seventy-five cents. Fortunately, the uniformed candy man had just pulled in to restock his wares.

"I'd rather travel the Maine Turnpike than the one in New Jersey," he said as he returned my change. "And I just hate it through New York—all those burned-out cars. It's only the southern half of I-95 that's bad here in Maine. For years they've been talking of widening it. It was very busy this summer, but in my business we need the tourists.

"The people of Maine enjoy the tourists as much as the tourists enjoy the people of Maine."

37

"What about moose?" I asked.

"My friend hit a moose once," he said matter-of-factly. "It tore the roof right off his Subaru sedan. He didn't know what had happened until he looked at his hands. They were filled with blood, fur, and moose poo."

Enough said.

At a larger rest area farther south I approached a bus driver, a garrulous black woman who had been driving the Interstates for twenty-six years. She was hauling a group of senior citizens that had been in Maine for the week. Now she was anxious to get them home and out of the rain.

"People need to be better educated as to what the Interstate numbers mean," she said. "It's certainly easy enough. Even-numbered routes run east to west, odd numbers north–south. If the first of three digits is odd, it's a spur into a city. If it's even, it goes around the city. What can be simpler than that? But numbers can be disorienting. And not all the Interstates have the same services and facilities. You'll certainly find that out by the time you get home!"

Back on the highway, with my time in the state running out, I saw another one of those proud signs that seemed to speak for itself. *If your business were in Maine you'd be home by now.* But my business was all over America.

By noon I had re-crossed the high bridge over the Piscataqua into New Hampshire, and when I reached Massachusetts I took I-495 to Lowell, where the weather suddenly changed. High winds replaced the mist and rain, buffeting the 'Vette in manic traffic. Leaves scuttled across the highway and litter swirled in circles as the wind shoved cars and trucks from lane to lane. I was happy to exit, although Lowell—old, ugly, and industrial—is full of potholes, bumps, and cramped avenues.

It took me awhile to find the large iron gates of the Edson Cemetery on Gorham Street, but once there the Corvette karma kicked in.

"Zat your cah?" said the middle-aged woman in the office. She was looking out the window at the 'Vette. "It's a very nice cah. I've owned three 'Vettes myself."

"I've come to see Jack," I said. "Could you take my picture? I want to plant a flag at his grave."

She handed me a map. "I cahn't leave the office 'til the other girl gets back. My boss was thinking of closing for the day, what with the wind. A lot of limbs are falling out theh. It was horrible lahst night, but the worst is ova." Then the door opened behind me—the other girl was back—so I hurried out to the 'Vette to fetch my stuff.

The Edson Cemetery is old and large, with many narrow tree-lined streets. Leaves whipped by, and limbs swayed overhead. Branches were strewn everywhere—in the paved avenues, on the brown grass, across the headstones.

For the record, Jack Kerouac's grave is No. 1 in Lot 76. Entering from Gorham Street you turn left on Oberlin, right on Seventh, then left on Lincoln, to the second big tree on the right. The grave is about fifteen yards straight in, a simple marker flush with the ground:

> "TI JEAN"
> JOHN L. KEROUAC
> MAR. 12, 1922–OCT. 21, 1969
> —HE HONORED LIFE—
> STELLA HIS WIFE
> NOV. 11, 1918–FEB. 10, 1990

To the left of the inscription is a dove from which rays of sunlight emanate. *Ti Jean* is short for *"Petit Jean,"* a French pet name bestowed by Kerouac's father. Kerouac's mother had Native American blood, making me glad I had stopped to see the Chief.

My banner, with note attached, at the grave of Jack Kerouac in Lowell, MA.

Someone had been at the grave a week earlier, leaving a dated handwritten message on a sheet of paper under a rock. Incredibly, it was still legible despite the rain. *Feeling is the essence of intellect, because without feeling nothing is known.* It was a direct quote, perhaps by Kerouac himself, and the note was signed *with much appreciation.* I couldn't make out the signature. My own note had been prepared back in Ohio, on a laminated three-by-five card in which I had punched a hole for a flagstick. It said, simply, *Ti Jean, I am lapping America.* Finding the nickname on the headstone thrilled me, a sign of subconscious sympathy.

"My fahtha grew up in Lowell," the 'Vette woman said as she clicked away with my disposable Kodak. "I wish I'd ahsked him about Kerouac. Kerouac's daughter Jan died not too long ago. She had wanted to get Jack out of this cemetery, you know. And you know what else? My cousin Pam once dated Kerouac's nephew. Paul Kerouac's about forty-eight now. He runs the PK Garden Center up in Nashua. Or is it ova in Amherst? Anyway, he's very quiet. A very nice guy."

Then we got the hell out of there before a tree could fall on my cah.

3

ON THE INSTRUMENT PANEL OF MY 'VETTE IS AN IMAGINARY DEVICE I CALL AN *idyllometer*. I invented it myself (patent pending). It has all the latest computerized gizmos. The idyllometer monitors a variety of conditions in search of the perfect Interstate ride.

An *idyll* is a short poem or prose piece depicting a rural scene in idealized terms. The scene is tranquil and simple and carefree, with overtones of a romantic interlude. Thus urban areas (Cleveland, for example) rarely receive a respectable idyllometer reading, although certain cities on my grand lap would offer pleasant surprises. Key factors include the weather (there must be abundant sunshine, clear skies, and a seasonable temperature), traffic (light to nonexistent), speed (steady at ten miles per hour above the posted limit), median (wide, with natural landscaping, no barriers or guardrails), road surface (freshly paved, with bright lines), and scenery (attractive and varied, with no billboards or overhead wires). Music is optional (your favorite tape, CD, or classical radio station; even your own voice, should you break into song). But time (duration) is crucial. The ideal conditions must be sustained for a one-hour minimum.

The idyllometer assigns each element a value of zero to one hundred and computes an overall rating. The lowest composite reading—absolute zero—is what I call an *Interstate idle* (pun intended). When you're stuck in traffic (as I was in Boston). At a dead standstill. Not moving at all. But as long as you maintain speed according to specifications, the idyllometer's digital read-out will show at least fifty, despite all other data. The perfect reading, then, is an even one hundred. If Olympic athletes can be perfect, why not the Interstates?

Needless to say, on the opening days of my grand lap of America, the idyllometer barely flickered past fifty. The wind and rain were persistent, a steady sun was lacking, and I was beginning to doubt that I would ever experience the perfect Interstate ride.

* * *

I spent the night in Southborough once again at my cousin's home, where heavy winds had flattened his son's basketball hoop and buried the driveway in branches and leaves. But by morning the storm had gone, leaving a magnificent New England day—clear blue skies, crisp air, total sunshine—the best weather I had seen in a week.

I got up early to walk, then washed the 'Vette, restoring the torch-red gleam it hadn't had since Ohio. Dennis saw me off at nine with a bag of apples and a CD of Eric Clapton's greatest hits. A few minutes later, as I retraced my route to I-90—to connect with I-95 South—the 'Vette began to make a grating noise. I ignored it until it grew louder, forcing me into the nearest service station, where I backed into the only available parking space, bouncing over the raised covers of the subterranean gasoline storage tanks.

The Elias Aoude Mobil Company was hopping with suburbanites on Saturday-morning errands, all with spiffy sports cars or SUVs in need of immediate attention, their hoods in the air like open mouths. But while the Southborough area thrummed with frenetic energy, Elias Aoude—tending to customers himself—was an island of calm. I must have looked distraught because he put a hand on my shoulder and took me inside for coffee and donuts. Ten minutes later, with me riding shotgun, he was slamming the 'Vette through heavy traffic on I-495—braking quickly, changing lanes, downshifting, testing the engine in all six gears. From the instinctive way he handled the car I could see that it was capable of so much more than I was demanding of it.

Aoude is from Lebanon and has been working in the United States for more than twenty years. "America is the greatest country in the world," he said, changing lanes once again. "Don't you ever forget that!" Darting between trucks, he exited the beltway and sped back to the station. "There is absolutely nothing wrong with this vehicle," he said jumping out. "It is a strong car, a powerful car. A muscle car." Then he laughed, bending over to pick up a long branch. It was from my cousin's driveway and I had dislodged it myself, backing the 'Vette over the raised storage covers on arrival.

I could feel the hot flush of embarrassment rising up my face like mercury in a thermometer. "What do I owe you?" I said sheepishly.

Elias Aoude smiled broadly. "We're not here to make money," he replied. "We are here"—he meant on this earth, not at this Mobil station—"to help people."

No charge. And I was back on the road, my faith restored. In mankind, America, and Corvette karma.

Unfortunately, the good feeling subsided immediately in the face of heavy traffic, a frantic Saturday-morning pace in every direction. Then an Interstate idle swallowed all vehicles at the I-90 toll. When the congestion loosened half an hour later, I headed south from Boston on I-95. Simultaneously the terrain began to change, the pines giving way to ash, oak, and elm. The birches were gone but granite outcroppings remained, in sharp relief against a royal blue sky. Only the brown medians, despite the recent rain, showed signs of lingering drought.

I flew by a fleet of yellow trucks from Hydro Quebec, the kind that service power lines from a basket with a maneuverable arm, and when I stopped at a rest area for a midmorning break, the convoy caught up with me. There were several dozen trucks en route from Quebec to Pennsylvania, all workers wearing plastic yellow helmets. When three of the crew came over to look at the 'Vette, I asked them what they thought of the Interstates. But a small man in a ski vest shrugged his shoulders. Another turned his palms to the sky.

"No English," he said. "No speak English."

I began again. *"Les Entr'états,"* I said, perhaps coining a phrase. *"Qu'est-ce que vous pensez?"* We carried on in French until the foreman came over, anxious to practice his English before they got to Pennsylvania.

"You have good road in USA," he said. "You protect well your road in USA. In Canada, a problem with the winter. But we love to drive the America." Then he raised an arm to signal an abrupt end to the break and I returned to the 'Vette, leaving the convoy in the rearview mirror.

A few minutes later I crossed a bridge into Pawtucket, Rhode Island, where Abbott Run enters the Seekonk River on its way to Narragansett Bay. Pawtucket is an old New England mill town—some factories, old houses on high rock ledges, a few churches with pointed steeples—made more grotesque by the likes of Burger King and Dunkin' Donuts. Then comes Providence, a classier city, where a series of chicanes snake past the domed capitol in four broad lanes and there's a structure like the Empire State Building. To the left, on a hill, sits Brown University—alma mater of my brother whom I was on my way to visit. Then I-95 leaves downtown along the lovely Seekonk. The road was exceptionally smooth, allowing the heavy traffic to stream right on through. Elias Aoude would have been proud of how I took the chicanes.

On I-95, Rhode Island is as brief as New Hampshire. I didn't think the traffic could get any heavier, but south of Providence it did just that, where the highway narrows to two lanes. The route was pleasantly rolling and tree-lined, with a wide median through the heart of hills and valleys, but the crazy traffic kept the idyllometer in check. Where were all these people coming from? Where were they going? And what the hell was the hurry?

At noon, entering Connecticut, I felt a surge of excitement. I was home. Certainly things would be more civilized here. To celebrate, I stopped at the North Stonington Welcome Center just across the state line, the very first rest area available—a good practice when traveling the Interstates since every state wants to make a good impression. Leaving a state's a different matter. The state no longer cares. Your business is gone and no special treatment's needed. Often, right across the highway from the attractive rest area that greets you, you can see its dilapidated counterpart, last on the list of state funding priorities.

The North Stonington stop was my favorite to date, a wooded area with circular drives neatly landscaped with hedges, mountain laurel, and rock ledges that had been blasted from the terrain. Each pavilion held a grill built into its own stone wall, plus a redwood picnic table on a cement-and-stone base. Wood chips and cedar mulch lined the sidewalks around a rugged stone comfort station and information area. Overhead, on high white flagpoles, the Connecticut flag flapped beside an American flag. And there was that Eisenhower Interstate sign with the five white stars—the first I'd seen since Ohio—gleaming in the seventy-degree sunshine. I was home, on an Interstate mission, and the 'Vette had never looked better, spanking clean and smartly parked between bright white lines in the freshly paved lot.

But I hadn't lived in Connecticut for more than thirty years, returning only once or twice annually. I was unprepared for the population density—the sheer volume of people—source of the harrowing ride that followed along the coast of Long Island Sound. For sustained terror over time, it was the worst stretch I would experience on my Interstate odyssey.

Leaving North Stonington for my brother's home near Stratford, I was instantly caught up in a mad race—cars, vans, trucks, and SUVs packed so tightly that they created an optical illusion. Every vehicle seemed to be towing another. But they were simply tailgating—all lanes in both directions—bumper to bumper at exactly seventy-five miles per hour. I passed a Toyota with a yellow kayak and a bicycle on the roof. The driver seemed headed for an Iron Man competition. But he was already in one.

Ironically, I had subconsciously prepared for the day's madness by playing Nintendo with Dennis's young son the night before, the kind of game in which it's all but impossible to keep your vehicle on the road. I had chosen a Corvette, of course, a newer model than my own, but through the fantastic cityscapes and challenging obstacles all I had done was crash and burn, blowing the sleek 'Vette into oblivion with an amazing blaze of graphics and sound. Now I was playing the game for real and it was no longer fun. Unlike the chicanes through Albany and Providence—or the wild ride with Elias Aoude—it was a matter of survival.

The weather couldn't have been more sparkling, the scenery more attractive—jagged granite cliff faces, rolling hills, and rivers that widen into spectacular views of boats and harbors on Long Island Sound. But I was too intent on the traffic to enjoy it. I sped by Mystic Seaport, site of a sixth-grade field trip, then Groton, home of America's nuclear subs. In New London sat the Coast Guard Academy, rival to my under-graduate Wesleyan. In tiny Clinton I searched for the backyard where my cousin Dennis had grown up, where I myself had spent some timeless hours of childhood. But there was no time for leisurely strolls down memory lane. The lane was congested and the stroller would be flattened.

In Branford I fought my way into the right-hand lane and exited to a service area. Heading inside for coffee, I noticed an employee catching a cigarette by a rear delivery door. He was from South Africa, aboriginal in appearance, and I asked him what he thought of our Interstates.

"They're very safe," he said in an accent not quite British, "but the speed of your trucks is totally unacceptable. You never see the police pull the trucks over. It's always the cars. Around here very few people even give a damn on the roads. During Floyd they were just crazy to get home. East or west, I-95 has terrible traffic at all times. It's been worse since they put in that casino at Foxwoods. When you want to change lanes the trucks sit on your tail. That's so dangerous. Ever try to change lanes with a truck on your tail? Your truckers go faster than in any country I've ever seen, and I've been to South Africa, Germany, and Australia. Don't misunderstand me, there are some good drivers here—some excellent drivers—but the speeds are unacceptable. Totally."

Braced by a large coffee, I rejoined the race in brilliant sunshine, turning on the AC, the temperature now up to seventy-six. In East Haven the eastbound traffic suddenly screeched to a halt, backing up for miles, an Interstate idle of absolute zero. But the westbound lanes, after slowing briefly, resumed the crazy pace. The psychological advantage of movement—with the opposite lanes stuck fast—made New Haven exciting. Sailboats, jetties, flags, and cranes spread across the harbor where the Quinnipiac River meets the Sound. I had done graduate work at Yale and looked for old landmarks—the treed cliffs of East Rock, the Hall of Graduate Studies, the Biology Tower—all glimpses as fleeting as the vehicles about me.

In Milford, I-95 rises into the sky above the Housatonic, with a barrage of power lines and smokestacks to the right. To the left the scene is far more soothing. The brackish river skirts the Shakespeare Theater on the far shore, then curves gently by the yacht club to Short Beach. Stratford, my hometown, lies just beyond the bridge, where I-95 was under construction, the rough pavement scored for resurfacing. Guardrails had replaced the green median of my youth and the highway was a maze of cones and barriers. All of which the barreling traffic simply ignored.

I exited abruptly at Exit 32 into the throes of a mid-afternoon Interstate ambush. But I knew the way here, and I was determined to revisit some scenes of my boyhood. Circling by the high school, I worked my way to Main Street. It was four lanes now, with a center turning lane, lined not only with tall trees but businesses. A few minutes later I was parked at the curb on the corner of Mt. Pleasant Avenue, across the street from the junior high school. Our house and yard looked smaller than I remembered, although the trees I had planted with my father were now enormous. A *Crime Watch* sign saddened me. There had been no need for such a sign in my youth. The corner is fed by three streets, and the traffic had increased to the point that it made my idling there dangerous. When a police car halted at a stop sign and lingered just opposite, I retraced my route to Main Street, heading for the south end of town.

At the intersection of Main and the Boston Post Road I stopped for a red light as I had done so often years ago when riding my bike to the dentist's. The intersection was so jammed with traffic that I never could have crossed it on my bicycle. But it was still *New York* to the right and *Boston* to the left, and as I waited for the light to turn I smiled up at the summer sun through the 'Vette's dark glass roof. Then the light changed and I turned toward New York, cutting back a block to I-95, where the entrance ramp proved much shorter than the one in my memory. Despite all the construction, the traffic was still flying, and when a speeding trucker refused to let me merge, I skidded to a halt a few inches from a battered guardrail.

So much for the reenactment of my first ride on the Interstates—an event that my brother, at his home a short while later, couldn't even recall.

* * *

Sunday—another crisp sky-blue day of abundant sunshine—was reserved for relaxation, my first day without travel. I was at the home of my older brother in the wooded confines of Shelton. To be honest, I was exhausted, not yet in a rhythm. I had been averaging three hundred twenty miles daily for the first six days, yet in days to come I would often do five hundred.

A columnist from the *Connecticut Post* came by in the morning and our interview produced an accurate headline—*At last, a stout defender of America's Interstate highways.* I hadn't known, when we talked, that the ride through Connecticut would prove the worst of my grand lap, and so a second article, written from a phone interview when I got back to Ohio, was less complimentary—*Connecticut drivers fail road test with this traveler.* But by then I was safely out of town.

Sunday afternoon my two younger brothers dropped by for a family reunion and a visit to my mother at a local nursing home, to which she had moved following my father's death. Mom was failing, but she recognized each of us and was surprised I had come from Ohio. I didn't explain my odyssey because it would have been futile. We pushed her wheelchair outside into the bright sunlight for some photos on the grounds, then returned her in time for her Sunday-afternoon movie. It was a poignant visit—I knew it would be the last time I would see my mother alive—but we made the effort and Mom responded. What more could one ask?

Back at the house, we began debating the Interstates. Brian's daughter was attending college in Providence. "I avoid I-95 at all costs," he said. "We always take the state routes through Connecticut to Rhode Island. You can't go anywhere without being delayed anymore. Still, I'm positive about the Interstates. I think they're great for the country."

But my sister-in-law was adamant. "I hate the Interstates," she said. "That time we came to see you in Ohio was one of the most grueling drives I've ever taken. The speed and the amount of traffic is getting to be too much for me. I find it confusing to have to make so many split-second decisions."

Bruce, who had come down from Hartford on I-84, disagreed. "I absolutely love the Interstates," he said. "They let me travel all over New England. Within two hours I can get to a lot of significant places in any direction—New York, Newport, Boston, the Berkshires, the Rhode Island beaches, the southern Vermont ski areas. The Interstates have been a great friend to me."

Bob, from the northeast corner of the state, had also come on I-84, but he was frowning and shaking his head. "Connecticut is one big traffic jam from one side to the other. Malls have destroyed the charm of New England, and one purpose of the Interstates is to get people to the malls. I saw a TV program about that recently. It was originally thought that the malls would relieve local traffic, but all they've done is spread it out along the Interstates. In Connecticut you rarely see more than one person in a car. And the road rage is incredible. On the way here today a guy passed in front of me and gave me the finger. What have we wrought upon ourselves with this system?"

He paused to let the Samuel Morse echo sink in. *What hath God wrought?* "There's this bus driver who takes my students to New York City each year," Bob continued suddenly. "He says we need a separate Interstate for the trucks. He thinks they ought to build it in Long Island Sound. Out in the water, right along the shore."

The idea reminded me of my colleague's husband who wanted to see trains in the Interstate medians. But *this* notion seemed ridiculous. A few days down the road, however—when I got to the Deep South— it would begin to seem more and more feasible.

"Actually," Brian said, "the New Jersey Turnpike splits into separate truck lanes right after New York City. That's a big help, at least for a while. They only go so far."

Bruce jumped back in. "I remember very distinctly the day that Dad took Great Aunt Vera to see I-95. He was giving her a tour and explaining about this new marvel, the Interstate. I was in the first grade then, and I told everybody in school that I had driven on the *turnpipe*. Somebody straightened me out later. It was just a short ride. We got on at Exit 31 in Stratford and got off at Exit 32."

I didn't mention my abortive return to the same spot the day before. I was on record as a stout defender of the Interstates and I didn't want to quell Bruce's enthusiasm. Or my own. But I was still piqued by Brian's inability to recall that day years ago when we had taken a shortcut to the beach on I-95. A day that had changed my life.

Bruce, the family historian, was still pumped. He had traced our ancestors back to the 1500s in England. His most recent find was a relative who had been one of the first settlers in upstate New York, in the very terrain I had crossed driving east. "He made his way into the territory in 1809," Bruce said, "traveling on ice! He had waited 'til winter just to do this. Then he built a log house in the total wilderness. How classic. How American! Today he would have taken the Interstates."

* * *

I dreaded leaving Monday morning. All the major roads in the Carolinas were heavily damaged. Many were closed or still restricted to north- or westbound traffic. Thankfully, Gert had moved out to sea, but now another tropical storm—Harvey—was threatening to sweep across the Gulf of Mexico.

None of this had anything to do with my dread. On Monday I was going only as far as Baltimore. But to do so I had to pass through New York City—a twenty-mile jog between the southwestern corner of Connecticut and northeastern New Jersey—one of the most intimidating stretches of Interstate in America. And twenty years earlier I had sworn that I would never again pass through New York City on I-95.

Like the candy man in Maine, I had always associated that bit of Interstate with burned-out cars—disabled vehicles that had been stripped, looted, and set ablaze the instant the unfortunate driver left the scene for help. It was a highway without shoulders, flanked by graffiti-laden retaining walls, divided by twisted guardrails and rusty chain-link fences. The road surface was a minefield of potholes as dangerous as the surroundings, so battered that all traffic bounced—*pa-dump pa-dump pa-dump*—as if on rumble strips. And on the curves the cars would slip and slide.

For a decade beginning in the late '60s, while teaching high school in the D.C. area, I had traveled I-95 frequently between Washington and Stratford, a three-hundred-mile trip I routinely made in less than five hours. But I was much younger then, the East Coast population was less dense, and I knew every lane, tollbooth, and trick of traffic. Still, it had always been a harrowing drive. The day I swore off New York City forever came in the early '80s. My wife and I were on the last leg of a ten-hour journey from southwest Virginia, a toddler and new-born aboard, when we hit an Interstate idle at the George Washington Bridge. Stratford was less than an hour away, but we crept and crawled for two hours, funneling from six lanes into one, just to cross the Hudson. It grew dark, both boys were screaming, and the car stank from the fumes of changed diapers. Finally arriving at the bridge, we found nothing but a few rubber cones. A maintenance truck was parked sideways to block the lanes, and a crew of workers was sitting about, laughing point-blank at the traffic. *Never again*, I promised. From then on we had taken a longer route, swinging north on the Garden State Parkway to the Tappan Zee Bridge, entering Connecticut beyond the grip of the city. Now I was going to confront that hostile cityscape one last time, against my better judgment, and in the most expensive automobile I had ever owned. For the greater glory of the Interstates.

49

I left Shelton at nine—the day clear and sunny and a cool sixty degrees—in order to hit New York at mid-morning. Bridgeport came first, two-thirds of the way through Connecticut on I-95 and as ugly as ever, an industrial port city of bricks and smokestacks and overhead wires, where the traffic immediately resumed the rapid pace of Saturday. The city had been fighting off bankruptcy for years, a condition Chief Big Eagle's tribe hoped to eliminate with a gambling casino—if the Bureau of Indian Affairs ruled in favor of their land claim. But the jury was still out, pending a ruling on the Paugussetts' appeal from Washington. And all I could think of was the comment of the aborigine at the rest area restaurant at the other end of the state. *It's been worse since they put in that casino.*

Beyond Bridgeport, raised above the terrain on high embankments, I-95 peers down into the backyards of Connecticut's middle class, a perspective I always find obscene. Swing sets, gas grills, and garbage cans fly by below in backyards barricaded with fences—wire fences and slatted fences and rail fences that catch the litter from the Interstate. I thought again of Emily Dickinson's poem, in which the train that laps the miles peers superciliously into *shanties by the sides of roads*. I felt like a voyeur, glimpsing the detritus of people's cramped and crowded lives.

But the view soon changes—to rooftops and high-rises, billboards and fast-food logos, then glass-and-steel corporate headquarters and turn-of-the-century neighborhoods. Electric railway lines parallel the highway all the way to New York and commuter trains pass on either side, the passengers bent over newspapers and briefcases. Occasionally to the left there are pleasant treed areas and quick views of Long Island Sound, but to the right runs the Boston Post Road, ever congested and claustrophobic. Passing above it at high speed is no consolation. There's simply no relief to the eye.

The megalopolis continued toward New York. Airplanes crossed above strip malls as urban sprawl yielded to suburban sprawl, the traffic relentless in never fewer than three lanes. Concrete barriers and galvanized guardrails divided the highway as a disturbing thought nailed my brain—I couldn't remember when I had last seen a grass median.

Short of the New York state line on I-95, a spate of trees and rock ledges offers a brief respite before the fury begins in earnest. Although I had seen it all before, it still came as a shock—towering dirty-brick apartment buildings, a steady barrage of garish billboards, concrete canyons, concrete walls, concrete barriers. The traffic intensified and the planes grew larger overhead, readying to land at JFK, LaGuardia, or Newark. But there was one very happy surprise. In the years since I had sworn off I-95 through New York City, the road had been marvelously resurfaced. The traffic swept right on through, although at breakneck speeds. In contrast with Boston, New York rates far down the list in terms of time lost in traffic—only thirty-eight hours annually, twenty-sixth place nationwide—an amazing statistic, given the potential for a perpetual Interstate idle.

Approaching the George Washington Bridge, you think you're going to drive head-on into the Port Authority building. You're walled in on all sides and there's no place to go except straight ahead. But at the last second the road dips and you go *under* the building. Then, after a brief tunnel, depending on which lane you get shunted into, you find yourself on the top level or the lower level of the George Washington Bridge, an old suspension structure devoid of aesthetics. The quick transition from tunnel to bridge is disconcerting, and crossing the lower level can be cramped and disappointing. But on this mad Monday I came out on top, with a gorgeous view of the Hudson to my right and a magnificent view of Manhattan to my left—a postcard sky-line with the Empire State Building, Chrysler Building, World Trade Center, and a host of other shoulder-to-shoulder rooftops. It passes quickly but it's worth the risk. Just to see at least once.

Beyond the bridge all lanes sweep north and west on a connector to the New Jersey Turnpike. It was ten-thirty and I was jubilant. I had crossed the George Washington Bridge for the last time in my life! To celebrate my successful passage I exited at the Vince Lombardi Service Area, the first point of relief. It's a large area, like Ohio's Commodore Perry Travel Center before the renovations, and at mid-morning only a quarter of the parking spaces were occupied.

In the men's room a group of truckers were discussing Harvey, the new kid storm on the block. Packing fifty-mile-per-hour winds, it was two hundred miles from Tampa Bay and heading northeast. Which meant that the Carolinas, already swamped by more than twenty inches of rain, were going to get hit again. Which meant that *I* was going to get hit again, perhaps harder than Floyd's battering in Bangor. When would it end? Where was the decent weather? The idyllometer had been reduced to an afterthought.

Outside again, strolling around to shake the tension of the drive, I munched on one of the apples that Dennis had given me. Across the way an industrious-looking young man with tousled hair was reading a book on the running board of a large tractor-trailer. He was a student from Budapest, Hungary, traveling east with friends from Los Angeles, and he snapped shut his book when I asked him about the Interstates.

"I'm afraid I have a negative view," he said apologetically, with a hint of a Slavic accent. "There is simply too much construction and there are too many delays. I heard on your television that there's not enough money, so the construction is spread over many years. The Interstates in Oklahoma and Arkansas are the worst I've seen on our trip. Western Europe has better roads than those states. The highways are good in Europe, but in Eastern Europe they are horrible."

I told him about the roads I had seen in Russia with Chief Big Eagle—that it was no wonder the Soviet Union had collapsed. He nodded knowingly. "The roads in Hungary are getting better now, with that Communist mess behind us. But you know—" He stood on the running board and reached through the open window of the door into the cab of the tractor trailer "—what is best about your Interstates, for me at least, is *this*." He handed me a large pair of expensive binoculars. "Try," he urged. "Try!"

I put the binoculars to my face, focused, and trained them on the gasoline pumps at the end of the service area. I could read the price—I intended to fill the 'Vette before leaving—a dollar forty-nine point nine.

"I am a bird watcher," he said. "A member of the Audubon Society. Do you know this group?"

I nodded, handing the binoculars back over. "And what does this have to do with the Interstates?"

"Your Interstates offer the best places for bird-watching. There are so many scenic stop places. We have come all the way across the country, and I have made my friends stop so often they want to kick me out! Several times I have seen your wonderful bird, the eagle. The symbol of your wonderful country, with the wonderful roads."

* * *

Three gasoline islands stood at the far end of the service area. Two of them held several vehicles, so I chose the free one, stopping at the very first pump. Immediately a car pulled in on my tail, idling while I filled up. When I reached for the squeegee, a woman in the front passenger seat—her husband was behind the wheel—leaned out the window and whined, "Anytime you're ready, sir!" Her tone was exasperated, her accent flat and ugly, a New Jersey original. I pointed to the free pumps all about me and she whined again. "But our gas tank's not on that side!" In the time they had spent idling, the woman fuming—I had no idea what her husband was thinking—they could have circled to another pump. Then their gas tank *would* have been on the right side.

A more subtle New Jersey welcome awaited me a few miles down the road when I stopped at a tollbooth for a ticket. All chutes had green lights, but a bottleneck had developed in the middle lanes. Cars were squeezing to the left and right and the traffic was stacking up rapidly. When I got there I could see why. Orange cones blocked the middle lane. The ticket machine was out of order.

"You oughta shut off that green light," I suggested to the uniformed attendant who finally handed me a ticket. She was middle-aged and plump, with rouged cheeks and plucked eyebrows that had been redrawn at a rakish angle.

"OK," she said. "We will." But her words were utterly devoid of sincerity. She had obviously heard it all before, was tired of hearing it, and wasn't going to do anything about it. And so the first two sour notes of my grand lap of America were sung as I entered New Jersey, a double dose of attitude with accents to match. As our forefathers wrote in the Declaration of Independence, *let facts be submitted to a candid world.*

The northern end of I-95 in New Jersey gives the state a bad reputation and makes it the butt of unkind jokes. In contrast, I-80 in western New Jersey is pastoral, especially through the Kittatinny Mountains and the Delaware Water Gap. But in the east the New Jersey Turnpike cuts through the meadowlands—flat, wide open, and ugly, especially along the coastal plain of Newark Bay. Smokestacks, power lines, refineries, and oil tanks sprawl across the salt marshes in a dense grid, a jungle gym of tubes, pipes, and derricks. Eerie white smoke leaks into the sky above cylindrical railcars. Storage tanks sit everywhere like giant aspirins.

Farther along, seagulls flock above garbage dumps, and old trestles span marshy inlets, black iron structures at odds with the natural beauty of cattails and angelhair grasses. It was seventy-six degrees now and clouding over, the grayness coloring my mood along with the landscape. I thought of *The Great Gatsby*, the famous ash heaps just to the east of me, where the neck of Long Island meets New York. Do people reflect landscapes the way some do their dogs? The women at the service center and at the tollbooth had convinced me.

But there was a plus, as my brother Brian had noted. Far to my right the trucks had their own lanes. For the first time since departure I was entirely free of them. But the glorious freedom was short-lived. North of Trenton the grand merge began for good—six lanes to three—trucks, cars, SUVs, you name it, barreling along madly again as through Connecticut.

In the late '60s a cousin of mine had lived in New Jersey, commuting the New Jersey Turnpike daily. This was decades before the term *road rage* entered the national vocabulary, but the behavior was widespread despite the lack of a label. Passing through New Jersey once en route to Connecticut, I had stopped to visit Barry, and all he could talk about was his daily battles on the Turnpike. "He was trying to kill me!" he said, explaining his most recent encounter with a driver who had pursued him right to his exit, trying to run him off the road. The disbelief and fear in his voice echoed in my mind as I passed the exit I'd taken to his apartment.

At eleven-fifteen I pulled into another rest area where an enormous St. Bernard, wedged improbably behind the wheel of a parked car, barked at me as I headed for the men's room. My attention diverted, I nearly walked head-on into another car just pulling out. The encounter left me tap dancing to avoid getting hit. Several elderly couples were in the car, and the driver rolled down his window, wagging a finger in mock warning. "We'll get you next time!" he laughed. What a contrast to the two sourpusses up the road! These folks were obviously retired. And in no hurry to kill anyone.

Back on the highway, we had a false alarm. As at the toll station earlier, the middle lane was suddenly closed, blocked off by cones, the traffic splitting to the right and left. Nowhere was there any evidence of construction—no workers, no equipment, no signs—but the middle lane remained closed for several miles. Then, just as suddenly, the cones were gone and the three-lane race resumed. Who makes such decisions? I wondered. What had been the chain of command—and the time factor—between the order and the execution? And to what purpose? I wanted to believe in the logic of cause and effect but my instincts told me otherwise. There had been that precedent years ago at the George Washington Bridge. But today, at least, the delay was brief. And there was no idle crew laughing at the traffic.

South of Trenton the New Jersey Turnpike becomes bearable because trees flank the way, but the cement median barrier gets monotonous. Soon the three lanes dwindled to two. And the gray skies darkened. An SUV was hugging my rear. Annoyed, I shifted gears and sped away. Finally, thirty miles before the Delaware Memorial Bridge, the traffic settled down and I was able to set the cruise control—for the first time in New Jersey. Other surprises followed. The sky parted, sunshine flooded the countryside, and a wide median returned. Grass once more! Then, despite the cruise control, my leg suddenly cramped from the morning clutch work, forcing me into the Clara Barton Service Area at one o'clock.

A state trooper sat in his patrol car at the end of the parking area, busily writing in his ticket book. He was still there after I had walked off my cramp, so I went on over and he rolled down his window. He was keen on the Interstates, especially the New Jersey Turnpike.

"It's a good road," he said thoughtfully, "and great for commuting. It's well cared for and well maintained, whereas I-295 is horrible. The funding's unequal. But our biggest problem out here is drivers falling asleep. They don't take advantage of these rest areas, like *you're* doin'."

The trooper seemed amenable, so I thought I'd ask him something I had been wondering about for years. "Why do you let the traffic go seventy-five when it's posted at sixty-five?"

He shook his pencil at me. "I'll stop you at sixty-seven," he said. But I could tell he was fibbing.

"And why do you pull over more cars than trucks?"

He looked up through his sunglasses. "Because there *are* more cars. Where you headed?" He wanted to change the subject, so I pointed to the 'Vette and told him what I was up to.

"You'll love I-10 out of Florida," he said. "It's a beautiful road. One of my favorites. Now if only this sun'd stay out."

And it did—for a while at least—through the toll at the end of the Turnpike (four dollars sixty cents) and the Delaware Memorial Bridge (two dollars). I had forgotten how beautiful that bridge is—twin green spans suspended side by side, rising high above the Delaware River. Up top, a wide country view spread out before me, marred only by a few industrial clusters along the far shore. The temperature had risen to seventy-eight, the radio calling for rain—from Gert this time. Harvey was in the Gulf of Mexico, ready to come ashore—still a tropical storm, not a hurricane, a lucky break. And it was just an hour from here to Baltimore.

* * *

As we leave New Jersey, here's an Interstate Item:

America's Highways: 1776–1976, a history of the Federal-Aid Program published by the U.S. Department of Transportation, won the Award of Excellence from the Society for Technical Communication. On page 467 of that book there is a large photograph of the Piscataqua River Bridge on I-95 that joins New Hampshire and Maine. It's an aerial view of the protractor-like, Erector Set structure that I had crossed earlier—twice—northbound and southbound. The photograph was taken from a helicopter or small plane. Its caption says of the bridge, *It fits gracefully into its environment and provides convenience, safety, and savings in travel time for the motorist.* But the same could be said for the Delaware Memorial Bridge, which joins New Jersey and Delaware—only more so, because it's a double span, a suspension bridge that resembles the Golden Gate Bridge. Imagine *two* Golden Gate Bridges side by side!

Since the 1920s the residents of New Jersey and Delaware had pressured officials for a fixed crossing between the two states. Beginning in 1926, a ferry served as a substitute. The present bridge, constructed between 1949 and 1968, runs a total of 13,200 feet, northbound and southbound. The towers rise 417 feet above the surface of the river. Their foundations are submerged 110 feet into the New Jersey side of the river and 70 feet into the Delaware side. The concrete pour for each caisson—approximately 27,000 tons—lasted seven days, the longest continuous pour at the time.

And so, in their next highway history, I hope that the U.S. Department of Transportation will replace the photograph of the Piscataqua River Bridge with a shot of the Delaware Memorial Bridge. Certainly we can expect such a publication in 2006, in honor of the 50th anniversary of the Dwight D. Eisenhower System of Interstate and Defense Highways. Meanwhile, if you're in the vicinity, treat yourself to a crossing of the Delaware Memorial Bridge on I-95. I think that George Washington himself, having crossed the Delaware into history, would have wanted his own bridge in New York City to be as pleasant.

* * *

Through Delaware the terrain began to roll, a welcome change from long and level New Jersey. Then the Delaware Turnpike spanned the Susquehanna River on a lengthy, flat bridge—no majestic suspension needed—with another wide view. Green hills rose and fell as if they hadn't heard of the drought. It was almost pleasant, except for the crazy pace of traffic. First three lanes, then four, pressed on toward Baltimore.

In mid-afternoon a siren screamed by me, red lights flashing. I caught up with it over the crest of the next hill. Several cars had collided and sat at odd angles off the highway. Slowing suddenly, the four lanes of traffic converged to two, skirting puddles of shattered glass. The delay was brief, and a sobering pace ensued, the good behavior lasting just a few minutes, the speed increasing with every mile from the scene. The sun was gone now, the afternoon gray and ominous. Gert's rain was very much on the way.

I dreaded Baltimore, remembering Eleanor's words in Maine. I had fought my own way through that Harbor Tunnel too many times. *No Hazmats* the signs warned, but I was carrying no hazardous materials. Just some apples and flags and an Eric Clapton CD. Happily, as in New York, the road was brand new, ascending gradually for a panoramic view of Baltimore Harbor—cranes, smokestacks, boats, docks, warehouses, and stacks and stacks of brick row homes. Then all traffic descended in a mad panic for the tunnel, fanning out and stopping abruptly for a one-dollar toll before continuing into the mouth of the yellow-tiled tube. Which brought another surprise. The tunnel was cleaner and brighter than I had ever seen it, bathing the red 'Vette in an otherworldly yellow glow. The tube bottomed out then ascended, curving as it went, emerging into daylight to continue rising south and west of the city. I had to hand it to Baltimore. It had finally cleaned up its act. Except for the traffic. The traffic was absolutely mad.

At the I-695 beltway I headed west for Bill and Kathy's in Reisterstown, suddenly finding myself doing seventy-five in fourth gear. The cruise control had gone the way of the idyllometer and in changing gears I had simply lost track. But the 'Vette never winced. I had more car than I needed and it was a powerful feeling—because there was a semi on my tail and it was raining again. Changing lanes to shake the truck, I had to swerve to avoid a car cutting in from an outside lane. But the sixteen-inch tires held true. The inside tread on the 'Vette's racing tires differs from the outside tread for maneuvers just like this. Bobbing and weaving, I shot northwest on the 795 spur into the heart of the Baltimore suburbs, country club and horse territory newly greened by the rains of Floyd.

Then the four o'clock commute stopped abruptly. The instant I exited. To a local four-lane in the teeth of an Interstate ambush.

4

THE FIRST TIME I EVER SAW A CHEVROLET CORVETTE WAS IN JUNE OF 1960. My older brother had just graduated from high school and one of his friends had dropped by the house to show off his graduation present— a brand new blue-and-silver hardtop Corvette with bucket seats and four-on-the-floor. This was definitely not the friend we had beaten to the beach a few years earlier by taking the Interstate. His name was Dick—*Dirty* Dick after that day—and he sat smugly behind the wheel at curbside on the corner of Mt. Pleasant Avenue across from the junior high school, leaning toward us on the sidewalk and caressing the leather of the passenger seat.

"You've got your education," he said slowly, letting each syllable sink in. "I've got my car."

He meant that his parents had taken all the money they'd saved to send him to college and turned it into a Corvette. The choice had been his. Whereas my older brother and I—and our two younger brothers and all of our friends—would be going to college instead. With no choice in the matter.

Dick spoke nonchalantly, as if it were simply a matter of taste, but I could tell by his tone of voice that he was convinced who had the better deal. "See ya later, alligator," he said finally. Then he peeled out and left us standing at the curb.

* * *

The rain increased, pelting the 'Vette beneath black skies. But Bill's directions proved sound. I found his street—free of cars beyond the tentacles of the Interstate ambush—then couldn't find the house. The street had been extended since my last visit.

Turning around at the cul-de-sac, I tried again, and the Corvette karma kicked in. A car with two teenagers was exiting a long driveway. I flagged them down, two blond kids, Bill and Kathy's. I hadn't seen them since they were in junior high. Thomas had just gotten his driver's license and was chauffeuring his younger sister to some after-school event. "Our folks will be home soon!" they shouted through the rain. "We left the door open for you!" So I parked out front and ran inside. Right to the nearest shower.

Bill, who looks a lot like David Letterman, arrived shortly. He's one of those friends you can count on one hand. But he's never been a fan of the Interstates. When we lived in southwest Virginia, he and Kathy came to visit once—a six-hour drive down I-81. Thomas was an infant, and the return drive took ten hours because Bill was at the wheel. Infant or no infant, he had to get off the Interstate.

"The rain's beading so beautifully on your 'Vette out there," he said. "You've gotta take Thomas for a ride after dinner." Then he lapsed into a discourse about his latest interest—CB radios on the highway.

"They say it's degenerated since the days of 'Convoy,'" he began. "Remember that song? Probably just a mirror of the whole society, really. I'm amused at some of the cars I see with CB antennas. The other day I saw a Fiesta, or some such small car, with an eight-foot antenna on the roof! I bought my outfit at a large truck stop down in Jessup. I've attached a PA speaker to it, so I can talk to other CBers on the radio. Or boom my voice to anyone nearby. I'm amazed, though, by all the trash on the airwaves. All the profanity. Driving out to Frederick the other day I switched to this channel and someone says, 'Quite a puss in that white van.' 'Well, send her up here,' somebody replies. 'Don't keep her back there all to yourself.'"

When Bill gets going like this I just kick back and listen. I had had a shower and was feeling brand new. I let my tape recorder do the work.

"Another astounding thing," he went on, "especially in the early evening, is how you can hear truckers talking from long distances. I've heard 'em in Mississippi, Kansas, Missouri, Minnesota, Kentucky, Michigan, and Massachusetts. It's got something to do with the sunspot cycles. The heavier the solar activity, the denser the iono-sphere, the more likely the signals will bounce down. I'm amazed at how many radio users actually have—or are faking—a southern accent. Nine out of ten, as I said, lace their talk with profanity. Fortunately, CB has another dimension. There are some actual, legiti-mate conversations taking place, and people use the thing for practical reasons. Most of the rotten stuff is on Channel 19, the truckers' highway channel. But you can still ask for—and receive—legitimate information on road conditions, speed traps, whatever you need. Some people are really friendly, especially when you're asking for directions. But it's surprising how many of these big-rig drivers don't even know where the hell they're going. I always imagined them as map experts, with any map they might need right under their seat. But they're not."

I smiled and clasped my hands behind my head, safe in Reisterstown and out of the rain, three hundred miles from my brother's home in Shelton.

"I like to scan the channels," Bill continued. "I've found truckers conversing with each other and their loading supervisor as they wait to fill up at the local gravel plant. It's not deep conversation, but for them the CB's useful, a special tool. On certain channels you can hear people talking across the country. The other day I picked up a guy from southern California. This is called DX-ing—long distance communication—technically illegal under FCC rules, but it's done all the time. Yet the typical CB outfit only has a maximum range of seven or eight miles, except during the sunspot activity, as I said. The whole CB thing is sort of fascinating. If I were a Communications guy, like my office mate at the university, there'd be enough concepts involved for a Ph.D. thesis. Or at least an interesting article."

Kathy had returned home and soon called us for dinner—crab cakes, a local specialty—and Thomas and Coralee scrambled to the table.

When it comes to the Interstates, Kathy's the opposite of Bill, relying on them frequently to visit family in Utah. "When my grandmother died back in 1964," she said, "we left Maryland on a Thursday for services on Sunday. The Interstates weren't complete then. I'll never forget my father on that trip, saying again and again: 'Of all the words of tongue and pen, the saddest are these—the expressway ends.' Then we'd have to get off and plod along the local roads until the next stretch of Interstate. Today, it's smooth sailing all the way."

"I prefer the oldness of country roads," Bill said. "It's just a matter of taste."

Thomas looked up from his crab cakes. "I like the numbers on the signs."

I must have looked confused because he continued quickly. "The speed limits, I mean! But the suburbs are following the Interstates right out here into the country. First there was I-95, then I-695, then the 795 spur. We used to live way out, but now we're close in."

"Speaking strictly as a passenger," Coralee added, "because I'm too young to drive yet, I'd have to say that I prefer the off-roads."

Bill smiled. "As you can see, when it comes to the Interstates, as a family our opinions are divided."

The rain hit hardest during the night—nothing to do with Floyd or Gert, according to NPR. Just a local cold front. Harvey had changed course, however, and was scheduled to hit Naples, Florida, by nightfall, lingering through Wednesday as a tropical storm. If my schedule held, I would just miss it. Still, I was starting my second full week on the road as I had started my first. In the rain. It was getting depressing.

I left Reisterstown at nine-thirty in a cold drizzle and was immediately locked into an Interstate idle, all lanes jammed along the 795 spur, on the I-695 beltway, and on I-95 South. Washington, D.C. ranks fifth, just above Boston, in terms of time lost in traffic, and with the idyllometer at zero I munched on an apple, gnawing it to the core like a caged rodent. A high terra cotta wall laced with ivy along I-695 was the nicest I'd seen, but it was offset by a corrugated blue metal affair on I-95—the ugliest to date—short of the Wilson Memorial Bridge on the Potomac. There was little else to notice in the drizzle besides the sea of vehicles. Finally, after many false starts, the traffic picked up, forcing me into my Richard Petty mode. A sign for the *Rosecroft Raceway* on I-95 was more than appropriate. No need to exit. The race was on.

The flat but stately Wilson Bridge—a wide drawbridge—offers a brief glimpse of the Potomac River as you enter Virginia. The nation's Capitol lies just out of sight to the north. After college, I had spent a decade in the vicinity teaching high school. But, as in Connecticut, the traffic killed all reminiscence.

* * *

Before leaving Washington, D.C., here's an Interstate Item:

Just three miles northwest of the Wilson Bridge is Shirlington, Virginia. It derives its name from Shirley Highway (I-395) and Arlington County. According to its web site, *Shirlington is a young professional playground. It is simply a bastion of convenience, located a stone's throw from employers in Washington and Arlington. A stylish collection of restaurants and entertainment options, surrounded by a mix of apartments, condominiums, and traditional neighborhoods, it is hip enough to attract crowds from other parts of the metropolitan area, but still quiet and quaint enough to be a relaxing home to thousands of residents.* Shirlington is featured in *America's Highways: 1776–1976*; that is, on page 482, there is a photograph of Shirlington's pedestrian bridge. The caption reads: *With safety for the pedestrian in mind, a 1,082-foot long pedestrian overpass was built over I-95 in Shirlington, Va., that safely connects a large apartment complex on the east side of the highway with a large shopping center on the west.* The overpass is a cage-like structure that curves up from the sides as if to form a canopy, but remains open directly overhead like the sunroof of the 'Vette.

Simply put, Shirlington would not be "simply a bastion of convenience" without its Interstate overpass. I would see a variety of such pedestrian bridges around the nation, always strategically placed, making similar urban villages possible while rendering the Interstates an innocuous feature of America's backyard.

* * *

By eleven o'clock, caught in heavier rain and miles of construction, I could tell it was going to be a long day. I exited near the Lorton prison, feeling like a prisoner myself, and at the nearest gas station the lively black attendant seemed to read my thoughts.

"The Interstate is the craziest, sorry-ass road known to mankind," he said. "They built it all wrong. They put a beltway around D.C. and ran three lanes into two, creatin' instant bottlenecks. Any asshole can see that. And as soon as they finished it, it was obsolete. But look at West Virginia. They get more because they don't have many people. This country has miles and miles of gorgeous Interstates that nobody uses. It's all pork belly politics with Senator Byrd. Mr. Smith goes to Washington with good intentions, then realizes it's all a big club. They shoulda put in six lanes between here and Boston right at the start. I tell ya, man, from five to nine each morning there are forty thousand cars coming into D.C.—into ten square miles! And never, never, never get on the Interstate around here between four and seven in the afternoon! They shoulda built the Interstates for a hundred years from now."

Across the street the steep embankment of the exit I had taken was studded with pieces of white PVC pipe about two feet high. "What are those?" I asked, peering through the dark rain. "Markers for the people who get killed here?"

The attendant cracked up. "Nope. There are little trees in each of those pipes. It's to protect 'em from the deer. The deer come out late at night and nibble the trees. Way after the rush hour. They're the only ones with any sense!"

Filling the tank of the 'Vette brought a psychological boost, but it disappeared as the traffic swallowed me again and swept on toward Richmond. In the rain. Past the *Rappahanock*, the *Ni*, the *Po*, and the *Matta*—rivers I couldn't follow with my eye because cement barriers flanked their brief flat bridges. There were unmistakable signs of the South now—a reddish tint to the sand along the shoulders, unkempt median grass, strewn black litter from blown retreads, and dirty floors in the rest areas, where all talk had a twang. Where country music was piped in and the stalls were etched with graffiti. *Get God and get free. Elwood was here. I saw you take that shit, now put it back.* The pines had returned—not the storybook pines of New England but southern Christmas tree pines—white pines in the medians and wooded shoulders.

Then came Richmond. I had been looking forward to it, but it was *garbage in, garbage out*, an Interstate phenomenon I would witness all too often. By *garbage in, garbage out* I mean that the least desirable local entities are shunted to the city limits and beyond. They get you coming and going—warehouses, failing industries, marginal businesses, old homes, junkyards, fast-food places, railroad tracks, power lines—all as drab as this rainy Tuesday itself. As I crossed the James River into Richmond proper, a small sign for the Museum of the Confederacy

61

confirmed that I was, indeed, in the South. Then the highway threaded left and right, commanding all my attention. Ever since D.C., truckers had been camped in the passing lane as if they owned it, their constant spray and mist challenging the rhythm of my wipers. It was all I could do to get to Richmond's *garbage out.*

At Exit 54 a sign for Virginia State University—a traditionally black institution—took me back in time. I had spoken there once when we lived in Virginia. North of Petersburg the reminiscences continued as I crossed the Appomattox River, a river my grandfather used to call *Applemattocks,* relating the tale of a relative in the Union army who had witnessed Lee's surrender to Grant. The road was two lanes again in each direction, with a flat, grassy median and moderate traffic. Then I-95 left the Chesapeake Bay Watershed, and the megalopolis that had begun way back in Portland, Maine, gradually ended. I was halfway to Miami on that great relief map in my mind, my little Hot Wheels Corvette again on cruise control. And the rain was letting up.

The Virginia coastal plain is flat, yet it could have been pretty had the median grass been mowed. Walls of white pines soothed the way, but spread out among them were homes unlike any I'd seen en route—bungalows, prefabs, trailers, shacks—stuck willy-nilly along the edge of the highway. And all the people poking about in the back-yards were black. In New Jersey I had crossed into a zone of obnoxious behavior, and south of Richmond I crossed a color line. Only the black road itself was in good shape. Everything else was ragged around the edges.

A yellow sign-on-wheels just off the berm ahead was announcing in scoreboard lights what I had feared: *Expect delays. I-95 in NC.* Whatever Floyd had left behind lay just ahead of me, the gap closing rapidly at seventy-five miles per hour. To prepare for the worst I stopped at a travel area at two-thirty in the afternoon. The facility was old, dirty, and in a state of disrepair. And suddenly I was one of three whites among a hundred or more blacks. Avoiding eye contact, I followed a series of handwritten signs to a temporary restroom upstairs. A final sign on a hallway door said *for the men to use.* It was signed, *manger.* I took care of business and returned to the 'Vette in a hurry.

I had parked in one of a few empty spaces in a far corner of the lot, where a black trucker was about to climb into his rig. When he caught my eye I asked him about the Interstates, and his earnest response left me ashamed for having fled the facility.

"I haul from South Carolina to D.C. all the time," he said. "It's *tur-rible* up there, ain't it? I like it better down here. It gets easier south of here, but they's crazy people driving all over the place in D.C. Truckers up there drive in *the ticket lane*—that's what we call the *inside* lane—so you cain't get on by. I'm always glad to get home. I been doin' this fo' ten years now. Damn good way of life."

I asked if he had seen the warning up the road, if I-95 was open farther south. There was a huge CB antenna on his cab. "From what I hear," he laughed, "it's wide open. Jes' like yo' eyes."

I laughed too.

"Not many white folks stop at this place," he said.

"I didn't realize—"

"—it was all black?"

I nodded.

"Now you know how *we* feels." He grinned broadly.

"Live and learn," I said. We shook hands.

"Yessah. We live and we learns."

Back on the road and reassured in all ways, I crossed the line into North Carolina.

It was a humid seventy-five degrees and the sun was struggling to come out. And quite suddenly the landscape was neat and trim—except for a shocking barrage of billboards, including the first of dozens for *South of the Border*, one of which featured a huge sombrero in gaudy day-glo colors. *Come on down, y'all!* Billboards flew by one after the other, tacky, relentless, unwarranted. The sheer number was unbelievable, reducing the few I'd seen in New York for Niagara Falls to a misdemeanor. But in North Carolina billboards are a major crime. Where was Lady Bird Johnson when we needed her? She had crusaded against billboards, but what had come of her campaign? We need someone to take an ax to America's billboards like Carry A. Nation had once taken an ax to America's booze. And they could start in North Carolina.

Crossing the Roanoke River, I pressed on for Fayetteville, my day's destination. A corridor of pine forests flanked the highway, and suddenly the median was a wild burst of yellow. Flower beds appeared out of nowhere, then disappeared just as suddenly, only to reappear again and again farther on—sometimes yellow, sometimes orange, sometimes red—interludes of beauty amidst the ugly billboards, a welcome North Carolina Interstate touch.

Then came my first glimpses of Floyd's damage, much less horrendous than I had imagined. Tall spindly pines, snapped like matchsticks, lay across the shoulder, right to the edge of the white line. Crews had been clearing only trees blocking the road. The shoulders would have to wait. A narrow sign on twin metal legs had been twisted like a corkscrew. It now stood bent over, its top stuck in the grass. Waist-high water wandered through adjacent pine forests, a neighboring creek that Floyd had left a muddy sea. The rain that had pelted me in Bangor had produced the worst flooding in North Carolina's history. Abandoned cars, some battered, waited to be towed from the median and shoulders, each tagged across the rear window with a bright orange sticker.

But another burst of median color spiced the damage—bright red this time—a stretch of tall flowers like gigantic poppies, as stunning as a float in the Rose Bowl parade. The rain had stopped and the sun broke through the moment I whipped by the dazzling display. Then the speed limit changed to seventy—the highest posting I'd yet seen—and the traffic immediately moved to eighty. The psychological boost brought a surge of adrenaline. There was something exciting about even digits on the speedometer. 80. This was more like it—speed, beauty, sunlight, and, after a brief search, classical music on the radio. I reached for my sunglasses, but the trucks across the median were coming at me with their headlights on. It was raining again farther south. I couldn't believe it. When would it end? I flung my sunglasses back on the seat beside me.

* * *

The rain caught me again in a construction area north of Rocky Mount, where a blinking sign warned that Route 64 East to Tarboro was closed. Occasionally, across the median, a host of rubber cones reduced the twin northbound lanes to one, the way littered with tree bark and slick debris. The first billboard for *Disney World* seemed like proof of my southern progress, but it was still a billboard, competing with others for *South of the Border* and *North Carolina Train Service*—a constant plague that will forever keep North Carolina from a respectable idyllometer reading. Despite all the gorgeous flower beds in the world.

The rain continued through the afternoon. South of Rocky Mount the shallow rapids of the Tar River ran rife with whitecaps. Twenty miles east it had inundated Princeville, sending residents fleeing for their lives. North Carolina, according to a travel-area place mat, is called the *Tar Heel State*. But it has nothing to do with the Tar River, or the quantities of tar, pitch, and turpentine produced locally. A livelier story involves a North Carolina Civil War regiment that threatened to put tar on the heels of another regiment so they would "stick better in the next fight." General Lee, hearing of the soldiers' tenacity, reportedly said, "God Bless the Tar Heel boys." And the name stuck. Like tar itself. Like the residents of Princeville. Although it would be more than a year before they could return to their homes.

At three-thirty I stopped for coffee at a nearly empty restaurant where I met two college students from East Carolina University in Greenville. They were heading north because their college was underwater. An attractive young couple, they reminded me of my own students. Having been forced to abandon their campus, they were happy to find a professor.

"Is the Interstate open north of here?" the blonde asked eagerly. "We're going to my home in Maryland. We're trying to time it so we miss the crunch in Richmond and D.C."

"Good luck," I said. But I was happy to tell her that the roads were no longer closed.

Her boyfriend, from Fayetteville, had never been north of Richmond on I-95. "I have no complaints about the Interstates," he said, "except that they're so boring in South Carolina and Georgia." He seemed apologetic, knowing I was headed south.

But his girlfriend, who was doing the driving, had a complaint. "The on–off ramps ought to be extended," she insisted. "They're not long enough to merge safely. At least for me." And she was adamant on another point. "I-95 in North Carolina is the prettiest Interstate of all. It attracts you but never distracts you. It's simply the best I've ever seen."

"What about all the billboards?" I asked.

She looked up from her french fries. "What billboards?"

I had heard that innocent intonation so often from my own students that I knew better than to pursue the issue. I just wished them luck and got back on the highway.

The closer to Fayetteville, the more trees were down. Entire stands of pines lay flattened. Portable roadside signs, in their yellow scoreboard letters, announced that I-40 East to Wilmington was closed. *No detours.* No wonder the students had been worried. Near a sign for Cape Fear Basin dozens of billboards were smashed—eerily ripped, shattered, and splintered—no cause for remorse. I wished Floyd would have taken them all, especially those counting down the miles to *South of the Border.* And those touting lewd thrills—*We dare to bare! Topless cafés! Food and fun! 24 hours!* I counted six of the latter in a single mile stretch—a desecration, an abomination unto the Lord. Right down here in His own territory. The *Saith.*

I was annoyed now, boxed in by a pickup running parallel to a VW van. The drivers were cruising side by side, a dangerous habit, either out of ignorance or, worse yet, on purpose—to keep the 'Vette in check, the one with out-of-state plates. That spiffy red sports car, while both North Carolina vehicles were dilapidated. It was the second time this had happened to me since crossing the state line, a bit of lunatic local color I could do without. But it continued for twenty minutes or more, through an intermittent drizzle, until our little trio passed what to me will always be the image by which I remember Hurricane Floyd—a tractor-trailer in the northbound lanes, upside down along the median's white line. It was now pointing south, without dent or damage, wheels in the air like a centipede on its back. High winds or water had somehow flipped it, turning it a hundred-eighty degrees and leaving it just out of danger, unscathed except for being upside down. Unlike the abandoned cars up the road, it bore no orange sticker. It didn't need one. You couldn't miss it.

But the grim sight had a salutary effect. The driver of the pickup weaved slightly in his lane, causing the VW van to weave in turn, and they nearly collided. Then the pickup cut ahead into the right-hand lane and I downshifted and left them in my sixteen-inch tracks. In a heartbeat the 'Vette was doing ninety—my fastest ever—a speed I maintained until my rearview mirror showed nothing but pines.

A few miles later I exited in Fayetteville, heart still thumping, all senses geared to a new challenge—to locate my lodgings and beat the Interstate ambush. I was batting zero so far when it came to finding my motel and wanted to raise my average. But it was easy this time, because the rain had let up and the ambush didn't materialize. I was free at last of the East Coast megalopolis. And for once the directory was clear. *Exit 49. Left over bridge to motel.* And there it was.

Inside at the desk I caught the headlines of the *Raleigh News & Observer* in a rack of daily papers: *Damage hits 1.3 billion. Many roads reopen as effort grinds on.*

The friendly woman behind the counter shook her head sympathetically. "Those poor folks over to down east," she said. "They really got hit bad. Even the president himself came down. He was here yestiddy, commiseratin'. You just missed it." But my attention had snagged elsewhere. She had said *down east.* North Carolina, like Maine, has a *down east* too. And for a weird moment I thought I was back in Bangor.

In my room the TV recapped President Clinton's visit, tracing Floyd's local damage northward through Virginia into New Jersey, where many coastal communities still were without power. But Floyd had left me relatively unscathed. Except for enormous fatigue. And the feeling that my Hot Wheels Corvette was Noah's Ark.

* * *

Wednesday brought the autumnal equinox, the last day of summer. It was still raining. The temperature had dropped during the night to forty-five. Lit by the yellow arc lights of the parking lot, the 'Vette gleamed in the chilly rain outside my window. There were exactly one hundred days left until Y2K—if we could survive all the rain. Up at five, I paced the long corridors of the motel until the restaurant opened at six. Then I had a quick breakfast and checked out, hitting the road in total darkness at seven-thirty as the rain beat a drumroll on the sunroof.

Traffic was deliciously light, and south of Lumberton I began to get excited. The sky was graying on my left shoulder, the rain thinning. As soon as I passed into South Carolina I'd be done with billboards for *South of the Border* for the rest of my life! One said, *Come see our great white shark!* Another was totally upside down, a pathetic last-ditch attempt to snag tourists. The place itself, set on several acres just off the northbound lanes, is as gaudy and tacky as its billboards—a cheap, chintzy, mini theme park filled with souvenir shops. Its crowning attraction rises right in the center of the place, an enormous sombrero atop a structure resembling the Eiffel Tower. I was so very glad to put it all behind me.

In South Carolina the posted speed remained seventy, so the traffic cruised at eighty, heading for Florence down a flat, straight, two-lane corridor flanked by tall pines. Pines graced the median as well, often obscuring the northbound traffic. The roadbed itself ran higher than both median and shoulders, the drainage creating swamps to the left and right—stagnant algae-filled water that seemed perfect for alligators. As did the Great Pee Dee River, which, agitated by Floyd, slugged along like brown soup as I whipped by.

At a rest area in Florence beds of red and yellow flowers—as tall as tulips—brightened the gray morning. Inside, I met a truck driver who had emigrated from India.

"Between New Jersey and Florida," he said, "I-95 is the best route I've ever driven. But it gets congested up north."

A black South Carolina state trooper was eavesdropping on our conversation. "Sure, it gets busy," he said, "but hey—that's what it was built for. It's well kept and it keeps you out of the country."

The implication seemed to be, down here in the South, you don't want to get stuck out in the country.

"I been twenty-five years on the force," he said, "and I love patrolling the Interstate. Faulk's the name, like right here on my shirt."

I hadn't asked, but was touched by his enthusiasm. I would speak to several hundred people in the course of my grand lap, but he was the only one to insist on telling me his name. Which I promptly wrote down. "With a *u*," he said. "L. J. Faulk."

Outside, a few blue holes had opened in the sky overhead, and I put on my sunglasses to encourage them. The rain had stopped, for the umpteenth time since Ohio. Meanwhile, Harvey had crossed Florida into the Atlantic and was heading for the Bahamas.

Before leaving the rest area I cleaned the windshield of accumulated grit, but as soon as I got back on the highway a truck ahead of me blew a retread, spewing large fragments of synthetic rubber through a dark cloud of rust. Fortunately, because the 'Vette rides so low, the brunt of the debris flew overhead, littering the road behind me with what looked like squiggly dinosaur turds. The windshield was a different matter. It was now coated with a thin brown film. The moment confirmed what I call Murphy's Interstate Law. *If you clean it, they will come.* As I would learn again and again around America. *They* being any local entity capable of dirtying what you've just cleaned.

Had I never seen a retread explode before, I would have been terrified. But the 'Vette hit ninety again—oh so easily—and I put the truck behind me. And out of the dust came a billboard featuring magnolias, enormous yellow flowers on a leafy green bush, perhaps the very flowers I'd been seeing in the medians and rest areas. Southern flowers for southern belles.

Signs for Sumter and Shiloh lent a further southern touch. This was Civil War territory for sure. So how'd all those soldiers, I wanted to know, ever get across the Great Pee Dee River swamp? Or the Santee Lakes, now a wildlife refuge? Or Lake Marion, where three side-by-side concrete bridges rise from the water on pylons of telephone poles? Humped like the Loch Ness monster, the triple bridges were as brown as the choppy lake just beneath, their green concrete side-barriers matching a spectacular green view of the countryside. The Lake Marion bridges are reason enough to take I-95 through South Carolina.

North of Savannah the sun came out again and the idyllometer hit eighty—exactly my cruising speed—whenever the billboards disappeared. There was blue sky now, sunshine, and a clear track through pine tree country. I munched an apple, totally content, disturbed only by occasional roadkill that I couldn't identify—something like a big dog that was shaped like a seal, some monster that had crawled out of these ever-thickening roadside swamps to take an unfortunate turn across the Interstate. Such sights are unnerving. On the Interstates you see dead things you've never seen before.

Stopping for gas at eleven-thirty, I noticed a big crockpot on the counter when I went inside to pay.

"Har yew?" said the fat woman at the cash register.

"Fine," I said. "You?"

"Fahn," she sang. "Jus' fahn." She caught me staring at the crockpot. "Reg'lar or Cajun?" It was filled with boiled peanuts, about four times the size of your take-me-out-to-the-ball-park peanuts. But I opted for a Slim Jim, a country compromise, which I gnawed on outside, standing around in the sun like a good ol' boy. The sun felt great on my face. There was no rain in sight. And although I wouldn't have believed it had you told me, I was to see no rain again until Oregon.

But a new complication immediately introduced itself. Crawling about on the 'Vette was something that would plague me for the next two weeks. There were dozens of them—hundreds of them—winged narrow black bugs about half an inch long, each with a small square orange head.

I thought they had mistaken the 'Vette for a big ol' red magnolia. They were crawling all over it slowly, as if in search of nectar. But they were in pairs, joined at the rear. Others floated above the car, likewise joined, their wings beating slowly as they hovered or drifted on the breeze. When the air was still they went nowhere, pulling in opposite directions and hence making no progress. I waved my hand to brush them from my face. Logy as winter wasps, they were alighting on everything—me, the car, the bench out front. And the asphalt was thick with paired corpses.

"What *are* these things?" I asked a man coming out of the gas station.

He seemed incredulous that I didn't know. "We call them *love bugs*," he said. "They mate in May and September. This is their season."

Love bugs, I later learned, are flies. Order Diptera, with the Latin name *Plecia nearctica*. But a scientific moniker doesn't make them any less of a nuisance.

As I pulled out of the gas station they were still on the windshield, crawling about slowly in their odd mating dance. And as I flew back onto the highway they were *still* on the windshield, unaffected by the air speed. I tried the wipers—a huge mistake. The bugs instantly turned to mush in streams of yellow goo that the wipers spread methodically, streaking the glass until the goo dried like egg yolk. The washer spray only made it worse. But I had just stopped and was not about to stop again.

The midday sun caused a different problem, casting shadows across the highway from the long tunnel of trees. The shadows were entrancing, their dappled patterns swaying on the road surface as the overhead pines swayed in the wind. But they made depth perception difficult. The effect was exotic, seductive, and dangerous.

Closer to Savannah the traffic picked up. Palm-like shrubs joined the flowers in the median, a new kind of flora. Then I-95 crossed the broad Savannah River and a large sign welcomed me to the state. *We're glad Georgia's on your mind.* Immediately the road surface changed to new asphalt, the lanes increased to three, and the posted speed dropped to fifty-five. There were many more trucks now, pushed about in a stiff wind, but otherwise it was a sunny seventy-two and entirely pleasant. Except for the ever-present litter of retreads.

Beyond the Savannah River comes a series of rivers with a new look—dark water winding through marshlands and tidal basins, scenic waterways through the heart of pine forests—the *Jerico*, the *South Newport*, the *Cathead*, the *Darien*, their shallows laced with tall rushes and waving cattails. Many of the bridges that cross these rivers have pylons like telephone poles, tilted slightly toward the road surface to form the Greek letter *pi*. The water beneath them sparkled invitingly.

Taking a break at twelve-thirty, I parked the 'Vette beside a Pepsi truck at a gas-and-food mart. The teenage driver of the truck turned to me immediately.

"Ain't nuthin' better than to ride in a 'Vette," he said, shaking his head wistfully. I immediately asked him about the Interstates. "Well," he began, in no hurry whatsoever, "they're fairly good around here, not too congested. But in Florida they're in worse shape. My favorite's I-16 between Savannah and Atlanta. It's wide open, smooth sailin' all the way. But if you go above eighty you're askin' for it." He shook his head again, eyes drooling on the 'Vette.

Inside, colorful glass jars lined the counter by the cash register, their contents explained by a handwritten sign on the wall. *Item closeout sale. Aunt Jilene's Jelly. Only $1.69. All flavors.* Another southern delicacy, like Cajun peanuts. I settled for a cup of coffee instead, then went outside to wash the love bugs from the windshield. The Pepsi truck was gone but the love bugs were back en masse, hovering about the car two by two, alighting in my hair, crawling up my arms, clinging to the very squeegee with which I scraped away their mushed cousins. The chore took an entire roll of paper towels and half a spray-bottle of washer fluid. Scrubbing away at the windshield, I had to pause every few seconds to flick away floating pairs with thumb and finger, an effort that reduced the marauders to airborne goo. Half an hour later I was exhausted, drenched with sweat, and angry.

Then it dawned on me. Was that really Aunt Jilene's Jelly on sale inside? Or some local concoction made from love bugs? I would be taking some with me after all, because a dozen pairs came with me as I dove into the 'Vette, drawn inside on the breeze of my hasty retreat. Slamming the door, I turned on the air conditioner, its frigid blast propelling the mating pairs out of reach, and for the next few minutes I twisted in my seat, swatting at them with the motel directories. It was the Civil War all over again, a Connecticut Yankee against southern insurgents.

When I thought I had killed them all, I got back on the highway. Dozens of pairs still clung to the windshield, but I knew enough not to use the wipers. It didn't matter. Murphy's Interstate Law applied anyway. Within minutes the glass was egg-yolked again as I flew through wavy black swarms. A few pairs still floated about inside, drifting in and out of view in the rearview mirror. I was on my way to Jacksonville, my destination for the day, and I already knew how I'd be spending the evening. Ridding the 'Vette of Aunt Jilene's Jelly.

* * *

Through Georgia, I-95 becomes tedious—long and flat and straight—and I was soon forced into a small rest area to stretch. But I was glad I stopped. The facility was all but deserted, a tiny green island of peat moss and pine. And it contained the only official *anti*-Interstate propaganda I would see in all of America, posted behind glass with other travel information.

Speeding your way through Georgia on dull Interstates? Heading for the I-95 stampede south to the Golden Isles? There's a shorter way, says the Georgia Department of Transportation, and a more scenic way. A country highway through southern towns and family farms, a quiet blacktop past antique stores and Revolutionary War sites, over glinting rivers and through historical coastal hamlets. Don't have time to see the sights? Don't worry. This is a quicker way, even at a slower pace. Take the Wiregrass Trail. You'll arrive beachside relaxed, not ragged from the rough ride.

Directions to the Wiregrass Trail followed, the route cutting across the corner of the state where I-16 meets I-95 south of Savannah. The suggestion was tempting, but I was committed to the Interstates, tedious or not. Besides, the Department of Transportation was making no promises about love bugs.

The first palm tree on I-95 is near Exit 7 in southern Georgia. It's planted in the median, but it's nonetheless a palm tree, top branches flopping slightly like the rotors of a helicopter at rest. Other palms follow in the median farther along, amidst marshy frond-like plants with tall fan-dancer plumes. And suddenly the forest to the right grew creepy with thick vines. The coastal plain was giving way to black mud-flats. Reeds and rushes filled the shallows. The Myrtle River runs through here, curving away to the west through luxuriant swamps. But to the east, smokestacks of an oil refinery mar its contours. Then tall bushes with red flowers lined the median, a thick green wall of camellias or magnolias. The names don't matter. All such flowers are gorgeous.

South of Brunswick two teenagers in the passing lane were busy kissing each other—love bugs of a different sort—their speed fluctuating between fifty and eighty. Their Ford Fiesta weaved dangerously, obliviously. I followed them carefully, saw my chance, and shot by.

It was clouding over as I crossed the Little Satilla River, then the Crooked River, where clumps of angelhair grasses laced the winding marshes. Near here the Okefenokee Parkway leads to the famous Okefenokee Swamp, a much larger version of the local landscape a few miles west. Then it was up and over the St. Marys River—with a long view to the horizon—right into Florida. *Welcome to the Sunshine State.* But the sun had disappeared behind a thin gray haze, and the temperature had fallen to sixty-eight.

By two-thirty the love bugs had forced me into Florida's very first rest area. Time to clean the windshield again. I had planned to stop anyway, taking my own advice about a state's initial welcome. And as I got out of the 'Vette I could instantly tell that I had crossed another invisible boundary. A kind of rain forest abutted the parking lot, thick with vines, pines, palms, and fronds. The air itself was balmy. Large scarab-like June bugs worked their way over the peat moss. Small brown lizards scampered across the sidewalks into yucca bushes and shrubs, reptilian cousins of the alligators I had imagined in the swamps along I-95. A friend had once told me that Washington, D.C. lies in the humid sub-tropical climate zone. But if D.C. is *sub*-tropical, Florida's the real thing.

From the forest came a cacophony of sounds—crows again, after a long East Coast absence, and the incessant twittering of smaller birds, all yielding to the loud and obnoxious call of the *Uh-Uh Bird.* Its piercing scream was haughty and hypnotic. *Uh-uh! Uh-uh! Uh-uh!* Like the annoying nasal *Nert!* of a game-show buzzer. But I couldn't see a single bird. They were all concealed in the dense jungle behind me, except for a silent variety just outside the restrooms, a flock foraging in the grass like pigeons. The size of large robins, they had big feet and were black like crows, but with brown breasts. A dull combination and a great disappointment. I wanted nothing but colorful cockatoos and parrots to emerge from the swampy rain forests of Florida.

As I paused to swat a cloud of love bugs from my face, an elderly woman passed on the sidewalk with her husband. "What do you call those birds?" I asked her. I meant the brown-and-black ones. Not the *Uh-Uhs.*

"Gackles," she said. Then she turned to her husband. "Ain't those gackles, Henry?"

"*Cackles*," Henry corrected. "Or *crackles.*"

The woman rolled her eyeballs. "We don't know!"

I didn't bother to ask them about the Interstates.

It took me half an hour to clean the windshield again, sweating profusely and drenching a clean T-shirt in the process. Fortunately, I had dressed for the day in khaki shorts. But it came at a price. Love bugs stuck to the backs of my legs as I leaned across the sleek hood of the 'Vette with my squeegee and plastic spray-bottle of cleaning fluid.

On the highway again and bound for Jacksonville, I noticed state police cars lurking everywhere—behind fronds in the median, behind bushes just off the shoulder. A show of force. Traffic had increased from light to moderate but was otherwise behaving itself. The way was flat—flat and straight and tedious. It can get so flat and straight and tedious in Florida that any overpass looms as a major event. One such overpass was lined with double rows of a new kind of palm tree—cigar-shaped pineapples with green tufts, an amusing variety compared with the helicopter palms.

But the lush coastal scenery was far behind me by the time the Jacksonville skyline materialized, waiting in the distance on the flat terrain and rising toward a shelf of gray clouds. Like so many American cities, Jacksonville has a stair-step structure that resembles the Empire State Building. And a sleek narrow affair labeled *Modis*. Then comes the modern gray BellSouth building. North of the city, adjacent twin bridges span the Trout River like protractors, but the real surprise comes minutes later, when I-95 turns briefly east across St. Johns Bay. Suddenly a host of glass-and-steel buildings line the waterfront in a palette of muted pastels—grays, blues, and greens—as soft as the South itself. The harbor is clean and inviting, a youthful city on its shores.

But the Interstate was under heavy construction, the traffic immediately heavy as well. On my right, tall white concrete buttresses paralleled I-95 like a monorail, waiting to be topped by a new highway that would yield an even more spectacular panorama of the city. And in a flash the Ohio Rust Belt and New England mill towns fell into perspective. This was the new America, a stunningly aesthetic city of the South—clean, bright, and vibrant—designed with care and literally rising into the future before me.

But it was also the rush hour, made doubly worse by plastic cones and concrete barriers shifting traffic from lane to lane. I had reserved a room south of the city to avoid the Thursday-morning rush. And I wanted to raise my batting average even higher, having missed two of my first three motels. But it wasn't to be, although I somehow found the exit. Once again the motel directory proved hopeless. *Turn left, then right on So-and-So Road. One mile on left.* But there was no sign for *So-and-So Road.* So I sailed right on by, stuck in the crunch of the four-lane highway to which I had exited. Into another Interstate ambush.

But for once I didn't mind. I was lost in a new idea, a vision of Jacksonville rating one hundred on the idyllometer, if I could sweep by and above it at sunrise—or at sunset—on that new highway being built in the sky. Interstates, I decided, can be compatible with cityscapes. I was convinced of that now. And thrilled by that knowledge, I turned the 'Vette around for another pass at Motel Find-Me-Not. In no hurry to arrive and face the love bugs.

5

"EET'S A STRAIGHT SHOT FROM HERE TO MIAMI," THE YOUNG LATINO DESK clerk said in the morning. "About five or seeks hours."

I had crossed another invisible barrier between Georgia and Jacksonville. There were Latinos now as well as blacks. Everywhere. "Sorry about thees weather," he continued. "We had a record cold last night. Low feefties. Very unusual."

"Just in time for the autumnal equinox," I said.

The clerk laughed. "Whatever you say, meester."

Because of the cold, I had traded yesterday's shorts and T-shirt for long khakis and a sweatshirt. Now I was ready for a big day—four hundred and seventy miles during which I'd plant a flag in Miami at the very end of I-95, then cross the Everglades on I-75, taking "Alligator Alley" to Naples. I had a niece in Naples whom I had intended to visit, but she had moved from Florida just a few days earlier, but not before issuing me a strict warning about Latinos in Miami. As in Maine, I had no idea what awaited me at the end of I-95, but one thing was certain— the scene would be urban, not rural, and my niece's warning lingered like a small dark cloud.

Leaving Jacksonville was easy. The college student in North Carolina had complained about entrance ramps, but here they were long and wide for easy access. This particular stretch of Interstate *had* been built for the future, as the black man in D.C. had argued they should. Long lanes made getting on and off easy.

Beyond the city limits I-95 returned to two lanes, the traffic light and fast. It was sixty degrees and overcast at seven-fifteen. And the Latino desk clerk was right. It *was* a straight shot south, with a wide and empty median, and lowland swamps to either side. The Atlantic Ocean lay but a few miles east, paralleling the Interstate down the Florida coast. But it would remain hidden from view until Miami.

At the intersection of International Golf Parkway came a burst of billboards for *World Golf* and Jack Nicklaus courses. The sun was rising on my left shoulder, a red disk rippled with thin gray clouds. Then more billboards revived an old message. *We dare to bare! Next exit!* Stark stretches of charred pine forests followed—blackened spindly shafts in wide swamplands—while the road ran ruler-straight ahead of me. And ruler-straight behind me. As far as the eye could see. So flat that it extinguished all perspective. There was absolutely no horizon.

Since Maine, except for a few hills in Delaware and Maryland, I-95 had been relatively level. But compared with the flatness of Florida, the earlier stretches seemed mountainous. The effect was oppressive, without relief. Rest areas lay farther apart than in any state so far—as much as eighty miles—adding to the psychological malaise.

Gradually, tall natural palm trees replaced the pines in the roadside swamps, their gray bark like elephant hide, a welcome change from the occasional planted palms in the median, a Florida touch that somehow seemed forced. The grass was different, too—a kind of sawgrass—each blade like a green plastic knife.

A Corvette exactly like mine was speeding northward, then another—a white ragtop convertible—and suddenly I knew the answer to a question that had been puzzling me since Ohio. Why were all the 'Vettes I saw always headed in the opposite direction? The answer was simple. I wouldn't see one on my own side of the road unless I passed one. Or one passed *me,* whereas the northbound lanes presented a steady stream of different vehicles. It had taken a dull stretch of Florida Interstate to produce the revelation. The Interstates, I concluded, reveal the obvious.

Traffic was moderate through Daytona, where those palm trees that look like cigar-shaped pineapples line the overpass at LPGA Boulevard. Large white rocks on adjacent embankments spell out *L-P-G-A.* At Spruce Creek Bayou—the first marsh with a French label—shafts of sunlight finally pierced the overcast sky. The French had borrowed the term *bayou* from the Choctaw (*bayuk*), but French or Indian, and despite the welcome sun, the terrain remained flat. Every overpass, miles apart, became a major event, a brief blip on the contour of the landscape, a contact lens on a tabletop. Signs for I-4 to Orlando promised a distraction, but the spur cuts off to the southwest with scarcely a fanfare.

* * *

Here's an Interstate Item from Walt Disney World Secrets:

Walt Disney, the pioneer cartoonist/showman-turned-entrepreneur, personally selected the site for Disney World while flying over Central Florida in his company's Gulfstream jet in April 1964. For several years before that, Disney had wanted to build an East Coast version of his successful Disneyland attraction in Anaheim, Calif. It had to be in the South because Disney wanted it to operate year-round, and he wanted it away from the beach so it wouldn't have to compete with the ocean for tourists. Disney chose the future location of Walt Disney World from the air when he spotted a vast tract of virgin land west of the junction of Florida's Turnpike and Interstate 4, which was then under construction.

Disney kept his plans quiet and set up dummy corporations in order to secretly buy the land for his park so that speculators could not run up the price. He was successful. By the time the plans for the park were revealed 18 months later, Disney's lawyers had purchased 27,400 acres straddling the Orange-Osceola County line at an average price of only $182 per acre.

No doubt the ready access to Orlando provided by the fledgling I-4 figured prominently in Disney's sneaky plans.

* * *

At last a rest area showed up, a far cry from the initial Florida facility. Porta-potties lined the outlying parking area to handle overflow crowds. But the place was nearly empty in the early morning, except for some unhurried senior citizens. Getting out to stretch, I abandoned my sweatshirt for a T-shirt. Small brown lizards darted across the sidewalks by the restrooms, and when I returned to the 'Vette, a husky black woman was parked beside me, bent over the engine of her station wagon, its hood up and hoses steaming. But she had everything under control. Unlike me, she knew all about engines.

"The problem with this Innerstate," she told me, "is that it takes too long to get to certain places and when you get there they's closed. With no warning. How can you get food or gas if they's closed? You can go for miles 'n' miles without any signs, even signs for what road you's on. You never know if you's on the right track. At least down here they do construction at night. That's a help. Now if they'd only put up some *signs*!"

Like the 'Vette, the station wagon's hood, windshield, license plate, and front bumper were streaked with love bugs. But the woman ignored them, while I scrubbed away at my own yellow goo for the next half hour.

Back on the highway at nine-fifteen, I immediately put on the air-conditioner. It was eighty degrees now, and I began to regret my long khaki pants. But there was a new distraction—cows—something I had never imagined in Florida. Brown cows, black cows, and gray cows grazed in flat meadows just off the shoulder. Then power lines began to follow the highway, strung along telephone poles with crisscrossed braces, ugly goalposts that added to the monotony. Narrow canals appeared, to drain the low-lying coastal terrain, a vast network that continued for miles into a stretch of pine barrens—where a yellow sign suddenly warned, quite simply, *Smoke*. Earlier, I had seen several signs for *Fog*. Fog I could understand. But not *Smoke*. Wide-open wildfires—like the one that had produced the charred forest in the swamp back up the highway—apparently present a danger to traffic, especially in times of drought. Another Interstate revelation.

At ten-thirty, two hundred miles south of Jacksonville, I stopped at a rest area to clean the windshield again. The plague of love bugs seemed to be lessening a bit, as if I had endured the worst through Georgia and northern Florida. If that was true, I would meet them again on Friday, leaving the Florida panhandle for the Gulf Coast.

Beyond the restrooms, a silver-haired supervisor from the Florida Department of Transportation was sitting in a state pickup truck, taking notes. When I asked him about the Interstates, he regarded me suspiciously. Fixing his eyes on his notebook, he fell silent. Then he looked up and drawled, "I'd ruh-tha not comment on they-it."

I was taken aback—the first refusal of my standard query, something that wouldn't happen again until Wisconsin. But southern highway officials had been criticized in the wake of Floyd. Maybe the supervisor was mistaking me for a journalist. It was nonetheless a breach of southern hospitality.

South of the rest area the flat landscape continued. Power lines flanked the highway, spanning tacky subdivisions. The traffic, moderate below Daytona, became heavy as hell by noon in West Palm Beach, where a vintage Corvette Stingray sat abandoned on the shoulder, in ominous defiance of Corvette karma. My own 'Vette, running precariously low on gas, rolled into the first available station when I exited into a midday Interstate ambush. Just off the exit, the four-lane highway was jammed, the temperature a humid eighty-five. I had killed the AC to save fuel.

"It only gets worse between here and Miami," an Ohio native told me at the gas station. He had noticed my plates. I was standing beside the 'Vette, catching my breath, as trucks, vans, and SUVs sped by on I-95 above me, simultaneously darting along the local highway to my right—a modern strip of mini-malls, palm trees, bright new sidewalks, and that knife-like grass.

"I've lived in Florida for years now," the guy from Ohio went on. "The Interstate's a great system but it's way too busy, especially around here. They were thinking of putting in a big cloverleaf over to Okeechobee west of Miami. And a toll station to discourage all the trucks. But so far they've been lollygagging."

When I told him I intended to plant a flag in Miami at the very end of I-95, he laughed, shook his head, and wished me luck. Then I scrubbed the love bugs from the windshield, filled the tank, and zipped back on the highway, teeth clenched in my Richard Petty mode.

* * *

From West Palm Beach to Miami is only a half-hour drive. But for density of traffic and intensity of obnoxious drivers, the stretch rivals I-95 through Connecticut. I made it safely only because of a classical radio station I picked up near Fort Lauderdale. It was playing a slow, soothing melody that I turned up full blast to counter the thumping bass sounds from the vehicles that whizzed by me, changing lanes without signaling, many with young Latinos behind the wheel.

An ambulance, lights flashing, was caught in a pack of cars behind me. It stayed in my rearview mirror for miles, unable to make progress despite desperately changing lanes. The midday pace was a frenzied race to the finish, the absolute antithesis of I-95 at the Canadian border, and the tension killed my impending sense of ceremony—of planting my second flag. My only concern was survival.

But Miami lived up to its postcard fame. It's all pink skyscrapers and pastel high-rises. Palm trees are everywhere, with blue ocean glimpses beyond. A vibrant city as attractive as Jacksonville, but much larger, Miami projects a lurid air of *anything goes*. Approaching by Interstate, you see a high narrow building with a stair-step top that creates a triangular look. Another building has a fly-roof with antennae. Others resemble the U.N. Then shorter apartments blend with higher glass façades, their gray and white balconies creating a waffled effect. But all I got were glimpses, the traffic too quick—five lanes moving at hyper-speed through downtown exits, vehicles running on top of one another like cars in a train. Following all signs for I-95 South, I tried to imagine a quiet space where I could stop to honor the Interstates.

But it wasn't to be. At its final exit in Miami, I-95 South becomes U.S. Route 1—the dear old Boston Post Road—barreling ahead for the Florida Keys as a four-lane tree-lined highway without so much as a pause. I took the first right turn possible, then an immediate left to a parallel access road, stopping at a crowded convenience store to recover. People were jumping in and out of cars to pump gas, chug a drink, and fly back on the highway. The fetid air jangled with rap music and unintelligible Spanish. I was about a mile from the Interstate and it would have been dangerous to retreat. Neighboring side streets were packed with shabby houses. People of all colors loitered at the fringes of the rush.

Squeezing the 'Vette into a narrow space beside a service van at the very end of the convenience store lot, I took my hammer, flag, and star drill to a muddy patch of grass along the curb. It was one-thirty and my T-shirt was sticking to my back, the bright sun like the eye of a Cyclops, the gutter rife with puddles from recent storms. When I kneeled to plant the flag, the knee of my khakis got soaked. But I didn't care. I just wanted to plant the flag and get the hell out of there.

Retreating to the 'Vette, I spread my atlas on the sunroof to determine the quickest way to I-75. A few yards away, my blue millennial
flag, with its crossed Stars and Stripes, hung limp as a rag. I hadn't
photographed it, so I grabbed my camera, went back over, and clicked
off a few uninspired shots. Simultaneously, a man who looked like Lee
Trevino—with a personality to match—got out of the service van,
where he had been eating a sandwich behind the wheel.

"Let me help you with dat," he said. "You wanna be in the picture,
doncha?" And he was right. I did. So I knelt in the muddy grass again,
holding the flag out with one hand, flashing two fingers with the other.

"Two thousand!" Lee Trevino squealed. "Yo, Millennium!"

"No," I said. "That's not it."

"V for victory," he guessed.

"Nope." Although in a sense it was true. It *was* a victory to have
made it this far, to have survived the crunch from West Palm Beach.
"This is the second flag I've planted," I explained. "The first was at the
Canadian border."

"Ho ho!" Trevino laughed. "You doin' the four corners? Zat why
you got such a hot car?"

I realized I was smiling. For the first time since Jacksonville. "How
many times have you been told you look like Lee Trevino?"

"Ho ho! I wish I had dat cat's money!"

"I gotta get outta here," I said. "Where's I-75? San Diego gets flag
number three."

Lee Trevino handed me the camera and stepped to the atlas. I had
been planning to continue south on Route 1. But it would have been a
mistake. Instead, as the happy fellow instructed, I got on I-95 North,
took Route 826 to the Palmetto Expressway, then connected with I-
75—overjoyed. Another spate of Corvette karma had dignified my brief
Miami flag-planting.

But by two o'clock I was snagged in an Interstate idle, munching an
apple by the Miami airport while large planes took off and landed, the sun
bouncing brightly off a thousand stationary sunroofs. My own included.
Then the idle loosened and the traffic raced in a mad pack by the dog track
at Hialeah, as if chasing a mechanical rabbit. And at Okeechobee Road I
understood what the Ohioan had said in West Palm Beach—why a
colossal cloverleaf was needed, why they needed to do something about
the trucks. The same volume of traffic that had converged on Miami—
sucked down the east coast of Florida as if by the force of gravity—was
now shooting northward as if launched from Cape Canaveral.

Another ambulance flashed behind me. And two fire engines. I saw
their lights but couldn't hear the sirens, the traffic out-racing them up

Miami, at the second of my four-corner stops, where I-95 becomes U.S. Route 1.

I-75, at the southern end of the Interstate on which I had begun my odyssey in Ohio. Minutes later the road swung dramatically west for the Everglades. Houses and apartments with flowerpot roofs flanked both shoulders. Then they disappeared and "Alligator Alley" began in earnest.

Everyone should drive across the Everglades just once. A second trip could prove tedious. Lily pads as large as dinner plates stretch away to the horizon across a broad flat swamp—a calm and shallow blue-green sea. The geography is simple, as it always is on the Interstates. I was headed due west under a hot sun and hazy sky, the road raised just above the level of the swampland. To the north and south there was nothing but water. And lily pads. The median held puddles in spots, from the incessant recent rains. It was a dreary landscape with one saving grace—the bulk of the mid-afternoon traffic had continued north. There was no one behind me as I cruised into the sun.

At two-thirty I pulled into a parallel rest area, a narrow open parking lot devoid of shade. The facilities consisted of two porta-potties. A lone car was parked by a cement boat ramp at the far end. It was ninety degrees now, and for the first time—as I got out and stretched— I felt the searing strength of the Florida sun. That Cyclops eye baked me like an oven, drying my T-shirt and khakis, glaring sharply off a glass display case provided by the Everglades Wildlife Management Area. According to the exhibit, fish in the wide waters all about me included every species I could catch in Ohio—bass, bluegill, catfish—except for something called a spotted gar. But other wildlife, all so colorfully depicted, was more exotic—river otters, wading birds, snakes. And alligators.

The Everglades came to the very edge of the parking lot, cut by long green channels through which airboats—flat boats with huge fans mounted in the rear—could speed at will. Thick vegetation lurked just beneath the surface. Close up, the lily pads were huge—green elephant ears, anchored to the muddy bottom by umbilical cords.

I headed for the boat ramp, where a fisherman was casting a line into the channel beside his car, working a surface lure along the chunky rock along the side of the highway. An enormous grasshopper was also making its way across the water. I kept waiting for a bass to explode and take it. But the water remained still. It was too hot for fishing and too hot for the fish. Too hot for conversation as well. But when the fisherman turned and saw me, I went on over.

"I'm in the Coast Guard," he said, "stationed on the cutter *Valiant* off Miami. But I live in Fort Myers." He nodded west, into the brilliant sun. "The old road that used to come across here had restricted speeds—fifty-five during the day, forty-five at night. There were only two lanes, and it used to take me forever to get home. They opened this Interstate about a decade ago. Now I can make the commute in two and a half hours. The Everglades are about eighty-five miles across, toll-gate-to-tollgate, and about three hundred miles north to south. I've been driving it twice a week for fourteen years." He grinned widely. "I'm supposed to be on my way home. My wife'd kill me if she knew I stopped to fish. But thanks to the Interstate, I've got the time. We just got back to port. Harvey chased us to sea. My wife says we had a lot of rain in Fort Myers."

I shaded my eyes from the glare of the sun, enjoying—despite the gritty heat—the extreme silence, such a contrast to the noisy congestion I'd recently escaped.

"All that crazy traffic you went through is normal for Miami," the fisherman said. "It's all those third-world drivers. I hate to say it, but it's true." He flicked his wrist and sent the lure glinting into the sun. It hit with a bright splash. "Look out for 'gators rest of the way. They like to crawl up out of the swamp and sun themselves beside the road."

I couldn't tell if he was kidding, but I continued across the big swamp with an eye out for 'gators. As with the fish, none were stirring. All the storms must have scared them away.

Just ahead of me, a wildlife officer was hauling an airboat on a trailer. And then—incredibly—came signs for an Indian reservation, the Miccosukee. A short while later I flew by the Big Cypress Seminole Reservation. I couldn't believe it. In Connecticut, Chief Big Eagle's ancestors had been displaced from prime territory, valuable land the tribe was still trying to reclaim. In Florida, the Indians had been stuck in a swamp.

The Everglades are full of surprises. Billboards crop up out of nowhere—ads for swamp-buggy rides and swamp safaris. The terrain holds a surprise as well. As I-75 cuts the corner of the Big Cypress National Preserve, the swamp becomes as forested as I-95 through the Carolina pines. Narrow channels still flank the shoulders, but tall cypress—a variety of evergreen—rise high above them, with strange scale-like leaves and spherical cones. A prison-like wire fence separates the trees from the highway—to keep travelers on the road. Or alligators *off*. Then, thirty miles from Naples, palm trees begin to appear in swampy groves.

NPR was discussing love bugs—the station was drifting, so I missed most of what was being said—but apparently love bugs had been introduced to the South in 1947 because their larvae have a positive effect on the environment. Whatever that positive effect might be, it remained to be seen—unless it was to provide the local population with steady exercise, in the form of scrubbing their vehicles, another session of which awaited me on the other side.

At the end of "Alligator Alley" I paid a dollar-fifty toll and exited in Naples, locating my motel with relative ease—but not easily enough to raise my batting average—and by four-thirty I was lounging in the pool with a pasty, sunburned couple from Ireland. Discussing the Interstates.

The woman's lilting voice was as refreshing as the water. "When our kids were adolescents we brought them to the States," she said. "We did a tour just like yours, only in reverse. And we skipped New England."

Her husband was floating on his back. "We flew into New York, rented a car, and went straight to Niagara Falls," he said. "Then we headed west. It was simply a wonderful way to see America. The kids loved it. We did nine thousand miles in three weeks."

"You must have been flying," I said. "I'm doing ten thousand in *five*."

The man chuckled, his brogue as infectious as his wife's. "In Oregon I got caught doing ninety-five, but the policeman let me off. I pleaded *kilometers per hour*. But that bloke didn't know his math. Ninety-five kilometers is well within the speed limit."

"I kept telling him to slow down," his wife needled. "But we only had three weeks."

Her husband waxed serious. "The Interstates are absolutely great for observing the landscape. You can see the subtle changes from region to region, the changes in the people as well. I love the big broad hats of the police in the Pacific Northwest—just like the Royal Canadian Mounties. And in Texas I never expected so many Mexican cops."

"We watched one of the Apollo launches from I-95," his wife said, "the one before the one that blew up. But the Miami area was just too crazy for words."

"Still is," her husband said.

I nodded in agreement, then dragged myself out of the pool. It was time to wash the 'Vette. To scrub the love bugs.

Later that evening, at a nearby restaurant, I chatted with a truck driver who, for twenty-two years, had hauled doublewide homes and oversized loads between Fort Lauderdale and Miami. Now he was hauling rock and sand, exclusively on I-75. He lived nearby. Yesterday's rains had flooded him out of his trailer.

"Any more, it's just too crazy on the Miami side," he said. "It got that way about ten years ago. Half the drivers are immigrants who never owned a car before. That's why our insurance is so high—we're payin' for all them immigrants. I'm from Homestead, south of Miami. It takes as long now to get from Homestead to Miami as it does to get from Homestead to Naples. I can make triple the money hauling to Naples. Time is money. It's that simple, so I stick to I-75. You'll like it north of here, by the way. It's a helluva lot prettier than I-95."

Outside, the truck driver's pickup was parked beside the 'Vette. When we left the restaurant he began digging around beneath a tarpaulin in the rear. Then he held up what looked like a large green pear. It was an avocado.

"I used to haul these to Chicago in the early seventies," he said. "Twenty-four in a case at a buck a piece. Keep it in a dark place until it gets soft." He tossed it over. "Just slice it up and serve it with salad. You'll love it. As much as I-75."

I tucked the odd gift beneath the privacy screen in the rear of the 'Vette, where it could ripen in the warm darkness. I suppose it was just what I needed. I was all out of apples.

* * *

Seven o'clock Friday morning I headed due north out of Naples on I-75. The day was muggy—seventy-six degrees beneath an overcast sky. Rain was forecast locally but I would easily out-run it. It was forty miles to Fort Myers, a hundred and thirty to Tampa, then another hundred and fifty to I-10. From there I would point my little Hot Wheels Corvette toward San Diego. But my goal for the day was more modest. Ninety miles west on I-10 to Tallahassee.

Traffic was moderate, heavier southbound, but it soon lightened considerably. And as the avocado man had promised, I-75 was delightfully scenic, once the local subdivisions dropped away and the country landscape resumed. The route skirts all cities, and since Florida's west coast is less populated than its east, it looked like a good day to dust off the idyllometer.

A large white waterbird glided above the wetlands to my right, trailing its long feet like landing gear. Thick birch forests had joined the palms and pines. I passed a brand-new tractor-trailer—hot pink from cab to mudguards—the perfect color for Florida. But a local bumper sticker seemed more appropriate for the Miami side. *Next time wave all your fingers!* Unfortunately, the love bugs, which had never really disappeared, were striking the windshield with alarming regularity, forcing me into a rest area just before eight. I had packed my own squeegee, and replenished my paper towels and bottle of washer fluid, but my supplies were dwindling.

Half an hour later I crossed the Peace River, a bloody sun rising on my right shoulder. Twin bridges, humped like a brontosaurus, spanned a misty bayou, its lengthy shoreline dotted with attractive white cottages. Suddenly a hot-air balloon appeared above the tree line—a potential postcard—but its red-and-white skin was drab and dirty. If I could scrub my vehicle before taking off, why couldn't the balloon man?

A sign for Venice reminded me of Naples, and I began to wonder—what is the source of the Italian influence in Florida? Perhaps the wetlands here had reminded settlers of the waterways of Italy. The classical names were well chosen, for it is classically beautiful territory with a constant variety of vegetation—mossy pines, palm trees, yucca-type bushes, rushes, angelhair fronds, and weedy underbrush laced with creeping vines. North of Sarasota, in a sudden stretch of fog, I passed a sign that seemed to sum up the exotic landscape. *Moccasin Wallow Road.*

As I continued north I began to watch the idyllometer. It was hovering at eighty, but I-75, like I-95 to the east, was simply too flat and straight for a higher reading. And there were too many love bugs. At nine o'clock I had to stop at another rest area to clean the windshield.

Across the parking lot a huge motor home—a Diplomat Morocco diesel pusher—seemed to dwarf the charter bus beside it. The elderly owner was attending to the hitch of an Oldsmobile he was hauling behind. I asked him what it was like with such a rig on the Interstate.

"This outfit's so big," he said, "I need a TV camera to see what's behind me. I can barely see the car we're trailing. My wife and I been all over in this thing—Nevada, Utah, California. We just came to Florida from Michigan, and I got nothing good to say about the roads up there, especially in the Detroit area. Why, the overpasses are falling down! But this machine does real well on the highway. You just gotta be careful. It's our home on the road. The other side there pulls out into an extra room."

"What do you do about all these bugs?" I asked.

He scratched his head and laughed. "They come with the territory."

But the love bugs were becoming less and less amusing. Dozens of vehicles in the rest area were absolutely striped with their dried yellow goo—windshields, hoods, headlights, radiators, bumpers, license plates—every square inch. Predictably, as I left the rest area for Tampa, Murphy's Interstate Law kicked in. A pair of love bugs smacked the windshield on the entrance ramp, *exactly* in my line of sight. Then three more pairs smacked the glass, leaving long yellow streaks. Out of perverse curiosity I began to count the hits—the first one hundred—a number I reached before Tampa, only twenty miles distant. Each new splat diminishing my visibility and increasing my anger.

North of Tampa, I-75 begins to curve and roll, a welcome relief, and the coastal salt marshes give way to unexpected farmland. As along I-95 to the east, cows—totally black this time—grazed peacefully in green dells. The terrain reminded me of the Maryland countryside. Traffic was light, the morning still misty, all vehicles running with headlights because of the lingering fog. And out of the gray mist a work crew emerged, sodding the median, working from square stacks of turf on a flatbed truck. The maintenance effort seemed more expensive than need be. I had seen medians seeded before, but never sodded. Maybe the heat simply baked the young seed. And I had seen sod rolled like rugs, but never in squares.

A sign for *Palmer Slough* introduced a new Interstate term, one I would encounter frequently from Florida all the way around to North Dakota. A *slough* is a stagnant swamp or marsh, part of a bayou or backwater inlet. In Ohio its counterpart is called a *run*, a drainage ditch linked to local streams and rivers. Here the term aptly suited the landscape—an area like the Camargue of southern France, or the way I imagine the Argentine pampas to be. But how to pronounce it? The only *slough* I had ever known was the Slough of Despond in "The Pilgrim's Progress"—a metaphorical bog, a sinkhole of mud and mire encountered by John Bunyan's Christian in the midst of a plain. My professor had pronounced it to rhyme with *know*.

Stopping again shortly to clean the windshield, I took advantage of the break to consult one of the locals. "Palmer Slough?" he said. "Down the road apiece? We say it like *cow*."

"Do you know the Palmers?" I asked.

"Not hardly."

As usual, cleaning the windshield proved useless, love bugs spattering the 'Vette as soon as I hit the road. And always—*always!*—the first pair struck between the eyes, blocking my line of sight, making me rearrange myself behind the wheel. I was beginning to hate the flighty narrow black critters with a passion. How could their square orange heads ooze *yellow*? They were grotesque creatures from a southern horror story. But when would the story end?

I had solved one problem, at least. It was slough as in *cow*.

South of Gainesville the morning mist burned away to reveal a lovely day. I was in the Florida citrus area now, a barrage of billboards touting orange juice, alligators, drag racing, swamp buggies, adult toys, and *We bare all! 24 hours!* The terrain was more hilly than earlier, a pleasant surprise. Only the love bugs and billboards kept the idyllometer in check.

At the Paynes Prairie Rest Area all vehicles showed the stress of love bug storms—they were absolutely coated—but I seemed to be the only driver concerned or annoyed. It was noon, a humid eighty-five degrees, and the surrounding shrubs looked like the green tops of pineapples. Heading for the men's room, I noticed an elderly couple beside a huge Harley-Davidson, a small trailer attached. They were easily in their seventies—snow-white hair and clear blue eyes. And the windscreen of their big motorcycle was absolutely clean. I wanted to ask them about love bugs, how they kept their glass so clean. And about the Interstates. Were they on a four-corner tour like the biker in Maine? But I was in a hurry to hit the men's room where I lingered too long, slammed by huge blasts of frigid air as I entered. It was one of the few air-conditioned facilities I would encounter nationwide, so I stood there as if in a walk-in freezer, enjoying the relief from the heat, and when I got back outside, the huge Harley was roaring away.

North of Gainesville green hills roll to the horizon in all directions and thick pines line the sides of the road. In the occasional cleared fields, hay shaped like huge segments of Tootsie Rolls waited to be gathered by local farmers. A few miles later, with a renewed air of excitement, I hung a left on I-10, heading west in light traffic—a pivotal moment on that great relief map in my mind. I had traveled east, north, south, then briefly north again. And now my Corvette was pointed west, like the pioneers, across the entire American continent. The road was smooth and brand new—a black velvet carpet—and I let out a whoop.

87

Psychologically, I-10 was new territory, a land of its own, and in the gently undulating countryside the idyllometer perked up, occasionally flashing above eighty. Set among oaks now, the pines thinned to a tall spindly variety. I had seen many like that in the backwoods of Russia, their stark branches staggered at the very top. It was farm country, with that Tootsie Roll hay, unpopulated except for an occasional doublewide trailer on cement blocks. The historic Suwannee River runs through here, rocky and shallow, green trees hugging its serene and wandering shores.

Beyond the river, where I-10 flattens out, the sky grew overcast and a swarm of love bugs chilled my enthusiasm, darkening the air ahead like a dirty screen. The encounter forced me into the Madison County Rest Area to clean the windshield. In the early afternoon the place was nearly deserted, but I was too angry to get to work on the love bugs, so I abandoned the 'Vette for a meandering sidewalk. I hadn't realized how tall the pines were, their thick trunks surrounded by circles of brown needles. Pines towered above the cement pavilions, curious structures with Y-shaped roofs—pseudo Frank Lloyd Wright creations that did nothing but collect needles and cones. Given the setting, teepee-shaped roofs would have been more practical.

Spanish moss draped the occasional oaks like ragged gauze—the first hanging moss I'd seen—giving the shadows a Halloween feel. In the shade at the far end of the parking lot, a member of the local Lions Club was selling hotdogs and soda from a small vehicle on wheels. *Free food. Donations gladly accepted.* I ordered a hotdog and Coke and asked about the Interstates.

"We had three hundred cars stuck in here last week during the Floyd evacuation," the vendor said. "It was a madhouse, but great for business. We have to renew our permit every two weeks. They don't allow no vending machines here, so we do OK."

"What about these love bugs?" I asked.

His response was typical. "What about 'em? They're almost done." He handed out my hotdog. "I-10's just been repaved through here. A few years ago it was one of the worst Interstates in the country. Still is, through Looseyana. A regular minefield."

I took a second hotdog, tossed five bucks in the coffee can, and headed back to work on the windshield. "Drive careful out there," the vendor called after me.

For the next hour I worked on the 'Vette, scraping the dried yellow streaks with my squeegee—then my fingernails—until my hands cramped in a knot. It was eighty-five degrees, the humidity unbearable, my T-shirt plastered to my back. Pairs of love bugs hovered overhead in their slow dance of death, alighting in my hair, crawling across the backs of my legs, crawling up into my shorts. As I was finishing up, an old beater of a Buick pulled in beside me, although there were ample empty parking spaces to choose from. Eventually, an old man climbed out, as beaten as his car. Leaning against a battered front fender, he began to pop peanuts into his mouth from a glass jar, watching me work. He wore a wrinkled short-sleeved shirt, crusty gray trousers with suspenders, and a straw hat with a large circular brim. He had to be very local—there were hardly any love bugs on his car.

"Back in nineteen and sixty-five," he said finally, "this here ve-hickle cost me fifteen hunnert. Wadya pay for thet un?"

I didn't have the heart to tell him. Brand new, the 'Vette had cost thirty times what he had shelled out. Besides, he was being nosey.

"I got it used," was all I said, moving from the windshield to the front bumper. "It's a ninety-six."

The old man popped another peanut in his mouth and came around to the front of the 'Vette. "What you need is a bra. It would cer-tainly hep."

I looked at him curiously, then understood. He meant those black leather protective covers. I had seen a few on the highway, fitted snugly around the headlights like the mask of Zorro. I had always dismissed them as pure affectation, but they had a purpose after all. Another Interstate revelation.

"Still," I said, "they'd be no help for the windshield. Or the license plate." My calling card—*LAP USA*—was virtually unreadable.

"Once't upon a time," the old timer said, "when I was a young feller like yeh-sef, I had a problem with love bugs. It was night and I had to pull into a gas station. Couldn't see a blamed thing. An' this good-ol'-boy comes out and says, 'Buy me a Coke and I'll take care of them bugs for yeh.' I thought thet Coke would be payment for the job. But what he did was, he poured thet Coke all over the windshield. And the bugs come right off. It's the acid in it."

"Thanks for the tip," I said as nonchalantly as I could. But I wanted to scream: *Now you tell me!*

Beyond the rest area I-10 continued to weave its way through lovely pine-lined stretches, up and down, left and right. By mid-afternoon the temperature had reached ninety, the traffic light beneath a bright sun and high white clouds. It was only the love bugs keeping the idyl-lometer in check now, the ugly yellow streaks still accumulating by the minute. But I watched the mounting corpses with a malicious interest. I had discovered an antidote, a bit of local knowledge that I hoped would prove as reliable as the old man's suspenders.

89

And it did.

Arriving in Tallahassee at three-thirty, I fought the Interstate ambush down a four-lane strip, found my motel without a hitch, and bought a liter of Coke at an adjacent convenience store. Then I went to work, in a nook of shade cast by pines in a corner of the parking lot. I applied the Coke sparingly so as not to damage the finish or leave a sticky residue on the glass, scrubbing and rinsing simultaneously, shooting streams of cleaning fluid from my plastic squirt bottle. The exhausting effort took two hours but worked like a southern charm, flushing the love bugs and restoring the 'Vette to its Ohio gleam.

Later that evening, after a leisurely dinner at a Chinese restaurant, I cracked open a fortune cookie as the ancients used to open the books of Virgil. Looking for a sign. The printed slip of paper seemed to applaud my good sense in taking the old codger's word. *Fortune truly helps those who are of good judgment.* I tucked it into my wallet as a souvenir, a reminder of my southern battle with the love bugs.

But in that moment of smug self-congratulation, I never imagined I'd be heeding the advice of that fortune cookie again—in much more serious circumstances—in less than twenty-four hours.

6

MY FIRST AND ONLY RIDE IN A CHEVROLET CORVETTE—BEFORE I TEST-DROVE my own in the summer of 1999—came when I was in college in the mid-'6os. The 'Vette was similar to the blue-and-silver beauty in which Dirty Dick had pulled up to the curb following my brother's high school graduation. Only this one was a convertible. It belonged to a fraternity brother of mine at Wesleyan. His name was Gary and he was quite a groovy guy—played guitar in a popular rock band, had a sexy girlfriend, and retired after college to a Caribbean island where he still plays guitar in his own restaurant. I don't know what happened to his 'Vette.

I was on the golf team at the time, and Gary, who occasionally played golf, drove me out to the course one afternoon for a quick nine holes. It was a sunny spring day and we had the top down, our golf bags wedged behind the bucket seats. When we stopped for a red light on Main Street in Middletown, Gary removed his shades, turned his face to the bright sun, and smiled.

I'll never forget that smile. It was not at all like Dirty Dick's condescending, blue-collar, public school *I've-got-a-'Vette-and-you-don't* smile. It was an unabashed prep school smile that said, *I'm cool, the car's cool, I know it, you know it, and I might as well take advantage of this red light to catch some rays.* Then the light turned, Gary floored it, and the 'Vette shot out of Middletown, flattening me against the passenger seat before we were out of second gear. The car was *hot* and I was a goner, the hair on my neck standing as straight up as my crew cut. And at that moment I made a promise to myself. Someday—*somehow*—I would have a Corvette.

It was because of Groovy Gary's cocky smile that I had lingered at the red light on Main Street back in Stratford. In my own 'Vette. Smiling up through the sunroof.

* * *

What I remember most about leaving Tallahassee is the moon. It was sixty-eight degrees at seven in the morning and there was an enormous yellow moon on the inky horizon. I was driving right for it and it seemed about to swallow me whole. The moon was full—as wide as the world itself—so bright it was casting long shadows from the trees. As I-10 dipped and curved its way west, pockets of fog lay in the dells, and the magnificent moon lighted them strangely, rendering superfluous the embedded cats' eyes in the pavement.

It was Saturday morning and I was alone on the road, headed for New Orleans on brand-new blacktop, the day's drive to take me out of Florida, then briefly through Alabama, with longer stints in Mississippi and Louisiana. A four-state day along the Gulf of Mexico. Pushing on to Baton Rouge—nearly five hundred miles distant—was never in the plan.

In the gentle hills near Lake Seminole the temperature dropped to fifty-eight. At the Apalachicola River a lone fisherman drifted silently in a bass boat through rising mists. Then a big orange ball of a sun began to rise in my rearview mirror, rippled through the middle by thin gray clouds. As it continued to ascend, the dew began to glisten in the median and parallel forests. It was too early in the day for love bugs— they seemed to prefer the warmer swampland to the chilly altitude of rolling hills—and so with a clean windshield I flew toward the autumn moon, Saturday's sun growing large behind me.

Due to the weekend, traffic remained light. It was time to sleep in. Only travelers like myself—people on a special mission—were taking to the highway. Like that lone fisherman in the bass boat, or some folks beyond the Apalachicola in a '50s-era bus, a green vehicle with white trim and a blank marquee, its name painted in white script across its rounded rear. *The Original*. It reminded me of the *Siloam* bus from upstate New York, that paisley vehicle with a somber cause. *The Original* seemed more intent on nostalgia.

About a hundred miles west of Tallahassee, as the sun and moon ascended in tandem, the pavement began to ripple rapid-fire. Unkempt double-wide trailers popped up along the roadside, and forests gave way to wide swamps. The tall pines looked desperate, branching only at the very top. Then the terrain leveled out and the love bugs returned, not as thick as on Friday yet annoying enough to force me to stop. But I was prepared this time, with an extra liter of Coke.

Leaving the Interstate was a mistake. The exit dumped me into the middle of a Saturday-morning ambush as wild as the one at Elias Aoude's. Pulling into the first fast-food place available, I thought I'd get a cup of coffee before attacking the love bugs on the windshield, but it was so crowded I abandoned my spot in line to seek out the men's room. A sports car with the mask of Zorro had just pulled in. I assumed the driver would come inside where I could talk to him, but when I came out his car was gone. And for a good reason. The parking lot was full. I took out my frustration on the love bugs then fled back to I-10, where my spirits improved immediately.

The road had smoothed out, the humidity was low, and the sun was creating deep shadows among the roadside pines, inflaming puddles of auburn needles about their trunks. Angelhair grasses blazed in the median. The moon was climbing, growing smaller, a pale disk. And suddenly blue skies and rolling hills opened up in the distance, each new crest bringing wide and scenic vistas. A sign for *Niceville* couldn't have said it better. The idyllometer took notice, rising to eighty-five, reviving my hopes of experiencing the perfect Interstate ride. Would today be the day?

High thick pines flanked the highway now, lining the median as well. The dry grass was freshly cut, a tan swath through green trees. By mid-morning the sun was sparkling, defining the clear day in bright bands of color—blue sky, green hills, tan grass, auburn needles, and black pavement edged with white and yellow lines.

At the Blackwater River a twin bridge humped like a river bass crosses a lovely tree-lined lake. A similar view follows on the edge of Pensacola, where the terrain flattens out and a *triple* bridge traverses Escambia Bay—a vast blue stretch of open water. It was the longest bridge to date, gradually rising across a long hump to fall away on the far side just as gradually. I was beginning to fall in love with these humpbacked southern bridges.

Through Pensacola the speed dropped to fifty-five, which made the traffic, suddenly moderate, seem to crawl. Urban strips replaced the country landscape. At ten o'clock, just beyond the city limits, I stopped for gas and coffee at a mini-mart where a bunch of twelve-year-old boys and girls—in shorts, T-shirts, and bathing suits—were holding a car wash under the guidance of several harried adults. The morning was very warm now, the mini-mart buzzing.

Two of the boys ran over the moment I pulled up to the pump—one chubby, one skinny, both sporting homemade haircuts and freckles.

"Wash the car for y'all?" they shouted in unison.

"Just washed it last night," I said. I got out, flipped down the rear plate, and inserted the nozzle as the boys frowned and turned to go. "But I *do* need some information," I added quickly.

The boys stopped in their tracks.

"What can you tell me about the Interstate in these parts?"

"It's *the bomb*," the chubby one shot back. "The safest I ever bin on. Other roads 'round here have too many wrecks and crap like they-it. But not I-10."

"They need more cops," the skinny one said. "Cuzz people speed. It's an OK road, I guess, but they need bigger signs with bigger words so the blind people can read 'em."

"The blind people?"

"And then they got they-it big bridge over to Mobile," the chubby one said.

"*What* big bridge?" I couldn't imagine a bigger bridge than the one across Escambia Bay.

"You never seen they-it bridge?" the skinny one said.

The chubby one rolled his eyes. "Geez!"

Then another car pulled in and the boys ran off shouting. "Wash the car for y'all, ma'am?"

I reached the Florida state line by ten-thirty, crossing the narrow Perdido River into Alabama where a host of marigolds waited in welcome. A portable sign was flashing a warning—*Cattle In Road!*—but I saw no cattle. Nor anyone with a banjo on their knee. Just billboards, detracting from terrain as beautiful as the loveliest stretches of the Florida panhandle. If my speed held, I'd be through Alabama in an hour. A brief Interstate visit.

On the outskirts of Mobile the Saturday traffic increased to moderate once again. And before long I realized what the fat boy had been talking about. Descending a slight hill to Mobile Bay, I-10 suddenly becomes a causeway—dual bridges, two lanes east and two lanes west, supported by *pi*-shaped pylons—across a seven-mile stretch of bogs and bayous.

Small fishing boats glinted in the sun across the far reaches of the bay. Others were anchored in the narrow band of shade cast by the Interstate itself. Elsewhere, speedboats carved white wakes into the wide blue surface. All craft looked like toy boats in an immense blue bathtub. Then a modest skyline materialized along the hazy western horizon—two or three pink buildings to the left, some cranes, then smokestacks and power lines to the right—an industrial melange that's home to about two hundred thousand people. Lampposts lined the causeway every hundred yards or so, flicking by like the tiny islands just off the highway—treed islands, islands laced with cattails, others that are mere dark circles. Time on the bridge seemed suspended, and the long crossing began to unnerve me.

Before you reach the far shore of Mobile Bay there's a sign for the city limits. Then the road descends into a round yellowish tunnel like the one in Baltimore. Only this one descends steeply and rises abruptly, its contour more a *V* than a smile. Emerging into bright sun again, I realized that the best Mobile has to offer already lay behind me—in the approach to, and crossing of, the bay. It'll test your nerves, but it's well worth the trip. And it left me reconsidering what my younger brother had mentioned in Connecticut—about putting an Interstate just for trucks through Long Island Sound.

Beyond Mobile, the first hint of Mississippi is a sign for Pascagoula, a city south of I-10 on Mississippi Sound in the Gulf of Mexico. Then a sign welcomes you to Mississippi itself, and the pavement suddenly bears a reddish-brown tint. The very first rest area promises *The South's Warmest Welcome*. How could I resist?

The area is huge—twenty acres or more—with a plantation-style brick home in the center, its white pillars reminiscent of Mt. Vernon. Lighted pavilions with shake-shingle roofs keep travelers out of the sun, while long sidewalks wind through an open lawn. The parking lot was half full, and out of habit I drove slowly to the far end, seeking empty spaces in which to leave the 'Vette. Happily, the windshield was nearly free of love bugs. I was outrunning the critters as I had outrun the hurricanes. But Mississippi brought a love bug of a different sort.

At the very end of the lot, a middle-aged woman in shorts and halter was leaning against the trunk of a large tree. She watched me get out, stretch, then check the windshield, and when I headed for the plantation house she called after me. "Welcome to Mississippi, y'all. Be happy to use your lap any ol' way you want."

Unsure of what I'd heard, I kept on walking.

A female security officer was sitting on a bench outside the plantation house, the first such rest-area officer I had seen en route. "Why does a place like this need a uniformed guard?" I asked. And as she began speaking, I understood what had transpired at the far end of the parking lot. I had been propositioned.

"Wherever you get truckers you get hookers," she told me. "But we pretty much got 'em cleaned out now."

I was too stunned to respond. *The South's Warmest Welcome* indeed.

"Considerin' the volume of people that come through here," she went on, "we don't get much trouble. Three to five thousand people a day sign the register inside. An' we're told about twenty-five percent don't even bother. Most folks are headin' to the casinos in Biloxi, Gulfport, and Bay St. Louis. Aside from the hookers, I gotta deal with people who let their dogs off the leash and cars that park in the truck lot out back. Some folks think this is a campground and try to stay the night. I commute I-10 to here thirteen miles daily. It's OK, I guess, but the traffic can be a pain near Pascagoula."

"I better go sign that register," I laughed—it had become apparent that the security officer was ready to talk all day—"before you arrest me."

Inside, pretty southern matrons were dispensing free Cokes from behind a counter. A sign said, *Please excuse the condition of the restrooms. We are in the process of renovation.* But the restrooms were superb, cleaner than any I'd seen en route—so clean that the sign seemed an affectation, a gratuitous flaunting of southern hospitality.

The centerpiece of the plantation house is a living room decorated with period furniture—an antique sofa and chairs, a coffee table, a Persian carpet on a firm brick floor. In the living room stood an elderly man wearing a cowboy hat, the first cowboy hat of my grand lap, a distinct change from the ubiquitous ball caps. I had never been anywhere before where men wore cowboy hats. Or cowboy *boots*, but there they were—grainy leather like fine alligator skin, with impossibly square, pinched toes.

Outside again, the sun struck me with a new texture, a dry heat unlike the humid heat of Florida, but equally intense. The temperature was in the low eighties, the effect much hotter. There was an intense Gulf breeze as well—a new geographical feature—and I could easily imagine how unbearable Mississippi would be in mid-summer. Shorts and a T-shirt were all I needed now.

I returned to the 'Vette warily, but the woman who had greeted me was no longer propped against her tree. I suppose I should have been prepared for such an event, and it got me to thinking. For lone male travelers on the road, women seem to come with the territory. The famous Charles Kuralt had certainly proved that. The full details of his twenty-nine-year on-the-road affair had been in the news before I left Ohio. A woman by the name of Patricia Shannon had sued his estate for rural property he had promised her in Montana, including one hundred-thirty acres and a home near Twin Bridges. Kuralt, father of two daughters from his first marriage, had led a double life, acting as father to Shannon's three children in Montana while his wife was at home in New York. Unlike Jonathan Raban, however, Kuralt had had the common sense to keep Shannon out of his book, *My Life on the Road*. Raban, in one of his American travelogues, shacks up with a woman near St. Louis, interrupting the book's journey for coitus that is definitely *not*. Then there's Kerouac, whose cars always had women in them, or else were en route to women. And in *Travels with Charley*, John Steinbeck complicates the issue. Traveling alone except for his dog, he twice had his wife fly out to join him on the road—once in Chicago and once in Texas for Thanksgiving. Which left *me* as the only celibate traveler.

As I learned when I telephoned my wife—I was in the habit of checking in once or twice a week—my grand lap had become a touchstone of sorts. Some of her friends wanted to know why she hadn't gone with me. Others expressed naive envy, wishing their own husbands would leave town. But from the beginning my grand lap had been planned as a solo adventure. I would have been bad company anyway—talking into a tape recorder while driving, taking notes when interviewing people, falling asleep exhausted soon after dinner. Besides, my wife didn't even like the 'Vette. On a joint test run to Chicago soon after I bought the car, she had complained that it rode too low to the highway. That it was too awkward to get in and out of.

The woman who welcomed me to Mississippi caused me to think of such things. And to rethink my vanity plates—*LAP USA*.

* * *

Here's an Interstate Item of a salacious nature:

According to the Center for Problem-Oriented Policing, one of the problems that needs policing along the Interstates is prostitution. It's an industry that grew with the Interstate System, and it's most often found at seedy, low-budget motels.

However, according to an article in *The Sandspur*, the Rollins College newspaper, *an unseen world—seamy and sometimes deadly— thrives inside the trucks and over the crackling citizens band radios in truck stops across the nation. Women who work truck stops are called "lot lizards" by their customers, or johns. Without a CB radio, they are almost impossible to detect. If you're not looking for prostitutes, odds are you won't see them.*

I beg to differ.

* * *

Thick trees lined the Escatoqua River like a canebrake. Bayou Casotte was rife with billboards—for alligator farms, for airboat rides, for casinos the security guard had mentioned. At the Pascagoula River a dual bridge on pylons ran flat for a mile or more, then humped high above blue water from which the view was all salt hay and pines. The humps, I decided, must be for boats to pass beneath. Without them, because of the flat terrain, such watery passages would be far less picturesque.

Beyond the bridge lay the Sand Hill Crane Wildlife Refuge, seventeen miles from Biloxi. It was high noon, the traffic moderate, and French names began to dominate—*Fontainbleu*, *D'Iberville*, then *Beauvoir*, home of Jefferson Davis, president of the Confederacy. Gulfport and Biloxi brought more humped bridges as well as large convoys of eastbound cars, purple flags flying above each roof, colors of the *Southern Jaguars*. Hundreds of fans were taking the Interstate to an afternoon football game.

Sixty miles from New Orleans a phalanx of billboards batters the skyline, one after another after another. Gaudy, crass, and shameless, they extend high into the sky above the trees flanking the highway. There is no escaping them—the I-10 corridor gives them a captive audience—and they began to dampen my enthusiasm for seeing Louisiana's largest city.

Near De Lisle another twin humpbacked bridge became visible miles in advance, its graceful curve rising and falling. On the far shore, after the exit for Bay St. Louis, the lovely Jourdan River curled away through marshes and pines. Ignoring the bright sun, two old black men were fishing with long cane poles in the bayou beside the highway. A few miles later, by a billboard for boiled peanuts, I exited in a long loop to a rest area in a grove of tall trees. Here the plantation-style facilities bore a sign that made me laugh louder than I had at the Canadian border. *No Solicitation.* No more warm southern welcomes.

Much smaller than the first area, the place was uncrowded—everyone was at the Jaguars game, I guess—so I lingered just long enough to walk and stretch. On my way back to the 'Vette, however, I came across an old black man with gray hair, sitting alone at a rotting picnic table in the shade of a high pine. When I asked him about the Interstates, he was silent. So I kept on chattering. "I'm amazed at all the water along I-10," I said. "It's built right through water."

Finally, the old man looked up. And his response was classic. "In the Sout'," he said slowly, "da Innastates are *causeways*. 'Cause dere ain't no ways else to go."

At the Pearl River, following a flat approach, I-10 ascended the highest humped bridge yet, putting me briefly above the tree line. Forests the texture of green cotton candy spread away in all directions, the Pearl River running below. And at the far end of the bridge it was *Bienvenue à Lousiane.*

The descent into Louisiana brought another revelation. There was a pattern here I had finally realized. So many states in America have rivers as their natural boundaries, something I would have never understood so thoroughly without driving the Interstates. Thinking back, I had crossed rivers between New Hampshire and Maine, Massachusetts and Rhode Island, New York and New Jersey, New Jersey and Delaware, D.C. and Virginia, South Carolina and Georgia, Georgia and Florida, Florida and Alabama. Now I was crossing a river from Mississippi into Louisiana.

But my meditation was cut short. Entering Louisiana, as the hotdog vendor had warned in the Florida panhandle, I-10 immediately became horrible—faded pavement, rippled and bumpy. I passed up the first rest area, breaking my habit since I had so recently stopped, but if the condition of the highway was any indication of the roadside facilities, it was just as well to bump on by.

The West Pearl River followed, more narrow than the Pearl itself, with another humped bridge through a bayou. Three lanes now careened for New Orleans, the traffic moderate to heavy at thirty miles out, the highway flanked by billboards and industrial sites. Dry weeds laced the unkempt median. Shattered glass and retreads littered the brownish berms. New Orleans, it was easy to see, would be *garbage in* and *garbage out*.

Farther ahead, another long humpbacked bridge lay in wait—ten miles or more in length—longer than the span into Mobile that had unnerved me. The span carries I-10 right across Lake Pontchartrain, a shallow blue expanse that looks as wide as the Everglades. And suddenly it seemed that the entire day from Tallahassee, with all of its swamps and bayous and smaller humped bridges—with all of those *pi*-shaped telephone-pole pylons that make the Gulf Coast appear to be one long morass—was simply in preparation for this Interstate surprise.

Across the blue surface of Lake Pontchartrain sailboats leaned like tiny white triangles in the buffeting breeze. Larger speedboats cut white arcs about them. The passage disturbed me more than the bridge at Mobile—I'd hate to have to cross it in heavy weather—but the steadily increasing traffic seemed unimpressed. Everyone was hell-bent for *N'Awlins*—the Big Easy—as if nothing else mattered but getting there.

Above the vast meandering shoreline of Lake Pontchartrain—a shoreline punctuated with a thousand tiny docks and cottages—a slight haze rendered the sky a light blue. The water itself, wrinkled in the breeze, was dark blue. Mid-way across, I was struck by another revelation. I was convinced now that a separate Interstate for trucks could indeed be built through Long Island Sound. My concept of the Interstates had always been limited to *terra firma*. The South is a swamp, yet no problem whatsoever.

Orleans Parish begins right in the middle of Lake Pontchartrain, the first in a series of parishes marking the French Catholic influence. St. John's, St. James, Baton Rouge, and Ascension Parish follow across the state, historic jurisdictions spread east to west. Meanwhile, far to the north, another causeway strung with tall power poles and wires paralleled I-10 across the water, angling south to converge at a distant point as in a perspective drawing. On the far shore, which was finally growing nearer, a series of bridges suddenly came together out of nowhere, crosshatched by an ugly array of power lines. Here all traffic meets in a manic approach to New Orleans.

Among all the French names, a sign for *Irish Bayou* seemed out of place. It reminded me of the couple I'd met in Naples. They would have crossed this very bridge with their family on their own lapping of America. *Bayou Sauvage* seemed more appropriate—a national wildlife refuge—preparation for the wild life of New Orleans. Then strip malls and brick tract housing began to fly by. The day was clouding over, threatening mid-afternoon rain.

An old black bridge that seems built from an Erector Set mars the New Orleans skyline. The Superdome sits off to the right, and there is a tall oblong building with a lopped-off top that looks like an electric shaver. The rest is a gray mass of towers, wires, antennae, and nondescript buildings, through which the traffic rattled and slid on a pockmarked surface. In New Orleans the tilted slabs of concrete of the Interstate are so battered that they produce no steady rhythm, just indiscriminate jarring and jolting across four or five lanes. The ride was worse than through Cleveland because it was longer, the pounding sustained from one side of the city to the other. I-10 had degenerated into a warped surface, a series of unpredictable speed bumps, punishing my neck and shoulders and the base of my spine, leaving my buttocks feeling skewered as if by an ice pick.

A study by the Federal Highway Administration had declared the roads in New Orleans to be the worst in the nation. But I didn't need a study to tell me that. As in Cleveland, the 'Vette's lumbar seats were no help whatsoever. Gritting my teeth in my Richard Petty mode, I hung on as the reckless traffic banged its way across the Huey Long Bridge. Named for a famous local politician, the bridge brought to mind *All the King's Men,* Robert Penn's Warren's novel about Louisiana politics. As the Groucho Marx guy had said in Boston, "The Interstates is all politics." Which was all too true for New Orleans, where all the king's horses and all the king's men couldn't put I-10 together again.

As the mad dash continued through the western outskirts, I was beginning to wonder if this was *it*. If I'd be forced to abandon my grand lap in New Orleans. My back was screaming in pain, but relief was in sight. It was three o'clock and my exit was coming up. And the directions to the motel couldn't have been simpler. *I-10, Exit So-and-So*. But the ramp dumped me into an Interstate ambush, on a one-way two-lane highway, where there was nothing to do but turn right. And the motel was nowhere to be seen.

That was the least of my problems. The area was less than desirable, a littered strip of gas stations, convenience stores, and cheap shops, where everyone—in the hectic traffic and hanging about on street corners—was black. Cars were darting from stoplight to stoplight as the highway swept me north away from the Interstate. After a mile or so I swung into a weed-filled parking lot by a string of discount stores. Jumping out, I locked the 'Vette and hurried back along the curb toward the Interstate. The humid gray sky that had begun at Lake Pontchartrain had thickened overhead, its drab dome enclosing a scene as frantic as Miami.

Finally, above the hostile traffic, loitering pedestrians, and overhead wires—above an indistinctive sprawling landscape neither suburban nor urban—I saw the sign for the motel. The place was just south of I-10, beneath an adjacent embankment, fifty yards from where I had exited. Unreachable because of the one-way traffic.

I turned immediately and jogged back to the 'Vette, sweating and frantic, searching for a way to make an about-face. Then I saw it—a center-lane turnaround beyond the discount stores where I had parked, the only access to a parallel highway in the other direction. A narrow esplanade of dirt and weeds separated the opposing lanes. To get there I had to cut across two lanes of oncoming traffic—no problem for the 'Vette—but as I did so, a small white car peeled out behind me and stayed on my tail, maintaining pace as I headed back toward I-10.

Eventually the road bent to the right, around a dirt park or central square, forcing me into a series of left-hand turns that finally brought me within the shadow of the Interstate. Without signaling, I swung abruptly into the motel parking lot. The white car followed. The lot was crowded and I took the only free space. Then I grabbed my suitcase, locked up, and hurried inside, while the white car idled in a delivery zone.

It was three-forty. Bypassing the desk, I crossed the lobby, took a long hallway to a rear exit, and worked my way around to the front of the building. The white car was still there, the driver talking on a cell phone. I began to tremble, my heart thumping. Years ago, when I had driven into New York City in a Chevy Nova with Virginia plates, the car had nearly been stolen out from under me—the ignition lock broken by a special tool, the culprits fleeing when I returned unexpectedly—in circumstances so strikingly similar to the present that I knew I had to get out of there. Then I remembered Friday's fortune cookie. *Fortune truly helps those who are of good judgment.* Retracing my steps to the lobby, I cancelled my reservation just minutes before the four o'clock deadline.

When I first dreamed of owning a Corvette, the car had routinely appeared on the annual top-ten list of stolen vehicles. But in the intervening years, things had changed. Today, the Corvette is not even in the top twenty-five, having yielded to the Toyota Camry, the Honda Accord, and similar cars. Even my '91 Chevy Caprice, the family car, was ranked higher at number eighteen. But I had nearly lost a Nova once in New York City. Now my entire body was warning me about the 'Vette in New Orleans.

The white car was gone when I returned to the parking lot, just as my 'Vette might have been gone in the morning. But in avoiding one problem I had created another. I still needed a room for the night. Sharp pains racked my shoulders, back, and buttocks, exacerbated by the tension of the Interstate ambush. But first things first. Returning to I-10, I headed for Baton Rouge, eighty miles distant, relieved to put *the Big Uneasy* in my rearview mirror.

* * *

West of New Orleans you encounter a new Interstate term—*spillway*, another version of the causeway. Between Lake Pontchartrain and the Mississippi River, I-10 runs through continuous bayous—marshy bogs thick with vine-laced pine forests, wet flatlands edged with rushes— where spillways and causeways, as the old black man had said, are the *only* way to go. Perpendicular to the highway, long canals carry greenish water beneath the traffic. But unlike so many other rivers and waterways I had traversed to date, I felt no desire to explore these avenues into the swampy interior. Not even with my imagination. The absence of sun didn't help. The gray sky was still threatening rain, and I was under the negative spell of the Interstate ambush.

Intimidating as well, in the space of a few miles I saw two roadkills I couldn't identify—something yellow like an armadillo and something furry like a ferret—strange creatures from the surrounding black lagoons through which I was fleeing in pain, on a relentlessly rough road that had begun at the Louisiana state line.

About halfway to Baton Rouge, when the Interstate returned to hard ground, I stopped at a rest area to phone another motel. The rest-area facilities were old and in need of repair, the dry open spaces begging for a gardener. But there were few people and fewer vehicles, a welcome relief. I phoned my doctor in Ohio as well, ordering a prescription to be sent on ahead by overnight mail. If the Interstates continued into Texas in the same hopeless condition as Louisiana, I would have to abandon the 'Vette and fly home.

From I-10, the initial view of Baton Rouge includes a Hilton hotel—a typical sight in many American cities—above the usual *garbage in*. Small bungalows cluster in neighborhoods along the Interstate embankments, and treed blocks of the LSU campus spread away to the right. Then the highway makes a sweeping turn toward the Mississippi, crossing high above the wide river on a great gray bridge that is arched in several sections like protractors. It's another Erector

Set bridge—all girders, bolts, and rivets. But this one ascended so high it gave me vertigo, the very top bringing a misty view of flat countryside beyond the far shore, where oil tanks lined the way through a stretch of industrial wasteland.

A short while later, well beyond the city limits in West Baton Rouge Parish, I exited into the kind of isolated, rural business block that dominates the Interstates as you drive west, a self-contained community in the middle of nowhere that exists solely *because* of the Interstates. No more than half a mile square, such blocks lie in open treeless terrain adjacent to the highway. All businesses in these places are run by local people who somehow materialize from the surrounding scrub. This one was brand new, with several gas stations, motels, and fast-food chains. Its main road had just been paved, running for a few hundred yards before dead-ending into a field. As a result, the 'Vette picked up oil and tar and spit it out behind, coating the flanks and undercarriage with a gritty residue.

According to the motel directory, the brief new road right off the highway was the ubiquitous "Frontage Road," a road that "fronts" the Interstate. Yet it always appears without a road sign, confusing the more literal-minded traveler. Thus, as a navigation aid—despite what the directory says—it's totally useless. Generally, the more expensive the motel, the closer it's located to the Interstate. The one I was looking for was at the very end of "Frontage Road," near a temporary cul-de-sac that would one day be extended farther into the wasteland beyond. The gas mart beside it was so new that its logo was not yet up. And like so many similar enterprises I was encountering en route, its windows were plastered with advertisements for ready employment within. The American economy was booming. People were desperately needed to attend to business along the Interstates.

A hundred yards beyond the motel sat The Cabaret, an innocuous flat-roofed establishment that, like the woman at the Mississippi rest area, seemed to cater to a variety of needs. Its parking lot was empty, the day too young for nightlife. By my watch it was five-thirty, but that proved an hour off. Somewhere along the way—perhaps in the middle of my New Orleans panic—I had missed the change from Eastern Daylight Saving Time to Central. But that was OK. It would mean an extra hour's sleep. The motel had an outdoor pool, and I was hoping to loll about as in Naples, to ease my aching muscles and let my body unwind at will. But the temperature had slipped to sixty-five.

"We been waitin' six months for cool weather," the desk clerk told me, "and we finally got it."

"And I've been waiting all day for the road to improve. The last few hundred miles have been murder."

"Well," he said rather philosophically, "you can't have everythin'. It gits a little better west of here."

In the utility room at the end of the office I tossed two weeks' worth of laundry into a washer. While it was churning away, I soaked in a hot bath, then went out to check the tar on the 'Vette. I had parked beside an old Ford draped with an ersatz mask that seemed made from a badminton net. Loose black straps dangled from the headlights like garter belts. The jerry-built thing was more Victoria's Secret than Zorro. And despite such protection, the car—with Florida plates—was coated with love bugs. From the way the goo had dried, I could tell it had been there for days.

I thought about seeking out the owner and offering my liter of Coke, but I didn't want to insult him. He had improvised his own solution, as I had done in New Orleans.

Sometimes on the Interstates you have to fend for yourself. . . .

About three in the morning I awoke to the sound of whining tires on I-10, the loneliest sound in the world. It reminded me of what Chief Big Eagle had said back in the days when he was willing to talk about his life as a truck driver. "There is a lonesomeness to it—life on the road. People don't realize that."

The whining meant that someone was out there on the highway, an individual consciousness perhaps fighting to remain awake as his headlights glared into the blackness. The very image left me unable to get back to sleep. I began to think about what had happened in New Orleans. About my aching back. About what F. Scott Fitzgerald had written—how, in the dark night of the soul, it's always three o'clock in the morning.

At five o'clock I gave up trying to sleep and went out for a walk, surprised by the chill. The brilliant full moon was back on the western horizon, marred by the yellow glow of arc lights along "Frontage Road." Up on the highway, tractor-trailers rolled by intermittently, their presence somehow a comfort now. I hiked over to the gas mart for coffee but the place was deserted, so I began to circle the motel parking lot for exercise, the main drag too full of oily tar. Half an hour later I returned to my room and showered. I wanted to check out as soon as the desk opened, to get out of Louisiana and into Texas. San Antonio was my goal—another drive of nearly five hundred miles. I was hoping the highway would improve at the state line. It certainly couldn't get worse.

It was still dark as I headed for the 'Vette, when a door opened to the room beside mine and two very attractive young women—in tight slacks and jiggling halters despite the chill—strolled right by me in a cloud of perfume. They carried no suitcases, no pocketbooks, just their sexy no-nonsense selves. They were headed to a small green sports car now parked beside the 'Vette where the fishnet Ford had been. Perhaps they worked at The Cabaret, perhaps they had partied there while I soaked my bones in a hot Saturday-night bath. They looked like the kind of women that the billboards had been advertising—*We Bare All! 24 Hours!* But there had been no noise in the night—no screeching of cars, no music, no loud voices—from The Cabaret or the room next door. Or if there *had* been, I had slept through it all.

Hurrying to the 'Vette, I thought I'd ask the women about the Interstates. Then I thought better of it. There are certain people you just don't ask about the Interstates. That's what I learned in Louisiana. At the Mississippi Welcome Center as well. The pair ignored me anyway, hopping into their little green sports car, backing out and zipping off, leaving me with nothing to do but reset the 'Vette's digital clock to Central Time. Then I filled the tank at the gas mart, bought a bunch of green bananas—the avocado was not yet ripe, nor am I an avocado fan—and headed for Texas, the sun once again rising behind me as I drove into the moon.

Sunday-morning traffic on the Interstates is always skimpy, and today was no exception. It was seven o'clock and misty, the road smoother than expected, running due west along a ragged median flanked by tall trees. Occasional headlights gleamed on the damp pavement. The terrain was firm now, flat and wide—absolutely the widest so far—the shadowy vistas to the left and right extending for miles. In crossing the Mississippi I seemed to have left the bayous behind for good. Nor did I miss them. But once again there came roadkill I couldn't identify—a gray wolf or coyote, something with skinny legs and a pointy snout—nothing as familiar as an Ohio raccoon, which I would have welcomed. My back felt better, but before long my buttocks began to sting again. There was nothing to do but gut it out. The long day's drive would determine if my grand lap would continue.

Forcing myself to focus on other things, I fished out the Eric Clapton CD that my cousin had given me in Connecticut. Then I put it away, saving it for Texas, to honor Dennis in the state where he had earned his first million. The radio news was full of the Ryder Cup, the American golfers woefully behind. It would take a Sunday miracle to pull out a victory—just the distraction I needed. I would catch the last hour of the event on TV in San Antonio. And ignore my aching back in the interim.

Up ahead, as the sun rose in the rearview mirror, the large yellow moon began to climb the sky. Near Lafayette, disappointingly, the highway reverted to *pi*-shaped pylons and bayous, checking my feeling of having left the South behind. The Interstate sign—*Swamp Freeway*—was all too literal. The highway cuts through thick cypress forests where long channels of water serve as a median, separating the east- and westbound lanes for miles. The total absence of a median was intimidating—nothing but a wide berth of *air* between opposing lanes, with water rippling a hundred feet below.

A sign for *Whiskey Bay* conjured images of bayou moonshine, white lightning distilled in backyard swamps accessible only by airboat. Other bodies of water came and went—*Bayou des Glaises, Atchafalaya River, Lake Pelba, Lake Bigeaux, Henderson Swamp*—all dotted with islands of dead trees, islands with stumps of trees, entirely green islands devoid of trees. Traffic continued to be light, mostly Louisiana vehicles with license plates boasting *Sportsman's Paradise*. But I saw no place where I personally would want to fish. The terrain was too wild. You can go fishing in Louisiana and not come back.

Beyond Lafayette the Swamp Freeway finally ended, but the next stretch of I-10 was under construction, the work mercifully halted now on Sunday. And here a simple idea struck me—all Interstate signs that announce *Construction Ahead* should instead read *Maintenance Ahead*. The psychological difference is crucial. Americans maintain their yards and homes and cars just as our highways are maintained. But *construction* connotes starting from scratch, conjuring images of dump trucks, bulldozers, and road graders—and miles and miles of orange cones and barrels—which mean frustrating delays. The term *maintenance* is less harsh. It could soften the tendency to road rage. In a few states I had seen special billboard-type signs in construction areas—*Your tax dollars at work*. Others explained the ratio of state and federal funding. More signs like that might create a different Interstate mind-set. Especially when faced with construction at the end of the Swamp Freeway.

It was great to see new blacktop again. Ironically, the ugliest median strip in all of Louisiana lay along this newly paved stretch of highway—nothing but weeds, dirt, and gravel. But I'd take it. You can hang the aesthetics when comfort's at stake. No doubt the median would be attended to later. But then the new blacktop ended and the jolting returned—*pa-dump pa-dump pa-dump*—at times as rapid as a machine gun. The bayous had given way to sparsely populated farmland, and more strange roadkill. But the battering road surface was all that concerned me now. I had to exit for relief. And it was only eight thirty.

The stop, at an isolated gas mart of gray concrete blocks, produced another first, a blue-and-white sign on a highway heading north from I-10, a sign I had never seen before—*Hurricane Evacuation Route*. In Ohio there are signs that say *Snow Emergency Route*, but in western Louisiana hurricanes are as routine as snow.

The small gravel parking lot was empty. Getting out of the 'Vette slowly, I stretched my back then limped around the flat-roofed building in search of the men's room. In the rear a lone metal door stood wide open, riddled with rusty bullet holes as if someone had been assassinated—Mafia style—while in a vulnerable position. Cinderblocks around the doorframe were likewise pockmarked. The room had no light, the gut-wrenching stench from within forcing me to retreat into the fresh Gulf breeze.

Inside at the counter, the heavy-set woman behind the cash register seemed happy for company. She was alone in the building, so I asked her about the Interstates.

"My son, he's forever complaining about I-10," she said. "Every week he travels on business from Lafayette to New Orleans and it just about kills him."

"Does it get any better?" I asked.

"No sir. That road's gonna bang your bones all the way to Lake Charles."

"Ever snow in these parts?" I needed a change of subject.

"No sir. Just a lotta wind and rain and mud."

"We could have used some of those hurricane signs back east."

"Hep yourself," the woman laughed. "Y'aller welcome to 'em."

Back on the highway, I was beginning to hate Louisiana. The median was thick with tall wild grass, the roadside trees sparse and scraggly. I watched the cars ahead of me bounce over the rough spots, trying to anticipate the jolts, posting in my seat as if riding a horse English style. But the horse I was riding was a bucking bronco.

This was farm country now, with ranches of black cattle. And walking the berm on this Sunday morning were more hitchhikers than I had seen anywhere—black and Latino—nobody you'd pick up just based on appearance. But I felt no guilt in not stopping. I had resolved before leaving Ohio not to pick up any riders, for the same reason I hadn't brought my wife. The ragged men stared meanly from the roadside, and when they raised their thumbs I averted my eyes to the billboards—billboards that were still advertising Cajun cooking when I saw a sign for Beaumont, Texas, the first promise of relief from Louisiana.

But Lake Charles would come first, a city of seventy thousand, with a bridge that even from a distance looks strange. It's a brown triangle, a teepee instead of a smooth hump, its apex bringing an ugly view of an industrial bayou—refineries, squat oil tanks, smokestacks belching white plumes. A place called *Sulphur* lies a few minutes beyond, perfectly named for the prevailing odor of rotten eggs. The road surface stank too, its battering rhythm as irregular as in New Orleans—not quite a ripple, not quite a washboard, not quite a rumble strip—but always punishing.

Unexpectedly, for a few miles at least, the unkempt median suddenly improved. Salt hay, rushes, and tall white fan-dancer plumes appeared, waving in the stiff Gulf breeze. But the sight could do nothing to relieve my aching back. At nine-thirty, just an hour after my first stop, I exited into an empty rest area to stretch.

Not surprisingly, the condition of the place matched the condition of I-10. The men's room was the worst I'd seen. Many of the stalls had no doors, and the few remaining ones were scratched with graffiti. The automatic hand dryers either didn't work or the knob you punch was missing. Outside, I took a brisk walk around the area to loosen up. Weedy, cracked sidewalks wound through several acres of open ground, through scruffy brown grass and patches of sand. T-shaped pavilions with flat roofs sat among clumps of enormous pines and pin oaks. Draped with Spanish moss, the pin oaks stood menacingly, like trees in scary cartoons. High in the pines hung cones as large as grapefruit, a threat to anyone walking beneath.

In an open area I sought out an old picnic table where I lay flat on my back for a series of exercises. High white clouds floated in the pale blue sky, occasionally shielding the sun. The temperature was already eighty and the humidity was increasing. And I was wondering if my grand lap was about to end.

7

BY THE TIME I LEFT THE REST AREA THE TEMPERATURE HAD JUMPED TO eighty-five, the road so immediately bone-jarring I felt I hadn't stopped at all. Horses grazed in the wide flat terrain, some pretty pintos in the sun, but the median, shoulders, and trees had a ragged look. I feared the state of Texas wouldn't be any different, and the Texas Travel Information Area was just a mile away. Meanwhile, across the highway just off the eastbound lanes, sat the most attractive rest area I'd seen in Louisiana—as lovely as the first one in Mississippi and the very antithesis of the one I'd just left—ready to mislead visitors from all points west in terms of what lay ahead across the state.

Then I crossed the tree-lined Sabine River into Texas—another natural boundary—where a barrage of industrial cranes greeted me. And an ungrammatical sign: *Drive Friendly, the Texas Way.* But *Drive Friendlily* would have sounded just as bad. Two other signs were more Texas-like—*Livestock Check Station 3/4 mile* and *El Paso 857.* The latter spoke volumes. Eight hundred and fifty-seven miles was farther than I had driven from Toledo, Ohio, to Portsmouth, New Hampshire! And all of it was in Texas and all on I-10. I laughed out loud, but my laughter sounded strangely unconvincing. This was the great state of Texas and I was about to cross it east to west. Which suddenly didn't seem so funny.

As I had hoped, the highway smoothed out just across the state line, allowing the light Sunday morning traffic to *ride friendly* for a while through rangeland of grazing cows and horses. But the bucking and bouncing resumed near Beaumont, another case of *garbage in, garbage out*—an industrial landscape of oil refineries reminiscent of New Jersey, fed by dismal strip malls and billboards. Beaumont, in French, means *beautiful mountain*, but in Beaumont, Texas (pop. 114,132), there's no mountain. Nor anything beautiful to be seen from the Interstate.

Across East Texas the road surface earned a *C-* at best, through a flat and desperate landscape, the population sparse. I could see no reason whatsoever for living in East Texas. It was time for Eric Clapton, a blatant diversion from the surrounding flatness, and the first cut on the CD—Clapton's rendition of "I Shot the Sheriff"—did the trick, conjuring images of the Old West, cowboy movies in which some guy always dreams of getting himself a little spread down by the bend in the river. *Spread* is the operative word in Texas. *To open to a fuller extent or width.* East Texas is one enormous *spread,* but so flat you can't see to its fullest extent. It just spreads away from I-10 in all directions. And keeps on spreading. Land without end.

Sixty miles east of Houston, where I-10 becomes three lanes, the big western sky begins for good, a blue dome over scrubby terrain. A concrete white barrier replaces the median strip—a monumental psychological loss, even though the shallow V-shaped median was dry and scruffy. Then the commercial *garbage in* begins—the omnipresent Stuckey's, souvenir shops, food marts, used-car lots—a tedious stretch even Eric Clapton couldn't drown out. As in Florida, any overpass becomes a major happening, momentary relief from the hypnosis of level geography.

I welcomed the wide Trinity River, but its high humped bridge gave me vertigo, the view as giddy as it is wide, the countryside extending from marshy tree-lined shores. The aerial perspective only confirmed what I had already sensed from I-10—that the highway ran straight ahead forever, only to vanish in a rippling distant haze. Immediately below me the river's blue surface was roughened by the Texas wind. Soon a brown wire fence rose from the concrete divider, a touch of prison in these wide-open spaces. Up ahead, strung across stanchions that resembled the Eiffel Tower, high-tension wires scored the sky. Large oil tanks squatted below them amidst a gridwork of pipes, ugly reminders of the source of Texas money. And the dirtiest air in the entire nation.

I kept the 'Vette in fourth gear now, hoping a slower speed would ease the jouncing as the *garbage in* of Houston began its assault— industrial wastelands beyond the San Jacinto River, then sprawling strip malls and more high-tension wires. But on the outskirts of Houston came an Interstate surprise—an astonishing maze of ramps and overpasses gleaming in the sun. White concrete pylons and brand-new bridges curled across the horizon like roller coasters, an impressive display of found art and engineering. Then the city skyline emerged beneath blue sky and white clouds—a cluster of dominoes standing on end. Traffic was moderate but increasing steadily as four lanes funneled toward the city, home to one and a half million Texans.

Closer in, buildings began to distinguish themselves—one with a teepee-shaped roof, others with tops like pyramids—in attractive greens, tans, and browns. Closer still came a brownish stair-step structure, another like a bell tower, and some like octagons. Then I was wheeling through the heart of downtown, running the gears in my

Richard Petty mode as a succession of modern buildings flew by on each elbow—towering facades of glittering glass and steel, their sheer edges sharp against the blue sky.

West of downtown the Interstate surprise continued. Enormous Y-shaped concrete pylons stood out starkly, waiting to be topped by an elevated highway. Then the excitement abruptly ended in heavy traffic—bumper to bumper in three lanes at high speeds. Rough pavement resumed through the *garbage out* of urban sprawl, the median divider but a concrete wall and wire fence. Ahead of me a pickup truck seemed to be towing a van, but it was one of those Interstate illusions—the van was tailgating. Houston ranks fourth in the nation in terms of annual hours lost in traffic. *Should be no problem*, a man at the rest area had said. *It's Sunday.* And all I could think was, I'd hate to see it on *Monday*.

It was two hundred miles from Houston to my motel in San Antonio, where I planned to soak in a hot bath and watch the conclusion of the Ryder Cup. Because of the weekend, the prescriptions I had ordered—a painkiller and an anti-inflammatory—were being sent ahead to Van Horn, Texas. I would catch up with them Monday evening, if I could last that long, and make a final decision about continuing Tuesday morning. Meanwhile, the heavy Texas wind was shoving the 'Vette around, bending trees in the canebrakes, rippling flags flat-out from high poles. A fleet of motorcycles roared by on my right, tacking like sailboats. The temperature had risen to ninety-three.

I didn't think Texas could spread out any farther but it was doing just that—wide spaces and flat plains without perspective. Was that car ahead of me a hundred yards away? or a hundred miles? There was no way to tell. The concrete divider had given way to grass as brown and brittle as the landscape itself—a brown tabletop with prefabs, doublewides, and single trailer homes clustered here and there in small glens.

But between Houston and San Antonio there are hints of hills. I-10 begins to dip and swell—a major change in the landscape—with scruffy stands of pine and oak to the left and right. The barren median assumed a reddish tint, and the surrounding terrain became a matching reddish-brown.

Cattle grazed to the north of the highway now as I continued toward San Antonio—black cattle and white cattle and brown cattle, not the Texas longhorns I had expected. Ancient oaks grew in scattered clusters amidst scruffy tan grass and sandy soil. Mercifully, I-10 continued to roll, not only dipping but curving left and right, an entirely new sensation. My back was beginning to feel better, massaged by the undulating landscape and a smoother highway beneath me.

Signs warned of loose gravel in the median. One for *Oak Ridge* seemed apt as well, for groves of oaks now dotted the distant ridges. But a town called *Flatonia* (pop. 1295) seemed out of place. With a name like that it belonged farther east, not in rolling terrain. Before long some attractive ranches began to appear—with white wooden fences and brown wooden fences, with horses and cattle grazing in fields the color of wheat straw—beneath high white clouds and a blue bell jar of a sky. These are the dream spreads of the old cowboy movies.

I entered Gonzales County, noting the Spanish name. The French had been left behind in Louisiana. And suddenly the idyllometer flashed eighty-five—the best reading since the Florida panhandle. Smooth new blacktop was partly responsible, an invitation to Sunday speeders. But the police were out as well, pulling over anyone doing more than eighty, their radar easily concealed in the ranchland dells. Drivers stood at intervals along the sandy shoulder, arguing their case with Texas' finest.

Eighty miles east of San Antonio some very lovely modern homes begin to crop up to the left of I-10—the nicest I'd seen in the state. Low and sleek, they were set in khaki-colored hills of brownish green trees, a landscape right out of Rembrandt. But a cluster of trailer homes soon marred the effect. Gradually, a new feature of the Texas landscape was revealing itself—a series of creeks. From a distance they look like lone furrows plowed into the earth—*Plum Creek, Smith Creek, Salatrillo Creek, Martinez Creek, Rosillo Creek*. Only yards wide, they wander south to cross beneath the Interstate, some with shallow water gleaming over smooth rocks, others as dry as gravel sandbars. My favorite is *Woman Hollering Creek*, as innocuous as the rest, invoking images of some pioneer bride who might have lost her sanity in these wide-open spaces. I could picture her getting out of a covered wagon, turning to her husband—perhaps she was a mail-order bride—and saying, "This is *it*, Silas? We're gonna live *here*?" Then she went hollering to the nearest creek to drown her sorrows. Or perhaps *herself*.

But another new feature of the landscape proved more dramatic. Each time I-10 crested a hill now, a wide oval vista opened up all the way to the horizon—a stunning earth-rim view to the very edge of the world. It was easily the most of America I had ever seen in a single glance. Earlier, the land had been too flat for such a perspective. Now the contrast was stunning. No wonder the woman had gone mad by the creek! I was virtually alone on the planet between Houston and San Antonio, zipping along in my 'Vette, devouring the miles that years ago had meant months of travel. The effect was both thrilling and frightening.

The first glimpse of San Antonio from I-10 is a needle-like tower on the distant horizon. Then the city materializes like a scale model on a boardroom table. As with Houston, the approach is *garbage-in*—warehouses, strip malls, industrial parks, urban sprawl—both outside and inside the I-410 beltway. As you draw nearer, one building resembles a giant thermos, with an upright handle that might be used to pluck it from the earth. Small brick houses in tree-lined neighborhoods spread away from the Interstate on both sides. It was almost four o'clock, the traffic light, the temperature holding at ninety-five.

Before long, I-10 skirted the city to the south, then turned due north, the abrupt change of direction taking the traffic through the heart of downtown. The shift changed my attitude as well. Suddenly San Antonio opened up above me on the right—clean, sleek, and colorful—as modern and attractive as downtown Houston. Shimmering glass-and-steel edifices rose into the sky, neatly stacked and matching the earth tones of the landscape. Then the highway split into an upper and lower level, and in the confusion of a detour I got stuck on the lower route. But the view from up top must be spectacular, buildings rising against the blue sky like a bar graph, large rectangular columns of light and shade.

Beyond downtown the city continues non-stop, spreading toward the outer beltway over gorgeous golden hills, a cityscape that seems the essence of modernity. And suddenly I realized that too much of my life has been spent in old cities of the Midwest and East. In such vibrant hubs all seems new and possible, certainly for the one million inhabitants of San Antonio. Even on Sunday.

I had come nearly five hundred miles from Baton Rouge, and with the rough road at last behind me and the stress on my back much relieved, only one thing remained to be done—to find my motel beyond the beltway in time for the Ryder Cup. There was no excuse this time. The late afternoon was bright and clear, and I could see the motel sign high in the sky as I approached my exit. Still, checking the directory, I had my doubts. I had seen these directions before: *Exit So-and-So. Turn left under I-10 to Frontage Road.* What could be simpler? But I had learned more about "Frontage Road" than I cared to know. What followed made me want to sue the CEOs of every Motel Find-Me-Not chain in America, compelling them—as part of my settlement—to follow their own directions to every one of their units in the country.

Exiting I-10, I turned left as instructed, but there was no indication of "Frontage Road," just a large overhead sign for *Turnaround Lane*, a road paralleling the Interstate in the direction of San Antonio. But I had just come from San Antonio and had no desire to return. I wanted to watch the Ryder Cup. So I continued along the highway on which the exit had dumped me.

Winding left and right, the road eventually ascended into some lovely hill country where I found myself in an exclusive neighborhood of modern homes and huge estates—each with watered lawns and well-trimmed hedges, the deep green of the grass an attractive contrast to the khaki terrain, certainly no location for a motel. I needed to turn around and go back. But now that I *wanted* to turn around, there was no place to do so. The clean well-paved highway ran farther into the country, split by a wide central divider as meticulously manicured as the area homes.

Hurrying on farther, I came to a golf course that was—an incredible coincidence—hosting a Senior PGA Tour event. But I didn't want a *Senior* event. I wanted to watch the Ryder Cup on TV. The local tournament had just ended and stragglers from the gallery were heading for the parking lots. At one green by the roadside, tournament officials were removing the flag, so I pulled to the curb, powered down the passenger window, and shouted over. They said I could turn around about a mile ahead.

Retracing my route to the Interstate, I took the only option remaining, heading down *Turnaround Lane* toward San Antonio. And there was the motel, half a mile farther, tucked into a hillside on the right, hidden by pines and a jungle of shrubs. Towering above it, on a fat round shiny metal pole, was the logo I had glimpsed from I-10. I jumped out, checked in, and raced to my room, tuning into the Ryder Cup just as the announcers were signing off, the slow-motion replays showing jubilant American golfers dancing in celebration. After the most dramatic comeback in Ryder Cup history.

* * *

In coming to San Antonio I had crossed another invisible boundary. Blacks had all but disappeared. Everyone was Latino or Latina—the desk clerk, the motel maids, the restaurant waitress. The television had three channels in Spanish, and seven of the first ten radio stations I tried were in Spanish as well. Even the Interstate had a different look, with a new kind of posted jargon—*loops* and *turnarounds* and *access roads*—terms the locals use around San Antonio as if they're common knowledge.

I checked out first thing in the morning, just as the headlights of Monday-morning commuters began to swish by on I-10. And the moment I left my air-conditioned room I was hit in the face with a new perception. My glasses immediately fogged over, meeting the warm air outside, steaming up so thoroughly that I had to stop for fear of tripping. The surprise continued at the 'Vette where, for the first time since Ohio, the car sat entirely devoid of dew. The simple discovery stopped me short, forcing me to reassess my entire notion of climate in America. I had driven out of a humid zone into an arid part of the country, land without dew. It is possible, I realized, to live without oppressive humidity. There are places in America where your morning shower leaves no steam on the bathroom mirror. Where perspiration takes on a new meaning. I never would have realized it if I hadn't driven the Interstates.

And this land without dew was just beginning.

Putting *Turnaround Lane* behind me, I headed west on I-10 for Van Horn, eighty miles short of El Paso on the West Texas border. Signs warned of deer, the first such warnings I could remember since New England. Deer carcasses lay mute along the shoulder, some battered, others seemingly napping. Live deer stood just off the highway like shadowy lawn ornaments, their eyes shining eerily when caught in my headlights. It was not yet seven, a full silver moon was crawling up the sky to my left, and the temperature was already up to eighty. Traffic was moderate towards San Antonio but much lighter heading west—into the teeth of the ever-present Texas wind. It was Monday morning, the start of another workweek. The start of my third week on the road. Already.

West of San Antonio I-10 begins to roll, dip, and curve, eventually discarding the *garbage out* beyond the beltway. Then comes a major surprise—mountains on the distant horizon. I blinked and looked again, but there they were, in low silhouette. I had been inured to the level terrain for so long that I had forgotten the psychological comfort of mountains. Mountains let you locate yourself. They say, *we are here and you are there!* I-10 was beginning its ascent from sea level, another milestone on that color-coded relief map in my mind. At this very spot I was leaving the green sea-level area of the East Coast and South to enter the yellow area of higher elevations. Halfway to El Paso that yellow would turn brown, continuing across mountain ranges and deserts to heights of more than six thousand feet, a magnificent stretch of the American continent that would eventually drop me—quite suddenly—back to sea level in San Diego. And it was beginning *right here*, west of San Antonio. Where those mountains appear. I could see it all happening from I-10.

There were creeks again too, dark furrows in the dawn, creeks that continue all the way to the New Mexico line—*Cibolo Creek* (Spanish for "bison"), *Little Joshua Creek, Holiday Creek, Cypress Creek*, intersecting a landscape that soon adds yet another distinct feature—round mounds like the knuckles on the back of your hand. A new West Texas contour.

Some of these knuckled mounds are topped by dark chaparral, dense thickets of shrubs, or small trees. Others are bare. Still others have eroded, exposing low rock ledges that I at first mistook at a distance for stone walls. Where the Interstate runs directly through them, their crests have been blasted away, leaving horizontal outcroppings flanking the highway—brief solid rock chutes not much higher than the 'Vette itself.

The first hint of sun appeared in the rearview mirror, a long red bar across the black shade of night. Soon deep colors began to proliferate across the landscape—golden mounds, olive vegetation, khaki median, purple sky. The highway was running through gentle valleys to distant mesas, flat-topped elevations with cliff-like sides. It was easily the prettiest terrain I had seen in Texas, but when I looked to the idyllometer the instrumental panel alarmed me. I was on reserve fuel. I hadn't been paying attention because of the deer.

The 'Vette's fuel information is displayed in a narrow column of horizontal bars. As fuel is expended, the bars disappear and the column falls lower. When only two lines are left, the word *RESERVE* appears. The warning must have been displayed for a while, because the moment I noticed it, the final two lines—like an equals sign in an equation—changed to one. I had never taken the 'Vette that low on fuel before. The computerized *RANGE* function indicated I was good for another thirty-six miles, but I had no idea if I could trust it. So I exited at the very first place available—Kerrville—the final vestige of civilization until Fort Stockton, two hundred and fifty miles distant. Had I not stopped I would have been stranded within the hour, in the middle of West Texas, reduced to an Interstate pedestrian.

* * *

The above frightening prospect calls for an Interstate Item from the American Automobile Association, regarding people setting foot on the Interstates:

In 1995, 543 people were killed on foot on an Interstate highway! Pedestrian fatalities on Interstates have claimed an average of 610 lives each year since 1989. Nearly 10 percent of all the nation's pedestrian fatalities occur on Interstate highways, even though the Interstate system comprises only about one percent of the nation's total road mileage. Furthermore, 12 percent of all Interstate traffic fatalities are pedestrians. These are alarming numbers, especially given that pedestrians are legally restricted from entering Interstate highways in all but 10 states.

The AAA Foundation for Traffic Safety's staff research analyst Christopher Johnson looked at a three-year sample of 400 police accident reports detailing Interstate pedestrian fatalities in Texas, Missouri, and

North Carolina to find out what pedestrians are doing on the Interstates and what factors are contributing to the crashes. Nearly one-third of the crashes from the sample involved "unintended pedestrians": people pushing or working on a vehicle, people involved in a previous crash, or people walking on the shoulder, all situations in which the average motorist could be involved. Forty percent of the crashes involved pedestrians crossing or entering a lane of traffic. These cases usually involved people exhibiting irrational or suicidal behavior, or simply trying to travel the shortest distance from one location to another. Less than three percent of the pedestrians in the sample were reported to be hitchhiking. Construction workers were involved in less than one percent of the crashes.

* * *

Kerrville brought a bonus. As I was filling the tank a rugged old-timer drove up in a pickup truck. He was the very image of Gabby Hayes from the old Hopalong Cassidy movies—full white beard, floppy cowboy hat, red-and-white polka-dot kerchief. The triangular fold of his kerchief was turned to the front, ready to pull up over his face like a bandit or to protect him from dust out on the range. Had we met farther west on I-10 he might have tied that kerchief to the antenna of my 'Vette while he drove me back to Kerrville for gas. I wanted to ask ol' Gabby about the Interstates, but each pump at the station was occupied, so he pulled out as suddenly as he pulled in.

Then, from behind a mesa to the east, the sun suddenly rose in a brilliant glare, so startling that I stopped pumping gas. I had been squeezing the handle—the metal flipper that holds the trigger in place was broken—while Gabby Hayes came and went. Then the sun struck me dumb, the red disk rising through the bright glare in slow motion until it stood fully round on top of the distant mesa. It only took a few seconds, but it was several long minutes before I realized that I had stopped pumping gas—that I was just standing there, pump in hand, mouth wide open, entranced by West Texas in the first red blaze of dawn.

Heading west again I could scarcely keep my eyes on the highway. Sunlight was flooding the hills to the right and left, flooding the knuckle-like knolls and mesas dead ahead. Scrub vegetation bristled from low rock ledges whose gray faces were striated in white. Angelhair grasses gleamed atop smooth mounds. The earth itself—laced with sparse purple sage—bore the rich bright texture of brown gravel. Several gray clouds floated overhead, their purple underbellies matching the purplish tint of the sage, the colors and contours a constant feast to the eye.

With the sun up, the deer began to disappear. Traffic was light to nonexistent. And with the gentle rise in elevation, the temperature dropped to seventy.

Then, unbelievably, a sign warned of a steep grade ahead, the first such warning for trucks since New England. As the 'Vette descended, a wide view of the countryside opened up below and beyond. The idyllometer went crazy, jumping to ninety-five. Then came an old-time windmill with wooden fan blades, its rudder shaped like the feathers of an arrow. It was set on a pyramid-shaped frame above a dumpy abandoned spread, not moving at all despite the steady wind. It was probably rusted in place, posing for a perfect Wild West postcard.

Groves of oaks dotted the shallow dells in all directions, with more signs warning of deer. But the deer were shy of the sun now. It was two hundred and twenty-five miles to Fort Stockton, then another one hundred twenty-five to Van Horn, across a strange and magical West Texas landscape.

Now the striations in the low rock ledges were changing color. Initially gray, some turned chalk white in the light of the sun. Others were pink, roseate, or purple. Scattered among them were wine-red bushes, dome-shaped vegetation that might have been sumac. And for miles around, the land stood empty except for occasional abandoned ranches—small spreads of weathered barns with rusted tin roofs, forlorn outbuildings, broken rail fences, and empty water troughs splintered in the dust. Some places with wire fencing might have kept cattle once, but certainly kept them no more. No one stirred in these ghost spreads. They told their own stark story.

And then the idyllometer hit one hundred! It happened when the sun began casting deep shadows, when every contour on the landscape—every mound, knoll, and mesa—had a purple shadow to give it depth, a dark complement to its own sumptuous color. Distant groves of olive-green oaks, in random clusters, gave the illusion of solid black forests across the horizon. But in the foreground the sumac gleamed brilliant red, the angelhair pure white, the ledges in the mounds a palette of pastels. The brown gravelly earth seemed edible.

It was the hawk that did it—kicked the idyllometer to a perfect hundred—a hawk hunting in wide circles above the highway. That hawk and another old windmill, this one spinning like mad. And the large pale moon, still nearly full. And the marble-veined cliffs of the mesas. And a hundred-mile-wide vista where I could see all this at once. It was near a place called Segovia and I'll never forget it. It left me breathless, and I knew then that the prescriptions waiting for me in Van Horn would be anti-climactic. I had much better medicine all about me. My grand lap had to continue.

I had to see if the rest of America could rival this perfect ride.

* * *

A deep gorge divided the east–west lanes and I looked down at clusters of trees as from an airplane. In the distance, glimpsed through scrub willow and cottonwoods, white rock faces gleamed like vertical scars. Other cliff walls stood brown and reddish—the color of crumbly sandstone—as if they'd disintegrate if you tried to climb them. Then I-10 swept into a gorgeous valley surrounded by foothills, rising and falling as it went. My ears popped and crackled, adjusting to the change in altitude—a milestone of minor discomfort on that giant relief map in my mind. There were only three cars now in the hundreds of sunlit miles of West Texas. And one of them was mine. And the idyllometer was at a perfect one hundred.

Near a place called Junction (pop. 2654), the Llano River crosses under the Interstate, a pan-for-gold type of stream—shallow, gravelly, and sandy along both shores. The surrounding territory is all edges, curves, and angles, an ever-changing array of trapezoidal buttes, knuckled mounds, rolling knolls, and flattop hills. West Texas had become a high plateau where turkey vultures flocked in a corner of the sky. Then the highway skirted a line of cliffs, and Interstate signs warned of falling rocks. But the tan cliffs seemed pebbled—all sandstone or shale—incapable of casting out boulders. In the dry grassland beyond them lay Tootsie Roll bales of hay rendered pure white by the bright sun. It was windy here, the 'Vette shoved between lanes, buffeted from straight on, but without traffic the danger was minimal. Still, I straddled the broken white centerline.

My ears popped again as I crested a rise, surprising three turkey vultures breakfasting on a dead skunk. Then the odor struck—a deep sweet pungent stench—and the birds lifted off, flapping their wide ragged wings in slow motion, three-pronged talons hanging limply beneath. Such buzzards are ugly—beady eyes, red oval heads, orange hooked beaks at the end of long crooked necks. *Who are you to intrude?* they seemed to be asking. They looked annoyed, circling briefly until I was gone, then descending on the skunk as if drawn back by a string. I watched it all in the rearview mirror—West Texas buzzards as persistent as New England crows.

It was only nine-fifteen when I pulled off I-10 to stretch my legs, yet with the idyllometer at one hundred I felt like I'd already put in a full day. The sign at the exit said only RM 3130. *Rural Maintenance?* It was just an exit in the middle of nowhere, a patch of gravel beyond the stop sign with not much of a view from below the level of the highway. Except for the vast sky, which was totally RM. *Really majestic.*

Stiff wind propelled a few clouds rapidly overhead, making the seventy-degree morning feel like fifty. I put on a jacket against the chill, hair whipping about my face. I needed long pants, not khaki shorts. Hopping onto the shoulder I hiked the exit back and forth, always keeping within a hundred yards of the 'Vette. And for half an hour I never saw another vehicle. Either on I-10 or RM 3130. The isolation was total. All I could think of was that I was glad I'd filled the tank in Kerrville.

And then, as in a cartoon depicting a man lost in the desert, two turkey vultures appeared high overhead, riding the rising thermals in wide circles, tilting from side to side like drunken sailors in the wind. There could be only one reason for their presence. *Me.* They were checking me out. Buzzard bait, courtesy of the Interstates. I was amused at first, even flattered. Then I got to thinking. What if I *had* run out of gas at this very spot? I might have stretched out for a nap on the warm hood of the 'Vette and awakened with a buzzard on my chest. Ready to peck out my eyes.

The birds were still circling as I continued toward Van Horn, the idyllometer impervious to my brush with death. I drove in a trance, snapping out of it only when the scrub trees took on a new look—like those twisted bonsai trees in Oriental gardens. The land was leveling out a bit. Near Exit 404 a herd of black cattle—hairy Black Angus?—grazed at the roadside. Then a sign warned of dangerous crosswinds, winds that began to slam the 'Vette severely as I crossed a blasted knoll.

All at once, for the first time on my grand lap, I felt an urge to talk to someone. That's how big Texas is. The wide-open spaces—stunningly beautiful as they are—can begin to wear on you, and at ten-fifteen a rest area brought a promise of relief. I considered passing it up, since I had stopped within the hour, but a sign put the next rest area at eighty-six miles, another hour at least. So I pulled right in.

There were spaces for about fifty cars, but only two or three were occupied. The small facility had been designed in quaint homage to the past. Enormous twin wagon wheels supported the slanted metal roofs of each pavilion, with thick concrete rims and spokes—all freshly painted in a tan color to match the landscape. Clean sidewalks led away from the parking lot to snake about the trim brown grass. Along the rear boundary of the place, behind the low brick restrooms, a wire fence kept the wide-open spaces at bay. Several large birds were walking about back there—turkey vultures, I feared at first, coming to get me again. But they proved to be peacocks.

Across the way someone waved and yelled. "Hello! We were just talking about you!" It was an elderly couple from Arizona—a large white-haired man with his little white-haired wife—whom I had met at a rest area in East Texas on Sunday morning. It seemed like a year since I'd seen them.

I hurried over. Despite having each other, the elderly couple was experiencing the same desire for company that I was. That's how absolutely large Texas is. But the Interstate, I was learning, creates its own family.

The husband was obviously excited. "Ever see so many dead deer in your life? And did you see that dead *pig*?"

"That thing with the *snout*? So *that's* what it was."

"Don't miss the peacocks back there," the woman interrupted. "They're so purty! And when you get to New Mexico, don't forget to watch for roadrunners!"

"Like in the cartoons," her husband added. "*Beep! Beep!* They're the New Mexico state bird." He was all excited, pulling an imaginary cord like an engineer on a train.

"Come along, dear," the woman said. "We best be going and leave the young man be."

As they started down the sidewalk, the man stopped and called over his shoulder, "See you next time! *Beep! Beep!*"

8

IN MAY OF 1970 I WAS TRAVELING TO CONNECTICUT FROM IOWA VIA INTERSTATE 70. The University of Iowa, where I was in graduate school, had shut down early for the season. U.S. troops had gone into Cambodia, the National Guard had shot the kids at Kent State, and students had rioted in Iowa City, burning down a building that held my office and a few meager possessions. The university administration responded by sending everybody home.

I'll never forget that ride. All traffic seemed headed to "Nap Town" for the Indianapolis 500. And there I was, tooling along in "Bullet," my '66 Chevy Impala, doing seventy on I-70, when a fleet of Corvettes passed me so quickly I thought my car had stopped. I had barely noticed the 'Vettes in the rearview mirror when they zipped by in a blur—*Zing! Zing! Zing!*—in all the candy colors of a pack of LifeSavers. Thirty or forty Corvettes, passing me on the left, passing me on the right, running me off the road. Then they disappeared into the flat and shimmering distance.

I was already a goner—I had been a goner for years—but now I was the *gonest.*

I wanted a Corvette.

Home in Stratford that summer I discovered, much to my chagrin, that an old high school acquaintance who lived down the street now had a big blue Corvette sitting in the driveway. His name was Lenny. I didn't know if he had gone to college or where he was working or if the only reason he could afford a Corvette was because he was living at home. But none of that mattered. The fact remained, Lenny had a Corvette and I didn't.

I immediately developed a theory to assuage my failure. Lenny was short—very short—not much over five feet. He was a nice guy and a polite guy but a short guy. I decided he was living at home with his mother and driving a Corvette to compensate for his lack of height, his manhood, whatever.

I was chagrined even further to read in one of those slick car magazines that, at six-five, I was *too tall* for a Corvette. Fortunately, the ergonomics would change in the years to come, enough to please even Shaquille O'Neal. But for the time being everyone had a 'Vette except me. Little Lenny. Groovy Gary. Dirty Dick.

It just wasn't fair.

* * *

Before I could reach the men's room a glass display case caught my attention. Historical information—*High wide and lonesome Van Horn: Crossroads of the West.* That's exactly where I was headed. *Superb I-10,* the display said, *is a literal lifeline across West Texas' sunseared immensities, making the traveling easy.* How true, how true. Unlike the official blurb in Georgia that had advocated abandoning I-95, this one made no bones about the crucial presence of I-10. To abandon the Interstate here would be to put your own bones at risk. Bleached bones picked over by buzzards.

Colorful photos around the text showed what lay ahead—Sierra Blanca and Sierra Diablo—the White Mountains and Devil Mountain. In Spanish *sierra* means "sawtooth" as well as "mountain range." According to the display, Victoria Peak on Sierra Diablo climbs to 6,350 feet, higher than Denver, the mile-high city. Other info focused on wild pigs, wayward rooting creatures that had become a new source of road-kill. Which left me thinking, given the choice, I'd rather hit a deer.

In the men's room came another surprise. The automatic hand dryers were the smallest I would see in all of America—five-inch trapezoidal snouts perhaps designed with wild pigs in mind. They seemed incongruous in the great state of Texas, where you would expect the biggest hand dryers in the world. But when I pushed the doorbell-like button, my dismay disappeared. The tiny contraption blew hot air like a sandblaster, fiercer than the West Texas wind.

Outside again, that hot West Texas wind seemed to have increased, shoving me from the top of a picnic table as I rolled back to stretch, rear end in the air. Thin gray clouds had pushed in from somewhere and all at once the morning was overcast. The temperature had reached seventy-five, but with the grayness and wind it suddenly seemed like winter. It was time to get moving, to see if I could catch up with the elderly couple from Arizona.

As I headed for Van Horn in dim sunlight, the idyllometer fell to eighty. Just ahead, an old white school bus was towing a car, the side of the bus proclaiming *International UFO Center.* Well, if you wanted UFOs, this was the place to find them. It was near Ozona (pop. 3181), a small town apparently named before anyone began to worry about the ozone layer. An uncannily perfect name for such a hole in the earth.

The road was level now, straight for the horizon, with power lines to the right and a few windmills ripping away. Across the entire FM radio band I could find but a single station, drifting in and out with the wind. The AM band was no better—two local talk shows, laconic voices in no kind of hurry. After all, it was only Monday morning.

I crossed the Crockett County line, wondering the obvious. Could it be? Yes! There was a sign announcing a monument to Davy Crockett, my Walt Disney boyhood hero. Ol' Davy had traipsed around out here in order to get to the Alamo. But we never learned about that part in school. Getting there was half the battle. *Getting there* was what American history was all about. It had taken more than two years for word of the Emancipation Proclamation to reach slaves in Texas. But today it's easy to get there—easy to get *anywhere* in America—on the Interstates.

A few lone hawks were hunting low on the landscape near Eureka Draw, a shallow gully where, given the name, someone had apparently struck it rich. It was a *draw*, not a *slough*, but I couldn't see the difference, unless a slough is always wet while a draw runs dry.

Traffic had increased from nonexistent to light, eastbound vehicles keeping pace with a state trooper, a welcome presence in such empty terrain, a bleak landscape that is forever changing shapes—flat-topped mesas, pyramid-shaped pinnacles, rolling hills, knuckle-shaped mounds—the constant variety challenging the potential monotony. My ears popped again, further proof of I-10's ever-steady ascent to Sierra Blanca. Trees were no longer tall, just those Oriental miniatures giving the land in the distance a stubbled beard. The two westbound lanes sported brand-new blacktop, but across the median the sun had bleached the lanes to gray. Resurfacing was obviously alternated in such isolated areas, insuring the lifeline across these *sunseared immensities.*

I soon encountered the kind of gorgeous scenery found on the cover of the Rand McNally Atlas. In the foreground lay rugged outcroppings of brown stone tufted with green chaparral. Then buttes and mesas spread to mountains on the circumference of the horizon— older mountains worn smooth by the eons, not yet the sawtoothed type of the Sierra. Even the cloudy sky couldn't kill my awe, and the idyllometer agreed, rising steadily to ninety. I put on Eric Clapton's version of Bob Dylan—*Knock, knock, knocking on heaven's door*—the perfect soundtrack. Given the steady ascent, it's exactly what I was doing.

A Texas milestone flashed by—my first oil well—a single derrick off to the left, a giant grasshopper bobbing up and down like a neighing horse. Either image fits the territory. Horse or locust, take your pick. Then I crossed an *arroyo*, a rutted dry gulch edged by scrubby vegetation, a new feature of the landscape announced by its own Interstate sign. How an arroyo differs from a *draw* I couldn't say. Both are narrow cracks in the earth, winding and wandering. But I suppose the local Texans would make a sharp distinction, just as Eskimos call *snow* by fifty different words.

My ears popped again and I swallowed to rid my head of the pressure. The mesas were hard by the roadside now, larger than I had imagined and shaped like loaves of bread, a new contour visible for hundreds of miles. Other forms followed through a succession of wide valleys—some perfectly rounded, some exactly like onions, still others like French berets—natural spectacles to delight the imagination. Then, beyond the valleys, the most distant mountains gradually changed in color from olive green to white. It was Sierra Blanca, not snowy but chalk-like. And it would be quite awhile before I got there.

Near the Pecos County line an enormous flag was rippling high above the horizon on a thick metal pole. Its three broad stripes—red, white, and blue—bore a large white star in the center. It was the flag of Texas, the Lone Star State, in the last place on earth I would have ever expected a flag. But that's exactly the point. The rugged windswept landscape deserves a tribute. The people of Texas are well aware of their desolate terrain, and so proud of it that they've planted a big flag in its honor, just as I was planting little flags to honor the Interstates. That grand banner of Texas, snapping madly in the sky, absolutely dominated the horizon, evaporating the loneliness I was beginning to feel. Like rainwater from an arroyo.

By eleven-fifteen, excited by the drive, I needed a men's room, and a rest area popped up just in time. *The eyes of Texas are upon you*, said a silhouette at the entrance—a figure of a state trooper in sunglasses, addressing all drivers. There was a five-star Eisenhower Interstate sign as well, brown instead of blue in homage to the landscape. Pulling in, I was pleasantly surprised—the place was literally an oasis in the desert. Sprinklers twirled at the end of long hoses in an attempt to water the grass, but the wind was blowing the droplets sideways, watering the sidewalks as well. Three palm trees surprised me—I thought I had left those behind on the far side of the state. Tall and sturdy, they stood like giant feather dusters, their gray trunks topped by green spikes. Cactus gardens edged the grass, filled with rubbery plants and spiny jackrabbit ears.

The parking lot was so small it had no white lines. You just pull in parallel to the curb and get out. But I had to battle with the door against the wind. Then the sprinklers drenched me, and I hunched over to fight my way to the men's room. There was only one other car in the parking lot, its driver ahead of me on the sidewalk, struggling like a mime. But it wasn't funny. It was only seventy-five degrees, the wind as fierce as Floyd's in Boston, and I was soaked and freezing.

Out of necessity all trash barrels here were tilted at an angle, welded to thick metal poles and anchored in cement. Wide-mouthed, they looked like medieval mortars. Their bright brown paint matched the color of the pavilion roofs, the same color as the wooden frame of the information case. The attention to detail was encouraging. Someone was paying attention, even in a land of gale-force winds. A run-down rest area in run-down terrain would have been depressing.

In the men's room the artistic touch continued with a tribute to Texas history. A bright tile mural covered an entire wall, a full-scale scene of a soldier with his horse at an old-style fort. I couldn't imagine being stationed at such a place, but the soldier seemed up to the task. Outside again, I paused at the glass case. This was Pecos County, home to stories of the mythical Pecos Bill, the larger-than-life Texan whom every schoolboy knows. But there was a quiz for the uninitiated. Question: *How did Pecos Bill die?* Answer: *He died laughing at the dudes who called themselves cowboys!*

Another text explained the famous West Texas welcome—*the friendliest greeting in the world!*—a combination yelp, scream, gee-haw, and Rebel yell, a wondrous whoop I never once heard in Texas, but I could easily imagine Pecos Bill letting it rip. Moments later my own attempt emerged as a curse when I was blown from a tabletop into the wet grass, a curse drowned by the West Texas wind. Then I fled to the 'Vette. I had hoped to talk to the other traveler, but he had more sense than I did. He was long gone.

Pushing toward Fort Stockton I encountered a sign for Bakersfield, a place so small it isn't in the atlas. Like most small towns announced by signs along I-10, it passes unseen. There was nothing across the vast wasteland now but occasional oil derricks bobbing in rhythm—*yessir, yessir.* Never the massive oil fields I had imagined.

Suddenly the fierce wind blew the gray sky away, leaving puffy white clouds floating in bright sunshine. Miles ahead, at the very end of the earth, appeared a massive white pyramid-shaped mesa, tufted in green and gleaming like a beacon. It was high noon by the time I reached it, the highway passing within a few hundred yards, constantly shifting the angle of my vision until that mesa resembled the Sphinx. Up close, it was sandy in color, and as it gradually receded in my rearview mirror I recited aloud the final lines of Shelley's "Ozymandias"—*Round the decay/Of that colossal wreck, boundless and bare/The lone and level sands stretch far away.* The words gave me shivers. You don't need to go to Egypt to see the Sphinx. It's right there on I-10 in West Texas.

There were a few more radio stations now, one mentioning the *basin area*. That was it! The term I'd been looking for. These were not *valleys* but shallow *basins* I was traversing, with ever-changing sky-wide vistas, incredible backyards for the few people who lived in the shacks and house trailers along the highway. One of the stations brought news of the road, a proposal to make America's highways safer by more testing of younger and older drivers. The same report decried the danger of SUVs—a report I could have issued myself—a danger I was exempt from now in the absence of traffic.

As I neared Fort Stockton, hints of civilization began to appear—a flatbed truck hauling an enormous steel cylinder, a strip of rusty silos, a few billboards, trailers and prefabs, a high school stadium with some modest homes behind it. Then came nicer homes in a small neighborhood with tree-lined streets. And that was it for Fort Stockton (pop. 8524) from where a Latina I had met in San Antonio had departed at midnight, heading east, only to encounter so many deer along the way. I couldn't imagine where those deer were hiding now.

Fort Stockton is a milestone of sorts. In leaving it behind you enter new territory as abruptly as west of San Antonio. The mesas disappear and suddenly there's nothing but flat prairie. Power lines parallel the highway, strung along goalposts with X-type supports, ugly structures that mean instant monotony. The scruffy dry land—dotted with sagebrush—is as flat and tedious as East Texas. Sensing the change, the idyllometer dropped to seventy-five. Then, as if in spite, the temperature soared to ninety.

At one o'clock, about a hundred miles from Van Horn, I stopped at a rest area to have lunch—peanut butter crackers and a bottle of water. A lone semi was idling at the far end of the lot, the driver presumably sleeping. Sprinklers twirling, this area too was an oasis, a lone Latino attendant on duty, his green coveralls matching the bright green grass. I wanted to ask him what it was like to work way out here on a daily basis, but he was muttering to himself in Spanish, in angry tones that seemed to have nothing to do with the sprinklers. Or *me*, I hoped. Maybe tending an oasis resulted in such behavior—an occupational hazard, like being stationed at a fort in the old days. But I didn't care to find out.

I turned instead for the nearest pavilion. Simultaneously, a moving van pulled in, the driver immediately hopping from the cab, and as if the stop had been choreographed, a well-endowed young blonde jumped down from the passenger side, removed her jeans jacket, and circled to the rear of the truck. The driver met her there, opened the rear door, and they climbed in, pulling the door shut behind them. It was siesta time in West Texas. Time for a little afternoon delight.

Like the other rest areas in Texas, this one had a distinct decor, a creative touch for which the state deserves applause. The pavilions suggested sod homes or lean-tos, their corrugated brown roofs supported by brick walls and horizontal beams. Flat on my back on a picnic table, I stared up at the crude rafters. Someone had tucked a small magazine up there and I had to stand on the table to retrieve it. Expecting pornography, I was surprised to find a Christian publication, *Awake*. I had seen it stuck like a motel Bible into nooks and crannies at other rest areas, but this was a new twist, stashing it high in the rafters. Someone was on a mission, but littering nonetheless. *Don't mess with Texas. The eyes of Texas are upon you.*

The strong winds had diminished to a stiff breeze now, welcome in the bright sun and dry heat. In the men's room I discovered another tile mural—a stagecoach with horses—but the colors had been dulled by the weather, the roof here raised above the cinderblock walls to admit the wind. Outside, a few palm trees were scattered about the oasis among curious taller trees that provided a modicum of shade. Oak-like, they produced long sickle-shaped brown pods like grotesque cigars.

I pirouetted in the wind, surveying the oasis. The mumbling attendant was moving the sprinklers. The semi was still idling, the moving van bouncing on its springs. There was no one to ask about the Interstates. But as I headed to the 'Vette a Native American couple pulled in, in a battered van that looked like it would never pull *out*. A swarthy pair, they were wrapped in drab blankets and made no eye contact, huddling together off the sidewalk until I passed by. Then a station wagon arrived at the far end of the lot, unloading half a dozen people wrapped in orange saris. It looked like the Dalai Lama and his entourage. I paused a moment until I could hear them speaking, but it was no language I could recognize, so I had to head for Van Horn unenlightened.

At Barrilla Draw a dry riverbed crosses beneath I-10, a kind of culvert where water might run in stormy weather—not quite an arroyo, not quite a gulch. The sandy mounds there are perfect hemispheres, with chaparral and sagebrush all around. And spiky Koosh Ball palms and yucca plants. Then flat plains of brown grass begin to stretch away for miles, and rugged mountains parallel the highway to the south. Turn north here and you'd fall off the earth.

But those mountain silhouettes provide comfort—Sierra Blanca, Sierra Diablo, and others in the same chain—steady company that always appear to merge with the highway at the farthest point ahead, a point never reached but ever receding into a rippling mirage. I was certain that the road was flooded dead ahead, where the hazy surface of the planet merged with gray sky. According to the radio, a driver had fallen asleep at the wheel, running off the road back at Ozona. I hoped it was no one I had seen or talked to, none of my Interstate family. This land could hypnotize. And make you believe in UFOs.

Suddenly, off to the right, thousands of flat acres of bright green rectangles stretched away to the horizon—lettuce maybe, or some similar crop—methodically irrigated by long thin contraptions like the wings of the Wright brothers' plane. Farther along, farmers were rolling that green stuff into bales. Then the green rectangles were gone and the landscape was empty except for a gray stone foundation of a tumble-down farmhouse. The radio mentioned *Pecan Creek Basin*, so maybe the crop I had seen was pecans. Or maybe those rest-area pod-like trees were pecan trees. The Interstates will test your knowledge of agriculture.

Eastbound, a brand-new 'Vette zinged by like a silver bullet, its black convertible top shut against the heat. I had been toying with the idea of removing my sunroof, but without air-conditioning the drive would be suicide. Texas is no place for convertibles. Another vehicle was zipping along far to my right, a pickup truck trailing a plume of dust along a dirt road parallel to the Interstate. The road was headed for a herd of black cattle on the open range. But you couldn't get there from here. In much of Texas, I-10 is just passing through. It's best to mind your own business. To keep the lid on against sun and dust. 129

The traffic, though scant, was becoming more familiar now. I overtook again the flatbed truck with the enormous steel cylinder that I had seen near Fort Stockton. There was a small black car trailing a U-Haul that I had passed several times, our rest stops not quite in sync. And I kept looking for the couple from Arizona. This was our caravan, our Interstate wagon train, our only defense against the West Texas desert, where the highway shimmers ahead of you endlessly.

The mountains to the left now resembled the Virginia Blue Ridge, the brown prairie in the foreground dotted with a new kind of shrub, a bluish sort of weed. "*Buy the Basin*," the radio was urging, a local economic message. But if *buying the basin* meant pecans, how many pecans could you eat? There wasn't much for sale in the basin besides pecans. And a strange sort of lettuce.

Gradually, I-10 began to rise toward a notch in the distant mountains, descending gently through a series of basins as it went. When the highway reached the notch, a deep valley lay beyond, a scene repeated well into the afternoon. But a definite line had been drawn across the mountain slopes now, above which the olive vegetation had simply stopped growing. The delineation was blatant. For want of moisture or air or some other crucial element, the dynamics of life changed exactly at that line. No vegetation could survive just one inch higher, and I found myself wondering what it would be like to hike way up there, to stand with one foot in the death zone. The line had been drawn, dramatically, in these high mountain deserts, making you glad of the on-going Interstate.

I crossed into Jefferson Davis County, obviously named for the president of the Confederacy, but a confusing link to the Old South nonetheless. A sign for the McDonald Observatory of the University of Texas followed, source of the NPR "Star Date" feature with Sandy Wood. Any of the surrounding mountains seemed perfect for an observatory. An interplanetary vigil.

A blue body of water by the roadside brought my thoughts back to earth, a small pond or catch basin perhaps related to irrigation. I couldn't remember when I had last seen water, but through the South water was *all* I had seen. Even the mountains were unpredictable, constantly changing in contour—irregular peaks, then smooth humps, then long ridges—any and all of them laced with vertical cliffs. In relation to the highway, the very position of the mountains changed as well. Sometimes they ringed the basins and valleys entirely. Sometimes they went three-quarters around, sometimes just half-way—a dizzying variety of world-rim horizons. But of course it was I-10 that was actually shifting, seeking the path of least resistance as it made its way west.

Often, between the mountain ranges, lay dune-like terrain, crusty and gravelly earth spiked in olive. In one such area I passed a pickup truck driven by the Marlboro Man, the stereotypical guy you see on the billboards. A short while later I overtook a cattle truck with open sides, a truck I smelled long before I ever saw it, a pungent odor that would drive all dudes back east. And then for the first time in Texas I saw a train—a line of black oil tankers far to the north, proof of oil fields beyond the few derricks I'd seen. Then it occurred to me. Maybe all those neighing grasshoppers were pumping water. I was an Interstate dude, out of my element, and I could hear Pecos Bill howling.

Beyond Wild Horse Road I found a rest area and pulled right in. It was two-thirty. I was four hundred miles from San Antonio and fully exhausted by the strange beauty of West Texas. I needed a break. But there was no oasis this time, no sprinklers twirling—just hard ground, brittle grass, and another *loco* attendant more frightening than the last, a dark-skinned Latino with a droopy mustache who was yelling at arriving vehicles as he swept debris along the shoulder of the entrance.

Several cars were scattered the short length of the lot, and I drove to the far end to distance myself from the attendant. The black car with the U-Haul was parked there, and its driver, a young man of twenty-seven, greeted me enthusiastically as I approached the men's room.

"You the 'Vette?" he said. "I'm the U-Haul. I've seen you ever since Houston! I'm going to California—San Luis Obispo. Ever hear of it? I'm going out there to start my own company!"

"I knew a girl from San Luis Obispo years ago," I said. "She attended Cal Poly."

"I wanted to study at Cal Poly as an undergraduate, but my folks didn't want me to leave home. They still don't want to me to go! I just finished grad school and this is my first time away. I've been driving with tears in my eyes ever since Houston."

"And missing all the gorgeous scenery?" I said.

"What scenery?" He swept his hand around the horizon. "You mean *this*?"

I had no time to answer. He had too much to say. He was choked up about leaving Texas and needed to talk.

"I once rode in a Corvette from Houston to Colorado," he said. "We drove straight through, and the next day I couldn't even walk!"

I began to tell him about the lumbar seat—how I couldn't be lapping America without it—but he wasn't listening.

"I'm writing a book!" he said. "I'm gonna call it *Seven and a Half Years of College Isn't Enough*. The current chapter is called *No Regrets*. It's about growing up in Houston and leaving home."

He finally paused, pensive, just when I was beginning to think he'd be a match for the loco attendant at the entrance. But he was part of our Interstate wagon train and I was glad to meet him. Texas gets to everyone in different ways.

"When I was your age," I said, "I quit my job as a high school teacher and drove out to Iowa to write a novel. I know what you're feeling. You're doing what has to be done."

The young man smiled broadly, nodding his head like one of those neighing derricks. Then I wished him luck and ducked into the men's room, an attractive facility of pink and gray stone with an open raised roof. There was no mural this time, no Texas history. The young man from Houston was writing the modern update.

When I came out, the black car with the U-Haul was pulling away, but an elderly woman was standing on the sidewalk, waiting for someone. She wore a white knit sweater despite the heat. I approached her immediately, needing to talk as much as the young man from Houston.

"I'm originally from Ohio," she said, "but we live in California now."

"What's I-5 like?" I asked. "I'm going to be taking it."

"Well," she said, "it's scenic, smooth, and straight. But my husband—he's retired now—does all the driving. You'd better ask him."

As if on cue, a tall elderly man exited the restroom and joined us.

"This gentleman wants to know about I-5 back home," the woman said. "I've been telling him how lovely it is."

"Well, now, Mama," her husband replied, "I-5 can get downright boring at times. Depends on what part you're taking." He looked at me as if he'd asked a question.

"All of it," I said. "Border to border."

The man chuckled. "In that case, you'll find out for yourself."

As the couple headed for their car, I sought out a picnic table on which to stretch. Once again the pavilions had a style all their own. This time, the brown corrugated roof was supported by slim vertical beams, one of which bore a sign I hadn't seen elsewhere: *No sleeping on tables.* Dang! I wanted to stretch out in the shade, but without testing the authority of the *loco* attendant.

Choosing a spot closer to the 'Vette, I dropped into the hot brittle grass. The ground felt like a pincushion, making me a fakir—a Hindu holy man on a bed of nails. With the sun hot on my face, I managed to roll back and pull my knees to my chest. And then, somehow, I managed to nap.

* * *

By five o'clock I was having beer and pizza in Van Horn—*Crossroads to the West* (pop. 2930)—the only place from which I sent a postcard on my entire Interstate odyssey. I sent it to a friend who always writes me when he travels. I wanted to reciprocate, and I chose Van Horn to celebrate a special occasion—the first day of a true Interstate idyll. After two weeks on the road, the idyllometer had finally hit a hundred. And stayed there. Hence the beer and pizza and the postcard, the kind divided into four or five different scenes—the mountains, the basins, the cattle, etc.— none of which adequately described the area. In snapping the shutter a photographer has to be selective, which automatically excludes something else. But in West Texas there's simply too much to see, and all in one glance, rendering postcards useless.

I sent the postcard anyway, from my motel, which was easy to find given the size of Van Horn. But after hundreds of miles of empty highway, the little Interstate community seemed bigger than New York City. There were the usual fast-food places, gas marts, billboards, and a few small ranch-style homes with flowerpot roofs. But no *Turnaround Lane* as in San Antonio. Or *Frontage Road*, for that matter.

In the men's room mirror at the pizza place, my sunburned face astonished me. The sun and wind were baking me. I had to be more careful. The total absence of humidity was deceptive, a bottle of drinking water a constant necessity. Yet to celebrate the day I was turning to beer. Alone in the restaurant, I had taken a table by a window with red-and-white-checked curtains, where I sat unnoticed for a while as the two employees—a heavyset Latina and a teenage Latino—shouted at each other in Spanish between the counter and kitchen.

Finally spotting me, the woman switched to English. "You ain't doin' shit, man!"

I assumed she meant her co-worker, but I suppose the remark applied to me as well.

Out the window, a long train of tank cars was chugging across the horizon parallel to the Interstate, the tracks closer than they'd been all day. Above the white smoke of the engine, mountains ringed the sky.

"How often does the train go through?" I asked, when the woman brought my beer. The boy had settled down in the kitchen, at work on my pizza.

"Every two hours," she said. "Every hour, maybe. Every thirty minutes, I *theenk*."

I was trying to determine if I'd be listening to trains all night, but the local answer revealed only that the locals don't bother much about trains.

Later, back at the motel, I opened the prescriptions that had been waiting for me at the desk. Now that I had them I didn't really need them, but I administered myself two pills as a matter of principle. Then I spent half an hour plucking burrs from my socks, the result of a short stroll through the weeds and gravel of Van Horn on my way from the pizza place. Area rocks had a curious reddish tint, and in studying them I hadn't noticed the burrs in the brittle grass.

As I plucked at my socks I listened to the nightly news, perking up at a special feature on highway safety. According to a poll, sixty-nine percent of Americans want the government to set new standards regarding speed. Fast cars, the report claimed, have contributed to a fifteen percent increase in highway fatalities since the fifty-five-mile-per-hour national speed limit was abandoned. All of which was undermining hard-won gains against drunk driving. Thirty percent of all crashes are caused by higher speeds, the report concluded, and damages cost the nation nearly twenty-eight billion a year.

That's fifty two thousand dollars a minute, I realized. The price of a new Corvette. But the report made me guilty. Having celebrated a perfect one hundred on the idyllometer, I now wanted to reach one hundred on the speedometer, flying in the face of the national poll.

As the sun began to set, I went to the window to watch the big red disk drop below the horizon—as rapidly as it had risen in Kerrville. The mountain silhouettes were streaked in red now, but I was too exhausted to absorb any more beauty. Flopping on the bed, I fell asleep to the drone of the Weather Channel. Snow was being forecast in the mountains east of Seattle. I'd be passing through those mountains in less than two weeks.

Snow near Seattle. Snow in the mountains. East of Seattle.

* * *

Up at six, I hiked around Van Horn beneath a pale egg of a moon and a peppering of stars, the darkness challenged only by sporadic patches of neon. It was seventy degrees, perfect at first but getting too warm as I walked, continuing my informal study of Interstate traffic. In the space of half an hour I counted twenty-four trucks and six cars rolling by on the highway—sparse traffic, but a far greater truck-to-car ratio than I had observed anywhere else.

Back at the desk, I asked the attendant about the time change. Where would I cross the line? I had missed the first time zone coming west from Florida and didn't want to miss the next one. Somewhere out there I stood to gain an hour and I wanted to use it to my advantage. My atlas was no help, showing four clock faces across southern Canada—from five o'clock in Quebec to two o'clock in British Columbia—but the vertical lines of demarcation stopped at the Canadian border. It was difficult to project them down the page.

"A few miles from Van Horn," I thought the desk clerk said, but I wasn't sure if I had understood her accent correctly.

The 'Vette waited outside, once again totally devoid of dew. And with another subtle change. The car was coated with a fine layer of greasy dust. The industrial air of Texas is the dirtiest in the nation and the evidence had sifted out of the sky overnight, as soon as the winds died down. That meant I'd have to wash the car at the end of the day. But first things first. Heeding the lesson of Kerrville I went to fill up the tank, the young Latino attendant jumping up—all eyes and excitement—as the 'Vette pulled into the gas mart beyond the motel. He flipped down the rear vanity plate, removed the gas cap, and stuck in the nozzle, attacking the greasy windshield while the hose was pumping. When he caught my eye, I asked him about the Interstates.

"The Interstates? Ooh, I love the Interstates, man! I wanna be a trucker like my father-in-law. Go all over the *cawn*try. I already got me a Class A license. I can drive those big eighteen-wheelers! With a life like that, you gotta love the Interstates. Especially out here in Texas! Hey, man, there's a big car show over in Odessa in October. You oughta go!"

"I'll be in New Mexico this morning," I replied. "Then Arizona tonight."

"Oh, man," he laughed, wagging a finger. "In this thing you must be haulin' ass!"

It was seven o'clock—still totally dark—when I left Van Horn, joining a small convoy of trucks heading west on I-10. On the crest of a hill not far from town, my headlights caught a sign for a scenic over-look. Then came the sign I had been looking for—*Entering Mt. Time Zone*. The desk clerk was right. But if there had been a similar sign for the Central Time Zone back east, I had somehow missed it. So it was now only *six* o'clock.

Driving away from the rising sun, I watched the inky sky bleed to purple-gray in the rearview mirror, above the sawtoothed silhouettes. As the sun ascended, the colors kept on changing—pink above gray, then yellow, then peach. The mountain formations changed too, much in the way clouds change shape in the open sky. There was a nebbish-shaped mountain with a bulbous nose, and another like an Indian-head nickel—all forms chiseled by erosion over the eons, beneath the ever-watchful eye of the morning star.

Then Sierra Blanco (pop. 900) came out of the blackness like a town seen from an airplane, a string of lights that ultimately revealed a few flat-roofed homes—mostly prefabs and trailers—nestled in a mountain notch. The mountains were becoming more rugged, ever increasing in size, as the highway ran ever higher into them. A pair of perfectly rounded peaks loomed ahead now. To their left, a modern A-frame topped a ridge with a full valley view, a luxurious chalet with ample picture windows. Huge reddish boulders lay along the roadside below, and I tried to imagine them tumbling from on high. With the increased elevation, falling rocks were not the only danger. The temperature had fallen to fifty-eight, as I-10 gradually descended into a series of valleys and basins—one after another—so incredibly vast I seemed to be driving through the bottom of the Grand Canyon. Shadowy earth-rim vistas lay in every direction.

Up ahead, a flatbed truck with slatted sideboards seemed to be carrying Christmas trees, but when I caught up, the load looked like bundled driftwood—the remnant of some sort of desert vegetation, maybe sagebrush without the sage. Meanwhile, far to the north, a long train of red boxcars moved silently through the graying dawn, a hundred cars or more pulled by five diesel engines. I tried to count the cars but grew dizzy at twenty. The train was clipping along, keeping pace with the 'Vette, and it was twenty minutes before it fell away behind me.

Soon a new Interstate sign proved puzzling—*Keep off median*—an order that seemed completely unnecessary. The median strip was wide and shallow, full of nothing but sagebrush and gravel, with the kind of scruffy vegetation that had laced my socks with burrs back in Van Horn. Why would anyone want to set foot on that strip of wasteland?

A barrage of other signs soon answered the question: *Grooved pavement ahead. Rough road. Attention wide loads.* Apparently I-10 was in bad shape farther west. The only escape was to cross the median and turn back. Which could prove dangerous.

But it was already too late. The tractor-trailer ahead of me was bouncing in the passing lane, which meant the slower right-hand lane—where it *should* have been—was no picnic. I passed the truck on the right and paid the price, the 'Vette suddenly jouncing about as it hadn't done since Louisiana.

It was eight o'clock now—really seven—the sun beginning to rise in a broad wash of yellow behind me to brighten the mountains like a celestial lightbulb. And following the yellow fanfare came *the rosy-fingered dawn*—the sun gradually extending long pink rays above the landscape like fingers from a hand. It was a phrase the ancients had been fond of—*the rosy-fingered dawn*—a description I had first encountered in *The Aeneid* of Virgil. And suddenly my six years of Latin seemed entirely worth the effort, a rehearsal for this very morning, to give me an image for another magnificent Interstate sunrise.

The undulating mountains cast deep shadows across the land. Then the wind gained force, knocking the 'Vette side to side across both lanes. Off to the north, some sort of brown dirt devil was swirling in place like a miniature tornado. Then I hit the *grooved pavement* announced earlier. But the warning proved misleading and far too mild. To me *grooved pavement* means parallel lines scored into the highway for added traction, like grooves on the face of a golf club. But these West Texas grooves were unintentional, running toward the median like waves to the shore, smooth humps and ruts a full foot deep from crest to trough. They shot the traffic left and right willy-nilly, the movement worsened by the buffeting of the wind. Maybe the wind itself had created these asphalt waves, blowing trucks back and forth on heat-softened pavement. Even with sixteen-inch tires the 'Vette couldn't hold a steady line. I had never seen anything like it, on or off the Interstates.

But a construction area soon cut the speed—the dangerous surface was under repair—and all trucks gathered in a long single file. The eastbound lanes were closed, funneling their traffic across the median to pass at arm's length beyond a concrete divider. And this arrangement created an amazing display. The sun, angled low from the right, struck the divider directly, bathing the westbound lane in a brilliant white glare while the eastbound lane remained in dark shadow. The stark contrast extended for miles, a black-and-white ribbon through the longest construction area of my entire grand lap, the full length of a basin surrounded by mountains. It was like a sculpture by Christo, the pop environmental artist. But *this* particular masterpiece was unintentional, a legitimate work of found art, a joint production of the sunrise and Interstate system.

Then the construction area ended and the way was smooth to El Paso—and the Texas border at last!

But first, as if to leave the traveler with an unforgettable impression, West Texas pulled out all the stops—with a sun-splashed sky-blue morning and a faint haze on the rim of the horizon, the terrain changing its face again and again—flat to the right, higher to the left, forests here, red rock there. Fertile green farmland lay in valleys and basins, then the sort of immense sand dunes you'd expect in Arabia. And then came the billboards, a sure sign of El Paso—*Chiquitas and mamacitas!*—non-stop beautiful ladies, adult videos, naked harems.

Excited, I found myself singing: *Out in the West Texas town of El Paso, I fell in love with a Mexican girlllllll. . . .* It was a country-western song so universal in its appeal that I had once heard it at the White Cliffs of Dover, crooned by a young German fellow who would show me bars in Germany where everyone dresses—and drinks—like a cowboy. Such Old West fame and notoriety had spread in song from El Paso—the closest my Interstate odyssey would take me to Mexico—where I-10 skirts the U.S. border at the Rio Grande.

Then it was civilization again after a two-day absence, a population of half a million caught in heavy traffic amidst El Paso's *garbage in*—a flat industrial approach, overhead power lines, a few tan buildings for a skyline. Big red boulders and sand dunes lined the way as well, but on approach the dominant feature is the mountains, looming close on the left and sloping right to the city. El Paso means "the pass," and on that great relief map in my mind it was notched in the highest mountains of the American Southwest, rugged terrain that had replaced the lower elevations beginning near San Antonio. I had been climbing for several days toward this city, to *El Paso*—the pass through the mountains. And here I was.

It was nine o'clock, towards the end of the morning rush, and a sign for *Lee Trevino Drive* recalled the merry man who had helped me in Miami. But this was the territory of the *real* Lee Trevino.

Then the traffic jammed up, squealing to a halt, as a car ahead hit the concrete divider, crumpling a fender and stinking the air with burning rubber. Incredulous, I watched it happen as if in slow motion. Then I was stuck in an Interstate idle, the idyllometer plummeting to absolute zero.

I toyed with the radio, passing five stations in Spanish before finding one in English. Meanwhile, beyond the sea of stalled cars, several Chinese restaurants sat incongruously on the streets of El Paso. There was a sign for *Pisano Drive* as well—Oriental and Italian flavors to complement Mexican salsa and West Texas chili. Happily, the idle lasted less than twenty minutes, and as the heavy traffic began to move, the appeal of El Paso improved with every mile.

Some attractive modern buildings crop up unexpectedly along the city's east side. Then I-10 threads its way beneath a series of overlapping viaducts, a geometric maze of concrete structures as striking as those in San Antonio. To the left several beige-colored banks dominate a downtown square. To the right, mountain slopes parallel the city. But the best comes downtown, a colorful Interstate surprise—retaining walls painted in bright colors—tans and blues and greens. Lovely murals depict mountain scenes, broad walls present Native American designs. The effect of this artwork is so instantly warm and friendly—the idea so very simple—that I found myself wondering why more American cities don't do the same. Spray-painted graffiti needn't be the urban Interstate norm. Downtown El Paso is a model for the nation.

The suburbs come next, across broad mountain slopes—small white ranch houses on a gravel landscape dotted with green shrubs, but not a single blade of grass. Desert colors dominate—tan, brown, red—with an adobe-style architecture in pink and salmon. And this dry sight sparked another Interstate revelation. There are places in America where rock gardens are the rule, where your entire yard looks like the pebbly bottom of an aquarium. I thought of my acre of thick green grass in Ohio—then life without a lawn mower—and was ready to move to El Paso.

As the city's *garbage out* pushed to the New Mexico state line, the terrain began to change yet again. Brown and gray sandy mountains rolled away to the left, with stretches of red gravel and sage along the highway. Sand lay everywhere in various consistencies—loose, coarse, crusty.

But just before the border, Texas turns ugly. All mountains disappear and the state becomes an enormous gravel pit, with I-10 running right down the middle. It's as if the last few miles of Texas have been quarried out and transported elsewhere. Unattractive neighborhoods fill the gray walls of the pit like bungalows crowd the hills of Pittsburgh. Then come oil tanks and power lines and sprawling industrial plots, all ringed by the high rim of the excavation.

Across the median sat the first rest area for eastbound travelers, nothing special in this final squalid stretch. It made me happy to leave Texas. At last.

* * *

Before we leave the great state of Texas, here's an appropriate Interstate Item:

Texas is big. According to the *Texas Highways Primer*, Texas is so big that it has 111 Interstate rest areas and 804 picnic areas. Its largest Interstate is I-10, which measures 878.7 miles from the Louisiana border to El Paso. Because Texas is so big, it has an overwhelming dependence on the automobile. Hence Texas cannot help but have the biggest highway system in the nation, with nearly 77,000 total miles of roads.

Along with its bigness, Texas claims an Interstate semantic oddity—its ubiquitous "frontage" roads, the state's official term for the roads beside the Interstates. Throughout the state, however, locals call their "frontage" road something different. In Houston they're known as "feeder" roads; in Dallas they're "service" roads; in El Paso they're "gateways." Texans are generally surprised when they go to other places and find no "frontage" roads.

Another oddity is the use of "turnarounds"—U-turn lanes that allow traffic heading in one direction on "frontage road" to head in the other direction on the opposite "frontage road."

And despite the fact that Interstate signs read *I-10*, *I-35*, etc., the official abbreviation for Interstate is *IH*, for "Interstate Highway."

During the mid-1980s the forerunner of the Texas Department of Transportation (TxDOT) introduced what would become an incredibly popular anti-litter campaign—*Don't mess with Texas*. Signs with that slogan went up all over the state. The slogan took off, and now you can get *Don't mess with Texas* T-shirts, mugs, stickers, key chains, you-name-it. *Don't mess with Texas* commercials have featured various celebrities.

Still, I was glad I didn't have to mess with Texas anymore.

9

LICENSE PLATES IN NEW MEXICO SAY *LAND OF ENCHANTMENT*, AND THE MOST enchanting Welcome Area in all of America lies just a few miles beyond the state line. It amazed me even as I pulled in.

A winding drive leads to a large oval parking lot beneath a wide-open sky. To the left sits a quaint adobe village—twenty or so pavilions in the form of adobe huts—all tan brick walls, flat wooden roofs, protruding brown beams. Each hut harbors a tawny ceramic picnic table. Clean white sidewalks lead to the village, where sand dunes roll away from each back door. To the right, the main facility is an old Spanish mission, with a low flat roof, arched portals, and a phalanx of those protruding brown beams. Its interior courtyards present a succession of tiled squares, each with low benches and bubbling circular fountains.

Surrounding rock gardens hold a variety of vegetation typical of New Mexico, from stubby cacti and yucca bushes to spiky grasses and cholla (pronounced *choya*, as I would learn inside). There are wiry shrubs as well, and a skinny kind of tree that seems to produce string beans. Other trees resemble Texas palms, but may simply be another sort of cactus.

I stopped at a small stone dedicated to the Jefferson Davis Highway, a monument erected by the Daughters of the Confederacy. Was there no escaping the Old South? There had been a Jefferson Davis County in Texas, now further homage here in New Mexico. But the fault, obviously, was my own—a Connecticut Yankee weak on his American history.

Another marker commemorates Oñate's route on the Camino Real: *Juan de Oñate, first governor of New Mexico, passed near here with his colonizing expedition in May of 1598. Stagecoaches of the Butterfield Overland Mail Co. began carrying passengers and mail from St. Louis to San Francisco, across southern New Mexico, in 1858. The 2,095-mile journey took 22 days.*

The mention of stagecoaches reminded me of Mark Twain, who had traveled the American West in such a conveyance, recording his journey in *Roughing It*. As Twain said, in order to comprehend the meaning of hundreds of miles of rugged mountains and dismal deserts, *one must go over the ground in person—pen and ink descriptions cannot convey the dreary reality*. And that's exactly what I was doing.

Except *my* stagecoach was covering the same distance in less than a week.

As his journey progressed, however, Twain found that *the romance all faded far away and disappeared, and left the desert trip nothing but a harsh reality, a thirsty, sweltering, longing, hateful, reality!* Recalling those words at the welcome area, I sensed my mouth turning dry. I was at the doorstep of the Desert Southwest, with no real idea of what lay ahead.

There was other information as well—on the Sante Fe Trail and Billy the Kid—images of the Old West that revolved in my head as I hiked from the adobe village into the mountain desert. Narrow footpaths snaked away between the dunes, the trails marked with paw prints, bird prints, and occasional footprints. The area wasn't crowded, but the few people out there were not from any world I knew. All were dark-skinned—Latino or Native American. One *hombre* in dirty jeans and a T-shirt seemed typical, his greasy black hair pulled back into a long ponytail. When he headed my way I went inside to sign the guest book.

A short, darkish woman stood behind the counter. "What do you call that stringbean-type tree out front?" I asked.

She stared at me strangely. "That's a desert willow." *A day-zurt wee-low.*

"And those tracks in the sand?"

"Naw-thing spay-shul. Just rabbits and quail and roadrunners."

But she omitted one thing, perhaps on purpose, something I had been happily oblivious to—until I noticed a small sign on the sidewalk when I returned to the 'Vette. *Beware of Rattlesnakes!* A perfectly enchanting note on which to leave.

Back on I-10, I tried the radio. Seven of the first ten stations responded in Spanish, the most since San Antonio. The New Mexican landscape was suddenly foreign as well, with a distinct lunar quality—miles and miles of rocky terrain that seemed formed from molten lava, all dunes and craters and no discernible horizon—just the curvature of the moon as seen from outer space. The vegetation was skimpy, occasional sagebrush and yucca, but a brazen billboard didn't seem to mind at all: *Welcome To The Old West, Where It All Began!* Given the moonscape, I couldn't tell what *it* might be. Unless this was the Bible Belt and someone meant Genesis.

Cattle came next—*Pee-yew, pee-yew!*—thousands and thousands of cattle penned up in stockyards to the right, the stench nearly knocking me off the road. There were scattered homes out there, too—bungalows, trailers, and larger dwellings with Spanish archways and flowerpot roofs. How could anyone bear to live in the vicinity when the wind shifted? There was nothing enchanting about the pungent odor. Then on the left came long stretches of bright green fields—maybe grass to feed all that cattle—irrigated by wings of the Wright brothers' plane. Sudden groves of trees surprised me too, carefully planted in rectangular orchards. One plot resembled New England birch, but the white trunks may simply have been bandages to discourage the nibbling deer.

Soon I-25 branched north from I-10 for Albuquerque, depleting the traffic even further. A specially marked white vehicle was closing in on me in the rearview mirror. I moved into the right-hand lane to let it pass. It was the Border Patrol—an Interstate first for me—with a no-nonsense wire fence between the front and back seats. The uniformed driver ignored me, and the reason for his presence became clear a few minutes later when I passed through Las Cruces, where I-10 crosses the Rio Grande.

The famous river is but a hundred yards wide—not so *grande*, and shallow enough to wade—the green grasses along both shores providing cover from the Border Patrol. I had seen the Rio Grande on TV programs, *wetbacks* wading across from Mexico to pursue the American dream, scrambling up the gravelly banks into hiding. The game is routine—Hide 'n' Seek. Red Rover. You come over, we get you, and put you back. But there were no players on this fine September morning. Because of the altitude it was only seventy degrees, with blue skies and a bright yellow sun. Too easy to get nabbed in broad daylight.

Las Cruces (pop. 63,000) passed largely unseen, except for a flurry of billboards marketing the Old West. And I thought, maybe *that's* what had begun out here, the marketing of the Old West. Everything imaginable was for sale—Indian jewelry, T-shirts, wind chimes, fireworks, Black Hills gold, polished rocks, agate bookends, desert critter souvenirs. Behind the garish advertisements, attractive Spanish-style subdivisions spread into the heart of a landscape that was lunar to the left, treed to the right. Presently, beyond the outskirts of the city, I-10 began yet another steep ascent to the western horizon—straight up toward the pale moon, the very moon mocked by the local terrain.

At the crest of the ascent a wide plateau commenced, with thousands of yellow wildflowers among red outcroppings of rock. Smooth hills lay beyond in all directions, then rugged mountains. Colorful grasses lined the prairies in between. Mesas and sand dunes came and went as well, variously edged with yucca and spiny shrubs. The high desert was proving more enchanting with every passing mile. Only the road surface—as rough as in East Texas—kept the idyllometer at ninety.

Then came a puzzling sign. *All Vehicles Stop Ahead.* Several miles in the glimmering distance a wide pavilion spanned the highway, a kind of white metal shed with a long fly-roof, not quite a tollbooth. Uniformed officers were strolling around up there, all in cowboy hats, talking among themselves. Occasionally they would turn to the driver of the vehicle at the head of an ever-lengthening line. It was ten forty-five and I was suddenly at a standstill. On a high pole by the pavilion a large flag was rippling flat-out in the breeze. There was nothing to do but watch it flap.

The trucker ahead of me leaned on his horn, then others joined in and—what the hell—I did too, sounding the horn of the 'Vette in anger for the first time ever. Finally, the line began to move. Slowly, intermittently. Traffic had been light but was backed up now nearly a mile, thanks to the chattering cowboys up ahead.

When it was my turn, I powered down the window with a simple question. "Why on earth—why on *the moon*—are you stopping us out here in the middle of nowhere?"

"Immigration inspection," the cowboy said from behind his sunglasses. Then he waved me on through.

And that was it. That was the extent of my *immigration inspection.* But had I not been a *gringo*—had that *hombre* from the adobe village hitched a ride with me—I suspect it might have been a very different story.

The first sign for Arizona followed—*Tucson 248.* But I was going only as far as Benson. My entire stint through New Mexico would be less than two hundred miles—less than three enchanting hours—and much of that in Luna County, which I entered next.

The sign made me laugh. *Luna County.* I was obviously not the first to see the similarity between New Mexico and the moon. But now prairie grasses were mixing with the craters, running to blackened hills that had been ravaged by fire, foothills of the jagged mountains on the lunar rim. I was traversing a basin in which translucent angelhair grass waved in the median, and under the spell of the surrounding vistas the idyllometer soared to ninety-five, the road surface still the only negative factor.

Then a happy surprise—the posted speed limit changed to seventy-five, the highest to date. Now I could cruise at *eighty-five,* fifteen shy of the goal I'd set in Van Horn. The sign was a blatant Interstate admission that the terrain in New Mexico is so very wide and vacant that speed simply doesn't matter. The traffic had spaced itself out after the immigration stop—a few trucks and even fewer cars—and I wiggled about in my seat, itching for an opportunity to *floor it,* hoping the posted speed would continue all the way to California.

Power lines soon appeared out of nowhere, cutting the idyllometer to eighty—ugly black wires on *pi*-shaped, cross-braced metal supports. A barrage of billboards dropped the idyllometer even farther, twenty-five or thirty billboards in orange, black, and gaudy Day-Glo colors, hawking everything from keychains to rattlesnake earrings. I-10 was in a basin now, with a moonscape horizon, making its way toward Michigan Flats, then Tequila Flats, both aptly named. Tequila Flats is not only *horizontally* flat but *vertically* flat—a Main Street cowtown-cutout like the backdrop in a Broadway musical, a brief roadside tourist trap as obnoxious as South of the Border on I-95.

Beyond Tequila Flats shreds of tires suddenly littered the highway—dangerous obstacles at eighty-five miles per hour, but still no match for the 'Vette. I swerved through them like a test driver dodging cones. The new speed was exhilarating, the Hot Wheels Corvette my Pony Express steed.

Far to the right a long train soon appeared, only the third I'd seen in the Desert Southwest, but easily the most colorful. Three black-and-yellow diesel engines were hauling a hundred cars or more. At such a great distance they seemed to be transporting children's blocks, in one long colorful line across the moonscape. Each boxcar was two-toned, like double-decker buses painted in contrasting colors. Such a happy-looking train—*The Little Engine That Could*! But when I finally caught up to it, the reality proved less enchanting. They weren't boxcars but semi-trailers without their tractors, stacked in pairs, to be hitched up later and hauled across the Interstates. I preferred that train as first seen from a distance—an enchanting page out of a New Mexico children's book.

Another puzzle replaced *The Little Engine That Could*. Several men in blaze-orange vests were working in the narrow median strip ahead, a median divided—for some reason—by a barbed-wire fence. The fence ran for miles through a gravelly stretch of spiky bushes, thistles, and ragged weeds. The same desperate vegetation dotted the surrounding terrain, where black cows now grazed as if in defiance of the landscape. I looked about for a pickup truck—some lunar lander that had brought these men out here—but the highway shoulders stood empty. These blaze-orange men had been dropped from outer space, and they were intent on something in the godforsaken median.

I saw what it was as I flew by, but I still don't understand it. Two of the men were standing about, as if waiting their turn. The third had a weedeater, and in the most incongruous and futile action I've ever seen on the Interstates, was whacking away at the scruffy median, raising a pitiful cloud of dust. But why bother? Those blaze-orange men could whack their lives away out there and never change that median one iota.

As the orange men receded in my mirror, the bright sun began to tint the miles ahead in rosy hues. It was as if I were running through a drugstore rack of sunglasses, testing the world in different colors—pink, aquamarine, fuchsia. Then, across a flat stretch of mauve prairie, I overtook again the truck I'd seen in Texas, the one with the puzzling bundles I'd mistaken for Christmas trees. Passing it again was no help—the stuff still looked like driftwood, sagebrush without the sage. This was near Deming, home to one of the most crass displays of advertising in all of America. Hundreds of billboards suddenly appeared, including several for the famous OK Corral—*True Gunfight Capital of the Old West!* I made a quick decision to stop, but not for the gunfight. The OK Corral is in Arizona. It was time to corral lunch.

* * *

Here's an Interstate Item for the discriminating traveler with artistic sensibilities, courtesy of an Interstate exit guide:

A mile and a half from Exit 85 on New Mexico's I-10 is the Deming Luna Mimbres Museum. Housed in an imposing old brick armory building, this large, rambling museum includes a very fine collection of Indian pottery and extensive exhibits of western and local memorabilia. The delicate white Indian pottery is decorated with remarkably sophisticated black and red geometric designs, animal figures, and scenes from daily life. It was found in the burial grounds of the Mimbres Indians, who mysteriously left this area some 800 years ago. Other exhibits include saddles and tack, a restored chuck wagon, a jail cell, a beauty salon, and household furnishings used by local settlers. Impressive collections of dolls, quilts, and lace, polished raw minerals, and Stetson hats are on view. Open Mon.–Sat. and p.m. Sun. except Thanksgiving Day, Christmas, and New Year's Day. Admission free but donations encouraged.

So why didn't I drop in, Native American advocate that I am? Because I had been so put off by the hundreds of billboards on the approach to Deming—as obnoxious as the touristy displays for Niagara Falls in the Northeast and South of the Border down south—that patronizing any of the local "sights" was simply out of the question.

* * *

I got a scare as I switched lanes to swing off the exit. A police car swerved in behind me, right on my tail. Was I going to be nabbed for speeding? My heart dropped as the vehicle passed me, screeching to a halt at a stop sign at the far end of the ramp. It was the Border Patrol again, two officers up front with two men in the rear, behind that bleak wire fence. The scene triggered a thought. Maybe the barbed-wire fence I had seen in the median was to keep wetbacks from crossing the highway. *Drybacks*, rather. Maybe the men in blaze-orange with the weedeater had been defoliating potential hiding places. It was the best explanation I could imagine as I rolled to a stop behind the Border Patrol vehicle.

An officer jumped from the front passenger seat, unlocked the rear door, and two of the meanest-looking *hombres* I have ever seen got out of the back. Both wore jeans and checkered shirts with the sleeves rolled up. Both had olive skin, greasy black hair, drooping mustaches, and flashing dark eyes. And those angry dark eyes told the story. This was the informal end to some official business, and the *hombres* didn't look too happy about it. They were being unceremoniously dumped beside the Interstate in a manner that seemed all too familiar to everyone involved. I was glad they didn't stick their thumbs in the air.

* * *

Deming (pop. 10,970) is no artificial Interstate community. Once you get by the doublewide trailers and lower-middle-class neighborhoods, there is a lovely downtown area with a homey western appeal.

It was eighty-five degrees at high noon—perfect for a shootout— but I had lost my appetite in the showdown at the exit. So I sat in the parking lot of a local restaurant, powered down the windows, and turned on the radio. NPR was reporting six more inches of rain in North Carolina, calling to mind the two college students who had been flooded from their campus. I couldn't remember the last time I had seen rain, but I would welcome it now—to wash the greasy dust of Texas from the 'Vette. To rinse the bad taste of the Border Patrol from my mouth. I hadn't felt such a strange sense of unease since traveling in Russia with Chief Big Eagle when the Soviet Union was collapsing about us. The Interstates can make you feel like you belong on a dude ranch.

Then a car rolled by with New Mexico vanity plates, a single word expressing just what I was feeling. Below the state motto, *Land of Enchantment*, the plates said, quite simply, *MERDE*. I laughed aloud, the sound of laughter just what I needed, even if it was my own. The people of New Mexico know their Spanish but certainly not their French. As those two *hombres* down the road were surely thinking: *SHIT*.

Beyond Deming, 252 miles from Van Horn, I crossed the Continental Divide, the extensive stretch of high mountains from which the river systems of the North American continent flow in opposite directions. It was a significant moment on that great relief map in my mind. My little Corvette was now moving downstream, albeit imperceptibly, headed for California from mile-high elevations with the momentum of an entire continent behind me. *Merde!* This was progress!

Then New Mexico became a land without shade, cattle grazing on angelhair acres surrounded by mountain silhouettes. And before long I encountered a new Interstate phenomenon—beyond the mountain ranges I could see *more* mountain ranges, a distinct succession of horizons, each more spectacular than the first. As I-10 wound its way up and through them, signs with arrows began to warn of sharp curves. But the 'Vette took them all without strain, clipping along at eighty-five.

Here and there wooden houses sat abandoned by the roadside, beaten to gray by the years, their dark broken windows like haunting eyes. I simply couldn't imagine anyone living in such bleak and empty spaces. Apparently the owners of these forlorn homesteads had come to the same conclusion.

Near the Hidalgo County line, thick black smoke suddenly choked the horizon. The world was on fire, I thought—thousands of acres parched by recent droughts. But I was wrong. A pale headlight soon peered through the distant dark cloud, beaming at the front of a smoke-belching train. The engine was enveloped in rolling smoke as if on fire itself. But there were no flames—just a horrendous black plume engulfing the entire train, obscuring the individual boxcars, spreading out to darken the sky like the aftermath of those oil refineries blown up during the Gulf War. The scene was hellish, apocalyptic. How could anyone stand to be in that engine? I wanted the storybook train I had seen earlier.

It was miles before the sky recovered and the last trace of blackness dissipated in my rearview mirror. Then New Mexico surprised me yet again. Pastel shades of purple suddenly covered the browns and tans, a scene out of that famous western novel *Riders of the Purple Sage*. Everywhere the land was suddenly purple, another color in the spectrum of drugstore sunglasses, while the 'Vette rose into a flawless blue sky.

Despite having crossed the Continental Divide, I-10 kept rising. Again and again my speedometer fell back from eighty-five to eighty-four, requiring a nudge of the cruise control. Such subtle indicators, I was realizing, are telling factors in Interstate travel. Especially when you're taking on a continent.

Passing through Lordsburg (pop. 2951) I was encouraged by some clear street names—*East Motel Drive, West Motel Drive*—none of this *Frontage Road* deception. Let's call a spade a spade, pardner. This is where straight talk began—the stark territory demanded it. But Lordsburg wasn't my destination. I was nearing the Arizona line, and New Mexico, like Texas before it, seemed determined to create a lasting impression. All at once I-10 appeared to be running along the bottom of the Grand Canyon. Spectacular ledges rose all about me, the highest I'd seen. The closest mountain ranges stood out starkly, with dark silhouettes behind them, the farthest but misty outlines, shimmering mists on the very edge of the moon. As if inspired, the road surface turned smooth and the idyllometer soared to one hundred, feasting on an array of enchanting data.

Behind the distant mountains lay vast plains, then wide green basins lined with outcroppings of rock. Interstate signs suddenly warned of dust storms—*Next Ten Miles*—and I soon saw why. A vague gray line striped the horizon ahead, an unsettling image across a wide and sandy basin. Minutes later it came into focus, a long flat dune. The slightest wind would stir it, the flying sand readily obliterating I-10. As if sensing the danger, the idyllometer fell to ninety.

Beyond the dune, through a brief work area, the speed dropped to fifty-five, then I-10 began to rise like a ramp towards a notch in the farthest mountains—big red rocky mountains, with pink and roseate slopes, ever sparkling in the sun. When the work area ended, brand-new blacktop took over, the high speed resumed, and I charged up the long incline ahead of two struggling trucks. Rocky outcroppings stood so close now I could reach out and scrape them with my fingernails. Then electronic signs appeared above the highway, suspended from what looked like huge croquet wickets. Higher up, their scoreboard lights warned of dangerous crosswinds, even wilder than the winds in the basins below.

Approaching that distant notch, the idyllometer shot back to one hundred. Humped mountain ranges rolled away beneath the roadway to the left. Jagged white cliffs gleamed on the right. I watched a truck ahead of me disappear over the crest of the horizon, and when the 'Vette followed all I saw was more mountains—range upon range—with stony pink faces and scrubby green beards. Then silhouette after silhouette of more mountains. Then all blue sky.

At the Arizona border, a large sign with an emblem of a star greets all Interstate traffic. Orange and red rays radiate from its center like bright spikes from the torch of the Statue of Liberty. It's a striking symbol of the sun, the perfect image for what you find in Arizona.

There's a verbal greeting too—*The Grand Canyon State Welcomes You*—but I felt I had already seen the Grand Canyon. The idyllometer had been perfect, and I couldn't imagine anything more spectacular than what I'd witnessed in New Mexico.

It was one-fifteen, maybe two-fifteen—had I neglected to change the 'Vette's clock?—and as usual there was a rest area just beyond the state line. It wasn't a welcome center, and there were only a handful of vehicles, but I pulled in anyway to get my Arizona bearings.

The absence of grass was startling—not a blade!—just pebbly red gravel across the entire few acres. Square red pipes fenced in the area, running horizontally between squat brick pillars. The main facility was triangular, with a slanted red roof topped by a steeple bearing some sort of crest—a bird, maybe, or another symbol of the sun. Each pavilion had a star-shaped roof to match the crest. Along the sidewalk, bricked-in gardens held spiny bushes and small trees.

Then I saw the proud sign: *It's a pleasure to have you in Arizona, a state blessed with some of the most breathtaking scenery—lush mountain forests, stunning red cliffs, sparkling high country lakes, Old West and Spanish towns, vestiges of the Indian past, and world famous canyons—all near or within a short drive from the Interstate highway.*

An elderly gentleman was waiting by the restrooms, and when his wife came out I went over to join them. They seemed in no hurry and glad for company. I had been so taken by the scenery in New Mexico that I had been neglecting to ask people about the Interstates. Then again, there hadn't been many people to ask.

"We're from Michigan," the man said thoughtfully, "from near Traverse City. I think the Interstates are fine, but as the population increases we must plan for the cities of the future. How else are we going to avoid the kind of bottlenecks like that one in El Paso? Did you get caught in that?" He seemed genuinely disgusted at what, for me, had been a minor Interstate idle.

"Ever been to Boston?" I said.

The man didn't seem to hear. "In Atlanta," he said, "it's so bad that, if you need anything, you better bring it with you. It's a total bottleneck every afternoon, from four to six."

I thought of the black man in D.C., where the bottlenecks last *three* hours. But I didn't push the point.

"We're from Michigan," the man's wife said enthusiastically, "and the Golden Gate has nothing on our Mackinaw Bridge! Why, it's five miles long—from the Lower Peninsula to the Upper! It goes right across the Straits of Mackinac!"

"We saw Steve Forbes' bus in Texas," her husband interjected. "*That* was a thrill. But I prefer our own rig." He pointed to a long trailer home in the parking lot, hitched to a sleek black pickup truck. "I see you got your C.R.S. book there," he said suddenly. He meant the black composition notebook in my hand.

"C.R.S.?"

"Can't remember shit!" The man slapped his thigh and laughed. Taking his cue, I told him about the vanity plates I'd seen in Deming— *MERDE*. But his wife seemed scandalized, so I changed the subject.

"Isn't the landscape spectacular?"

The old man laughed again. "Buddy, you ain't seen nothin' yet."

"You mean it gets better?"

"Oh God, yes."

Then he took his wife by the arm and they set off for their big rig. "When you get to Michigan," the woman said in parting, "don't forget the Mackinaw Bridge!"

I went into the restroom, then took a walk along the red pipe fence at the rear of the property. Train tracks paralleled the highway not far from the edge of the red gravel. A few hundred yards farther to the north, low mountains crossed the horizon, etched sharply against a solid blue sky. I had never seen such a deep blue. It was like the blue dye with which you color Easter eggs, that royal blue in the teacup before you drop the egg in. A solid, rich blue.

"Isn't it beautiful?" someone whispered behind me.

Turning abruptly, I discovered an attractive young woman of not more than twenty. Her hair, pulled into pigtails above each ear, was as dark as her eyes. She was wearing a short black sundress with spaghetti straps—almost suitable for a prom or garden party. The white skin of her shoulders was as luminous as the cliff faces I'd seen. Her sandaled feet sported bright pink toenails.

"You're going to get sunburned," I said, "if you're not careful."

As with the elderly man earlier, the young woman didn't seem to hear. "Isn't it just incredibly gorgeous?" She was still whispering.

"Incredibly," I replied. "And I'm told it gets better."

"Me too!" she said. "Me too!"

I wanted to ask her about the Interstates, but somehow it didn't seem appropriate. I tucked my C.R.S. book behind my back.

Folding her arms on the top rail of the fence, the young woman stared out across the railroad tracks into the vast blue sky. "I'm from Portland, Maine," she said finally. She seemed to be talking to herself, working things out. "I went down to Miami to work for a while. Now I'm moving to Phoenix."

"All on the Interstates?"

"Of course."

"How was the drive?"

"It went badly at times, like when I got caught in the rush hour in San Antonio, but *wow!*—after San Antonio, isn't it just fantastic? It's like someone raised a curtain out of nowhere and suddenly there's this incredible view. And all those hues at sunset! Did you ever see so many shades of violet?"

For a moment I thought she was going to cry, which would have made me cry too, but she switched gears unexpectedly. "Did you see those dead dogs?"

"I saw a few things I couldn't identify."

She nodded, then turned from the fence, and I realized she was smiling. "Excuse me," she said. "I've got to pee."

* * *

Beyond the rest area, as I-10 rose straight toward barren mountains, the cruise control continually slipped to eighty-four. The high desert temperature was holding at a dry ninety, and soon the Interstate signs carried a new warning—*Dust Blowing Area*.

Occasional irrigated orchards defied the landscape, small trees planted in orderly rows that shift geometrically as you speed by. They were pecans, maybe, or walnuts. But they looked like apple trees. These orchards flank the highway in basins that slope to foothills, hills rising in turn to jagged mountains on the hazy horizon. And all about them, the colors and contours change constantly—green, brown, purple. Knuckled, jagged, smooth. Sand mounds lay out there too, spiced with yucca bushes and small cacti. In these arid wastelands I had seen but a single bird—one cocky crow on the shoulder—but any roadkill, I was certain, would bring vultures.

A lone billboard for a cider mill suggested that the basin orchards I had seen earlier might indeed produce apples. Then a sign for *Cochise Stronghold* left me wondering about something else. How had Native Americans ever been driven from these mountain hideaways? A Chiricahua Apache, Cochise had directed Apache resistance against U.S. troops in Arizona from 1861 to 1872. The effort to oust him must have been as rugged and persistent as the terrain itself.

Miles later I saw a sign for a place called *Sunsites*. But the whole of Arizona is a sunsite, every view stretching for hundreds of miles in clear sunshine, as I-10 rises farther and farther into mountain deserts of sparse chaparral.

Just when I thought I was getting my Arizona bearings, I crested yet another mountain and dropped into a world of immense red cliffs. The sheer vertical walls seemed quarried from the landscape. Then they closed in, funneling I-10 through enormous chutes of red rock. A dead porcupine lay in the very center of the road, quills rising from its dark fur like the spiky rays of the Arizona logo. But the roadkill somehow cheered me. It was good to know that something could survive out here. If it learned to keep clear of the Interstate.

By three o'clock I was running out of adjectives. West Texas had been gorgeous, one of the most beautiful places on earth. But West Texas is still America, whereas New Mexico takes you to the moon. And if New Mexico is the moon, I decided, then Arizona is Mars. The red planet. The idyllometer had been stuck on one hundred for so long I had ceased checking. I needed a break from all the beauty. I needed to get out and walk and catch my breath.

But the next rest area, on a small scenic overlook, didn't help. It was a shelf, an open balcony on the edge of Mars, a ledge on a mountain of red boulders, domed by a solid blue sky. To the south, seven successive mountain ranges fell away one after another, each less distinct, the farthest but a mirage. Only two or three cars sat in the parking lot, the brilliant sun skating on brand new asphalt, a few travelers huddled in quiet pairs like parishioners in a cathedral.

Getting out, I leaned against the 'Vette, folded my arms across my chest, and stared at length across the universe. The stony interplanetary silence was humbling. I must have napped upright, dozing in a trance, because I was suddenly aware of the sun baking my forearms. Then I hiked the brief white sidewalk, finding two disturbing signs. *Defacing Rocks Unlawful.* And, *Danger! Poisonous Snakes and Insects Inhabit This Area!* The second warning no longer bothered me—I was glad that living creatures could make this barren land their own. But the other sign disgusted me, breaking the cathedral-like spell of the rest area. Other living creatures all over the Interstates make it a habit to mar the very beauty to which the Interstates take them. Even here on Mars.

At the end of the sidewalk, a middle-aged man in Bermuda shorts was taking a photo of the wall of rocks behind the parking lot. I stopped short of his camera so as not to ruin his picture. Then I realized I had seen this man in Texas, talking with another woman at one of the rest areas.

"Sorry to keep you from your exercise," he said. "Aren't you the guy who's always walking?"

"That's me," I said. "Where's your wife?"

He pointed up the sidewalk. "Here she comes now. But she's not my wife. We just keep bumping into each other when we stop."

The woman, in safari shorts and a white blouse, joined us cheerily. "Hello, again! How y'all doing?" She had a notebook in her hand.

"Your C.R.S. book?" I said.

She looked stunned. "Don't tell me *you* met that guy too?"

We laughed simultaneously. Then the man pointed his camera at the woman. "This here *walker man* thinks that we're married."

She winked seductively. "A secret Interstate affair. I'm from South Carolina, and I'm writing a journal of my travels. Where you headed?"

"Benson today," I said. "Sierra Vista in the morning."

"Ha!" the man said, winding his camera. "I'm retired from the service near Sierra Vista. *Fort Huachuca.* I'm on my way home. Sierra Vista's lovely. It's got a population of about thirty-three thousand, but it's the third-fastest-growing area in Arizona—besides Phoenix and Tucson. Be sure to see Tombstone while you're there. And the OK Corral. Catch a bit of the Old West."

The woman shook her head. "He's such a tourist! I keep telling him to put that damn camera away."

"On Thursday I'll be in California," I said. "But I can't imagine it at all."

"California," the woman said reverently, "is a world of its own."

It was only twenty minutes farther to Benson, so I lingered at the rest area after the couple had left, fortifying myself for the scenery ahead. And it proved spectacular—aerial vistas falling away for hundreds of miles from red rock cliffs at the roadside. Happily, the Arizona Department of Transportation was in tune with the color scheme. The sturdy guardrail, necessary on critical curves, was reddish brown. The cement divider, occasionally splitting the median, was pink or salmon—all so perfectly pretty that I began to fear for the idyllometer. How much beauty could it stand before it exploded?

I entered an enormous bowl—the largest basin to date—completely surrounded by five mountain ranges. Rolling hills to the north had eroded to red sand cliffs, the sort where Native Americans had thrived centuries earlier. I could imagine Pueblo people climbing ladders to adobe dwellings, their multi-level apartments cut into the steep faces. Sheer rock ledges dropped straight from the sky, striped horizontally by narrow bands of red and brown. The effect was primeval. In brilliant, ancient sunshine.

Just short of Benson I crossed Adam's Peak Wash, a small dry streambed—another gully or draw—that handles all the water from Adam's Peak, mountain run-off that could surge like a tidal wave. Lime Peak, just to the north, rises to nearly seven thousand feet. And suddenly I was happy I hadn't come in the rainy season.

On the outskirts of Benson (pop. 3824), the San Pedro River stood as dry as Adam's Peak Wash, a flat white bed of sand about fifty yards wide. Benson itself followed, spread out along the highway, a flat Interstate community of billboards, white bungalows, house trailers, and an adobe-style inn.

A few flags on high poles rippled straight out in the breeze as I rattled across a cattle guard at the end of the exit. There were no cattle in sight, but I had been similarly jarred at exits in Texas and New Mexico. The cattle guards always came as a surprise—narrow parallel pipes worse than any speed bump. Anything that wandered there would break a leg for sure. I suppose they serve a purpose, keeping livestock off the Interstates, but they startle out-of-town dudes in the process.

Then it was *Welcome to Benson*, where I found my motel without a hitch, where the Marlboro Man was lounging on a porch swing, in a bar of shade beneath the brief front roof, the very essence of rugged repose. A thermometer behind him matched the idyllometer at an even one hundred. It would be too hot to wash the 'Vette—there was simply no shade anywhere—a good excuse to postpone that chore until morning.

Sierra Vista is just half an hour south of Benson, but I wasn't due at my old friend Dilby's until Wednesday noon. Tomorrow would be a day off from driving. And I needed it—time to recover from the beauty of the Desert Southwest. As for now, there was an inviting pool at the end of the parking lot, its rippling blue surface reflecting the glare of the afternoon sun.

The Marlboro Man followed me inside to get me registered, and as I reached for my wallet I was startled by the clock above the desk. It was two hours earlier than I thought.

"You're on California time now," the cowboy explained. "It switches in New Mexico."

I couldn't figure out where I had gone wrong, but it didn't matter. I had been traveling in outer space anyway, in a trance and a time warp. All that mattered now was that pool outside. I tossed my stuff in my room, pulled on my bathing suit, and hot-footed it across the baking sidewalk. The poolside thermometer showed one-twenty in the sun— the highest reading I would see on my Interstate odyssey, the hottest temperature I've ever experienced. Yet it was more comfortable than ninety in the Everglades.

There was only one other bather at the pool, a paunchy pale businessman who wrapped his towel about his waist and grabbed his briefcase as I approached.

"Too cold!" he said, passing me at the gate. "It's all yours!"

I couldn't believe it. Another thermometer, hanging into the pool on a string, had the water temperature at an even eighty. But I soon discovered why the businessman had fled. The stiff Arizona breeze makes for such rapid evaporation that any wet body is instantly chilled. I had to keep submerged to my nose to avoid freezing. Pools in Arizona need windchill warnings. At temperatures of one hundred and twenty.

By six o'clock the sun was going down—a glorious blaze above the surrounding sawtoothed mountains—and still there was no shade, even up against the side of the motel. Benson was deserted, but as I walked off in search of supper I noticed a woman working in a rock garden at the edge of the motel parking lot. An attractive blonde with sun-streaked long hair, she wore white shorts and a brief blue top. She was tanned as dark as the Marlboro Man. In fact, she was his wife. And she was busily weeding the gravel.

"I thought only *grass* needed weeding," I said.

"You'd be surprised." She pointed to a few spiny slips that were sprouting among the rocks. I wouldn't have noticed them otherwise. "When these mesquite trees drop their seeds, they fly all over the place and root everywhere. You've got to keep after them, or else they'll take over." She was digging in the gravel with a tool like a screwdriver, plucking the pesky wiry shoots and tossing them into a bucket.

"Tell me about the Interstates out here," I said.

"Well," she said, "we get terrible winds in winter, but instead of closing the Interstates, the troopers line up the traffic like a wagon train, then proceed at thirty miles an hour, two lanes side by side. It helps block the wind." She stood up and wiped her forehead with the back of a gloved hand. "But in the rainy season—July through mid-August—we get a lot of bad accidents. A lot of older people have poor night vision and just run off the road. Speed's no problem. The main difficulty is hydroplaning. When it gets wet, vehicles just slide off the road. We have quite a few accident victims stay with us while their cars are being repaired."

The woman kneeled in the gravel again as I crossed the street to a local restaurant, grateful once again that it wasn't the rainy season. Or winter or summer, for that matter.

Dinner proved as hot as the day itself, the chunky chipotle peppers in the sauce on my roast chicken sending me to the ice water again and again. Then the sun dropped from the sky, bathing Benson in a rosy glow, and I returned to the motel to catch the evening news. One item featured a Georgia state trooper talking about the Interstates.

"Sleepy drivers act like drunk drivers," he was saying. It was exactly what the state trooper had told me in New Jersey. "Quick naps help, but many drivers simply don't get enough sleep. They turn up the radio or air-conditioning or even the heater, but it just doesn't help. These are temporary solutions. Caffeine's temporary too, no matter how much coffee you drink."

But *I* had discovered an antidote to falling asleep on the highway. Just drive the Interstates in Arizona. The startling scenery will keep you awake. And on that thought I fell asleep myself.

* * *

155

It was chilly at dawn but began to get hot the moment the sun rose in the east. I ate a quick breakfast and then, despite the No Parking Zone on the west side of the motel, moved the 'Vette up against the sidewalk into the shade of the building. I figured I had two hours to wash the car before all shade disappeared for the day.

Soon the blonde woman came by with a load of trash for the dumpster. I gave her a cheery good morning but she didn't respond—my punishment for breaking the rules. But it would have been too warm to clean the 'Vette in the sun, too difficult to see in the constant glare. Besides, the parking lot was not at all crowded—no more than a dozen vehicles amply spaced.

I drew my finger across the sleek red hood. The 'Vette was now covered with a soft red powder as fine as paprika. It had settled down out of the night sky once the winds had quit, adding to the greasy film of Texas and the dust of New Mexico. I had my work cut out for me, courtesy of the Desert Southwest, but I had slept well and was ready for the task, methodically lining up my rags, paper towels, squeegee, and squirt bottle along the edge of the curb.

I began with the windshield, and as I lifted the wipers a small business card fell out. It was from an electronics firm in Northern Ireland and there was a message scribbled on the back: *Nice car! Enjoyed meeting you! Have a nice trip!* It was signed *Mal and Eileen*, the Irish couple from Naples, Florida. I had stopped using the wipers even before I got to Florida—and hadn't used them since—or I might have discovered the card sooner. Mal and Eileen, I remembered fondly, had lapped America with their kids on the Interstates. It was great to hear from them again on this sun-struck Mars morning. *Good ol' Mal, my Interstate pal.*

Two hours later, as I took my rags and paper towels to the dumpster, a young woman exited one of the units and began loading several suitcases into a Jeep Cherokee with Connecticut plates. Here was a kindred Connecticut Yankee, an opportunity I couldn't pass up. She was from Salisbury and knew a Yale friend of mine who had been a high school principal there. She and her husband were lapping America too, on an extended honeymoon.

"We were going to take the same route as you," she said excitedly, "but the weather was so bad on the East Coast we thought we'd go in reverse. We're camping at all the national parks along the Interstates. Out here the Interstates certainly have all the best scenery. And to get from A to B, you simply can't beat 'em. I love the high speed."

I told her about Mal and Eileen. And the biker from Maine.

"Our numbers are growing!" she said. "And you're doing it your own way. I love your Corvette!"

By the time I had showered and packed it was time to leave for Sierra Vista, southwest of Benson down Route 90 from I-10. But Route 90—through the heart of rolling sandhills—was under construction, and Murphy's Interstate Law kicked in. The 'Vette was soon covered in red dust. Because I had just washed it.

Disgusted, I made a mental note to ask Dilby about this Martian paprika.

10

WHEN IT COMES TO OWNING A CORVETTE, MONEY'S ALWAYS THE PROBLEM, especially for a small-town professor like me. As they say, if you flinch at the sticker price—or even dare ask about the miles per gallon—you have no business driving a 'Vette. It's a totally impractical vehicle, a contradiction in values, and the realistic side of me deplores it. But my romantic side has always wanted one. Born a Pisces, those two fish swimming in opposite directions describe me perfectly, as well as my relation to the Corvette. I love it and hate it.

My father, who never went to college, had always wanted a Cadillac and finally bought one before he retired, after putting four sons through college. His example became my inspiration. If *he* could manage a Cadillac, *I*—who, as my father once said, have more degrees than a thermometer and only *two* sons to put through college—could somehow manage a Corvette. The perfect vehicle for a symbolic lap around the country.

Purchasing a new Corvette was out of the question, so I began to follow ads for used ones, scrutinizing the daily offerings in our local paper:

1976 CORVETTE, 350, air, power steering,
new interior, 47,000 miles. $8500. Call:
[phone numbers were listed in all ads].

1982 CORVETTE, body in good condition.
Runs good. $9400.

1984 CORVETTE red with 2 tops,
excellent condition. $7500.

1985 CORVETTE L98, gray with glass
top, 80,000 miles, $8500, must sell.

1990 CORVETTE, 58,000 miles, convertible,
Greenwood package, chrome coverings
on engine. Asking $18,000 + tax & title.

1996 CORVETTE convertible, automatic,
red/black top & interior. 3,000 miles,
perfect condition. $33,500 or will trade
for real estate.

1996 CORVETTE Grand Sport, 1200 miles,
all options.

As for the '82, I preferred a 'Vette that would run *well*. But I needed a later model, one with a lumbar seat for back support, and a seat that goes up and down and back and forth, allowing for maximum headroom and legroom.

As for the '90, I had no idea what the *Greenwood package* might be. It sounded like a model home in a residential development. And chrome coverings on the engine suggested a show car, not one for lapping America.

The '96 convertible in *perfect condition* bore a perfectly outrageous price tag, and my wife warned me about swapping the house for it. Which left—for that day's musings—the '96 Grand Sport, with all options and only 1200 miles on it, no price listed. But a quick phone call confirmed my suspicions. The owner wanted $35,000, too grandly sporting for a professor of poverty.

* * *

I hadn't seen Dilby in years. We had been in graduate school together in the '70s. A craggy clone of Clint Eastwood, he was seventy-seven now and retired from the Merchant Marine. And he was having health problems, fibrillations of the heart.

His wife Ché—a Filipina half his age—was at home alone when I arrived, their two sons at school. They live in an attractive but modest subdivision of ranch homes spread along curving streets, at the very bottom of those jagged mountains I had been seeing from I-10. It was another bright blue day with intense dry heat, and at noon the trees of Sierra Vista—a variety of palms, pines, willows, and a host of gnarled things I couldn't identify—provided scant shade.

Dilby's concrete driveway radiated heat like an oven. Beside it was a small rectangle of green grass. The front yards of all other homes on the street were rock gardens, like the kind the Marlboro Man's wife had been weeding back in Benson. But Dilby's an original. He's always been his own man. So in the desert Dilby has grass.

I greeted Ché with the large avocado I had been given in Florida, now perfectly ripe, unlike my bunch of bananas. Inside, the house was dark and cool, with a kind of Mediterranean decor. Dilby was at the supermarket, expected any minute, and as I settled in, Ché readily offered a frank opinion of the Interstates.

"Too busy!" she said. "Too much traffic! Too busy and too noisy! And it's a long way to Tuscon just to get what you need. Sure, it's easy for drivers, but if you live nearby it's too noisy."

"*Nearby?*" I said. "You mean you can hear I-10 way down here? And you think it's too *busy?*"

Ché had no time to elaborate. A nurse's aide at a local hospital, she had to get ready for work.

Dilby arrived just as she was leaving. We had lunch, then stepped outside, pulling two chairs into a square of shade on the narrow front porch. The sawtoothed mountains seemed right at the end of the street, so close I could have propped my feet on them. But Dilby ignored them. He wanted to talk about his lawn, which he kept green with a rusty sprinkler and a coil of green hose.

"You see," he said, "everybody else has gravel out front. But what does that do? It reflects the heat right at the house. At least here, with a few blades of grass, I get a little relief. The heat's oppressive in Sierra Vista from May to September. The monsoon season just ended. Today we've got a southeast breeze."

"What about this red dust?" I asked.

Dilby groaned. "What about it?"

"I just washed my car."

"And now you've got to wash it again."

"Exactly."

"You sound like my wife," Dilby laughed. "But let me tell you something. We get dust storms out here. And no matter how tight you shut up the house, when you open your bureau there's dust in your underwear. It drives Ché nuts."

"She doesn't like the Interstates," I said.

Dilby hiked his chair away from the creeping sun. "Let me tell you a thing or two about the Interstates. The best thing about the Interstates is that they go around the big cities. Those beltways are convenient. But Interstate tolls are repulsive. Whenever I see a toll station I get right off the highway. I won't give the government the satisfaction. I'll go *anywhere* to avoid paying a toll, even if it takes me out of my way. It's a matter of principle."

I adjusted my chair too, gaining an inch of precious shade.

"But I've had some lovely moments on the Interstates," Dilby went on. "When we lived in New Mexico I used to drive up I-25 to Magdalena. At night, coming through the Magdalena Mountains, you could see the lights of Socorro in the distance. It was just like being in an airplane. And that reminds me," he said suddenly, "when you head out of here tomorrow, look for the saguaros. They're that tall kind of cactus you always see in the movies, like fat green scarecrows. Some of them have appendages that are really phallic. In season they've got white flowers and edible red fruit. But if you look closely you'll see that many of 'em are mutilated. People drive out here on the Interstates from all over America and go home with a chunk of saguaro in the trunk as a souvenir. I can't get over it."

Dilby fell silent, until I mentioned the Border Patrol and *los dos hombres*.

"Don't get me started," he said. "Those two guys were probably picked up on suspicion of being illegal. But they had their papers in order and so were dropped off. That's why they were pissed. It'll get worse in December, when all the illegal immigrants visit family in Mexico for the holidays. Then the Border Patrol beefs up its personnel. They take to the air in blimps. They lengthen the steel walls along the busiest sections of the border. Southeast of here, near Douglas, they've welded steel panels to a 12-foot-high barrier. It extends for more than ten miles. Near Naco, just a few minutes south, there's a barrier of railroad ties set in concrete. It was recently extended to three miles. The Border Patrol has a network of motion sensors and video cameras and infrared cameras for the dark. They've got mobile observation posts and high-intensity lights, and they're always increasing the number of their agents. More than six hundred thousand illegals were caught in the Douglas–Naco corridor last year. The numbers keep rising, with increased patrols in Texas and California."

As Dilby spoke, I saw again those swarthy men dumped at the Interstate exit by the Border Patrol. It was a problem with no easy solution.

Merde.

"These people only want what anybody wants," Dilby concluded. "A decent life. But I'll tell you one thing—I trust these Latinos more than the white politicians who built the Interstates."

I didn't respond. This was vintage Dilby, but I knew talking was difficult for him, given his weakened heart. Soon he excused himself for his afternoon nap. A siesta sounded good to me too, so I stretched out inside and fell asleep immediately. Washing the 'Vette in the morning had exhausted me more than I thought.

Later in the afternoon Freddie arrived home from junior high, all dark hair and dark eyes like his mother. I told him his mom was at work and his father was sleeping.

"My brother Dom won't be home until midnight," he said. "He works in the supermarket after high school gets out. 'Zat your car out front?" he asked sheepishly.

I nodded.

"Must be great on the highway."

I nodded again.

"I love to go to Tucson on I-10 with my mom. I love to see the big trucks and all the construction. And I like to see all the mountain ranges. Every time we go I see something new. And you know what? If you do *this* when you pass the big trucks"—he made a downward jerking motion with his fist—"they blow their horn real loud. My mom doesn't like that because it scares her. But I always do it out the side window when she's not looking."

When Dilby awoke, he showed me the backyard, a small fenced-in area of hardpan beyond which a series of dry arroyos cuts through the neighborhood like alleys in a midwestern town. I couldn't imagine them filled with rushing water, but from the ruts and erosion it was plain to see that they had seen plenty. The late afternoon was hot and still, and I listened for the distant whine and rumble of I-10.

"Freddie's such a sweet kid," I said finally.

"Isn't he, though?" Dilby agreed. "Another year or two and he's going to lose that lovely innocence. The move from New Mexico killed him. They had to keep him back in school."

"Why'd you come to Sierra Vista?"

"I'm not getting any younger, you know. Ché wanted to start nursing school, but as soon as she got hired as a nurse's aide, she stopped taking classes. I keep telling her to continue but she's content with the ways things are. *Too* content, if you ask me, with all those bedpans."

"What about Dom?"

"He doesn't like having an old man for a father, someone who's always writing cranky letters to the local paper. He hears about it from the kids at school. Freddie not so much. But Dom—I embarrass him."

Dilby had been married once before, before I knew him in graduate school, with a Swedish wife and two daughters somewhere in Scandinavia. One of those daughters had become a TV star. But that was long after his wife had asked him to leave.

As Dilby spoke, I began to see that great American relief map in my mind in a new way. Little homes sit at every Interstate exit like the green houses on a Monopoly board. And in all of those houses all over the country, quiet dramas are being played out. And the Interstates put you right in the front row.

* * *

The evening grew dark the moment the sun went down. We shared a quiet supper with Freddy—a stew of Dilby's making that was too hot for my taste—then turned in early, long before Ché or Dom returned from work.

At six in the morning, as I took a "power walk" around Sierra Vista, it was still dark and only fifty-nine degrees. I checked the 'Vette when I returned. As I feared, it was coated with more of that red Martian paprika. But there was no time to wash it—it would have been useless, anyway, given the construction in the dusty sandhills between Sierra Vista and I-10.

Today was my Balboa Day—the day I would discover the Pacific—and I wanted to get to San Diego before the afternoon rush. Growing up in Connecticut, I was very familiar with Long Island Sound and the Atlantic Ocean, but I had never seen the Pacific. Still, my excitement was checked as I said goodbye to Dilby. As with my mother in Stratford, I knew this would be our last visit, and as I climbed into the 'Vette at seven o'clock there was only small talk.

"Don't forget those saguaros," Dilby said. "And look for the date farms in California. Those dates are delicious. You oughta get yourself some. Watch out for mist and fog in the mountains."

I promised I would. Then I backed from the driveway, beeped the horn, and left Dilby standing there grinning. On his rectangular patch of grass in the desert.

From Sierra Vista it's forty-five minutes to Tucson, then four hundred and ten miles to San Diego. It was another sky-blue day, a big sun behind me, a three-quarter moon ahead. The day off had revived me. I had been running on the adrenaline of a perfect idyllometer, and now I was ready for whatever the Interstates would bring next.

Having bequeathed my avocado, I moved my bananas to the passenger seat, hoping they'd catch some sun and ripen a bit faster. They were still tinged with green, like the sandhills between Sierra Vista and Tucson, reddish gravelly mounds with tangles of waist-high vegetation.

I crossed Davidson Canyon—bigger than a draw or wash, but no gulch or arroyo. And definitely not a *slough*. The perspective of the landscape was changing radically now. At times sandhills flanked the shoulders, I-10 weaving through them like moguls on a ski slope. Then the highway would crest a ridge and the entire vast blank surface of Mars would open up before me, littered with large piles of red rock. At the Saguaro National Park—nothing but hilly desert, really—I began to look for those large green cacti, but there were none to be seen from I-10.

Then came Tucson, where the approach is *garbage in*—a low stretch of billboards, industrial parks, factory outlets, telephone poles, house trailers, and ranch-style subdivisions reminiscent of Dilby's. The median was all sagebrush and weeds, the shoulders flanked by large

163

piles of industrial sand processed in long drab buildings nearby. Dry mudflats stretched away to the right, with oil tanks and more factories and sandpits. Railroad tracks paralleled the Interstate, and then a few schools and baseball diamonds began to appear in the distance. Three mountain peaks commanded the sky above the city itself.

Tucson has no beltway. I was headed straight into the city, home to four hundred thousand. As a kid I had called this place *Tuckson*, just as Puerto Rico for me was *Pewter Rice-o*. Now I waited with the eyes of a child for this *Too-sahn* to reveal itself. Its skyline was nothing spectacular—three or four buildings higher than the rest. Then I threaded a viaduct and suddenly, as in El Paso, all underpasses and retaining walls were pink and purple, painted in bright pastels to match the landscape.

Downtown Tucson is attractive as well. There's a brownish building, a tiered affair with an octagonal observation deck, and some tall glass structures framed by mountain peaks. Then comes a mission-style building with twin towers, some pink buildings, and two like the United Nations with iridescent faces. Riding low in the 'Vette, my view was vertical—all towering facades and blue sky.

It was eight-thirty now, traffic moderate across three lanes, the mountains close enough to grab. I saw a saguaro but it was on a billboard, a huge cactus with three or four outstretched arms. To the left, housing developments spread across the desert all the way to the mountains. Then tile murals decked the Interstate walls—prettier than El Paso's—the prettiest I would see anywhere. It's worth a drive to Tucson just for the Interstate art, a simple touch that readily transforms the urban center. The street names of Tucson are picturesque as well. *Sunset Road. El Camino del Cerro.*

Then came the usual *garbage out*, but with a new shrub in the median—a kind of blue broccoli, thriving along a divider of metal fence posts and thick cables. There were cacti in there as well, Mickey Mouse ears spiked with long needles, and then—for the second time in the Desert Southwest—I passed a highway worker with a weedeater. He was standing up to his knees in scraggly vegetation, whacking away furiously at something or other, a whirlpool of dust at his feet. But once again the gesture was futile. He wasn't improving that median one bit.

* * *

Before we leave Tucson, here's an Interstate Item:

As you can imagine, construction of the largest public works project in history resulted in the discovery of a plethora of fascinating artifacts that had lain buried in the earth for centuries. What to do about such finds? The U.S. government has been involved for nearly a century, beginning with the Antiquities Act of 1906. This was followed by the Historic Sites Act of 1935, the National Historic Preservation Act of 1960, the Archaeological and Historical Preservation Act of 1974, the American Indian Religious Freedom Act of 1978, the Archaeological Resources Protection Act of 1979, and the Native American Graves Protection and Repatriation Act of 1990. This last bit of legislation requires consultation with Native American tribes before excavation or removal of cultural items. Chief Big Eagle, whom I had visited in Maine, had invoked the statute to halt construction of a road in Connecticut that was passing through an Indian burial ground.

According to the *Archaeology in Tucson* newsletter, an organization called Desert Archaeology excavated two parts of an ancient settlement for the Arizona Department of Transportation that was discovered during the construction of a Tucson interchange on I-10. *Two pithouses and several pits found in one area may date to the Hohokam Rincon phase (A.D. 950–1100). The other part of the settlement, a little farther north of the interchange, appears to be much earlier, dating to the early ceramic period before the appearance of decorated pottery—perhaps before A.D. 500. Most of the ceramics from this earlier area are from plain brownware seed jars; house forms are either circular or rectangular with rectangular plastered hearths and plastered adobe pillars flanking the entries. The rectangular hearths are particularly interesting, as this form is virtually unknown within the prehistoric Tucson Basin culture sequence.*

Also, near Grant Road along I-10 in Tucson, the University of Arizona Department of Anthropology conducted tests on the site of an ancient refuse dump, where a deeply buried layer of trash revealed Papago Red shards as well as ethnic Chinese artifacts.

Thus the Dwight D. Eisenhower System of Interstate and Defense Highways provides one long avenue from the ancient past into the present.

* * *

A golf course breezed by on the left, the first I'd seen since San Antonio, then cultivated groves of trees appeared on both sides of the highway, fruit trees according to the overhead signs—*Orange Grove Road* and *Tangerine Road*. The landscape changed yet again, flat to the left and straight ahead, but with mountain ranges to the right. All the way to the bleak edge of Mars.

Billboards pushed Native American wares now—*kachina dolls* and *moccasins, Black Hills gold* and *jewelry*—as the cruise control fell to eighty-four. I nudged it to eighty-five. I-10 was climbing toward jagged peaks, a long flat grade toward tall mountains that would eventually dump me into California. The peaks ahead were like giant upside-down molars. But other scenes would pass before I reached them—*Red*

Rock, Casa Grande, Pichacho Peak—after which the red rock molars claimed the horizon.

Suddenly something strange popped up in the red foothills to the left—a haphazard array of enormous green dill pickles. A dill pickle forest. *What the hell?* And then it hit me. They must be saguaros. Farther along they stood closer to the highway—tall green pickles with one arm raised at the elbow, the other straight out. Some had incredible penises. And Dilby was right, many were mutilated—chopped, hacked, mangled—these magnificent green sentinels of Mars.

Soon saguaros appeared to the right of I-10 as well, not a hundred yards off. They occurred intermittently, spaced apart as if afraid of pricking each other. Mark Twain had gotten out of his stagecoach to stretch his legs among the saguaros, but outside Tucson there's no place to stop on I-10. Still, souvenir hunters had found a way, perpetrating an Interstate shame.

At the bottom of Pichacho Peak a resort gleamed in the sun, a hotel like the Alamo, its sandstone walls a pretty pink. An array of orchards followed, then open desert again, with a distinct new look. Flat brown hard-packed sand extended for miles, dotted with scrubby tufts of vegetation. The ground was like an enormous dry pudding garnished with parsley, in a spacious bowl fringed by red mountains. A sign for *Gila River Casino* added an ugly desert image—the Gila monster, a venomous black-and-orange lizard. But it suited the terrain, which was turning ugly itself.

Presently, a sparkling green sign revived my spirits—*San Diego 350*—and minutes later I bade I-10 goodbye. For two thousand miles since northern Florida, I-10 had been my faithful Interstate guide. Now I swung south on I-8, its parallel Interstate sibling, California within reach.

On I-8 the posted speed remained the same, the traffic still cruising at eighty-five. The temperature was eighty-five as well, rising as steadily and gradually as the highway. Saguaros loomed at arm's length through parsleyed sandhills, and on the edge of a cliff near Casa Grande a few modern homes perched magnificently, the most elegant I'd seen. But west of Casa Grande, through the Sand Tank Mountains, the territory grew uglier than ever, giving the idyllometer—and my own sensibilities—a much-needed rest. The landscape matched my feelings. I couldn't stop thinking of Dilby.

After Tucson most traffic had continued towards Phoenix on I-10, so I was virtually alone now on I-8, a ruler-straight road across a basin bottom, a slight haze distorting the junction of land and sky. Irrigated green acres surprised me, a luxuriant cabbage-like crop, perhaps the dates Dilby had mentioned. Closer still, the green stuff looked like grapes, wiry and waist high. Irrigation was the key here, transforming an unarable stretch of desert into a highly productive land.

The Santa Rosa Wash came and went, a long dry crevice awaiting flash floods.

Yet I-8 itself seemed constantly flooded, the highway so flat that mirages become a problem, tricking the mind into fears of hydroplaning. At nine forty-five, looking ahead and behind, I thought I was parting the Red Sea. There were no other vehicles for hundreds of miles, just range upon range of mountains. And all that imaginary water. And I kept on thinking, *Surely California's just over that next peak.* But each time I-8 finally shot through a distant gap—a notch it would take an hour or more to reach—the expectant moment only duplicated the previous panorama. More sand flats, scrub grass, and saguaros waited below, the highway running dead ahead. Through yet another basin in the mountains.

A subtle noise caught my ear—*tick, tick, tick*—as if someone was flinging sand at the 'Vette. And suddenly the windshield was laced with black dots. Mosquitoes? Gnats? Desert mites? Whatever they were, they scared the hell out of me. But unlike southern love bugs, they didn't obscure my vision. I wouldn't have to stop. I focused my eyes on a pair of brown mounds ahead, rising from a mesa in a stretch of tan wasteland.

A short while later I swept by those mounds, headed for yet another mountain peak, after which bright new blacktop began. Then the familiar Martian landscape resumed—entire hills formed by red rocks and gray rocks the size of basketballs. Piles of rock sat in shimmering mirages before me, with the haze of distant mountains as a backdrop, more mountains waiting to be crossed by the proverbial bear. The setting was all too bleak, the idyllometer, perhaps frightened by the flying mites, holding steady with my cruising speed. And all I could think of was that man at the rest area. *Buddy, you ain't seen nothing yet.*

A new sign brought a puzzle. *Elevation 735.* Apparently I-8 had not only been going up into the mountains but coming back down. Now there appeared to be just one final mountain range to conquer, higher than all the rest, as if this lower elevation was the very last chance to catch your breath before entering California.

My scalp prickled with expectation, and at ten-fifteen I exited to a gas station to prepare for the final push. I wanted to fill the tank and check out the windshield. But something else grabbed my eye. *Gila Bend. Founded 1872.* The realization was startling. How very young the West is! My hometown of Stratford, Connecticut, had been founded in

1639, less than two decades after the Pilgrims landed at Plymouth Rock. Now here I was in Gila Bend, Arizona (pop. 1747), which had been incorporated after the Civil War. Interstate cities share similar age discrepancies, but somehow the disparity seems more drastic with small towns.

It was ninety-three degrees now, the 'Vette's windshield and bumper coated with rice-like mites. Fortunately I had my Coca-Cola, still as potent as ever.

Back on the road by ten forty, I noticed a few small yellow butterflies fluttering across the highway, no bigger than moths. Earlier, NPR had been discussing the migration of butterflies through Arizona and California—monarchs, I think—and as I recalled that very feature the yellow butterflies began to increase in number, a few dozen at first, then a few hundred—then suddenly thousands—a yellow snowstorm that lasted for twenty minutes. Each butterfly that struck the windshield left a six-inch yellow smear. Here was Murphy's Interstate Law at work again. This time on Mars. And *this* time I could barely see the road.

The moment the storm ended I pulled onto the shoulder to break out my liter of Coke. Hundreds of miles of flat sand extended from both sides of the highway. Stark red mountains lined the horizon. Intent on the windshield, I didn't notice where I was until safely back inside the 'Vette. The temperature had risen to ninety-five in the brief interval since I had stopped for gas, and the air-conditioning gave me a sobering jolt. This was no place to be outside cleaning your windshield. This was no place to be, period.

On the move once again, I passed a roadkill—something like a coyote—then nudged the cruise control back up to eighty-five. I-8 was ascending again, imperceptibly, on a stretch of smooth new blacktop by Agua Caliente. But here wasn't any *agua* anywhere, although I could vouch for the *caliente*. It was *hot*, approaching the century mark.

As I entered Yuma County near the Arizona border, the desert scene mutated once again. Black rocks littered the horizon like large chunks of coal, as if the red planet had been scorched by a conflagration. Incredibly, the remains of homes occasionally sat by the roadside—piles of rotted wood on forlorn stone foundations. I had seen such remains in other states, but none more desolate than these, in the starkest of landscapes. Who could ever have even *wanted* to live out here? The very next sign suggested an answer. *Aztec*. Of course. Indians. Native Americans. People with the courage of Cochise.

I checked my mirrors. There was but a single car miles behind me and a long straight stretch ahead. The time had come, and the decision was involuntary. I punched the accelerator and the 'Vette eased to one hundred—then *one-oh-one, one-oh-two, one-oh-three*—putting more miles between me and that lonely car in the rearview mirror. Then I took my foot from the pedal, coasting into a shimmering mirage.

It was my first time ever at more than a hundred miles per hour. And it was all too easy. The realization depressed me. The 'Vette was obviously capable of so much more, but now I had met all my goals—I had experienced a perfect one hundred on the idyllometer many times over, and I had exceeded a speed of one hundred miles per hour. Yet my Interstate odyssey was only half complete. What to shoot for next?

I decided to try for a *double-hundred*—one hundred on the idyllometer and one hundred on the speedometer. *Simultaneously.* And each successive time I would seek to exceed my former speed. It was an exciting idea, but any attempts, I knew, would have to wait until I was out of the mountains, perhaps until Montana—where speed limits, I had been told, don't exist. Content for the moment, I resumed the legal cruising speed. This was near a place called *Dateland*, which suggested an answer to those green crops I'd seen back down the road.

Now desert driftwood was strewn across the wastelands like driftwood on a beach. And the mountains of western Mars were outdoing themselves. Every bald range before me seemed the highest I'd ever seen, pronounced sawteeth and utterly desolate. Satellite dishes and radar installations added a queer outer-space look. A tall white globe sat on a white cylinder like a giant thermometer, a UFO perhaps. And there were unexpected groves of palm trees—absolutely the tallest I'd seen—like telephone poles with giant pineapples on top.

A house trailer hugged the shoulder, then a doublewide, inexpensive homes of local Martians. I had to nudge the cruise control again to eighty-five. The road was still rising, with occasional canals and aqueducts—always a shock—ferrying blue water through brown basins of red mountains.

Shortly before noon I stopped in Welton (pop. 1066), rattling across a rugged cattle guard at the end of the exit. *Welcome to Welton*, a sign said. *Incorporated 1970.* The place was obviously a stepchild of the Interstates, an entire century newer than Gila Bend.

Pulling into the only gas mart, I stretched, walked about, and scrubbed more yellow butterflies from the 'Vette. One of the butterflies had survived the blow intact. I lifted it like a fingerprint from the bumper and pressed it between the pages of my C.R.S. book, a Martian souvenir. Then I fled the blistering sun for the air-conditioning inside. It was time for lunch but I was too excited to eat. The only other customer was a young mother with her child, but they soon left, admitting a blast of hot air as they pushed out the door.

The friendly attendant seemed happy for company. "When they built I-8 through here," she told me, "it pretty well killed Tacna down the road. There's only about five hundred folks living there now. But Tacna used to have three gas stations." She paused to light a cigarette. "The other day I was lookin' at my older sister's high school yearbook. All the businesses in Tacna used to take out ads. They were glad to do it, you know? Now all those businesses are dead. The main road used to go right through Tacna. Now there's I-8. Here in Welton there's nothing but farming, like those valley ranchers across the street. And that's only possible because they bring in water. I-8 gave us a way out of here. Before it was built, everybody stayed put. Now, to all the young people around here, the Interstate is a means of escape. It showed us that Arizona is connected to the rest of America. So the first chance you get, you get the hell out."

"*You're* still here," I said.

"Don't get me started."

She paused—I seem to have struck a nerve—as I excused myself to use the restroom. By the tone of her voice, she seemed ready to talk all day, and I didn't want to give her a reason to bolt from Welton. I needed to get going myself in order to reach San Diego before rush hour, another two hundred miles at least. Still, the woman's story was touching in one respect. It was difficult to believe that anyone could thrive in this desert wilderness, where the Interstate had killed one community and created another. Giving folks an excuse to leave in the process.

The temperature was ninety-seven now—bone-baking dry—and down the road *Dome Valley* had to have been named for the landscape. *Red Top Wash* likewise. Then Arizona took on an entirely new look. The entire planet resembled a king's crown. Spiky red mountains encircled a bowl-like valley, with that big blue dome for a sky. This was Central Mars, I decided, where I-8 begins to slope steeply upward, winding its way through high red cliffs, curving and twisting through challenging chicanes that were still no match for the 'Vette. Signs warned of *Falling Rocks* and *Rocks On The Road*—rocks that would tumble down miles into steep, chiseled gorges, creating giant landslides as they went. Unless they clobbered you first.

Soon I-8 rose into the sky like a roller coaster, and over the first big hump Western Mars spread out below, a deep valley with gray gravel slopes, dropping from foothills into a flat central plain. The city of Yuma was down there somewhere, home to one hundred thousand people.

Fortuna Wash came first, as dry as sand, then Mesa del Sol, an attractive suburban community behind a handsome Spanish wall, its pretty ranch homes sporting pink roofs along curving avenues. There were lesser communities too, of trailers and doublewides, and one neighborhood that looked starkly out of place—ranch homes with black-shingled roofs, side by side on streets in straight rows. A desert Levittown defying local style.

The approach to Yuma is flat and ugly—brown sand, billboards, warehouses, oil tanks, lumberyards. And a sign of the times. *Last auto truck plaza before California prices.* I kept waiting for a skyline— tall buildings against the wide sky—but there wasn't much of one at all. Yuma's too spread out to define a city center. Downtown brings only more oil tanks, three of which in succession present a mural, a standard scene of the desert landscape—nothing but mountains, sun, and sand.

Then I crossed the Colorado River—winding and blue and several hundred yards wide—and on the far side, unexpectedly, was California. *Entering Pacific Time.* To the left lay Mexico and the Baja, the Fort Yuma Indian Reservation straight ahead. Beside the highway, the All American Canal flowed like pea soup, its cement shoulders thick with weeds and tall bushes. Then I-8 barreled on for San Diego, through desolate sandhills that serve as foothills to distant mountains—mountains no longer red, but brown as chocolate.

Traffic was halting up ahead, at one of those brief stations in the desert outback. When it was my turn, I powered down the window, and a woman in sunglasses handed me a brochure. Essential California information. Besides free Cokes at the Welcome Center in Mississippi, California is the only state in America that greets you with a gift.

"Where you comin' from?" the woman asked officiously.

"Ohio," I said. "The long way."

She was not amused. "Inspection," was all she said. "Any fresh fruit?"

"Nothing," I said without thinking. But my ripening bananas were right there on the passenger seat. Fortunately, 'Vettes are so low to the ground that the inspector would have had to kneel to see my contraband. Besides, the bananas were *not quite* fresh. Fresh fruit is *ripe*, I could imagine myself telling the judge. As President Clinton might have said, it depends on what the definition of *fresh* is.

Then she waved me through and I gunned it out of there, entering California from Western Mars like an alien. Transporting illegal goods on my very first visit.

* * *

It was ninety-nine degrees now as I headed for San Diego through terrain like the Sahara Desert. Nothing but sand dunes all around, rising and falling in bright waves, before all those stunning chocolate mountains.

At twelve forty-five, spotting the first rest area, I stopped briefly to hide my bananas. I was expecting a facility as attractive as the first one in New Mexico, but it couldn't have been worse—a few open acres of sandy gravel with no services besides a few porta-potties. A circular dirt drive gave the place the look of a stock car track, the infield clumped with dry grass. At the far end of the oval a lone station wagon was tucked in a grove of wilted trees. As I got out, the heat slapped me in the face. The porta-potties, buzzing with insects, emitted a gut-wrenching stench. I popped the hatchback of the 'Vette, tucked my bananas beneath the privacy cover, and was back on the highway in less than two minutes.

The outside temperature soon reached an even hundred. Then black smoke filled the horizon to the right, rising in the form of a capital T to eventually dissipate in a vague gray haze. California was on fire. And these sand flats were ugly, with monotonous power lines adding to the loneliness.

As the horizon burned I passed a place called *Gordon Well*. Water was at a premium, as more and more canals were attesting. At Cochella Canal, blue water rippled through a deep cement trough about ten yards wide, a conduit flanked by thick rushes. An amusing sign followed—*Rock Research Center*. Well, if you wanted rocks, this was certainly the place to be, for rocks lay everywhere—iron-like boulders and basketball-sized black rocks, and red gravel and gray gravel, and chunks of granite and quartz. Take your pick (no pun intended).

Tall palms—or cacti—flew by next, in occasional stark groves, with mountains to the far left and more mountains straight ahead. Sandhills fell away in the rearview mirror, behind flat reddish hardpan spiked with tall sage. Telephone poles replaced the earlier power lines—the only constant feature—dissolving at a hazy point in the distance, ever retreating and hypnotic.

Then, in an ominous moment, a futuristic power plant loomed to the north, a desert version of Three Mile Island—eight large funnels emitting thin white smoke. The scene got me to thinking. Perhaps the canals in the vicinity—so electric blue—carried nuclear waste. But the area was too highly agricultural. Outside El Centro (pop. 31,000) green acres suddenly appeared, covering hundreds of square miles of rich brown earth. Golden hay bales were stacked by the highway in long rectangles. And there was a local sign for *Dogwood Road*. If dogwoods could thrive out here, anything could, Three Mile Island or no.

Through El Centro, I-8 rises above ticky-tacky neighborhoods—Levittowns again—beyond which a sign warns of strong winds ahead. Then the median, long an eyesore, began to sparkle with red and white wildflowers, as soothing as other large blocks of sudden color—bright green fields, dark brown earth, deep blue canals. I crossed the New River, its white bed bleached dry, its banks thick with brush. The temperature was a hundred and one now, a hundred and six miles from San Diego.

An Interstate sign put the elevation at 759. The valleys and basins were working their way back to sea level. Still, I-8 was ascending, for what I hoped would be the very last time. The molar-like mountains of Mars had been replaced by clay-like ranges with smoother contours, a kind of galactic magma molded willy-nilly, changing colors like a chameleon—gray to purple, tan to orange, red to brown—range upon range. Strange worlds without end.

An exit sign for *Desert Parks* seemed redundant. I was in the desert parks already, driving through them on I-8, with scarcely another vehicle for company. And it was time for a break. I was hungry now, despite my excitement. I needed to prepare myself one last time for San Diego.

The Desert Kitchen Café sits high on a ledge to the left of I-8. You can see it for an hour before you reach it, and from its front window you can look back across the valley you've just traversed, following I-8 from the foothills to the perimeter cliff rims. Seated at the counter, I pushed a juicy Reuben sandwich into my mouth, watching a lone truck I had passed half an hour earlier thread its way like a toy through the valley, puffing little white balls of smoke.

I was alone in the restaurant, eating the best damn Reuben I've ever had. Then I said something that betrayed me as just another Interstate outsider. Wiping my mouth with a napkin, I confessed to the stocky waitress how absolutely stunning—how utterly staggering—I found the scenery.

"Yeah," she said flatly. "But that's *all* it is."

It was two o'clock, and she said I could beat the afternoon rush in San Diego if I kept on pushing, so I wiped my mouth again and hurried out, taking the 'Vette straight up into the most challenging mountain range in all of America.

Avoid Overheating. Turn Off Air Conditioning Next 10 Miles. They had to be kidding! Turn off the AC in one-hundred-degree heat? But I didn't want to chance it. The highway was ascending through steep curves, rockslide areas, and deep red canyons. I had come this far unscathed. San Diego was just beyond the summit. So I killed the AC, opened the windows, and the 'Vette became an instant oven.

My ears crackled, then popped. Water hoses and water pipes appeared at regular intervals along the shoulder, announced by small but crucial signs. *Radiator Water.* Crossing Devil's Canyon—*Elevation 2000*—my ears popped again. Mountains of red boulders rose immediately from the roadside as I-8 twisted through chicanes posted at sixty, sharp curves I took in fifth gear at seventy-five. Then, beneath a canopy of blue, came a sign for the San Diego County line. But where was San Diego?

Ascending to the next crest, I could see behind me for light-years. *Elevation 3000.* I had left behind the earth, the moon, and Mars itself in a spectacular conclusion to my westward journey. And I was still ascending.

Blown aloft by rising winds, meager seeds had secured a dry hold in these red rock canyons, desperate vegetation clinging to a perilous existence in narrow cracks and deep crevices. Every chicane now brought a view from outer space. I was an astronaut, my Hot Wheels Corvette a red spaceship, flying over the final mountain range in America on that great relief map in my mind.

At four thousand feet my ears popped a third time. Incredibly, a luxurious home sat near the crest of the mountain, a room with a view all the way to the Big Bang. Then Crestwood Summit topped out at 4190 and I began to descend. Shutting the windows, I cranked up the AC. The short span had been hellish.

Through the La Posta Indian Reservation the panorama before me turned olive, with white granite rock faces and convoluted hills. The sun had bleached I-8 to a pale stripe, a white squiggle through the valleys ahead, valleys now green and thickly forested. The next summit was lower, 4000. I was descending into San Diego proper, up and down through Pine Valley, then across the Laguna Summit, where an empty school bus, miles ahead of me, putted blithely on its way. So there were schools up here! In a few minutes that yellow school bus would be filled with chattering children, for whom the daily Interstate ride skirted the rim of the universe.

I followed the school bus across Pine Valley Creek on a divided two-lane bridge, rocketing into the sky above a pine-filled chasm, a succession of eight mountain vistas rolling away to my left. Signs warned of crosswinds that soon arrived as advertised, knocking the 'Vette left and right as the descent continued.

Overtaking the school bus, I was again alone on the road, speeding down a six percent grade lined with stark warnings—yellow signs with black trucks on steep inclines. At three thousand feet the valley to my left was sloped with khaki fields. At two thousand, a blue lake graced a canyon to my right. At one thousand, the temperature, which had been dropping ever since the summit, leveled off at a balmy seventy-eight. Then I was at sea level, half an hour from the Pacific.

Of all the Interstate approaches in America, San Diego's destroys the notion of *garbage in*. From the very first glimpse, the San Diego suburbs are civilized. Attractive homes with a Spanish flavor sit tastefully on the hillsides, in classy neighborhoods the very essence of style. Bougainvillea and fleshy ice plant grace all slopes, with manzanita and ferny anise as well. All yards are flower gardens, filled with crepe myrtle and pink oleander and morning glories and flowering plum. Exotic palms rise everywhere, as do orange trees and lemon trees, acacia and eucalyptus. I had crossed the final mountain peak in America into San Diego—the Garden of Eden.

In paradisiacal California.

11

"AND THE BOYS?" I ASKED MARG. SHE WAS STANDING IN THE KITCHEN, AS slender and pretty as on her wedding day.

"All grown! You can use Paul's room. He's at Carnegie-Mellon now, where you did your doctorate."

"John mentioned that in his e-mail."

I was in La Jolla, in a gated community of town houses, the highway still moving beneath me at the kitchen table. I had followed I-8 to its western end, cut briefly north on I-5, and exited near the famous Torrey Pines Golf Course. The afternoon traffic, increasing from light to moderate after my descent from the mountains, had been remarkably genteel, with drivers actually signaling before changing lanes. Now I was waiting for John, a boyhood friend, to return from his dental office. I hadn't seen him or Marg—I'd been best man at their wedding—in thirty years.

"I never thought much about the Interstates," Marg said, "until you told us of your project and said you were coming out. They're always working on I-5, widening it, expanding it, because southern California is always growing."

Then John arrived and we spun into our boyhood, back to the days when I-95 was being constructed through Stratford, before John abandoned Connecticut to make his fortune in California—the very place to which my father had said the Interstates would one day take us. Now I could finally believe him.

Like Marg, John hadn't changed at all—tall, trim, and healthy.

"You've got me all excited," he said. "I've been checking some websites about the Interstates. They even tell you where the speed traps are."

"Doesn't matter where the cops are lurking," I said, "as long as you cruise at ten above the posted limit."

John laughed. "Well, you can kiss the speed limit goodbye north of here. You're gonna be crawling through L.A. It's always been sprawling, and San Diego's always been small. But the population's spreading out now. There's an enormous bottleneck where I-5 meets I-805. It's called *the merge*, and it's always jammed. You'll see!" He shook his head. "L.A.'s a different story. It's impossible *any* time, a complete standstill from six to nine every morning and three to six every afternoon. But hey—let's go see the ocean! We can talk on the way. Then we're taking you out to dinner."

"Catch you later," Marg called after us. "I've got some errands to run!"

I followed John into the attached garage where we climbed into his SUV. Unlike getting into the 'Vette—which I enter as if crawling into an oven—getting into John's SUV is like climbing into a bunk bed.

"These things are the bane of my existence," I said. "Especially when they sit on my tail."

"But they're great for the beach. You just wait."

Minutes later we were jouncing through deep ruts atop the cliffs of La Jolla. Then we parked and got out and there it was—the Pacific Ocean—wide, flat, and calm. People were strolling the beach far below us, as small as midgets, while others sailed by on hang gliders. A film crew was shooting a movie along the bluffs, patiently waiting until we ducked out of range. And that's when it really hit me. I had driven the Interstates across the continent. Ocean-to-ocean.

"When I was an undergrad at Penn," John said, "a friend of mine borrowed his parents' car and we took off. We had two weeks to kill, and we told our folks we were going to New Orleans. But with the Interstates, we got there from Philly in less than twenty-four hours. *Why not keep going?* we said. So we headed west and were in Texas the next day, with twelve more days to kill. So we headed to Mexico, where we naturally assumed they had Interstates. *That* was a big mistake."

He paused, then pointed down below. "See over there?" he said. "That's the famous Black's Beach. All those people are nude."

"Paradise," I said.

"Where was I?"

"Mexico."

"Oh yeah. Our goal was Acapulco, but the roads were horrible— nothing but potholes, worse than the bluffs back there—so bad we could hardly steer the car. We had to stop every so often to patch the tires. They simply couldn't stand the punishment. By the time we got back, that poor car was a wreck." He paused again as a hang glider slipped by, apparently part of the film being shot along the bluffs. It was after five now, the sun beginning to color the blue Pacific with a yellow sparkle. All the way down the curving coastline.

"As a kid in Connecticut," John went on, "before we moved to Stratford and I started kindergarten, we lived in Greenwich. In those days, it was a major event just to visit my grandparents in Stratford, such an adventure along Route 1. Getting there and home again took an entire day. But when they built I-95, it only took half an hour."

"And out here?"

"When I-5 was under construction through a pass north of L.A., some physician murdered his wife and dumped her into the concrete.

He was never convicted because they couldn't find the body. Then, of course, there was O. J. Simpson's famous ride."

"I watched it on TV."

"You and the rest of the nation! The rumor was that he was heading for San Diego, then on to Mexico. Seriously, though, if it weren't for the Interstates, Marg and I couldn't enjoy our vacation home on Big Bear Lake. Because of the Interstates, it's possible for us to surf here in the morning and ski Big Bear in the afternoon."

A short while later we joined Marg at the town house for a brief drive to a local Italian restaurant. The area reminded me of Georgetown in Washington, D.C., yet with a tropical San Diego charm all its own. The palm trees were remarkable—green helicopter blades, atop tall trunks the color and texture of elephants' legs. Rows and rows of palm trees spread across lawns as short and lush as golf greens. I was still in shock, never expecting to find—at the edge of that final slope beyond the mountain desert—such luxuriant foliage, elegant homes, stylish people. And such a peaceful, wide ocean.

Friday noon, as a pristine white mist obscured the Pacific, we had lunch at John and Marg's club. Gray-green waves rolled toward us in graceful swells, frothing along the beach just a few yards away. It was the first of October, I realized. Already. A new month in a new land.

"That's the first such mist of the season," Marg said. "But you saw how clear it can get yesterday. This should burn off by noon."

We were waiting for John to join us from his office. In the interim I chucked my shoes and socks and went wading—to empty a small container of well water I had brought from Ohio, refilling it with a bit of the Pacific for midwestern Christmas gifts. Marg snapped my picture in the act of pouring, and that photo later revealed something bizarre. Out of the mist three seagulls had appeared, forming a perfect triangle right above my head—*The Father, Son, and Holy Ghost,* as I would later write to John and Marg, both far better Catholics than I. I had been attributing my good fortune to Corvette karma, but in retrospect that simple photo seemed a tacit blessing. There is something miraculous about it. And sinister. Lurking to the left, near the edge of the frame, is a barely perceptible ultralight plane. And *that,* I'm now convinced, was the Devil. Who would catch up with me in Montana.

Meanwhile, it was time to plant the third flag of my grand lap—at the Tijuana border, at the very beginning of I-5. John joined me for the ceremony, and we headed off in the 'Vette before three, hoping to get down and back before the Friday rush, a round trip of not more than sixty miles. The white mist had cleared, leaving a bright eighty-degree afternoon in the Garden of Eden.

Well water from Ada, Ohio, meets the Pacific Ocean in San Diego, California.

But a red light flashed on the instrument panel. It was time to change the oil. Corvettes can go seventy-five hundred miles between oil changes— I had figured on getting the car serviced in Seattle—but the rugged run through the desert had been harder on the engine than I thought.

"No problem," John said. "I know a Chevy dealer on the outskirts of town. We can stop on the way back."

So we continued toward I-5, stopping frequently for a series of traffic lights.

"Interstate access is a problem out here," John explained, "because the population's so dense. They don't want too many people on the entrance ramps during the rush hour. It just backs up traffic. So rather than jam cars onto the freeway, we have all these stoplights. They allow access to a few cars at a time. The idea is, once you're on the freeway, you can keep moving."

It was, in effect, a pre-Interstate idle. "A perfectly practical and civilized concept," I said. "They ought to try it in Boston!"

But John was off on another idea. "I once read about the colors of the Interstate signs. They did a study to find out what would work best. First they tried black letters on white, then white on green, then white on blue, which won hands-down. So today the numbers are white and the background is blue, on a chevron-shaped sign, with a highly visible red bar that says *Interstate* across the top. So all those red-white-and-blue signs have nothing to do with Old Glory, as I had originally assumed."

"Me too!"

We were on I-5 South now, winding beneath a triple overpass, through green urban hills as classy as those on the western edge of the desert mountains. Then a small sign revealed a big concern—*Wild Flowers And Vegetation Control*—evidence of the kind of care I had seen nowhere else in America. On a hill to the right, the white buildings of the University of San Diego gleamed in the sun, the campus high enough for a view of the ocean. But the Pacific wasn't visible from the highway, just billboards for world-famous attractions—*San Diego Zoo, Sea World, Mission Bay Aquatic Playland.*

Above such billboards, skyscrapers line the San Diego waterfront. One circular building has a top like the cap of a ballpoint pen. The Hyatt Regency sits to its right. The prettiest structure, with upper floors slanted like the head of an electric shaver, is all shimmering glass and tan concrete.

"Those waterfront buildings are highly controversial," John said. "They block the ocean view of the people who live on the hillsides." He twisted in his seat, looking for something. "My favorite Interstate sign is down here somewhere. Ah—there it is! *Cruise Ships Use Airport Exit.* But I've yet to see a cruise ship on the freeway!"

Traffic was moderate to heavy as we passed beneath a viaduct, buildings rising above us on both sides of the highway, a jetliner directly overhead. We were approaching Balboa Park, a beautiful green stretch with helicopter palms. Then the first sign for the international border popped up.

John pointed to his right, to a long dark stretch of land. "That's the Island of Coronado in San Diego Bay. See that gray battleship? They often bring aircraft carriers in here. And that's the Coronado Bridge straight ahead—twenty stories high!"

Out in the blue bay, the gray battleship looked like a toy. The long bridge was equally surprising—spanning both city and bay—the highest structure across the horizon as you zip through downtown. Moments later we flew beneath it towards the Mexican border, the traffic thickening across four lanes in each direction.

"Everyone in San Diego's going to Tijuana for the weekend," John laughed. "And everyone in Tijuana's going to San Diego!"

High to the left I could see the mountains I had crossed into California. Then, three miles from the border, came a warning—*Guns Illegal In Mexico*. A minute later it was repeated with a clarification—*Guns And Ammunition Illegal In Mexico*.

The San Diego–Tijuana border crossing is the busiest in the world. A long concrete facility spans all lanes in both directions like a gigantic tollbooth, with a lighted caged walkway across the top. Vehicles were lined up at every chute. Rather than drive across the border only to turn around again, I took the last exit possible and pulled into Camino de la Plaza, an immense parking lot adjacent to the highway for people entering Mexico on foot.

As I paid the seven-dollar parking fee, the mood changed dramatically, the scene before us a teeming replay of Miami. Blacks, whites, and Latinos were abandoning their cars and streaming for the border in a chaotic holiday mood. The lot was littered and dirty, with restrooms like construction-site trailers—not much better than the porta-potties at the first California rest area on I-8. Popping the hatchback, I grabbed my hammer, star drill, and millennium banner, then followed John through the throngs of pedestrians making their way to the stairs for the border walkway.

"Three years ago," John said, "a local developer submitted plans for a pedestrian bridge to connect downtown Tijuana with a conference center in San Diego. Supporters argued it would ease traffic on the Interstate and encourage more U.S. tourists to visit Mexico. But it'll be a miracle if it ever gets built. The project needs the approval of the Border Patrol, Customs, and the state Departments of Transportation and Agriculture. Federal departments have a say too—Justice, Defense, Commerce, and the EPA. Until everybody's happy, this place will remain jammed."

We halted a few yards from the border, at the very last patch of unpaved earth—a triangle of packed dirt, ice plant, and manzanita—where I promptly hammered home my third flag. As in Miami, the ceremony was brief, and John dignified the moment with my Kodak.

That snapshot shows the border in the background. Vehicles are entering and exiting as people hurry through the wire cage above. A telephone box hangs on a pole to my right. I am kneeling by a green bush, my right hand holding out the millennium banner, my left prominently displaying three fingers. My wristwatch shows three forty-five.

Then we got out of there as quickly as we had come.

181

Here's an Interstate Item about the far-flung corners of the Interstate System, a result of my being in San Diego, the closest I've ever been to the state of Hawaii:

According to an urban legends Web site, the state of Hawaii has three Interstate highways. All are found on the island of Oahu. But how can they be *inter*states, way out there in the Pacific Ocean? Because all roads developed under the Federal-Aid Highway Act are considered as such, even though they may fall completely within the borders of a single state.

Hawaii's interstates differ from others in that they are identified with a number preceeded by the letter *H*, instead of the standard *I* (*H-1*, *H-2*, etc.). The *H* obviously stands for "Hawaii." Similarly, Alaska's interstates are designated *A-1*, *A-2*, etc. Puerto Rico's are *PRI-1*, *PRI-2*. I assume that the *I* in *PRI* stands for "Interstate." (I wonder if the people of Puerto Rico ever confuse their Interstates with Public Radio International, my frequent companion on my grand lap of America?)

At any rate, according to the *Honolulu Star-Bulletin*, Hawaii's H-3 has a curse (*hewa*) on it because of its routing through the Halawa Valley, the legendary birthplace of the Hawaiian earth mother Papa. (How a Papa can be a mama? That's another thing I wonder about.) Native protests led to a costly $10 million rerouting.

"To me, H-3 is a temporary thing," said Laulani Teale, a native woman who chose to have her baby on a hill in the Halawa Valley instead of a hospital. "The land is permanent."

She reminded me of Chief Big Eagle on his mountain in Maine. At the other end of America. Near another far-flung outpost of the Interstates.

In leaving the U.S.-Mexico border, my Interstate odyssey assumed a new direction. My little Hot Wheels Corvette was now headed due north on that great relief map in my mind, a course I would maintain to the Canadian border beyond Seattle, at the very end of I-5.

But for the moment I had a more practical concern. Changing the oil.

City-By-The-Bay Chevrolet, on the southern edge of San Diego, is enormous, the largest dealership I've ever seen. Cars of all makes and models waited in line at a dozen service bays. I didn't think we'd have any luck without an appointment—especially in the middle of the Friday-afternoon rush hour—until I approached Mike Kennedy, the service adviser. Mike's a 'Vette fan, the West Coast reincarnation of Elias Aoude. My vanity plates caught his attention and Corvette karma kicked in. Within minutes the 'Vette was up on the rack, and I joined John on a bench in the shade.

"Gotta question for you," I said, "since you're such an Interstate expert. How do you pronounce s-l-o-u-g-h."

"That's easy. It's *sluff*. Like *enough*."

"You sure?"

"Hey, I'm a periodontist. We use that term every day. It's what happens with gum disease. When your gums shed tissue, we say they *slough*."

"I passed a sign for *Gum Slough* in Texas," I said.

"No thanks," John laughed. "I've got all the business I can handle in San Diego."

Then the conversation turned serious—family, the nature of success, spirituality.

"Both Marg and I participate in discussion groups," John said. "We're trying to glean a measure of comfort from the Catholic religion."

"Ever read Thomas Merton?" I asked. "Or Teilhard de Chardin?"

"No, but I'll put them on my list."

As we spoke, I kept seeing in my mind those little green Monopoly houses by all the Interstate exits. The Interstates had put dear friends within reach, and I wanted to take advantage of every moment.

Then Mike Kennedy came over. "All set," he said. "But you've sucked in a lot of bugs that should be hosed from the radiator. We don't have time for it now. It won't be a problem—just be sure to check it out when you get back to Ohio." 183

"Love bugs," I said. "Courtesy of the Deep South."

John's eyes flashed. "I remember those things in Mississippi, when Marg and I were in Biloxi for my hitch in the Air Force. What a pain! That's what killed Jayne Mansfield, you know. Her car ran into a cloud of love bugs one night. She was decapitated in the crash. Remember?"

"The blonde love-goddess done in by love bugs," I said. The irony was fitting, but the story wasn't true. I checked it out later. On the date of the crash—June 29, 1967—the love bug season had been over for a month. Jayne Mansfield was riding with her children in a car driven by her lawyer, somewhere between Biloxi and New Orleans. It was two in the morning, and they ran into the back of a truck that was spraying for mosquitoes. The kids were unhurt—I don't know about the lawyer— and Jayne was killed, but not decapitated. She had been wearing a blonde wig that flew off in the crash.

"One great thing about San Diego," John said, "there are simply no bugs out here at all. The climate's too mild. So your windshield and radiator always stay clean."

"Reason enough to move to California!" Mike Kennedy chided. He handed me the bill. Eighty bucks. It had cost me fifty to get the oil changed before leaving Ohio. And suddenly I remembered the warning on I-8—*Last auto truck plaza before California prices.* But I didn't care. It was worth the extra thirty bucks for the drive-up service, for the conversation with John, and for the chance to meet Mike Kennedy.

Returning to La Jolla, I studied more closely something I had seen when arriving on Thursday—a magnificent alabaster structure, like Disney's Fantasyland Castle. It sits to the right of I-5, with prominent twin towers that resemble the Empire State Building. Or rocketships. Or wide minarets. One tower comes to an arrow-like point above a large golden ball. The other sports a golden angel with a trumpet.

"What *is* that thing?" I asked John.

"The Mormon Temple. Like the one outside the D.C. beltway. But the Interstate here puts you right in its lap."

The large white structure sparkled in the sun directly above us, colossal evidence of the power of faith. Right here in paradisiacal California.

Friday evening, while John grilled salmon in the back yard, Marg brought out a photo album from their wedding. They had been married in Stratford, and I had driven them from D.C. to Connecticut up I-95 when John first introduced Marg to his parents. Now the Interstates had brought us full circle.

"Remember this?" Marg asked, turning a page of the album. "It's the speech you made at our wedding!" I couldn't believe it, but there it was in my own handwriting, churning the years.

I shook my head. "Now I can finally tell you all the crazy things John and I did when we were single."

John stuck his head in from the patio, apron about his waist. "Don't you dare!"

Marg laughed. "We're heading to Big Bear Lake for the weekend. I wish you could join us."

But I was taking the weekend off myself—to visit another old friend from Stratford in Rancho Bernardo just up the road. I needed to wash the 'Vette beforehand, which I did on Saturday morning. In the fresh and perfumed San Diego air. Then I headed north on I-5 through rolling brown hills, a dry landscape brightened by flower gardens, where the streets are named for picturesque valleys, from *Carmel* to *Sorrento*.

A large blue sign beside the highway bore the image of a sleek train—*The Coaster*—part of the area's rapid transit system, an alternative to the growing congestion on the freeways. It was ten-thirty, I wasn't due at Nancy and Bill's until noon, and my Florida bananas were finally ripe enough to eat. In no hurry, I peeled one to munch on as San Diego receded in the rearview mirror.

Consulting a county map, John had advised me to take Route 56 east from I-5, to connect with I-15 below Rancho Bernardo. The exit came up quickly, the highway curving away from the Pacific into parched and rolling terrain. But after several speedy miles the shortcut ended—right in the heart of a suburban neighborhood. I turned left, then right, and was soon lost in a maze of intersecting streets. Area residents, I was told when I stopped for directions, *didn't want* a connector between I-5 and I-15. At least not through their own country backyards. So Route 56 was on hold. Indefinitely.

Three times I had to ask for directions, finally exiting the far end of the tidy subdivision on a narrow dirt road along the side of a steep dry slope. Yes, I was told again, this was Route 56. That is, Route 56 would be constructed through here *someday*. In the meantime, hot dust covered the 'Vette, canceling the morning's wash. There was no place wide enough to turn around, and nothing but dry ruts and potholes ahead. Half an hour later the road mercifully ended in the vicinity of I-15, and I scooted north into Rancho Bernardo just before noon.

Nancy and Bill's ranch home sits in a cul-de-sac at the very top of an attractive neighborhood, the slope so steep that the neighbor's roof is at the level of your feet. Unlike in San Diego, the effect of recent droughts was more palpable here, the thick vegetation underscored by parched hardscrabble. Still, the hilly landscape retained a tropical flavor, the yards adorned with palm trees, orange trees, and lemon trees.

Nancy had grown up across the street from me in Stratford. An only child, she was the little sister I never had. Bill had played trombone in our junior high band, to my trumpet and Nancy's clarinet. Their daughter Britainy, a sophomore at the local high school where Nancy teaches, greeted me at the door. I had watched her grow up in Christmas card photos—absolutely no substitute for her precocious lively self.

"My folks are out," she announced brightly. "They'll be right back!"

In the interval I was reacquainted with Nancy's mother, alert and sassy as ever, though then in her eighties. She didn't recognize me until I quizzed her about Stratford.

"Who was your paperboy?" I asked. And her watery eyes blazed.

"Why I never!"

Then Nancy and Bill arrived and we swirled in a time warp, giddy teenagers once again. "I can't believe it," Nancy squealed as she hugged me. "My big brother in Rancho Bernardo!" Short and peppery, she hadn't lost an ounce of her mother's spunk, the same spirit she had evinced as a high school cheerleader. Bill, more sedate by nature, watched us with wonder, tugging on his full beard.

Once the past stopped spinning, we returned to the present. And the Interstates.

185

Nancy jumped right in. "Brit and I like to take I-5 into San Diego, don't we, Brit? The Diamond Lane's a big help. It's just for cars with two or more people."

But Bill had only horror stories. An independent software consultant, he often drives north to L.A. "About five years ago," he said, "it was scary as hell. There were snipers firing at random through people's windshields. That's L.A. for you—a real treat, as you'll see on Monday. But we get road rage right here in Rancho Bernardo."

He pulled a stool to the kitchen counter, where Nancy was setting out plates and napkins.

"Not too long ago," he went on, "some folks were going to a wedding on I-15. One member of the wedding party passed somebody, cutting him off. So this guy catches up and fires a shotgun at him, right into the car, mangling his hand. We happened to be at the medical center one day when the guy came in for physical therapy. He was trying to regain the use of his arm, but he's lucky to be alive." Bill reached for a slice of bread. "Then there's always the noise. On certain days you can hear it more than others. As you know, we're just a few miles from I-15."

"But let me tell you something, Big Brother," Nancy said from the kitchen. "The Interstates have given me a clear metaphor for America, something I never would have realized otherwise. I came up with it on a ten-day blitz from Connecticut to California." She brought a platter of cold cuts to the counter. "It goes something like this:

"In New England the trees grow close together. They have deep roots, just like the people, people who have been there for generations. They're strong, sturdy, and rugged. But the Midwest is flat and boring, although I grant you it's easygoing. Again, it's just like its people.

"Then there's the desert climate, with all its brilliant colors and gorgeous flowers. But the roots are shallow and the people are mobile. And that's the way it is here in California, isn't it, Brit? Brit hates it out here. She wants us to move to Connecticut. Whenever we visit back home, she wants to stay there. You don't realize these things unless you experience the country all at once. Taking the Interstates across America gives you a perspective you just can't get in an airplane."

I looked to Brit but she seemed content to listen, a young Californian with Connecticut Yankee roots. A citizen of two worlds, a continent apart.

"On our honeymoon," Bill recalled, "we had this '77 Maverick without air-conditioning. The car was loaded with wedding gifts and we had our skis on a rack on the back. Remember that, Nan? We were coming cross-country from Connecticut, passing through Nebraska on I-80."

"It was the Fourth of July," Nancy remembered with a laugh, "so hot we had buckets of ice cubes on the seats in an effort to keep cool!"

"Then we see this handwritten sign for gas and hotdogs," Bill said, "and we pull off the Interstate. Just beyond the exit there were a few picnic tables. So we gas up and are sitting there with our hotdogs at one of those picnic tables, and these two old guys at the next table keep looking at us, old codgers in bib overalls and no teeth. This goes on for a while, and finally they speak up. 'Say,' one of them says, 'we was wonderin', them is *skis*, ain't they?' 'Yes, those are skis,' I told them. And he elbows the old guy next to him and says, 'See, I *told* ya!'"

We all laughed simultaneously.

"I'm sure they thought we were nuts," Bill concluded. "Talk about your local color. It's at any Interstate exit."

Just like those little green homes on the Monopoly board, I was thinking. And I was in one of those little green homes once again.

* * *

Sunday morning, while Nancy drove her mother and Brit to church, Bill lost himself in his computer while I took the 'Vette out for a local loop on the Interstates.

On Monday I would be taking I-15 north to Route 78, to connect with I-5 again just south of Oceanside. This would put me well beyond *the merge* and get me to L.A. by mid-morning, minimizing the Interstate idle that would be waiting for me there. But in order to have driven I-5 from border to border, I needed to complete the stretch between Route 56 and Oceanside. Sunday, another sky-blue day, provided the perfect opportunity.

The clockwise loop took a leisurely hour. Heading south, I picked up I-8 and retraced my original entry into San Diego. Then I headed north again on I-5 by the Mormon Temple. Beyond La Jolla, where the brown hillsides resumed, sprinklers twirled everywhere, glinting in the sun, each drop of water so crucial in the face of sustained droughts. Many area homes, perched on mountains of granite, would be in danger of mudslides. If the rain ever returned.

Near Del Mar, upscale homes lined the highway. Then I slowed for construction—*Your Tax Dollars At Work: Project Funded By Federal Highway Trust Fund Plus State Tax Dollars*. And every single penny is worth it, I was thinking, for the opportunity to cruise along the Pacific on a sunny Sunday morning.

Smooth waves lapped brown beaches to my left. Green valleys—irrigated for agriculture—opened and closed on the right. Cardiff-by-the-Sea came next, a quaint seaside village much like its namesake in Wales. When had the *Welsh* come to California? I wondered. And the

Mormons, for that matter? The Interstates, I was realizing, can raise more questions than they answer.

Encinitas followed, then Carlsbad—one of the top-ten retirement areas in the nation, according to NPR. Lovely inland bays and blue lakes cut into the hillsides. Baskets of pink flowers adorned the whitewashed homes, houses with wrought-iron balconies and flowerpot roofs. Stately palms rose everywhere. Would I never get accustomed to their exotic presence?

All too soon I was five miles from Oceanside, turning east on Route 78, reconnecting with I-15 to complete my Sunday circle.

Back in Rancho Bernardo, I set up shop in the sunny driveway to wash the dust from the 'Vette. But the lofty cul-de-sac proved a distraction. I kept looking up from my squirt bottle and paper towels to gaze about me, over adjoining rooftops and leafy trees to smooth brown hills. Neat neighborhoods with tropical backyards were tucked efficiently into the steep slopes, the bright view extending for miles.

Then Nancy returned from church, helping her mother inside. Brit disappeared into the kitchen, popping up again just as quickly—with a plate of sliced apples and peanut butter. "My favorite snack," I said. "How'd ya know?"

"'Cause it's *my* favorite too!"

It was easy to see, as we chatted, that Brit was no "Valley Girl." Attractive, vivacious, and intelligent, she was struggling with her roots, her California sensibilities challenged by her Connecticut heritage.

"I want to go to college back East," she said. "Or maybe in Europe. What do you think?"

We discussed the possibilities, and when the 'Vette was clean, Brit posed me for a photo against the sleek red hood. Then we went inside for lunch.

"Come on, Big Brother," Nancy said when we were done. "I'm going to show you where I work! We'll take my car."

Minutes later we were at the local high school, the kind you see in the movies and on TV—a large open campus with courtyards and walkways extending from building to building. Parking out back, we walked the track in the sun, talking at length. Nancy had taught high school in Stratford before moving to California, and she detailed the differences, all consistent with her experience of the American Interstates. Beautiful surfaces, shallow roots.

Every Garden of Eden, I was beginning to see, has its serpents.

By the time we returned, Bill was firing up the grill for steaks on the side patio, on a rocky ledge overlooking the neighbor's roof. I joined him with a beer.

"See that dark haze to the north?" he said. "That's a forest fire."

I studied the distant sky, a charcoal smudge in the blue canopy. Had Bill not pointed it out, I wouldn't have noticed. But somewhere far to the northeast, flames were blackening the tinder-dry hills of California.

"You can get a better view from up there." Bill pointed behind him, above the roof of the house, to a quaint gazebo-like structure he had built on the highest point of their property. "We don't use it too often. It's too difficult to get to!"

He was right. Leaving my beer on the patio, I scrambled up the loose hillside on a nearly vertical path, my thighs burning with the effort. Up close, the romantic perch was less attractive, a net of cobwebs across the open entrance. But the view was wider than from the driveway. Once again southern California lay at my feet—its fashionable homes and people, its flowered hillsides, its palm trees and fruit trees, its bright tropical air. Yet somehow it now seemed so foreign.

My place of birth lay diagonally across the continent at the other end of the Interstates, beyond that charcoal smudge in the blue sky and all the mountains I had crossed, one after another. In Rancho Bernardo, for the first time on my Interstate odyssey, I was experiencing a twinge of melancholy. I had never been farther from home— while in my own country—than I was at that moment. So I scrambled back down the hillside to the comfort of my beer.

189

* * *

A thick fog choked the area on Monday morning. Nonetheless, everyone was up and gone early but me. Nancy and Brit had school, Bill was off to L.A.—on the very route I'd be taking later—and Nancy's mother had to be dropped at an adult day-care center.

The fog worried me. I couldn't even see the roof of the house next door.

"This is one of the worst days we've had all year," Bill said from his car phone, checking in at eight-fifteen. I was alone in the kitchen, nursing my coffee until the traffic lightened. "Don't be in any hurry," he cautioned. "There's an accident here on Route 78. It's bumper to bumper and going nowhere. Be sure to stop at the rest area when you get to Oceanside. It's got a great view of the Pacific. If the fog ever lifts!"

I poured myself a second cup of coffee, then turned on the TV. It was fifty-three degrees outside, the fog dominating the local news. Recent San Diego brushfires had blackened seven thousand acres, and two firefighters had been injured in the attempt to contain them. But the news only made me impatient. I preferred to be moving, no matter how slowly, so I tossed my luggage into the 'Vette and crawled away in the fog, carefully descending the steep hillsides to I-15.

L.A. lay just a hundred miles distant. I hoped to put it behind me before noon. But I was dreading the drive as I had dreaded New York City. L.A. ranks first in the nation for time lost in traffic. The fog only compounded my fears. Having visited three old friends in the last six days, I was striking out on my own again, leaving the comfort of those little green Monopoly houses for the anonymity of sterile motels.

Embedded reflectors in the road showed the way, marking the lanes like airport runways. Pale headlights approached in an eerie procession while red taillights flared before me—again and again—as drivers touched their brakes, all cars slowing in turn. By the time I reached the accident scene on Route 78, the damaged cars had been cleared to the shoulder, the traffic limping on in the fog. I settled for a classical radio station, sputtering along in first gear, starting and stopping, then starting again. Finally, at the intersection of I-5, the Interstate idle loosened. But the fog wasn't budging at all. Without Bill's recommendation I wouldn't have stopped at Oceanside.

Wrapped in a cloud, the forested rest area sat on a crest above the ocean, more crowded than any I'd seen at that hour of the day. Well-dressed commuters were lined up in the restrooms and at the vending machines. Others hurried to their cars like ghosts. But what struck me was the soft grass. The open areas were mowed like putting greens, fed by sprinklers gently twirling in the mist.

I lingered at the information station, where the display detailed everything from California wildlife and land formations to vegetation at different elevations. The variety was impressive—gray whales, terns, bison, coyotes; sagebrush, oak, chaparral, juniper, creosote bushes, Douglas fir, and cactus-like ocotillo. Standing alone before the glass case, I studied the illustrations while gray reflections of commuters passed before me.

Then I hiked to a slight rise at the north end of the parking lot, hoping for a view of the Pacific. I looked first to the east, searching for the sun, the terrain beyond like the moors I'd walked in England, rolling stretches of scrub brush with shelves of white mist—a stark and lonely contrast with the crowded facility. The rising sun, a vague white circle now, lit the scene but dimly.

Then I turned to the ocean—so haunting in the fog—not half a mile distant. Blue-green waves rolled to shore in a continuous smooth line, breaking gently in sudsy foam along the beach. The pervasive grayness was thicker than the pure white mist I'd seen in San Diego. I had caught California in a shift of seasons, in the very act of putting on its autumn shroud. All of which only seemed to annoy the Monday-morning commuters.

"How far to L.A.?" I asked a man with a briefcase as I returned to the 'Vette.

He never looked up. "About an hour."

North of Oceanside, the I-5 median becomes a narrow strip of asphalt and gravel, with a tall wire fence between twin guardrails. Prison-like, it runs on for several miles. *Prohibito* warn the yellow signs in Spanish—a parent leading two children by the hand in silhouette. Farther north, the warning changes to *Caution*, with a silhouette of two parents leading a child. I assumed the signs were about access to the beaches, the Pacific shores a temptation for passing motorists who might dare to dart across the lanes of high-speed traffic. But as I learned later, that isn't the case. Those signs warn of illegal aliens.

I ate a banana as the traffic pressed on in the fog. Now that they were finally ripe, I had more bananas than I needed. My goal was to eat them all before reaching the Oregon line—two days and seven hundred miles distant—in case any environmental fruit-watchers were waiting for me at the border. Unlike my illegal entry, I intended to leave California with a clear conscience.

A checkpoint soon followed. *All Vehicles Stop One Mile.* But the police were waving us through without stopping. It was just as well. I would have thrown my hands in the air and surrendered my bananas instead of having to eat another one at that point. Instead, I just smiled and saluted. A legal citizen with illegal bananas.

The temperature soon climbed to sixty-one, the sun trying hard to disperse the fog. Then the median became the ugliest I'd seen in days— a double guardrail through sand and litter, although the tall wire fence was gone. Near San Clemente, upscale communities lay to the west, where the San Mateo campgrounds and the San Clemente State Park offer final public access to the Pacific. Then I-5 turned inland for San Juan Capistrano, home to the famous Spanish mission with its loyal swallows.

Brown hills replaced the moor-like land to the east, hills made green by palms, sycamores, and juniper bushes. A lone billboard touted *Tarzan's New Treehouse* at Disneyland. And as the heavy traffic pressed on for L.A.—all vehicles with headlights still shining—I couldn't help but notice the carpool lane. It stood absolutely vacant.

And I couldn't believe the next sign: *Carpool Lane Violation. Minimum Fine $271.* But why such an odd figure? Surely the beautiful people of California could afford the extra dollar. What they couldn't afford was sharing their morning with another commuter. Fog or no.

By Mission Viejo the temperature reached sixty-four, the sky lightening considerably, the brown-topped hills a feast of attractive modern homes. But through Irvine, modern industries flanked the highway, the median a long cement barrier. The road surface deteriorated with the surroundings, just bumpy enough to be annoying. Finally, forty miles from Los Angeles, the fog began to lift and the thick traffic clipped along at seventy-five, six lanes in each direction. The only constant was the carpool lane—still vacant except for an occasional car or bus.

One of the strangest sights on the Interstates lay in wait up ahead—three or four enormous figures off to the right, each as large as the statue of Lenin I'd once seen in Leningrad. Their broad backs to the highway, the figures stare across the fields into distant eastern valleys. All are olive-skinned and painted in bright colors. These were obviously migrant workers, their silent tableau a somber tribute to the laborers whose backbreaking work was responsible for much of California's wealth.

I remembered the mural at the coffee shop in Maine—the rustic family of potato farmers—but this scene represented a larger family, one historically much maligned. Still, there was an unsettling air of propaganda about it, like the scenes on factory walls in the former Soviet Union, smiling young workers with their hammers and sickles. Such propaganda seemed out of place here. It was unexpected, catching me off guard, reducing me once again to an Interstate outsider.

Twenty-five miles from L.A. the fog suddenly thickened through a construction area. The lanes dwindled to three and the posted speed dropped to fifty-five, but the traffic plowed right ahead at seventy, all vehicles tailgating, bouncing wildly, pressing for advantage. An attractive pink wall accompanied the highway here, curving like a bay window between segmented columns. But the median was ugly—a battered double guardrail topped by a rusty wire fence—herald to the *garbage in* at the L.A. County line.

Suddenly the sky turned brown, the fog turned to smog, and a gritty haze hung above a barrage of billboards. Just as suddenly, a young Latino cut me off in a rattletrap Plymouth, weaving from lane to lane, continuing his caper all the way to the L.A. city limits, where—despite his reckless effort—he remained just two cars ahead. I'd never seen such dangerous driving in all the years I've had a license. But no one else on the highway seemed to notice. Or care.

And I'd never seen such smog. Even the palm trees looked sick—like smokers with lung cancer. Mercifully, I-5 was skirting L.A. to the east, on a stretch known as the Golden State Freeway. But there is nothing golden about the Golden State Freeway. And it isn't a freeway, but a *free-for-all*—a race for survival, a demolition derby—no signaling, no courtesy, no quarter. Beneath a brown and claustrophobic sky. There is only one word to describe it. *MERDE.*

Then the traffic skidded to a halt for an Interstate idle like the one I'd endured in Boston. There was nothing to do but console myself with another banana. Anxiety food. But that banana, plus the certain knowledge that this would be last time I'd ever come near Los Angeles, gave me courage—to ignore the brown sky and the flat terrain and the jam of cars and trucks. I found another classical station on the radio, then laughed at a sign on the shoulder. *L.A. Zoo.* Right here on I-5.

The minutes ticked away, and by ten-thirty I seemed condemned to a slow death in Los Angeles—crawling in first gear, clutch in, clutch out. Then the traffic picked up in fits and starts. Finally, just as all lanes were moving again at seventy, a large brown plastic garbage can came rolling across the highway, scrambling traffic in all directions. I punched the accelerator and roared clear, but the car behind me struck the can squarely, sending it off the windshield of a vehicle in the far left lane, and all traffic screeched to a halt in my rearview mirror, horns blaring.

Out of danger, my heart thumping, I began to wonder where that garbage can had come from, if someone had purposely launched it from the shoulder. Given what I'd seen of L.A., it seemed entirely possible. That can, I decided, *is* Los Angeles—large, brown, plastic, garbage. All the ensuing signs for *Hollywood* couldn't change my opinion. There's no glamour whatsoever in Los Angeles. If San Diego is heaven, L.A. is hell.

Another ironic symbol immediately followed, an appropriate parting shot. Highway walls were up for "adoption" along I-5, in the way that municipalities across America offer the care and maintenance of local roads to civic groups. Miles of walls awaited adoption—to be cleaned of graffiti and litter along their urban lengths. A conspicuous sign proudly announced the program. *Adopt-A-Wall.* Nearby stood a wall much in need of adoption, with a smaller sign saying *This Wall Adopted By—*.

But the space was blank. An orphaned wall. No takers.

* * *

Relief lay ahead—beyond Burbank in the San Fernando Valley, where khaki hills sloped to olive valleys and I-5 began its ascent from sea level, leaving civilization behind.

Suddenly the terrain was mountainous again, with sandy deserts and sparsely populated canyons, the wind gusting intermittently, shoving the 'Vette from side to side. But the wind served a much better purpose—helping to keep the brown sky of Los Angeles at bay behind me. By the time I reached Santa Clarita, so aptly named, it had succeeded. Blue skies prevailed once again.

Then the traffic thinned dramatically, and I stopped at a gas station to celebrate my escape from L.A. It was after eleven. There was only one other customer at the pumps, a thin braless hippie in jeans and a T-shirt, with long stringy hair. Here was a California stereotype from decades ago, reminiscent of the flower children of the '6os.

"What's it like up ahead?" I asked.

"Incredibly gorgeous!" she replied. "Grape territory—our wonderful wine industry! But beyond the mountains it's basically a truck route. And I better warn ya, man. The road's not the best."

I thanked her and went inside to the men's room, then bought a roll of mints at the front counter—from a cashier as olive as the terrain, a modern descendant of the workers in that propagandistic roadside tableau.

"*Seexty-five cents,*" was all he said.

On my way again, I passed a truckload of red tomatoes, imagining them being picked by hand. Then came a warning I'd seen entering California—*Avoid Overheating. Turn Off Air-Conditioning. Next 6 Miles.* So we were going up again—up and up into the cool of the morning, into the tan and purple mountains of the Angeles National Forest, where the dry brown grass looked as brittle as straw. Roadside watering stations marked the ascent, the pipes and faucets an attempt to keep all radiators functioning.

Elevation 2000. And the hippie was right—there were only trucks ahead, laboring up the steep grade in the right-hand lane. I flew right by them, watching them drop one by one from my rearview mirror. The temperature had risen to eighty, but I left the air-conditioning on, the road not as rugged as on my California entry, although the views were much the same—deep valleys, brown mountains, granite peaks, sandy mounds, all dotted with parsley-like vegetation. Only the power lines detracted, strung on stark metal towers, traversing high slopes and bald crests for miles.

Tan and sandy at first glance, the farthest mountains turned to granite up close, their rugged faces vertically scarred, like ski slopes in the sun. As the highway twisted through them, the asphalt median narrowed to a double guardrail. Pyramid Lake lay far below and to the left, its flat blue water reflecting a blue sky, the lovely light blue of architectural drawings. *Hungry Valley* followed—a perfect name. In centuries past, it would have been easy to go hungry up here. And it would take more than a few bananas to survive the present.

Suddenly the surrounding territory resembled the setting for *M*A*S*H*. Any minute I expected helicopters to swoop over the brown hills, their blades raising clouds of dust from the sandy green stubble. Then the asphalt median ended, replaced by a stretch of knee-high scrub. I was at four thousand feet and still climbing—straight up—a convoy of trucks struggling to my right. Then, quite incredibly, the entire surrounding valley turned *golden*.

California's nickname is *the Golden State*, a label I'd mistakenly associated with the Gold Rush. But it is the *hills* of California that are golden. The most distant hills now seemed covered with gold foil. Through Tejon Pass (*Elevation 4144*) the colors multiplied—golden hills, green pines, turquoise lake, blue sky—all sharp and clear in brilliant sunshine. And the idyllometer, comatose through L.A., shot to one hundred.

Then I-5 started to descend. At three thousand feet, runaway truck lanes began. My ears crackled, and I blinked in disbelief—another stunning valley lay beyond, a flat stretch between steep golden slopes, green rectangles flanking the highway for miles ahead, running from the shoulder to the very edge of golden foothills. A sign for a place called *Grapevine* confirmed the local crop.

But beyond the bright air of Tejon Pass, as I-5 continued its descent, a grainy haze appeared over the distant valley, a gritty curtain as heavy as chain mail. Headlights shone from all on-coming vehicles, my own somersaulting from the hood in self-defense. The clear skies, it was easy to see, were gone for good.

Nonetheless, the posted speed increased to seventy and the traffic adjusted at eighty. In the smoky grayness I zipped by trucks with bales of hay. One carried what looked like large onions, the membranous skins flying about like crazed moths. Among the local vineyards came occasional lemon groves and orange groves—so neat and colorful—but the fields of grapes, cultivated in sandy terrain, had a ragged edge to them, not as pretty or pastoral as the rolling vineyards of upstate New York. I had entered the southern end of the San Joaquin Valley, which drains the San Joaquin River to the north, and pervasive smog began to choke the idyllometer.

South of Bakersfield, where I-5 veers northwest for Sacramento, sudden warnings offered a clue to the hazy air: *Severe Dust Area Next 40 Miles*. Was blowing dust the source of the granular sky? Whatever the reason, that chain-mail curtain was trapped between the mountains. With nowhere to go. The entire length of the valley.

I crossed the California Aqueduct—*Nile of the San Joaquin Valley*—a life-giving waterway that follows I-5 for several hundred miles. Traffic was light, mostly trucks, but the basin was all business, thrumming on a Monday. Farmhouses, barns, and outbuildings spread away in all directions, and everywhere farmhands were at work—hoeing, shoveling, gesticulating. All were olive-skinned, dressed in jeans, checkered shirts, and straw cowboy hats, laboring in the very valleys toward which those giant figures near Los Angeles had been staring. Irrigation systems twirled and sprayed. Pickup trucks sped along local roads adjacent to the Interstate. Farm equipment moved slowly in the fields—tractors, tillers, harvesters.

Essential to the agricultural effort, overhanging power lines seemed to lower the sky, their slight droop, from pole to pole, growing more tedious with every passing mile. Incredibly, the smoky haze was thickening—I could no longer see the surrounding mountains—just a steamy, polluted smog in the central bowl.

And I began to resent I-5. The practical activity of it, the mechanical ugliness of it. I had been spoiled, I realized, by I-8. I wanted my Interstates uncluttered, pristine.

And the idyllometer, in total agreement, turned itself off.

12

THERE WERE MANY TIMES WHEN I SERIOUSLY DOUBTED I WOULD EVER GET TO tour the country on the Interstates. As with all ambitious undertakings, doubts crept in. The idea was too crazy. I was asking too much.

In one such dark moment I turned for advice to the *I Ching*, an ancient book of Oriental wisdom that I have consulted for more than three decades on behalf of family and friends. The question was simple—what did the *I Ching* think of me lapping America?

Tossing the three sacred coins, I determined the hexagram, *Kuan*. It means "contemplation"—both the act itself and in terms of setting an example. The attendant image is a tower characteristic of ancient China, one commanding a view of the country. Exactly my goal in lapping America. The hexagram is linked with the eighth month of the Chinese calendar, September to October. Exactly the time I had reserved for my sabbatical travel.

The *Judgment* for *Kuan* reads as follows: *The ablution has been made. But not yet the offering.* An ablution is any ritual of preparation—twenty years' worth, in my case. The offering, then, would be the journey itself, my Interstate odyssey.

Every hexagram has an *Image* as well. For *Kuan*: *The wind blows over the earth. Thus the king of old visited the regions of the world, contemplated the people, and gave them instruction.* Again, the *I Ching* was right on target. I wished to be "king of the road," to visit all regions of America, with hopes that my Interstate experience might prove instructive.

As I read further, the *I Ching* warned of naive egotism, a quality that must be defeated to render true objectivity—a bull's-eye once more. Finally, the book warned of a future retreat, preparing oneself to *leave the field.* To end the journey and return to work, that is. Always a difficult task.

Greatly encouraged, I raised one more question. What did the *I Ching* think of me lapping America *in a Corvette?*

* * *

The farther I went, the more I-5 deteriorated. Beaten hard by constant truck traffic, the surface rated a C+ at best. The median had given way to sand and scruff.

For relief, I tuned in NPR just in time for the news. Students were back at school in Tarboro, North Carolina, after three weeks off due to flooding. And suddenly, in this drought-ridden terrain, all that water on the East Coast seemed impossible. Yet I had driven through it, like Noah in a red ark. It felt like years ago, until a puzzling billboard reconnected me with the present. *How Did The Golden State Get Its Name? It's The Cheese!* Could I believe that? What about the golden hills? Was this just a commercial?

At twelve-thirty, two hundred and thirty miles from Rancho Bernardo, I stopped at the Buttonwillow Rest Area, intrigued by the name. The temperature had risen to eighty-four. A sign at the entrance warned of a thousand dollar fine for littering—a stiff penalty—but no one was paying attention. Paper cups, plates, and napkins blew about the parking lot, swirling in circles in the wind. Chewing gum wrappers glistened in the gutter and pop cans lay in the grass—grass like putting greens gone to seed, weedy and ugly, despite its short length. The few trees had ragged leaves, but at least the pavilions offered some comfort, their flat brown roofs slatted for shade above tan brick walls. Beyond them lay vast orchards, each slender tree trunk wrapped in white beneath a bushy green top.

The facility was deserted, except for a middle-aged man outside the men's room who seemed to sense my annoyance.

"I-5 is not meant to be scenic," he said. "It's strictly utilitarian. The truck lanes get pounded pretty bad. Then again, it's a major truck route. But it's well policed and most people observe the speed limit. This is the San Joaquin Valley. The valleys of California are named for the rivers that drain them. You'll hit the Sacramento Valley above Stockton. The scenery changes up there—more farmland, lots of cotton."

I pointed to the orchards beyond the pavilions. "Almond trees," he said, "wrapped for protection from the deer and bugs. They used to just paint them white, but now they wrap them. It helps keep in the moisture. In the desert, moisture is the key."

"What's a buttonwillow?" I asked.

"I have no idea."

I was soon back on the road, watching a bright yellow biplane—the kind you see in air shows—maneuvering across the fields, looping and turning, then circling back. It might have been a crop duster, but the pilot just seemed to be having fun. Miles later another yellow biplane appeared—maybe the same one—coming in low beside the highway as if for a landing, then skirting the ground and taking off again.

Or it could have been the police. Leaving the rest area I had seen a simple sign. *Patrolled By Air.* For the moment, that biplane was the only excitement in the entire San Joaquin Valley. But I couldn't follow its flight for long. An enormous brown dust cloud was billowing towards me out of the distance.

Something was up there, about a mile ahead, raising a plume of dust like an old-time stagecoach. Then the cloud was upon me and I couldn't believe what I saw. A Highway Department dump truck was racing through the median, endangering traffic with its rolling brown cloud, when all it had to do was use the paved shoulder. When the air cleared, I found myself behind a white pickup truck, passing a long line of tractor-trailers. Then the pickup refused to return to the slow lane, so I blew by it on the right. The driver, in straw hat and sunglasses, was playing mind games. But I had had enough of such games in the South.

As if by magic, the very thought of the South brought cotton fields—acres and acres on the right—knee-high brown plants topped by white puffballs. There were more almond groves too, in rows planted aslant of the highway, the pattern immediately hypnotic. I averted my eyes, but there was little else of interest.

Traffic continued light, fast, and spread out. Then, a hundred yards ahead, a car suddenly veered into the median, raising a shower of sand as it slid to a stop. It had been passing a farm truck, but the other vehicle hadn't swerved. As I gained on the truck I could see the problem. Long black nylon ropes were snapping wildly behind it, cracking like horsewhips, having worked loose from the load. The other car had been forced into the median in self-defense. But the 'Vette was too low to be in danger. I hit my horn as I sped by, and the truck driver, his face hidden by the brim of a ball cap, ignored me. More Interstate mind games.

Two hundred eighty miles from Rancho Bernardo, the Kettleman Hills brought a welcome change. I-5 began to rise through golden sandhills, with furrowed brown acres and sprouting green fields spreading away into gentle valleys. Still, power lines dogged the way. A sign for *Pleasant Valley* got me wondering. Was this area the source of that song from an earlier era—*another Pleasant Valley Sunday?* A sign for *Pleasant Valley State Prison* canceled the association.

Occasional cotton fields appeared in the golden hills now. Then I-5 passed the prison, where dozens of inmates were hoeing in long dark furrows, attending to a stubby green crop. Hence the expression *a long row to hoe*, for which too many people say *road*. But *I* was the one with the long road ahead. The prisoners, watched by armed guards in sunglasses, had only short winding furrows. With nothing but scruffy sagebrush beyond their Pleasant Valley farm.

I passed the onion truck again—it had slipped ahead of me when I stopped at the rest area—its onionskins still flying about madly. Another truck bore a Napa Valley logo, no doubt from the vineyards. Still another was hauling what looked like twin coal cars in tandem,

199

each filled to the brim with hard green tomatoes. It was one forty-five, and the temperature had dropped to eighty—through hills the color of wheat straw, hills suddenly rife with a strong gaseous odor.

The sweet stench hit long before I saw the cattle, thousands and thousands just off the shoulder of the highway, crowded into hundreds of muddy acres entirely devoid of grass, muddy ground on which the cattle stood dumbly, their heads bent low. It was the kind of scene I had expected in Texas, not in a California agricultural range. The pungent scent lingered in the 'Vette long after the cattle had disappeared, gradually replaced by the oily stink of chemical fertilizer.

A sign for the *Apricot Tree Family Restaurant* got me thinking about lunch. It brought another thought too—I might have been mistaking apricot groves for almond. The golden color certainly suited the hills. Apricot or almond, it didn't matter—my stomach won the debate, and I exited for a quick hamburger at a local restaurant.

It was a poor decision. Fly-ridden, with annoyingly slow service, the place was filled with Hispanic migrant workers in cowboy hats, blue jeans, and drooping mustaches. There were olive-skinned women with them, infants and children in tow. I had walked into a modern version of *The Grapes of Wrath*, but all I wanted was a quick hamburger. What I got was a slow one. Then I was back on the road.

Were it not for the constant haze, the surrounding territory could have been pretty. But the haze was endemic, wrinkling the air above the channeled blue water that followed the highway to the right, apricot hills to the left. There were signs now for the California Highway Patrol, an outfit made famous by the toothy smile of Eric Estrada on TV's *CHiPs*. The man at the rest area had said that I-5 was well policed, but I had seen only one officer so far, on the shoulder with a car he'd pulled over. The police were definitely about when needed. Maybe working in tandem with those playful yellow biplanes.

* * *

Here's an Interstate Item about California, where I-5 runs for almost eight hundred miles from the Mexican border to the Oregon border, and where the Interstate highways are the busiest, most congested— yet still the safest—in the nation:

According to *Transportation California*, California's highways save 573 lives per year. However, a recent study confirmed that California's highways have a critical need for maintenance. Nearly half of the state's roads are rated mediocre or poor; roads rated good and fair provide a higher degree of safety.

Funding is a problem. Bert Sandman, chairman of Transportation California, feels that the state has done a good job with the transportation dollars available in terms of maintaining roads that are heavily traveled at every hour of the day. He wants the federal government to do its share in meeting the transportation needs of the 21st century, which at the present time means a commitment to safety, maintenance, and mobility.

California's recent budget woes couldn't come at a worse time for its Interstate highways. Sandman wants Congress to ease California's economic difficulties by living up to its original commitment.

The California Highway Patrol operates on all of the state's Interstates. The CHP's web site contains answers to the following Frequently Asked Questions:

Q: Is it illegal to use my cellular telephone while I'm driving?
A: No. But use your common sense.
Q: Can I put after-market tinting on the windows of my vehicle?
A: Legislation signed into law effective January 1, 1999, exempts specified clear, colorless, and transparent material that is installed, affixed, or applied to the front driver and passenger side windows for the specific purpose of reducing ultraviolet rays.
Q: I'm pregnant. The HOV lane requires two persons in a vehicle. Now that I'm eating for two, can I use this lane?
A: California law requires two (or, if posted, three) separate individuals occupying seats in a vehicle. Until your "passenger" is capable of riding in his or her own seat, he or she does not count.
Q: How can I find out if it's OK to bring a particular kind of plant or animal into California?
A: This information is available at the web site of the California Department of Food and Agriculture.
Q: I have heard that some gangs are initiating new members by driving with their headlights off and when people flash their lights at them, they must shoot the drivers of the cars who do this. Is this true?
A: The California Highway Patrol has received many inquiries from people who have seen this message on the Internet. The simple answer is, it is not true. To our knowledge, nothing of this sort has taken place. Of course, as a law enforcement agency we would caution people not to do anything in their vehicles that could anger or upset other drivers.

Author's note: In lapping America the only thing I was doing to anger other drivers was lapping America. When they had to work.

* * *

More cattle followed—widespread this time—grazing beneath the hazy gray sky.

All vehicles were still running with headlights burning, dull yellow disks in the dim afternoon light. A sign for *Crows Landing* started me thinking again. I couldn't remember the last time I'd seen a bird, let alone a crow. Maybe, like the swallows of Capistrano, the birds were all gathered at Crows Landing,

I tried the radio, then switched it off, unused to Spanish voices and stations with call letters beginning with *K*. The highway was ascending again, with golden vistas to the left. The blue water of cement canals bisected green fields to the right. The V-shaped canals had gravel shoulders, creating a precise desert architecture. *Roll Up Windows*, a lighted scoreboard sign warned. My nose caught the reason. More chemical fertilizer.

By four o'clock the temperature had dropped to seventy-eight, and soon the golden mountains—still shrouded in haze—began to drop away in the rearview mirror. To the left and right the terrain was entirely flat, the traffic increasing before Stockton (pop. 211,000), my day's destination.

A stretch of construction worsened Stockton's *garbage in*—orange cones, blowing dust, shifting lanes, stop and go. The rush hour was just beginning, creating an Interstate idle, and I slowed to a halt just a few miles from my exit.

Resigned, I tried the radio again, catching a brief note of interest on NPR—Francis C. Turner, chosen by Dwight D. Eisenhower to be the chief engineer of the Interstate System, had died in North Carolina at the age of ninety.

If he could only see me now.

* * *

I reached Motel Find-Me-Not, with the usual difficulty, at four-thirty, the temperature down to seventy-five. I was surprised to see palm trees again, rising like giant feather dusters in clumps here and there. They had been conspicuously absent through the San Joaquin Valley.

Dust swirled in the afternoon air. It was time to wash the 'Vette again. I had a free evening in which to do it, yet I felt strangely sullen. And when I checked in at the desk I realized why. The calendar on the wall showed October 4. Tomorrow—Tuesday the 5th—was the anniversary of the death of my father, whose casual dinnertime remark in the days of my youth had sparked my interest in the Interstate System. Given the coincidence of the death of Francis C. Turner, the realization unsettled me.

I washed the 'Vette, had only bananas for supper, and turned in early. But I slept poorly, and by four-thirty Tuesday morning I was out walking—beneath a moon like the Cheshire Cat's smile. It was sixty degrees and I had to put on long pants. Out of habit, I counted the cars and trucks rolling by on I-5. The ratio was fifty–fifty, same as in Buffalo.

A local restaurant opened at six and I was waiting at the door, the waitress the first non-Hispanic I had seen in days. I asked her about the morning rush hour in Sacramento, forty miles north.

"It's your typical rush hour," she said with a flat drawl. "It can be slow between seven and nine. If there's an accident, of course, it'll be at a standstill."

"How big is Sacramento?"

"Several hundred thousand. My folks live there. You'll like it!"

I left Stockton at six-thirty in total darkness, expecting delays in Sacramento. The traffic was moderate, moving at eighty across three lanes. Far to the east, a pink shelf lined the inky horizon, a frosting of bright stars higher up. Then the three lanes became two, only to widen to three again beyond the Sacramento County line.

Swinging northwest, I-5 curved through the darkness toward Sacramento in a long sweeping line, the oncoming headlights strung before me like a pearl necklace. From what I could tell, there was no *garbage in*. Today would take me out of California to Roseburg, Oregon. But my thoughts were of my father. I tried to imagine him in the seat beside me. He had bought himself a Cadillac when he retired, which had dared me to dream of owning a Corvette. Now my dream had come true. But the 'Vette's passenger seat was dark and empty.

Having neglected to refuel the night before, I stopped for gas just short of Sacramento. Garish neon lights lit the isolated asphalt strip. The price of premium shocked me—a dollar eighty-nine nine—the most I would pay on my entire grand lap. I had based my budget on an average of a dollar-fifty per gallon. But I had been duly warned about *California prices*. All I could do was grit my teeth as the digits rolled higher and higher before my eyes. Then I was back in the flow of traffic—moderate to heavy across four lanes now—the sky beginning to lighten in the east at ten to seven.

The Sacramento skyline is sedate and conservative—mostly rectangular, with nothing outstanding. One building curves at the top like an electric shaver, a popular urban style. Above the silhouette of the cityscape, purple and gray clouds streaked the sky like jet trails. I darted beneath an underpass, then several more. Some sort of bridge loomed in the darkness, its twin pillars like huge goalposts. Old buildings sat on the left, glassy new ones to the right, one with a pagoda-like fly-roof. Then came a sign for—of all things—a *marina*. Boats were the last thing I expected to find north of the California desert. But the Sacramento River follows I-5 to the west, intersecting with the

American River just north of downtown, creating an attractive urban riverfront and a playground for watercraft.

Sacramento has no *garbage out*, but the terrain is flat and bland. On the outskirts I-5 continues due north, intersected by I-8, which heads west to San Francisco and east to Reno. A bushy median killed the glare of morning headlights. Brand-new blacktop made the ride a smooth treat.

As the sky grew lighter I caught a sign for Redding, California, posted in both miles and kilometers (155, 250), the first indication of the metric system. That could mean only one thing. Canada. Farther along, a flock of birds dotted the pink sky—Canada geese, I hoped, not crows from Crows Landing. Then I-5 crossed the Sacramento River on high twin bridges, the tree-lined shores half a mile apart. From the raised vantage point I could see a dark mountain ridge crossing the horizon miles ahead. But a kind of Louisiana marshland followed, the highway supported by *pi*-shaped cement pylons. The temperature had dropped to fifty-four, the rush hour over. Sacramento had been a breeze. And a psychological boost.

The road began to roll toward golden mountains, the sun climbing in a yellow circle behind me. A community of doublewide trailers marked the end of surburbia. Beyond Yolo (pop. 650), mountains rose to the left, cutting across the horizon farther on. But the sky was too hazy for domed vistas. Nor was the countryside scenic, just a continuation of yesterday's utilitarian barns, billboards, and telephone poles, through a wide agricultural plain. In one bleak stretch thousands of charred acres stood out starkly, evidence of wildfires in the lingering drought. But there were pretty moments too—white mists rising above fields that sloped to golden foothills, granite-faced mountains laced with green higher up. Still, along the Interstate north of Sacramento, picturesque farmland competes with the trappings of commerce.

Orchards and sycamore forests soon gave the plain of the valley a new look. Bales of hay were stacked like bricks along brown fields. Near Arbuckle (pop. 1912), small neighborhoods of ranch homes lined the highway. I had to turn on the heater. The temperature had dropped to fifty.

Shortly before eight I pulled into a small rest area to put on a sweatshirt, as the temperature dipped into the forties. For all my careful planning, I suddenly realized what I had neglected to pack—a ski hat and gloves. The way things were going, I might need them before the day was out, let alone through the Pacific Northwest. I couldn't imagine the hundred-degree heat of Arizona now. But the brisk air felt good as I hurried along the sidewalk, stopping at a glass case with a lengthy display about rice—a product you don't associate with California. Maybe that was rice I had been seeing all along.

I ducked into the men's room, then headed back to the 'Vette. Only three cars sat in the parking lot, plus a tractor-trailer, but I didn't feel like speaking to anyone. My mind was on my father. He would have loved it here, especially a little farther along the highway, by a small white farmhouse, where lovely horses grazed in a golden swale as the dew glistened in the morning light—a pinto, several black horses, and a reddish one, pawing the ground like thoroughbreds. Dad had hoped to retire to such a place, but his own ill health—combined with that of my mother—had prevented it.

Through the Sacramento Valley, I-5 is in better shape than in the San Joaquin. There are cattle ranches too, but smaller than before.

Slowing for a construction area, I spotted a crumpled bird on the shoulder, brilliantly feathered, with a roundish head—a hunting bird two feet in length—its talons limp but fierce in death. I tried to imagine that bird soaring among the geese I'd seen earlier, or eye-balling the pilot of those yellow biplanes. A hedge-like stand of ole-ander spliced the median here, flowered with red, white, and pink blooms, an appropriate funeral spray for that magnificent bird.

A billboard offered free olive tasting. No doubt I had been seeing olive fields along the way, too—olives, rice, apricots, grapes—exotic agriculture for a transplanted Yankee used to Midwestern soybeans and corn.

Beyond Rice Creek sheep grazed on golden hills. Gray in color, they were mixed with varieties of brown and black I'd never seen before. A new variety of cattle appeared as well—with shaggy skin, hanging wat-tles, and short horns—not quite buffalo. Testing the radio, I found only one Spanish station among the first ten on the band. My Interstate ver-sion of *The Grapes of Wrath* was drawing to a close.

I passed a sign for Elder Creek. Maybe the smallish trees I had been seeing were elders—with dark clusters of red and purple berries. Another sign signaled an impending change. *For Sale. One and One-Half Miles of Freeway Frontage.* Prime land for Motel Find-Me-Not. Another Frontage Road community in the making.

Soon I-5 recrossed the Sacramento River, its tree-lined shores wider than before, but the water was more shallow, with a long gravelly sandbar right down the middle. The highway was tree-lined now too, by noble oaks near the Noble Oak Estates. Then came Red Bluff, with a few lovely homes perched on a high red cliff. *Buckle Up*, a sign warned. *Speed Enforced By Aircraft.* I scanned the sky. The grainy haze was lessening, but there were no yellow biplanes above the tree line. Just golden hills patched with green oak. It was nine o'clock. Time for another break.

Down off the side of the highway, the rest area was rustic this time, its sidewalks winding through the shade of sturdy pin oaks—no grass anywhere, just bare dirt and acorns. Half a dozen cars were scattered the length of the narrow lot. I parked at the far end to ensure a longer walk, and as I headed back to the facility a bare-chested young man stopped me short. He reminded me of the *hombres* I had seen with the Border Patrol in Arizona.

Olive-skinned, with long scraggly black hair, he was standing beside the open door of a battered vehicle at the center of the parking lot. He seemed to be getting dressed, and as I came down the sidewalk, something flashed in his hand. It was a knife—the size and shape of a Bowie knife—the sun reflecting dully off the blade as he tucked it into a leather sheath in his jeans. He was unaware of my approach, and at the sight of the knife I turned up an adjacent sidewalk, away from the lot, watching him out of the corner of my eye. He was putting on a long-sleeved checkered shirt now, buttoning it up without tucking it in, keeping the weapon concealed.

I hurried to the men's room, then doubled back to the 'Vette. As I had learned elsewhere, there are certain people you don't want to ask about the Interstates.

* * *

Beyond that rest area, the landscape along I-5 began to change. There was an absence of peripheral valley views. The golden hills were still there, rolling and mound-like and flecked with green, but they swallowed the road, obscuring long vistas. Grass grew like wild wheat along the shoulder, brightening in the early sun and diminishing haze.

I passed a placed called *Cottonwood* (pop. 1747), named for the same tall trees that grow in Ohio. Cattle grazed on the hillsides again—black and brown-and-white. Then I rolled on towards Redding, through small communities of nothing classier than doublewide trailers. The lank median grass lay matted in clumps.

And then I saw it up ahead, something I hadn't seen since Maine, another sure sign of the North—a long flatbed tractor-trailer hauling thick logs, the pile chained in a tight high triangle. The sawed ends, each bigger than a serving platter, looked like roast beef, and I caught their scent, a delicious cedar whiff, as the 'Vette sped by.

South of Redding the highway descends, and the terrain—spiked with so many groves of oak and cottonwood—seems totally forested from a distance. The palm trees had yielded to pines in thick clusters, their color more blue than green. I crossed the Sacramento River yet again, its shallow water now choppy and whitecapped. The first Interstate sign for Oregon lay beyond—*Portland 430*. But Redding came first (pop. 66,462), beyond which I seemed to be driving toward the dead end of a forested horseshoe. Rolling hills and rugged ridges paralleled the highway, converging at a point in the distance where the road disappeared in green fir—a pretty preview of the Pacific Northwest on that great relief map in my mind.

But I was getting ahead of myself. California is as long as Texas is wide. Oregon was still a hundred miles distant—beyond the Shasta National Forest and the Cascade Range, where the traffic dwindled and brand-new blacktop smoothed the way. Then the landscape turned green and the golden hills were gone for good as bright white clouds pushed in with a high-pressure system, clearing out what was left of the haze. It was sixty degrees at nine thirty, the sky suddenly powder blue.

Soon I-5 began to rise towards a notch in the distant mountains, straight up between vertical outcroppings, into the Shasta Lake National Recreation Area, where a sign for *Dunsmuir* (pop. 2129) seemed familiar. British-born John Muir, who had become an American citizen and noted naturalist, had devoted much of his career to promoting the creation of national parks. *Dunsmuir* is Scottish— another California influence to add to the Welsh and Hispanic—and the Scottish Highlands themselves seemed to lay before me.

The idyllometer came to life, rising steadily, and soon I saw why. Lake Shasta suddenly spread out below the highway, the deepest blue I've ever seen—dark blue water that meanders like an inkblot, bound by a shoreline of bright red earth. Steep forests slope to the very edge of this red band, creating distinct zones of color—green, red, blue—as the lake wanders for miles in and out of finger-like fjords. Then the highway began to twist on itself, again and again, working its way higher through a series of tricky chicanes. I found a classical station on the radio—all Spanish programs were gone now—and the idyllometer hit one hundred.

The 'Vette was loving it, every mile—up and up, down and around—and I was loving the 'Vette. Alone on the highway, I crossed Lake Shasta on a long inclined bridge that rises into outer space. The surrounding scenery was stunning—light blue sky, royal blue water, dark green forests, gray rock faces. White clouds, black highway, red 'Vette. Coloratura courtesy of the Interstates.

At nine forty-five I stopped to catch my breath at the first rest area beyond Lake Shasta, a miniature version of what I'd been seeing from I-5. Beyond rustic picnic tables in a grove of oak and pine, the waters of the lake formed an isolated cove, the surface rippled by a slight breeze. Horizontal striations marked the red shoreline in thin bands of subtle color—orange, brown, burnt umber. Above this band, vertical planes of green—textured like wool—angled straight into the sky. Puffy white clouds drifted high overhead, nudged by the same breeze wrinkling the blue water below.

Two or three cars and a camper sat in the parking lot, spaced apart for privacy as if in awe of the setting. But I saw no one. From the men's room I hiked a winding sidewalk to the shore of the cove, sitting alone, eating the last of my bananas while absorbing the heavy silence. Intermittently, the sun broke through overhanging branches to illuminate circles of pine needles. The pine cones—fallen or hanging—were the size of softballs. But it was chilly in the shade, with a hint of morning dampness that touched my bones, forcing me back to the 'Vette all too soon.

The temperature reached no higher than sixty as I-5 continued to climb—through rugged mountains with granite faces, through sandy hillsides with dark green foliage, all rising immediately from the shoulders of the road. A sign for *Klub Klondike* said it all, despite the childish *K*. Northern California is on the way to Alaska, to the Yukon. But I was already there.

The wide median rippled with tall grass now as valley vistas spread away below. A sign warned of a six percent grade. Another warned of deer just in time—in the middle of the next curve lay the tawny carcass of a doe. The descent was thrilling, the chicanes challenging, the 'Vette spiraling downward through pine-filled ravines. The more narrow and runty pines looked like rocket ships trying to launch themselves from nearly vertical slopes.

Then, with a sudden panic, I recognized a car up ahead. It was laboring in the right-hand lane behind a line of ascending trucks—the rusted beater of the *hombre* with the Bowie knife. But a wave of chagrin washed over me as I passed him. He didn't seem at all threatening now. The knife, given the rugged terrain, seemed a necessity, and I felt silly for not having one myself. What good would my hammer and star drill do me at the bottom of one of these forested gorges?

I abruptly forgot about the *hombre* as I emerged from the next chicane to find a snow-capped mountain on the horizon—the very first of my Interstate odyssey, a perfect calendar cover. The sun was gleaming off its snowy cone, the backdrop blue sky and white clouds. I had entered what my father would call *God's country*. And I thought of my father as I stared at that snow-capped peak. At that moment—on the anniversary of his death—I had never felt closer to him.

Descending again, I found the left lane closed. Parked behind orange cones and barricades, a CHiPs officer watched me whizz by. I hoped he was just admiring the 'Vette, not looking for speeders. I downshifted anyway to slow my descent. The curves were posted at fifty as a flashing scoreboard warned—*YOUR SPEED 60!*. The radar was right on the money, but I was taking the curves with ease, the officer well behind me now, the road simply too much fun.

At *Elevation 2000*, white granite faces marked the mountains like ski trails. Then, just when I thought that California could stun me no further, I rounded a corner to yet another Interstate surprise. Clouds were floating *below* the mountain peaks, among jagged outcroppings like rugged castles, and a sign confirmed the image—*Castle Crags State Park*. A different face of paradisiacal California.

In the treetops below the highway, a sign advertised gas at a dollar eighty-five. If that was for regular, the price for premium would exceed what I'd paid in Sacramento. Maybe gasoline prices depended on altitude here. Given the scenery, I wasn't complaining. The only possible complaint was the median—too often a single concrete barrier through the winding chicanes, rigidly dividing opposing lanes on the steepest climbs. It's for safety, of course, but it brought the occasional traffic too close, keeping the idyllometer at ninety.

Shelves of clouds obscured the craggy faces of the highest mountains. But to the north, the gigantic snow-capped peaks remained untouched—aloft and aloof—mountains so high that forests can't reach their summits. Halfway up, all trees abruptly ended, well below the line where the snow begins. Between trees and snow lay only barren escarpments.

Then a new sign brought a new worry. *Chains Required One Mile Ahead.* Somewhere in the Desert Southwest, the Weather Channel had warned of snow in the mountains east of Seattle. I hadn't expected such a threat in California. The temperature was only fifty now. At these altitudes frost and ice could appear in a minute, rendering the 'Vette's sixteen-inch tires defenseless. *Ski Area First Right.* All the ski season lacked was one good snow.

Thin ribbed clouds began to overtake the sky, dimming the mountains to drab greens and sandy tans. Then the land leveled out, leaving I-5 in a long brown plain. The wind increased, punishing the 'Vette, continuing to blow through a place called *Weed* (pop. 3062). The name got me to thinking. I had not yet encountered any tumbleweed, that classic image of the great American West. I imagined tumbleweed as a sort of rolling sagebrush. Maybe sagebrush was out of season, or didn't occur in the mountains. At any rate, the surrounding terrain didn't seem especially weedy, despite a series of small towns named in its honor—*South Weed, Weed*, then *North Weed*. Havens for pot-smoking hippies.

Unperturbed by the wind, a few cattle grazed across brown foothills. Sloping right to the shoulder of the highway, these hills turned a darker brown higher up. Lava outcroppings marked open stretches like dark eyebrows. The temperature had risen to fifty-nine, and it was exactly fifty-nine miles to the Oregon border, the traffic light and moving steadily at eighty.

The fields held horses and cows now, on quaint fenced-in spreads. But up ahead a large animal stood *outside* the fences—an antelope, perhaps. I watched it carefully as I approached but it never wavered in the buffeting wind. It was a sculpture of a brown cow, head twisted upwards as if to moo at the sky—some sort of monument to area ranchers, a symbol of a rugged away of life. A fitting tribute, without an ounce of propaganda.

I whizzed by *Yreka* (pop. 6948), where thick oaks join the pines along the highway. Yreka? Perhaps someone had discovered something out here—*Eureka!*—but didn't quite know what they'd found. Or didn't know how to spell. No matter. The country could speak for itself and was certainly doing so, creating a final impression of California as spectacular as my first.

The terrain changed yet again. I was speeding down one of those six percent grades, through a series of chicanes skirting deep mountain gorges, as valley vistas opened through steep notches to the left. Green trees laced brown ridges on the right. My ears crackled and popped. At the very bottom of the descent lay the Klamath River, dark and smooth, following the highway through the contours of the landscape. Forested hillsides hugged its shores. The river looked cold—like some of the rivers in Maine—perfect for trout. But virtually inaccessible.

Increasingly overcast, the sky seemed closer now, deepening the shadows in dark hollows along the river. A sign for *Ditch Creek Road* brought another perfect image. To live on Ditch Creek Road you'd need a canoe, a four-wheel drive, a Bowie knife, and a lot of luck.

Then it was *Welcome To Oregon*. The sign gave me goosebumps.

* * *

There is nothing at the forested border but that brief welcome. No police, no checkpoints. Then I-5 climbs again—through a *Snow Zone* into the Siskiyou Mountains—three hundred miles from Portland, thirty from Medford. Several logging trucks were laboring in the right-hand lane, hauling their scented slabs toward the top of the world. Vertical granite ledges had been blasted away here to make room for the Interstate, leaving large round rocks strewn along the shoulders. The difficult ascent ended at the Siskiyou Summit. *Elevation 4310.*

Immediately beyond the crest, the rapid ride down begins with a six percent grade, the posted speed decreasing at each chicane—*65, 55, 45*—curves I took at seventy in fifth gear. But near the bottom came a moment of fright. I rounded a bend into a snowstorm of litter. Brown bags and newspapers were blowing from the back of a rusted pickup truck. The driver seemed oblivious, ambling along in the left-hand lane at half my speed. I blew by him on the right and he didn't even blink. I didn't bother to lean on my horn.

I-5 approaches Medford, Oregon, through the heart of a narrow valley where the hillsides are cluttered with ramshackle houses. And with the *garbage in* comes the ugliest wall in all of America—plain gray cinderblocks, eight feet tall. Hang the aesthetics, it's purely functional. Behind this wall sit apartment houses, duplexes, campers, and RVs, but despite the population—47,000—Medford's anything but urban.

Beyond Medford I-5 runs on towards Grants Pass, continuing a gradual descent from the Siskiyou Summit through terrain dotted with trailers, doublewides, and what can only be called shacks. Especially on some of the cowboy-like spreads. It was noon, and the sky, now totally overcast, hung a gloomy grayness along the hills and highway. My ears popped again, and suddenly the surrounding hills surprised me with a hint of autumn—subdued oranges, yellows, and browns, colors certain to deepen in the days ahead. I had forgotten the month. October.

There is a sparseness to Oregon that I liked immediately, a don't-bother-me attitude, an atmosphere of plainness and informality even evident in the Interstate signs. Unlike in the rest of America, yellow deer warnings in Oregon have no silhouettes, just large black letters stating the point—*DEER.* Enough said. The *Rogue River* cut through here, a name I loved instantly. And there was a sign for *Savage Rapids.* Another accurate and blunt assessment of the territory.

At twelve fifteen I pulled into a rest area that provides historical notes on the Rogue Valley Trail of Tears. In 1846 Jesse Applegate had discovered the famous Applegate Trail, a southern route into Oregon, a much-needed alternative to the treacherous Columbia River. In 1850 the Congress of the United States, through the Oregon Donation Land Act, had offered free land in the region of the Rogue and Klamath Rivers, land situated along an ancient Indian trail. Thus the Indian massacres of 1855 were a foregone conclusion.

Cut into the forest, this small rest area seemed timeless, more rustic than the simplest one in Maine. Lank grass and long pine needles softened the earth. Dark moss mottled the wooden picnic tables. A long green-and-white tractor-trailer was parked in the narrow lot, its driver coming from the men's room as I returned to the 'Vette. In tune with himself and the landscape, the guy walked with an enviable bounce in his step. I caught up with him as he leaped onto the running board of his cab.

I felt like talking now. Oregon had put me at peace with my father.

"I drive this Interstate every week," the driver said excitedly. He looked to be about thirty. "And I absolutely love it. Every minute of it. I live in California, below Sacramento, but my wife wants to move up here. Oregon's a beautiful state, even better than Washington. The roads are better, for one thing."

"And the chicanes?"

"Oh boy," he laughed, "ain't they fun? You just gotta slow down and pay attention, is all. I got the best job in the world, buddy, and I wouldn't trade it for nothing."

Given what I had seen since Sacramento, it was easy to believe him.

Minutes later the trucker tooted his horn as I caught up and passed him on the highway. My destination was Roseburg, just sixty miles distant, through rugged land rendered somber by the lack of sun. The surrounding forests were growing dark. I was on a stretch of I-5 called *The Redwood Highway*. Another apt image.

Traffic was nonexistent now, and for the first time in days a hitchhiker stood on the shoulder, the mountains rising steeply right behind him. He wore greasy overalls and was jerking his thumb arrogantly— almost defiantly—high in the air. He stared at the 'Vette as I approached, then gave me a dirty look as I sped by, thumb replaced by his middle finger. But hitchhikers had never been part of my game plan. From day one.

My ears crackled yet again. It was sixty degrees near Wolf Creek, where the right edge of the highway drops immediately into pine-filled gorges, the same pines ascending sharply on the left. The Interstate had been carved around the mountainside here. Ahead of me, long flat trucks struggled up steep grades with their loads of chained logs, racing down into the valleys beyond. Passing one such truck, I swerved to avoid a furry roadkill—a large beaver, traditional prey of trappers in the Oregon territory, according to a historical note at the last rest area.

Near Coyote Creek, granite ledges cut through pines both above and below me, sheer rock faces that would have been visible for miles through distant mountain notches if only the sun were out. I had all but given northern California my Interstate chicane award, but these Oregon curves were proving terrific—around and down, then around and down again, each new S-turn such a surprise and fun to drive. Only the absent sun kept the idyllometer from one hundred.

At *Jumpoff Joe Creek* I laughed out loud. How perfect! Like *Woman Hollering Creek* in Texas. Apparently the isolation of the West had overwhelmed both men *and* women. This area could drive the average Joe to distraction, forcing a dramatic leap into a local dark gorge, lending a name—and a legend—to one of the many creeks that wind along the Interstate. The only difference between here and Texas was the claustrophobic nature of the landscape. Just as deadly as wide-open spaces.

Even without the sun, autumnal yellows stood out in the surrounding forests as I flew through *Canyonville*—another perfect name, for what were these immense ravines and crevasses if not *canyons*? I was in the bottom of one now, with sheer cliff walls rising on each side. Another understated Oregon sign soon followed. *Slides.* Rockslides? Landslides? Avalanches? It didn't matter. The warning was suitably apocalyptic.

The next sign, for *Ocean Beaches,* jarred me more. I had been picturing myself deep in the interior of the Pacific Northwest. But I was neglecting the *Pacific* part, just eighty miles west. I had paid homage to the Pacific in San Diego, and my container of ocean water was tucked away in the back of the 'Vette. Now I had to add an entire ocean to that giant relief map in my mind.

In midafternoon I reached Roseburg, my driving done for the day. Spread out along seven exits of I-5, Roseburg (pop. 17,032) is a lovely little place in the plain of a shallow wooded valley. The gray sky had given way to a steady drizzle, enough to require the wipers—the first rain I had seen since South Carolina, since the days of Floyd and Gert and Harvey, storms I could scarcely remember. Now here in Oregon it was raining again. But it was just the Pacific Northwest being true to itself. It would spare me the chore of washing the 'Vette.

I exited the Interstate and pulled into the nearest gas station, and a teenager in a jumpsuit immediately leaped to the car. Snapping down the rear plate, he fixed the nozzle in the tank, then was all over the windshield with a rag and a squeegee. I watched him, bemused. I had been expecting to serve myself. Nowhere in America had the 'Vette provoked such unsolicited and devoted service.

Just as quickly, an older attendant stepped from the garage and called the younger one aside, pointing to the hose at the rear. "You don't mess with a car like this," he said in a loud whisper. "Hold that pump yourself! Don't spill any gas on the finish!" Then he smiled at me and went back inside.

The teenager sheepishly returned to the nozzle. To ease his embarrassment I asked him about the Interstates.

"It's about an hour up I-5 to Eugene from here," he said. "But there's too much construction. Then everything levels out, and it's a smooth run all the way to Portland."

He fell silent. Apparently that was all he had to say. I tipped him a dollar anyway, on the basis of his enthusiasm for the 'Vette, and he averted his eyes as he stuck the bill in his pocket.

Motel Find-Me-Not was just around the corner, complete with pool and Jacuzzi. It was a flagship unit, the newest of its kind in the Pacific Northwest. I had seen the sign from the Interstate, but of course couldn't get there. New roads were under construction in the north end of Roseburg, crisscrossing open fields of dirt and weeds. But I was in no hurry. Since I'd left Sacramento so early, I'd arrived with time to spare. I had nothing to do but soak in the Jacuzzi. So I drove around the block a few times, gradually homing in on Motel Find-Me-Not, where the large parking lot was all but empty.

Outside the new office, the bright paint was fresh on the stucco facade. Inside, the teenage girl at the desk was as bright and fresh as the paint. And more garrulous than her gas station counterpart.

"I commute to work on I-5," she said. "From Sutherlin, about ten miles north. You know Sutherlin?"

I shook my head.

"Anyway, the highway gets a lot of ice and snow in winter, but they keep it really clean. Know what worries me most?"

I shook my head again.

"All the *other* people. Who don't know how to drive in ice and snow. I take the Interstate for granted, I guess, but I know it hasn't always been there. At Abby's Pizza in Sutherlin—you know Abby's Pizza?"

I shook my head yet again.

"Well, they have these large black-and-white aerial photos on the wall—they're about five feet by four feet—taken way back in the fifties or sixties, before I was born. And there's this one that shows just a single car on the I-5 overpass. They put that photo on the wall because I-5 put Sutherlin on the map. It created all the business. You know how many people live in Sutherlin now?"

I shook my head one last time.

"More than five thousand! The Interstate put Sutherlin on the map!"

13

I-5 HAS BEEN KIND TO ROSEBURG, OREGON, A PLACE THAT IS GROWING RAPIDLY but without ugly sprawl. Expansion is limited by the valley's perimeter, and the mall in the center of town is modest and clean. The people of Roseburg are friendly, the pace unhurried. Everything is as soft as the rain that lingered through the night.

Early in the morning a gray mist slipped over the mountains and I watched it settle in, bringing a heavier rain that cut short my walk. It was a chilly fifty-five degrees and I didn't want to get soaked, despite the temptation to keep strolling through the muted colors of the surrounding terrain.

An older woman was behind the desk when I checked out.

"My wheels were slipping on the Interstate ramp coming in this morning," she warned. "You be careful now. It's kinda slick this morning."

In the parking lot, as I tossed my suitcase into the 'Vette, I met a middle-aged man who had arrived late in the night.

"I was afraid this drizzle would turn to snow before I got here!" he said with relief. "I'm coming from L.A. I was trying to make it to Albany, north of Corvallis. That's nearly nine hundred miles. I hoped to drive it in two days, but I didn't want to chance the weather. I'm on my way to visit a sick friend."

The man looked tired, his fatigue causing him to ramble.

"Ordinarily," he went on, "I wouldn't have even considered it, but the Interstates make such trips possible. I cheated in California—I took Route 99 through the San Joaquin Valley. It runs parallel to I-5, just to the east. The trucks have beat the hell out of I-5. Did you come that way?"

I nodded, then asked how long it would take me to get to Seattle. The man didn't seem to hear me.

"To tell you the truth, I avoid the Interstates whenever I can. I only use them when I have to. They can wear you out. Like on this trip. I'm on my way to visit a sick friend. You headed to Seattle?"

I nodded again.

"It's about six and a half hours from here. But you know, the Interstates up there can be as bad as L.A."

"I didn't know that." It was not what I wanted to hear first thing in the morning. I was already wary of the weather, but I had never heard anyone utter a single negative word about Seattle. I'd be arriving during the afternoon rush.

But it was only eight o'clock now and the rain had let up. Heavy clouds hung overhead, with a light mist to the east, giving a lulling effect to the Roseburg morning.

Not since Maine had I seen conditions like this.

Purple mists skirted the horizon as I headed north on I-5. Despite all the pines in the plain of the valley, the mountain colors seemed to have deepened overnight—nothing brilliant, just a somber reminder of autumn. The few trucks ahead of me were churning up a constant spray, forcing me to use the wipers as well as headlights. I put Roseburg behind me with this parting thought—I hadn't seen any roses.

Ahead of me now was something I hadn't seen either, in my entire Interstate odyssey—a truck hauling three trailers in tandem. I had seen plenty of doubles, but no triples. I couldn't imagine how the driver could maneuver such a long rig through the mountain chicanes or windy stretches. But it was smooth sailing north of Roseburg—all new blacktop—thanks to the construction the teenager at the gas station had complained about. The semi with the triple load was safe for the time being.

Despite the lack of sun, the fall colors were striking. Evergreens made the dull foliage more pronounced, an autumn collage mellowed by angelhair grass. Cows and sheep grazed in fields through the crooks of the valleys as I-5 rose and fell through the foothills. In the higher elevations clouds and mists loomed below me, as if I were piloting an airplane. All Spanish influences were gone now. And there was a blessed absence of billboards.

In the quiet and picturesque conditions, I found myself contemplating the phenomenon of motion. I'd once had a roommate who would fall asleep the moment you put him in a car. Motion for him was the ultimate soporific. And that's entirely logical, I was thinking, because what *are* we if not atoms in motion? Movement is natural, an organic part of our bodily constitution. Riding in an automobile is treating the body to what it does anyway. Which makes cruising the Interstates—where the ride can be sustained indefinitely—the perfect avocation.

Patches of blue sky peeked through the grayness now, promising a bright day ahead. By eight forty-five, the sun was steady on my right shoulder. More and more blue sky was opening up, a robin's-egg blue. Creeks and rivers wound through the valley bottoms, inviting imaginative exploration like the waterways in Maine. The narrow Row River was too shallow and rocky for rowing a boat, but it was a perfect little trout stream, an up-the-creek-without-a-paddle kind of river. There was nobody around to go boating, anyway. Except for an occasional small farm on a hump or knoll, the region seemed largely uninhabited. Yet there must have been a family named *Stalver* in the vicinity because I passed a sign for *Stalver Slough*. A different kind of waterway. Which raised again that old Interstate question, the pronunciation of *slough*.

Around the bend was a truck hauling cedar logs, the sudden aroma putting the question on the back burner. Years ago in Stratford I had helped my father build a split-rail cedar fence. What I remember most is the smell of that cedar—the same sweet perfume now filling the 'Vette, letting me cruise in my childhood once more.

South of Eugene the terrain flattened out in a wide valley surrounded by dark pine mountains. Large piles of timber were stacked in open yards beside the highway—triangles of logs as long as telephone poles and several feet in diameter. The sun broke through momentarily, splashing through the valley and brightening the yellow and orange foliage, deepening the green of the fir and casting long purple shadows. And suddenly I was driving through one of those nineteenth-century paintings that extol the beauty of the American landscape—white mists rising ahead like Indian smoke signals, gray clouds floating higher up, backed by silhouettes of mountain ranges and a pale blue sky.

Thankfully, Eugene (pop. 133,000) has no *garbage in*. There's no room for it. The trees and valleys come right to the shoulder of the highway. The Williamette River, running alongside, helps too: wide, shallow, tree-lined, curling—and enticingly fishable. Then Eugene was gone, nothing remarkable that I can remember, and in the flat plain that followed, with the sun peeking in and out, I stopped at a rest area to stretch.

The place was rustic, the few truckers suiting the place precisely—bearded men in baseball caps, flannel shirts, blue jeans, and work shoes, moving slowly among tall pines and white birches. The pavilions were simple—flat oblong roofs supported by gray metal poles, the kind that hold up the beams in your basement. Despite today's mist and yesterday's rain, sprinklers twirled everywhere, wetting everything—cars, sidewalks, picnic tables—and as I headed for the plain gray restrooms, a gentle sun shower began, adding a sparkling glaze to the already glistening grass and foliage in the shady little park. Rain fell harder as I returned to the parking lot, sending me scurrying to the 'Vette. But the truckers went about their business at the same unhurried pace.

Beyond the rest area I-5 flattened out as if for good, despite dark mountains to the far right and left. There were green and brown mountains too, reminiscent of California, but contoured like miniature volcanoes. Where the land had been plowed, long brown furrows cut through golden fields. Clear skies were moving in from the west, pushing the grayness to the east. Purple foothills completed the palette. It was ten o'clock now, just seventy miles to Portland, all rain and mist gone.

Closer to Portland (pop. 437,319), the traffic thickened from light to moderate, with an annoying characteristic. Trucks were moving into the passing lane to overtake slower trucks, causing all vehicles to gear down into a loping two-lane convoy. Then came the construction I had been warned about in Roseburg—*I-5 Widening Process. State Funds At Work.* The minimum two lanes were being extended to three.

A variety of industries and neighborhoods signal Portland's *garbage in.* About forty miles south there's an ugly gray wall to the right and an even uglier brown one to the left. Then a small sign in the median jangles your sense of geography—*45th Parallel. Halfway Between the Equator and the North Pole.* Nothing like knowing exactly where you are! But I realized *I didn't know* where I was. That great relief map in my mind only included the forty-eight states. I had thought Oregon was much farther north on the globe. That little sign in the median had shifted an entire continent.

Beyond the construction, three lanes ran on past *Woodburn* (pop. 13,404)—a perfect name for a less-than-perfect place, a tangle of fast-food joints and motels. I was in the Willamette Valley, named for the river I'd crossed earlier, pronounced, according to a local radio station, *Will-AM-it.* The going was tedious—flat, a scruffy median, incessant power lines, and a sprawling population. Billboards were back, including one with a pun to advertise a turf farm—*Instant Lawn: We Keep Rollin' Alawn.* Another sign alerted drivers to a speedometer check ahead, a posted one-mile stretch to confirm the accuracy of your odometer. I looked for it, began the check, but the *garbage in* was too distracting. I never saw the second sign at the end of the mile.

At ten-thirty I pulled into a rest area across from a stretch of noisy construction in the southbound lanes. The facility was set beneath a woodlot of tall pines, trees with trunks so gigantic that I couldn't get my arms around them. Stately, statuesque, and hundreds of feet high, these trees had been ceremoniously planted here to represent all the pine forests in the state of Oregon.

I could barely see the sky through the canopy of branches. Wispy white clouds scudded about overhead. The day had suddenly turned gorgeous—almost a touch of New England, despite a chilly fifty-nine degrees. Historical information on *Boone's Ferry* reflected the landscape: *During the period of Oregon's Provisional Government (1841–1849) residents traveled by Indian trails, water courses, or on primitive rough-hewn wagon roads etched by emigrant settlers. Alphonse Boone established a ferry crossing on the Willamette River near this marker.* Later, Boone's son had begun to clear a path through the surrounding counties, creating the present-day Boone's Ferry Road.

As at the earlier stop, lumberjack-style drivers tended to their rigs, while a few tourists strolled the artificial pine forest. But the din of construction from across the highway made conversation impossible.

An hour or so later, all was quiet at the next rest area, where I immediately sought out a trucker in charge of an oversized load. He was hauling half of a prefabricated home, a cargo necessitating pilot cars on the road, both in front and behind him. As I approached, he was securing a lengthy sheet of plastic along the side of the house.

"I love driving I-5," he said in a flat Canadian accent, "even though it's tough going. Everybody hates you when you're hauling a wide load! It's really rough through the construction areas because the lanes narrow down, like those stretches south of here. But I got an escort. You can't miss us with all those yellow lights flashin'. I'm goin' from Medford up to the Canadian border. I've driven all over America on your Interstates and there ain't a better way to go. I-5 is one of my favorites."

I had heard similar testimony from the men of Hydro Quebec on the other end of the continent.

"Do you get extra pay for wide loads?" I asked. I had heard that truckers hauling dynamite and nuclear waste always earn a bonus.

The driver laughed. "Nope! No combat pay! I just take it slow. In a rig like this, you gotta be a defensive driver."

"Any snow ahead?" I said. "I'll be heading east through the mountains after Seattle."

"Nope!" His certainty was reassuring. "Been too warm for snow this time of year. And that's a good thing, given that red toy you're driving. We seen you earlier."

A woman had returned to the rear pilot car, a cup of coffee in hand, and when she waved at us the trucker headed to his cab.

Outside the restrooms stood a spartan kiosk where the driver of the pilot car had purchased her coffee. It was operated by the Longview Masonic Lodge #263. A group of retired Masons, in baseball caps and flannel shirts, were standing about, tending the store—cookies, several air voids of coffee, and water for hot chocolate. I chose the hot chocolate and took the last of the oatmeal cookies from a plastic plate. I hadn't seen an operation like this since the Lions Club's hotdog stand in North Carolina.

"It's a great fund raiser," one of the Masons said. "We used to just have a plywood table, but old Sid Roberts came up and got permission to build this little stand. Now the folks have a choice between us and the vending machines." He spoke as if the new stall was a vast improvement. It reminded me of the shabby kiosks I had seen on the streets of Russia.

An elderly woman was chatting with the men. "I represent Beta Sigma Phi," she said proudly.

I blinked. "College sorority?"

"No, no," she laughed. "We're a female service organization. We want to do what these gentlemen are doing, but you've got to apply to the state a year in advance. We never got the honor." Watching the styrofoam cup in my hand, she gave me a kind of *tsk-tsk* look. "You're gonna have some watery hot chocolate unless you put in more powder!"

I added another dose to the steaming brown liquid, stirred it with a plastic spoon, and took my cup and cookies to a picnic table for a sunny morning snack. The surrounding stillness was palpable. I listened for birds but could hear none. Just the distant hum of traffic from the highway.

Approaching Portland, traffic became moderate to heavy across three lanes. But it was remarkably polite, the going pleasant despite a *B-* surface. A special truck lane kept all trucks to the right. Tall pines rose from the roadside, concealing any *garbage in*. Small middle-class homes dotted the hillsides. Unlike any other urban approach in America, the Interstate arrives in Portland through a series of tree-lined chicanes, dropping and rising as it goes, a refreshing entry.

The Willamette River returned through the trees to my right. I kept looking for a city but could see only forest. Soon a flat iron bridge and some modern buildings cropped up, only to disappear just as quickly. False alarm. An industrial stretch from an earlier era followed, with tall cranes towering above low-slung factories. Then I was on a large gray bridge over the Willamette, the old structure beginning level but rising abruptly—teepee-like—bringing a magnificent view of the earlier iron bridge on the left. Modern white buildings now stood on the right.

Then one of the prettiest cities in all of America suddenly opened below me, completing the tantalizing Interstate preview. A variety of bridges spanned the glinting river. Clean downtown buildings glowed bronze in the sun. I passed the domed facility of the Portland Trailblazers, a pink skyscraper, and twin glass towers pointed like rocketships. Many more bridges followed, one gray and humped in the middle. Low brick buildings with industrial chimneys lay beyond. I had been expecting another Bridgeport, Connecticut, but Portland is a modern Pittsburgh with touches of Jacksonville, Florida. An Interstate surprise that serves to prepare you for Seattle.

* * *

Before we leave Portland, here's an Interstate Item from page 484 of *America's Highways: 1776–1976*, where the caption to a map of "The Oregon Trail as of 1848" contains a typo. The caption reads: *The east-*

bound lane of I-80, east of Pendleton, Oreg., is built on the site of the Old Oregon Trail and takes the motorist into tortuous, but spectacularly scenic, mountain country. In this area, the east- and westbound lanes may be more than a mile apart. That caption should read: The eastbound lane of I-84 . . .

Below the map of "The Oregon Trail as of 1848" is a photograph of a lone truck winding its way up a long curving chicane through a V-shaped notch blasted out of the mountaintop. I-84 reaches its western end in Portland, Oregon, cutting through the same mountain ranges that I would traverse on I-90 when I turned east for home. Taking the path of least resistance through the rugged territory of eastern Oregon, the pioneers who traveled the Oregon Trail often met stiff resistance from Native Americans, particularly the Cheyenne. Thus the Native Americans, who knew the surest way from A to B, have to be counted among the engineers of the Dwight D. Eisenhower System of Interstate and Defense Highways.

Meanwhile, passing through Portland reminded me of the good friend to whom I had sent the only postcard of my grand lap back in Van Horn, Texas. He is from Oregon, and he taught me how to pronounce it—it's Oregun, not Oregon. Because of this friend, I own a bathrobe from Pendleton, Oregon, where the textile mills are world famous, and where I-84 takes the motorist into tortuous, but spectacularly scenic, mountain country.

* * *

North of Portland, I-5 crosses the Columbia River on an old green bridge of the Erector Set type. It's a double bridge, three lanes in each direction and three sections per span. The river is wide and deep, marked with buoys in several channels. Industrial sites line both shores. A sign says Leaving Oregon. You Come Back Again Soon! Under the spell of Portland, I was reluctant to leave.

Beyond the river the highway begins a long, steep ascent straight through pine forests into Washington. The Evergreen State. A bank of red and yellow flowers waited in official welcome, then the posted speed limit—which had dropped through Portland—returned to seventy and the traffic cruised at eighty.

Over the crest of the long incline the sun disappeared and I removed my sunglasses in the face of an overcast sky. The cloud cover seemed part of the welcome, as if to remind travelers that Washington is not Oregon. The Columbia River was following the highway to the left, a comforting historic presence. Then a sign for the Mt. St. Helens National Historic Monument signaled a presence of a more infamous sort. Tucked away in a drawer back home in Ohio was a small plastic bag of gray ash—volcanic dust from the eruption of Mt. St. Helens—the unique gift of a friend.

Near Kalama (pop. 1210) the wind increased, turning up the silver undersides of deciduous trees along the highway, their shine contrasting with the dull reds and yellows among the pines. The mountains had given way to hills, as the smooth blacktop followed the valley of the Columbia. It was a chilly sixty degrees, the day trying to make up its mind about the sun. Occasionally, the gray overcast gave way to blue sky and white clouds, forcing me to reach for my sunglasses again.

The first impression of the state of Washington is that it's remarkably clean, and a diamond-shaped sign soon explained why—*Ecology Youth Working*. Volunteer crews were making it their business to keep their state free of clutter. Other signs confirmed the effort. *Keep Washington Green*.

A yellow light was flashing ahead, from the rear pilot car of the trucker with the wide load. I hit my horn as I blew by their convoy and the trucker responded with a startling blast of his own. And suddenly I understood all too clearly why Ché in Arizona disapproved when Freddie encouraged truck drivers to sound their airhorns.

The thought soon evaporated. I was on a double Erector Set bridge over the Cowlitz River, wondering why these old bridges are always painted army green. Washington has so many. Why not take a lesson from Tucson and paint them bright colors? *That* thought disappeared with a sign for Toledo, which produced a twinge of homesickness, something I'd never expected. In two more days I'd be pointing the Corvette east toward Ohio.

But I was getting ahead of myself again. At the moment I was heading north through what looked like a gigantic Christmas tree farm, except that every tree was hundreds of feet high. Traffic consisted of mostly logging trucks, each carrying only a dozen or so logs, a testament to their size and weight. Signs for *Mt. Rainier National Park* and *Mossyrock* followed—the large and the small. A black Corvette parked on the shoulder seemed out of place. I hadn't seen another 'Vette since the oil change in San Diego. Given the terrain, I realized how ridiculous I must appear in my red Hot Wheels toy.

Signs for *Ocean Beaches* were disconcerting as well. I was headed for Seattle, which I didn't associate with ocean beaches. San Diego was for ocean beaches. Seattle is a port city on Puget Sound, a setting I imagined from *Snow Falling on Cedars*. Here along I-5, where pale yellow and orange hues accented the pine-filled autumn landscape, there was no room for sandy ocean beaches.

The Skookumchuck River put me psychologically back on track. This was more like Washington—another drab green Erector Set bridge, the dual spans only a few feet apart. Telling city signs followed.

Olympia 22, Tacoma 50, Seattle 75. But despite the cities ahead, I-5 remained just two lanes, with the added annoyance of trucks passing trucks, all vehicles now fighting dangerous crosswinds.

Scatter Creek refocused my scattered thoughts. *Who* or *what* had been scattered here? Indians? Settlers? Dreams? Once again there was no time for musing. I-5 had broadened into three lanes for Olympia (pop. 33,840), Washington's state capital, where the brownish dome of the State House rises above the green horizon, tiered like a wedding cake and topped by a small nipple-like structure. Pleasantly surprised by Portland, I was prepared for another attractive cityscape. But I-5 skirts Olympia to the east, in four tree-lined lanes, offering only a glimpse of the city, plus some of the inlets and bays that stretch to Olympia from the southern end of Puget Sound.

The surprises came just north of the city—another Corvette, southbound, the yellow banana style of 1970. Then a large body of water across valley vistas to the left. This was Capitol Lake below Budd Inlet, framed by mountains, a scene well worth the drive. Another pair of Erector Set bridges—drab olive—spanned the Nisqually River. Then I-5 continued toward Tacoma in heavier traffic.

* * *

A jetliner crossed the horizon just above the tree line. There was a hitchhiker ahead—appearing so suddenly he seemed to have dropped from that plane—a distinguished-looking old man in a camel-hair blazer. Sporting a trim gray moustache, he was managing to keep his dignity intact with his thumb in the air, despite whatever circumstances had forced him to the shoulder of the Interstate. He was the only white hitchhiker I would see on my entire Interstate odyssey. Sticking to policy, I passed him by, but a vehicle in my rearview mirror slowed to his aid.

It was one-twenty now, with four lanes to either side of a cement divider, as Tacoma brought on its *garbage in*—one long strip mall, then an industrial valley. A church spire with a cross popped up, then the Tacoma Dome, flying an American flag. Across the way, orange cranes and smokestacks rose above factories along the flats. White bungalows crowded green hills beyond. Then it was *garbage out*, making Tacoma (pop. 176,664) a disappointment from I-5.

Shortly before two o'clock, twenty miles south of Seattle, I pulled into the Sea-Tac Rest Area—a scruffy, congested facility at the very edge of the highway—to prepare for the last leg of the day's drive. The warning of the man in Roseburg worried me. *The Interstates up there can be as bad as L.A.* Tacoma hadn't helped. I didn't know what to expect now, and the scrappy rest area, jammed with harried commuters, was a letdown.

I consoled myself with a history lesson. *On Oct. 10, 1805, after 17 arduous months, the Lewis and Clark Expedition entered what is now the state of Washington. The group canoed down the swift and hazardous Snake River, traveling as far as 40 miles a day.* In the state of Washington, travelers can visit the actual Lewis and Clark sites, which are marked by signs bearing silhouettes of hiking figures. On their historic trek, Lewis and Clark had covered thirty-six hundred miles in seventeen months. I was doing ten thousand miles in less than five weeks. The mathematics left me reeling. I felt like Lewis and Clark myself, as I got back on I-5, about to discover Seattle.

Accelerating into ever-thickening traffic, I passed a truck hauling a tall white yacht with a sleek keel—twice the size of any boat I'd seen on the East Coast. A sign for *Vancouver 158* served further notice of Canada. Sea-Tac followed, flanked by valleys with suburban homes, a city of 23,000 formed by spillover from its abbreviated namesakes. The road surface was deteriorating, commanding too much of my attention as I began to search for the Seattle skyline.

The first glimpse of Seattle from the Interstate comes as I-5 crests a long rise. Suddenly, above the treetops, five buildings stick up above others like a bar graph. There was blue sky now, with sun-splashed white clouds, and the hillside foliage—largely devoid of pine—gleamed in patches of orange and gold. A busy airport soon appeared on the left, long and wide. Then I-5 ran a high ridge, like the approach to Scranton on I-81. Orange cranes rose like giraffes from below, with industrial steam from dirty brick smokestacks. A large bridge loomed ahead. The surrounding hills were flecked with small white houses. The five major buildings of the initial skyline had disappeared.

Minutes later I passed the very beginning of I-90, where I would be turning homeward in two days. Then the Seattle skyline began again and—*wow*—this time it was as brilliant as the sudden sunshine. An Empire State–like building fronted darker structures to the left. Other buldings, high and white, sparkled from the hillside. Then the city spread out before me like a Mediterranean seaport, a stark contrast of light and dark across the green hills that hug Puget Sound. The abrupt appearance was a total surprise—the most magnificent Interstate debut of any city in America, for which Portland is but a rough draft.

I raced through downtown wide-eyed, the 'Vette passing within inches of iridescent facades, a dazzling display of modern architecture in an array of colors—glassy copper, shiny silver, shimmering green. White clouds floated overhead in a light blue sky. Colorful flags danced and snapped in the breeze. I recognized the King Dome on the left, a gleaming white hemisphere, home to the Seattle Mariners and

Seahawks. Then the city center was behind me all too soon, gleaming like Oz in the rearview mirror, giving way to attractive white homes that overlook the Sound from suburban hillsides.

The glittering water of Puget Sound accompanied I-5 northward on my left, a darker blue than the blue of the sky. Up ahead, high above its rippled surface, a great black bridge spanned the horizon left to right. I began to hunt for my exit, along a raised stretch of highway with a lovely view of the surrounding country, where thick foliage all but concealed densely populated developments.

Exiting at two-thirty, I headed east for several miles, uphill and downhill through a series of neighborhoods, following directions to the wooded hilltop home of friends. I'd known Ann and Ed for a decade through the Hemingway Society. They had built their place themselves—a modern split-level with rustic touches, including a long deck overlooking a forested gorge along the back. The house sits on the pinnacle of a steep hill with three other homes, accessed by a narrow private drive so nearly vertical that I had to pull it in first gear.

I checked the clock on the dash. The man in Roseburg was right on the money. The drive had taken exactly six and one-half hours. But I was early—both Ann and Ed were still at work—so I stretched my legs then washed the 'Vette in a small clearing cut from the woods beside the driveway. Tall trees formed a canopy overhead, from which large yellow leaves occasionally floated. Out of a sunny sky with fluffy white clouds. On a deliciously warm afternoon in Seattle.

* * *

Ed arrived shortly before five. Bearded and burly, he only needed jeans and a flannel shirt to pass for a lumberjack. He's the athletic director at a local private school.

By six o'clock we were having dinner at a shorefront restaurant downtown, relaxing with a beer, as large white ferries came and went from distant islands. It was a scene out of Hollywood, the beer making me sleepy in Seattle. Ann, teaching at the University of Puget Sound in Tacoma, would join us later back at the house.

"I-5 is woefully inadequate for the Seattle corridor," Ed said. "Seattle's such a long and narrow city. There's the Sound to the west and Lake Washington to the east. I-5's the only route through, north to south. So it's a parking lot every morning and again in the afternoon. There's really no way to rectify it because there's no place to go, no place to build. The land's simply too narrow."

It was growing dark. Beyond the large picture window, a massive white ferry progressed slowly toward shore, lights blazing. Its steady, unhurried pace was like a balm, not quite in sync with what my body was feeling—the residual sensation of the 'Vette moving beneath me. I took another sip of beer.

"What this town really needs," Ed insisted, "is a rapid transit system, a monorail or something, and plans are being made. It's getting so bad that people out here buy inflatable dummies to put in their cars, so they can use the carpool lane. Going east on the Interstate is fine, because I-90 is finished now between Seattle and Bellevue. Bellevue's on the other side of Lake Washington, across our famous floating bridge. That bridge is amazing. It's built on pontoons anchored to cables. But the wind and rain sometimes restrict the traffic. And before you get on it, you go through one of the largest tunnels in the world. But you're heading north tomorrow, right?"

I nodded, floating in the darkness with the bright lights of the ferry.

By the time Ann caught up with us—her chipper self despite a long day at work—I was feeling guilty about my earlier response to Tacoma, to which she commutes three times a week. The campus of the University of Puget Sound, she assured me, is very attractive.

"It's a sixty-three-mile commute, door to door," she said. "So you have to pry me out of the house if it means getting on the Interstate on my off-days. It normally takes me an hour and fifteen minutes, but last year, the Wednesday before Thanksgiving, it took me three hours. I carry a cell phone to call in late if necessary. I always leave at eight in the morning for my first class at eleven. The express lane helps, as I'm sure you found out."

But I had been too captivated by Seattle to know if I'd taken the express lane.

"The population growth here," Ed pointed out, "has probably doubled in the last ten years. But the roads haven't changed at all. It's actually worse than L.A. But we're slower here. The terror factor is worse in L.A."

I nodded vigorously in agreement.

"But there are times," Ann said, "that Seattle is simply so stunning from I-5 that I feel it's worth it just having a job to commute to."

I nodded again, more vigorously.

"Then there's that industrial part down by Boeing Field. Not too pretty," she said. "And the I-405 beltway is a nightmare. It bypasses Seattle to the east. In general, I hate driving because I have to drive to work. Until our folks moved here, we made the trip from Seattle to Spokane about eight times a year. But that's easy compared to driving around Seattle. You'll love it. I-90's really pretty."

It was Ed's turn to nod in agreement. "I-90 goes right through the Cascades. They're snow-covered year round. Then comes the central Washington desert, which has been brought to life by an irrigation project. It's really spectacular. The land's been converted for agriculture."

His comment caught me off guard. I had heard of the Cascades, but hadn't expected a desert in the state of Washington. It had been a long day and I was beginning to lose focus.

"My commuting strategy," Ann was saying, "is to drive I-5 unthinkingly. I think of anything but the drive—shopping, ideas for my classes, *anything*. Or I entertain myself by watching the people. I've seen some pretty strange things—guys shaving, working out with free weights, flossing their teeth while driving with their elbows. But on the weekends I just can't get in the car. It's like I've reached some sort of limit and can't go beyond it. If you put me in a car then, I feel like jumping out."

* * *

In the morning I lounged in bed while Ann and Ed got off to work. Then I took a long shower, giving the rush hour time to clear while readying myself to head north on I-5—to plant my fourth and final ceremonial flag at the Canadian border, a drive of about one hundred and twenty miles.

The weather had turned gray. Yesterday's sun, it seemed, had been an exception. Today was more typically Washington—overcast, sixty-five degrees, a slight drizzle. Outside, I found 'the Vette covered with broad wet yellow leaves—true to Murphy's Interstate Law—since I had just washed it. The leaves left curious fossil-like imprints all over the hood and sunroof as I carefully peeled them away.

227

Stopping for gas before reaching the Interstate, I noticed a classy cubicle in the corner of the parking lot of the service station. It was a coffee shop, attended by an attractive, well-dressed young blonde. Such drive-up facilities are fashionable in Seattle, with more names for coffee than I had thought possible. But I had had my two morning cups before hitting the road. As I pulled out, the blonde craned her neck to admire the 'Vette. I hoped my Ohio plates would explain my ignorance of Seattle coffee etiquette.

By ten-thirty I was leaving the city in light to moderate traffic, up a long tree-lined slope where the I-405 beltway crosses Lake Washington to join I-5. I was trying to imagine the end of the Interstate at the Canadian border. But the wind was distracting me.

Incredibly, it was a stronger wind than I had experienced anywhere in America—a kind of wind shear, slamming the 'Vette sideways with forceful gusts. All vehicles had their headlights burning, the pale disks doing nothing to brighten the leaden sky.

Immediately north of Seattle I-5 runs in four lanes through industrial and suburban terrain. Vehicles were darting in and out of the carpool lane, and I soon found myself doing the same. The road is tree-lined, with a wide median and valley vistas all about. To the east, the Cascade Mountain Range parallels the highway, as it does the entire length of the state. But today the Cascades were a brooding dark presence. Then the highway crested a rise, and pretty countryside spread away below, bodies of water to the left and right—Puget Sound and the north end of Lake Washington.

Signs indicated Canada now—*Vancouver, BC, 113.* Then came *Union Slough,* that old Interstate puzzle, and I made a mental note to ask Ann and Ed how it's pronounced in this neck of the woods. Logs were piled in high triangles along the highway for miles and miles, as long as telephone poles but much thicker, with freshly cut planks stacked beside them.

At *Steamboat Slough* I began to wonder if all these *sloughs*—no matter how you pronounced them—were critical to the logging industry as a kind of sluiceway. My grandfather had once told me that one of our relatives had been killed in a logging accident in upstate New York, falling into the river while riding a logjam. That bit of family folklore had always struck me as romantic. Now, with so many powerful logs stacked against the somber sky, it seemed all too violent.

It was forty-four miles to Bellingham. Then I crossed the Skagit River, low and curling, imagining salmon running inland from the Pacific to spawn. But it was October—the salmon would run in the spring. So where were they now? Burlington followed (pop. 4349), bringing signs for the Burlington Northern Railroad. Both names seemed familiar, but I may have been confusing them with Vermont.

Near *North Cascade Park* the traffic became annoying—only two lanes now, with trucks passing trucks. The day was wet, drab, and increasingly windy, the temperature down to fifty. North of Seattle, the I-5 corridor is potentially spectacular—a natural for the idyllometer in sunny weather—but I was seeing it at its worst, as I had seen the Mohawk Valley in upstate New York.

At eleven thirty I stopped at a rest area south of Bellingham. Mist was falling all about me, fine and cold, but it couldn't keep me from taking the travelers' quiz at the glass information case: *What is Washington's favorite recreational vehicle?* The answer—I should have known it after last night's dinner—is *the ferry.* Ferries, the display proudly explained, allow visitors to enjoy the mountain scenery, the islands and inlets, and the quaint coastal towns of Washington. All year round.

But the rest area had a touristic feel that seemed out of character for Washington—more advertisements and brochures than historic notes. *Take I-90 from the mountains to the Sound,* one ad touted, *on a national scenic byway through the central Cascades.* Well, I'd be doing that soon enough, in reverse. For the moment, I turned to a man in a *Michigan Wolverines* sweater to ask if he had driven all the way to Washington from Michigan. On the Interstates.

"No," he smiled. "We flew to Seattle and rented a car. My wife's in the ladies' room. She refused to drive out. It's such a long way and she hates the Interstates.

"Michigan has a great Interstate system, and they've been doing a lot of needed repairs around Detroit, but out here it's a different story. Our tour guide in Seattle said they'd have no more room for another Interstate unless they filled in Lake Washington! Then they got that floating bridge going east. Maybe they could put another floating bridge north to south."

I told him what my brother had mentioned in Connecticut—putting an Interstate for trucks down the middle of Long Island Sound. It was certainly possible, as I had learned in the South.

"Similar creative solutions are needed in Seattle," he said thoughtfully.

Back on the highway, a sign for *Alger*—like yesterday's sign for *Toledo*—brought me a moment of homesickness. Alger, Ohio, near my home in Ada, has a population of 864. Alger, Washington, is so small it's not in the atlas. I wondered if both places had been named for Horatio Alger. Rags to riches. The big and the small. *Wondering* was about all this day was good for, anyway. But I was glad, finally, for the prevalent gray mist. It's what I had expected to find in Washington— what I had imagined but never before experienced—a steady drizzle that's not quite a drizzle but a spray. Like the spritz from an atomizer. As soft and pervasive as fog.

The rude wind, however, I could do without.

Now I-5 was rising from a plain into mountainous terrain where white mists floated in rockslide areas, limiting visibilty to a few hundred yards. Large boulders sat along the shoulder at the very edge of pine forests. Despite the lack of sun, the approach to Bellingham, through a notch in the mountains, was exquisite. Thick pines topped the crests of granite outcroppings, sheer faces worn clean over the ages. A sign for the Noosack Indian Reservation reminded me of Chief Big Eagle in similar terrain in Maine. Then construction clogged the two lanes into Bellingham (pop. 52,179), canceling the idyllic approach. I switched on the radio and the antenna rose into the mist. One in ten stations was in French now, a language I could follow, unlike Spanish. Local newscasts carried a severe wind warning.

Eighteen miles before Blaine (pop. 2489)—the last town on I-5 at the Canadian border—the wind and rain, incredibly, began to abate, just when the cold, wet conditions couldn't get more nasty. Flags appeared, snapping loudly overhead. Mustard tones of deciduous trees lightened the green pine forests, and occasional white birches flashed their silver leaves. A sign for the *Peace Arch Factory Outlet* preceded one for the *Peace Arch* itself. But what was this *Peace Arch?* Given the terrain, I was expecting nothing more spectacular at the end of I-5 than the lonely sign at the border in Maine. *End 95.*

It was twelve-twenty, and I was alone on the highway. *Freeway Ends One Mile. Canadian Customs.* I took the very last exit, which puts you on a brief connector to the Peace Arch State Park, a touch of officialdom that suddenly had me intrigued, a pot of gold at the end of I-5's rainbow.

The large parking lot was empty except for one other car. Abandoning the 'Vette, I headed for the green acres beyond, armed with a millennial flag, hammer, star drill, and camera. The wind was whipping again, the temperature down to fifty-five, but without the rain I braved the elements in jeans and a sweatshirt.

An information case on the path contained a map of the area, plus an inspiring story, *If Not For The Children: Through their donations of pennies, nickels and dimes, the schoolchildren of Washington State and British Columbia helped to purchase the land surrounding the Peace Arch for an international park. Today 16 hectares (39 acres) of gardens are jointly managed by Washington State Parks and British Columbia Provincial Parks.*

A statement by one Sam Hill followed. Could that be the guy responsible for the famous exclamation, *What in Sam Hill?* Maybe the phrase had originated in response to what others considered a preposterous idea—a Peace Arch on the border between the United States and Canada. *I would not have the United States and Canada bound by other ties than friendship,* Sam Hill had said. *Let each work out its own form of government. Let each learn from the other, but let not any right or fancied right be settled except by peaceful arbitration, and may the next one hundred years find each nation seeking its neighbour's good as well as its own.*

Other information addressed Sam Hill himself, one of Washington's foremost citizens. *Sam Hill, founder of the Peace Arch, was a renowned builder of roads and railways in the Pacific Northwest while President of the Pacific Highways Association. In the early 1900s he became the driving force behind the creation of a monument that would represent his firm belief in world peace and brotherhood among nations. To this day the Peace Arch remains the only monument of its kind in the world and represents international peace along 3,000 miles of undefended borders.*

Fittingly, it's right at the end of the Interstate. What in Sam Hill, indeed!

* * *

The setting for the Peace Arch resembles the Mall in Washington, D.C. The arch itself is like a brief covered bridge, as white as the White House, with thick walls and a shallow triangular roof. Two flags fly from twin poles up top—one American, one Canadian. Through the arch, at the far northern end of the mall, a large sloped flower garden depicts the Canadian flag, a maple leaf at its center. On the opposite end, a garden of equal size portrays the Stars and Stripes, each flag like a float in the Rose Bowl Parade.

Other gardens, with a variety of flowers, shrubs, and trees, surround the long green sward on three sides. To the west lies the Pacific, the shallow waters of the Straits of Georgia separating the mainland from Vancouver Island. Railroad tracks parallel the mall just short of the shore, where slate-gray waves chopped at the brown beach. Near the tracks, a plain white board nailed to square wooden posts says, simply, *USA CANADA BORDER.*

The Peace Arch itself spans the international border. Within its thick walls are metal caskets containing pieces of the Pilgrim ship *Mayflower.* Kneeling beneath it, I planted my fourth flag, my final tribute to the Interstate system. Then, as in Maine, I began to search for someone to take my photo. There had been one other car in the parking lot. So there had to be someone about the premises.

Finally, a Canadian college student, her mother, and an Australian foreign exchange student appeared at the far end of the mall by the Canadian flag. When they approached the Peace Arch, I enlisted their assistance. The Canadian student obliged, taking my Kodak. Her photo shows me kneeling in the green grass beneath the white arch, my hair blown straight back by the wind, the flowered Canadian flag in the distance, a dark gray sky overhead. My left hand holds the blue millennial flag taut against the wind. My right hand holds up four fingers.

The click of the camera came as a revelation. I had done it! This was the fourth and final flag of my Interstate odyssey. But it was no time for rejoicing. My fingers were numb. Given the windchill, the temperature was nearly freezing, and when I complained about the weather, the Canadian mother only laughed.

"Why it's positively balmy today!" she said, looking at me as if *I* was the balmy one.

I changed the subject to the Interstates. And now it was the daughter's turn to laugh. "*Brrump! Brrump! Brrump!*" she said, pantomiming her hands on the wheel of a car. "Your Interstates are concrete, but ours are asphalt. *Yours* always get me *right here.*" She reached behind her neck and jabbed a finger between her shoulder blades.

"The best thing about I-5," her mother concluded, "is that it brings all you Americans north to the Peace Arch!"

I smiled and nodded. I wanted to talk to the Australian student too—my flag ceremony seemed to have amused him greatly—but the threesome had been about to leave the park when I encountered them, so they excused themselves and continued on their way.

The final corner, beneath the Peace Arch at the U.S.-Canada border in Blaine, Washington.

I left soon after as well. My jeans were damp from kneeling in the wet grass, and the wind suddenly seemed colder and stronger. Keeping its force at my back, I took a brief stroll into Canada to the maple leaf flag, then put my head down and fought my way to the parking lot.

Two miles south of Blaine, as if on cue, the soft misty rain began again. Volunteer litter crews in yellow slickers were working the ravines along the highway. *Keep Washington Green.* The driving was a distraction now, the wind at a different angle. And suddenly I realized that driving the Interstates in Washington is an art form. You've got to stay far enough behind the vehicle ahead of you to catch the mist on the right wiper cycle, or else the blades rub and stutter across the windshield—*bup bup bup.*

Before long, the mist solidified into a pins-and-needles drizzle, then finally a downpour. To my right lay the wind-chopped Pacific, the early afternoon darker than ever. The curved side window of the 'Vette began to drip water on my left knee, the leak the result of jamming my umbrella in the door back in Buffalo. Or was that Bangor?

I had been lucky, I realized, at the Peace Arch. There might have been a downpour. I could have been drenched. But the Corvette karma was still intact. In the northwest corner of the state of Washington. America's Ultima Thule.

14

SO WHAT DID THE *I CHING* THINK OF ME LAPPING AMERICA *IN A CORVETTE?*

The hexagram was *Chieh,* which means *Limitation. In relation to ordinary life it means the thrift that sets fixed limits upon expenditures.* (Buddha, you bum!) *In relation to the moral sphere it means the fixed limits that the superior man sets upon his actions.* (So who wants to be superior?) But the *Judgment* was encouraging: *Limitation. Success. Galling limitation must not be persevered in.* (Oh Buddha, I take it all back! Thou shalt not gall thyself by not buying a Corvette!)

I read on eagerly: *Limitations are troublesome, but they are effective. If we live economically in normal times, we are prepared for times of want. In nature there are fixed limits for summer and winter, day and night, and these limits give the year its meaning. In the same way, economy, by setting fixed limits upon expenditures, acts to preserve property and prevent injury to the people. But in limitation we must observe due measure. If a man should seek to impose galling limitation upon his own nature, it would be injurious. Therefore it is necessary to set limits even upon limitation.*

Bless you, Buddha!

As if to confirm the wisdom of the *I Ching,* the morning paper on the day after my consultation featured a full-page section devoted to the latest Corvette—a steal at $45,464.

All I needed to do was find the money.

* * *

Before returning to Seattle, here's a scary Interstate Item from the Associated Press that I noticed in the newspaper a few days after heading east. The headline ran:

Bus driver kidnaps woman, speeds across border to U.S.

The dateline was Bellingham, Washington.

According to officials, the driver of an airport shuttle bus in Vancouver, British Columbia, kidnapped a woman passenger, raced past a U.S. border crossing, then fled the wrong way down Interstate 5 with authorities in hot pursuit.

The bus was finally stopped by a state trooper, who found that the driver had choked the woman almost to unconsciousness. According to Whatcom County, Wash., sheriff's deputies, the driver had also chased three drivers off the road, although no one was hurt. The kidnapped woman was treated at a local hospital and released.

Vikram M. Menon, 37, from the Vancouver suburb of Surrey, was booked for investigation on five counts of first-degree assault, including driving cars off the road and kidnapping. Officials said he could also face charges in Canada.

Menon, a driver for Vancouver Airporter, picked up a man and a woman in downtown Vancouver, stopped before reaching the airport, and asked the man to get out and check for a flat tire. He then drove off with the woman, raced through the Peace Arch border crossing at Blaine, Wash., and sped a brief distance the wrong way down the northbound lanes of Interstate 5.

Border Patrol agents and others chased the bus. According to Sgt. Larry Flynn, two cars, a motorcycle, and a state trooper were run off the road, but no one was injured. Vancouver police Constable Anne Drennan said the driver apparently told his bus dispatcher he had been hijacked by men carrying machine guns.

A likely story.

And then it hit me. Had the timing been different, I might have met that van head-on.

* * *

At one-thirty I stopped at a rest area, in no hurry to return to Seattle. Ann and Ed were at work. We would be dining in town again this evening, then Friday morning I'd be heading east to Spokane—a day earlier than originally planned because I had serviced the 'Vette in San Diego.

Like its northbound counterpart, this rest area pushed advertisements with an eye to the tourist dollar. But the Interstate information was helpful, including a list of I-5 junctions with scenic byways—the Columbia River Gorge, the Lewis & Clark Trail, the Spirit Lake Memorial Highway, the North Cascades Pacific Coast Scenic Byway, and the I-90 Mountains-to-Sound Greenway. The last listing—my intended route out of Washington—sparked my imagination, adding a touch of excitement to tomorrow's departure. But the scenery would depend on the weather.

And for the moment the weather was fickle, constantly changing. Occasionally the skies cleared, bringing tantalizing glimpses of the Cascades to the east, such high and mighty mountains. But despite what Ed had related, I was yet to see any snow-capped peaks. The clouds hung too low.

Sixty miles north of Seattle a sign for *Martha Washington Creek* raised a question. Had the state itself been named for the father of our country? If so, it was an association that had somehow escaped me. The *Stillaguamish River* followed. As the locals might say, *once* a guamish, *always* a guamish. Whatever a *guamish* was.

Twenty miles from Seattle the dual lanes spread to three and the traffic increased to moderate for the suburban reentry. I passed *Steamboat Slough*, a wide river with a bridge, stretching the definition of *slough*, if not the pronunciation. I hadn't yet seen a slough big enough for a steamboat. A marina off to the right held no steamboats, but it harbored more boats in one place than I'd seen anywhere else in America. It was like a state park for boats—yachts and dinghies, motorboats and sailboats—all bobbing at their slips in the rain.

Approaching Seattle from this angle I could see the large bridge I had noticed when northbound, rising up and over the water of Puget Sound. The roadside pines were tall and slim, the kind I'd seen in the forests of Russia. Then all traffic abruptly halted for the afternoon Interstate idle. My first in Seattle. It halted my musing as well. It was three o'clock—I was within several miles of my exit—but it was after four before I got back to Ed and Ann's.

"That's nothing," Ann said, when I complained of the delay over dinner. We were at another of those lovely downtown restaurants, with the dark water and glittering lights beyond. "On my very first commute to Tacoma, when I was starting my job at the university, it was raining hard. The traffic was a madhouse, and my car began to have engine trouble, something electrical. It was such a nightmare, but somehow I made it to Tacoma through all that rain. And at the end of the day, the moment I pulled into the driveway, the engine blew up in smoke. 'That's it,' I said. 'I quit! I can't do this day after day!' But now I have this new van Ed got for me. I sit up high above the traffic and it's not too bad. I feel superior sitting so high. It gives me a feeling of control. But as I told you last night, I mainly try to avoid thinking about driving the Interstate." 235

I sipped my beer, then turned to Ed. "I'm going to spell you a word," I said, "and I want you to tell me how you pronounce it. OK?"

He looked at me queerly.

"*S-l-o-u-g-h.*"

There was no hesitation. "*Slew*," Ed said. "Like the famous racehorse, Seattle Slew. Why do you ask? How *else* would you say it?"

I didn't want to get into it—*slew, sluff, slow, slough-as-in-cow*. Dinner was too pleasant, and I didn't want the puzzle revolving in my head all night long. I was leaving in the morning and wanted to savor every last minute. So I sloughed it off, leaving the troubling word to the gods of the Interstate.

To whom I was indebted for a memorable visit with friends in Seattle.

* * *

Friday morning I lingered over coffee after Ann and Ed left for work, waiting for the rush hour to clear before heading east. The local TV station said that traffic was "slow" on I-5—a euphemism for the kind of Interstate idle I wanted to avoid.

It was raining again, the temperature only fifty, and by nine-thirty, growing impatient, I left for I-5. Heading up a steep hill, I ran a red light, cutting off a black Corvette in the process. I didn't want to have to start from a standstill on an upslope, on wet pavement. There was a long line of commuters behind me, and they all stopped for the light as I sped on through. Once again, I hoped my out-of-state plates would explain my behavior.

Then I crawled into the express lane on I-5 South, amazed as much by the snarl of vehicles as by the politeness of all drivers. As in San Diego, people signaled to change lanes. People let you in ahead of them. People exchanged brief waves and thank-yous, even smiles. Nonetheless, traffic was bumper-to-bumper, a full scale Interstate idle, made more testy by the changing intensity of the rain. Again and again I adjusted the speed of the wipers.

A yellow sign flashed on the shoulder—*Express Lane Closed Ahead*—so I jockeyed to the left. Then came a sign for the University of Washington. *U-Dub*, as Ann and Ed call it, short for *U.W.* And then I turned east on I-90—the final momentous turn of my Interstate odyssey—pointing the little Corvette toward home on that giant relief map in my mind. I whooped in excitement, but the rain drowned me out. My spirits too. I had been hoping for a quick escape from Seattle on I-90. But I-90 was just a continuation of the Interstate idle on I-5.

The snag of traffic extended behind me, ahead of me, on all sides of me—as far as I could see beneath gray, rainy skies. Red taillights glowed whenever a driver touched the brakes, the lights flaring softly in the wet sheen of the pavement. Incessant headlights plagued the rearview mirror. Rain pelted the sunroof. I was stuck in Seattle, which ranks third nationally in terms of time lost in traffic. Behind L.A. and Atlanta.

Eventually, I reached the tunnel Ed had mentioned—five lanes eastbound—easily the largest tunnel I have ever driven. It's oddly rectangular in shape, unlike the roundish tubes of the Baltimore Harbor Tunnel. But Hemingway would have loved it. It's a clean, well-lighted tunnel and it brings an Interstate surprise—it splits in two. Suddenly there were two tunnels eastbound, side-by-side, and before long I could detect a pale light at the far end, so reassuring on such a gray day. Then all traffic inched across Lake Washington on Seattle's famous floating bridge, a modern Erector Set structure that extends to Mercer Island in the middle of the lake, then continues to the far shore.

Dark clouds hugged the choppy surface, where the kind of floats that line swimming pools seemed to demarcate lanes of traffic. The rain was letting up, the bridge swaying gently. But it could have been my imagination. Peering below me from the long flat surface, I tried to picture steel cables descending to concrete anchors in the blackest depths, hoping they would hold until I got to the far side.

On the eastern shore another Erector Set bridge appeared—more modern than the first—and beyond it lay yet another tunnel. Traffic was still bumper to bumper, the rain pelting again. Then I-5 ascended through pine-filled hillsides of suburban homes. I had been on the road an hour and had come but twenty miles, in an Interstate idle rivaling the one in L.A. But the civilized people of Seattle made it bearable.

By the time I reached Lake Sammamish, the traffic had loosened. Then I headed up Snoqualmie Mountain towards Snoqualmie Pass (elevation 3022). I was entering the Cascade Range now, where peaks rise to more than six thousand feet, where a sign soon alerted all drivers—*Advisory Information When Flashing.* Fortunately, nothing was flashing. But the thought of advisories was disconcerting as I sped up into the mountains through a cold, slanting rain.

I was worried about snow in Snoqualmie Pass. At least I'd have company—a few truckers and other motorists. But as the pine-filled hillsides rose higher and higher above me, the traffic began to spread out, thinning dramatically and climbing steadily. The pace finally reached eighty, despite low visibility, a wet surface, and ear-popping chicanes.

At Echo Glen came a blunt warning—*Severe Wind Ahead*—another cause for alarm. I couldn't imagine winds tougher than those I'd fought near the Canadian border, where there are no warning signs. *Spokane 250.* Here, at least, was an innocuous sign. But if there was snow up top, I might never see Spokane, my day's destination.

The temperature soon dropped below fifty, edging lower with every curve upward, threatening to make the next two hundred fifty miles the longest of my life. Then I couldn't believe what I saw in the rearview mirror. An old mid-sized car—with a vanity plate I couldn't decipher—was gaining on me rapidly, sending up a long gray wake behind it. I was in the left lane, and before I could move right the car flew by me, spraying the 'Vette like an automatic car wash. I put the wipers on high just in time to catch the license plate—DPRIVED. It couldn't have been more fitting. The driver was in danger of being deprived—of his license, if not his life—if he kept on attacking the mountain like that. Then the rattletrap disappeared into the mist around the next bend.

I passed the South Fork of the Snoqualmie River, which made geographical good sense. The river would flow *down* the mountain while I-5 curled *up*—into the woolly-textured Cascades, mountains that were getting more rugged by the minute, their great humps rising through the mist whenever the rain abated and the wind momentarily cleared the sky. Still, I could see no snowcapped peaks. Thick clouds obscured them.

About twenty miles from Snoqualmie Pass, signs warned of deer. That was all I needed—leaping deer in the rain and fog, on the curving chicanes of Snoqualmie Mountain, where the visibility suddenly dropped to a few hundred yards, smothering my headlights.

Fire Training Academy Next Right. Despite widespread droughts nationwide, I couldn't imagine how the forests of Washington could ever burn in mountains like these. There was too much moisture— lakes and rivers and rain—and as water steamed across the highway ahead of me, I feared the 'Vette would hydroplane on the chicanes. Or the water would glaze to ice higher up, sending me sideways despite my sixteen-inch grip, rolling me over the guardrail into a pine-filled ravine. The weather was worse than what I'd endured in Hurricane Floyd. And suddenly I was in second gear, climbing cautiously, searching for the wreck of the mad ship DPRIVED.

Severe winds hit as advertised the moment the lanes dwindled to two, making passing all trucks a problem. I had entered the Snoqualmie National Forest and was certain of just one thing—I was missing out on some terrific scenery. High pines and rugged humps and valleys lay all about me, all gone the second I glimpsed them through the scudding clouds and driving rain.

West Summit 7. East Summit 8. I was approaching the twin humps of Snoqualmie Pass, hoping that conditions would miraculously clear on the far side—that the Cascade Range would keep the wind and rain behind me. The sun was rising due east and I kept waiting for it to flood the horizon, to greet me in a blaze of glory. Instead, I saw a small sign that riddled me with fear—*You Must Have Chains When Traction Required!* The 'Vette *did* have a special traction gizmo—I had read about it in the driver's manual. But this was no time to be leafing through the manual. What you need in the Cascades is a 4x4 with chains.

Just short of the summit, rocky cliffs rose sharply on my left. Deep ravines dropped away to the right. Then, mercifully, I-5 added a third lane for trucks. I could give the lumbering rigs a wide berth now, avoiding their spray, keeping to the middle as the wind knocked me about.

A sign for *Cle Elum* (pop. 1798) stumped me. How could anyone manage to live up here? The name of the place was strange enough, perhaps French Canadian. *Clé* in French means *key*. But *Elum* doesn't mean anything, in French or Latin. Maybe the tiny community had been named for a *person*—old Clay Elum of the Elum clan. It gave me something to think about as I crawled through the rock ledges of West Summit, then over to East Summit, to begin the descent of Snoqualmie Mountain in—*Yes!*—much clearer weather.

* * *

Charred stumps dotted the valley floor below. Sawed off waist high, they protruded from black water in a swampy area that drained a nearby river. Red, yellow, and orange patches of leaves colored the mountains left and right, the moist air giving them a shiny brilliance. I was on the Mountains-to-Sound Greenway now—as pretty as promised despite the gray morning.

Kachess Lake lay off to the left, long and narrow like a reservoir. Then came *Cabin Creek Road*, a pastoral address. But if I had to live on Cabin Creek Road, I decided, it would have to be in summer.

A steep hill descended into the Wenatchee National Forest, where I encountered a welcome sign—*Chain Enforcement Ends Here*. I had crossed the crest safely. No snow through Snoqualmie. No qualms besides my out-of-state fears. I was free now to enjoy the view. Weather permitting.

In the spectacular territory of the Cascades, every road sign brings a pleasant image—*Iron Horse State Park, John Wayne Trail, Yamika River*. Minute by minute the sky was growing lighter, brightening the wheatstraw median near *Salmon Le Sac*. Fish in a bag? Salmon so plentiful that you can catch 'em in a sack? In such wilds it seemed entirely possible.

Yellow trees lined the black water of the Cle Elum River—shallow and rippling as it wound along beside the highway. Higher up, dark pines and tall cedars rose vertically above the deciduous yellow band. A few small houses, barely noticeable, were tucked away in the woods, and here and there small roadside parks sheltered trailers or campers. I-5 had returned to two lanes, making the occasional trucks a nuisance when they attempted to pass each other.

It was only eleven o'clock but I already felt exhausted, ready for a break just as the Indian John Rest Area appeared. Surprisingly, it was crowded—all truckers and travelers ahead of me had gathered here, the first point of relief after Snoqualmie Pass. I checked the vehicles as I entered the parking lot, but the mad ship DPRIVED was not among them. It began to rain again the moment I got out of the car, a fine gentle rain that everyone else ignored. I reached for my umbrella, then grabbed my jacket and hat instead, not wanting to act like an Interstate outsider.

The rest area was named for John Quititit, a Kittitas Indian. Well known among white settlers in the late 1800s, Indian John had owned property on this very hill. He and his wife were buried nearby.

Welcome to the eastern side of the Cascade Mountains, a marker said. *Travelers along I-90 are literally "in the middle of it all." You are near the center of the state, traveling in the Yakima River Valley, which is rich in history and opportunities. The most prominent land features are formed by deep alpine glaciers. The glaciers scoured out U-shaped valleys, leaving the jagged peaks of the Cascade Range. This area features a variety of ecosystems due to the rain shadow effect. Warm moisture-laden air from the Pacific loses its temperature as it rises over the mountains in the area to the west of Snoqualmie Pass. The higher elevations along the crest of the Cascades receive much more rain and snow than areas farther east. Changes in moisture lead to a variety in vegetation and animal habitat.*

Well, it was an informative marker, but totally unnecessary. I had just witnessed it all, driving the Interstate.

* * *

Heading east again at eleven-thirty, I noticed that the temperature had risen to fifty-five. Indian John Hill (elevation 2141) preceded Elk Hill (elevation 2359). I could see for miles now, the sun beginning to crack the dark clouds. Black and brown cattle grazed in golden fields cut from the forests. White sheep held the hillsides, too. Then the road surface, for the first time all day, ran clear and dry—a significant moment. Was this the very spot where the Pacific Northwest surrendered its wet grip? I certainly hoped so.

I was in the flat plain of a bowl surrounded by pine-filled mountains. Horses grazed on the hillsides now, too. Traffic was moderate, many campers mounted on pickups, their attempts to pass each other slowing the speed to sixty. The few French radio stations had disappeared. Ironically, I found one in Spanish, perhaps for migrant workers who worked the area farms. I-5 had entered an agricultural zone, where a dark green lettuce-like crop contrasted with angelhair meadows.

Another great change soon followed. The pine forests abruptly ended—as if they had been felled on purpose right up to this very point, leaving the mountains ahead all tan khaki. It was thirty-eight miles to Yakima and the state was taking on a new look. Cattle and horses roamed on wide ranches, across golden hills stubbled with gray sage. A place called *Ryegrass* (elevation 2535) offered a clue to a new local crop. And then the central desert Ed had mentioned began in earnest.

Quite suddenly, a planetary view of brown terrain opened before me, a smooth and craterless moonscape. Cauliflower scrub laced the wild ryegrass for hundreds of miles. Then I-5 ran a flat plain through mound-like hills. The sun slanted through and I reached for my sunglasses. Large blocks of blue sky were opening up, white clouds piled high on long shelves. High dark mountains lined the eastern horizon.

Soon a lovely new plant appeared, textured like broccoli and tufted with yellow flowers, shining in the sun across the brown terrain. Traffic was light, I-90 curving now through rolling hills. With the return of the sun, the idyllometer soared to ninety. But central Washington couldn't sustain the favorable reading. The highway passed through a huge gravel pit, then crossed a brown Erector Set bridge painted to match the landscape. *Severe Sidewinds Ahead,* a sign warned. But a barren river basin on the right took all my attention.

There was a wide, winding river out there, with steep walls for a shoreline. It was the Columbia! I had crossed it entering Washington and now I was crossing it again, where it runs north to south through the middle of the state—before turning west in its run for the Pacific.

On the bridge above the Columbia, stiff crosswinds knocked me from lane to lane. To my right, down river, stood the Wanapum Dam, a broad and bland concrete face. To the left I could see to the edge of the planet—thousands of miles of brown and yellow mounds, with purple shadows darkening the dry swales between them. Directly ahead, beyond the river, I-90 seemed to dead-end at a cliff as great as the Wanapum Dam itself, a wide, brown wall. But at the last second the highway turned sharply north, to climb the obstacle sideways.

As I snaked my way into the sky along vertical cliffs, the Columbia fell away behind me with a canyon-like view. I was in the Columbia Basin Federal Reclamation Project, where a sign announced the Gorge Amphitheater. Van Morrison had given a concert here once. But the entire landscape was an amphitheater now, gouged with brown crevasses that seem newly formed by earthquakes and glaciers.

Silica Road sounded just right. What else could there be in such wasteland but basic minerals? And oblivious cows grazing. And one Corvette, from which I could see curtains of rain moving on the right, blue sky to the left, and in the mirror a long, gray horizon. But directly overhead, through the 'Vette's glass roof, the sun was beating down brilliantly.

It was twelve-fifteen—high noon—and suddenly a few trees began to return in haphazard groves. This was definitely farmland now, irrigated by long triangular frames that could be wheeled across the fields. The Grand Coulee Dam lay to the north, where for thirty miles the

Columbia River carves out the Grand Coulee Gorge. *Soap Lake* followed—another mineral effect.

Crop Names In Fence Line, a small sign said. But I searched for crop names without success, curious to know what was being grown in the reclaimed desert. A slatted fence paralleled the highway now—for drifting snow, I assumed, because of high winds. Then the territory leveled out and I was speeding east through a basin rimmed by a hint of distant hills. It was a dish more than a basin, where rectangular bales of hay lay beside the highway, stacked in blocks large enough to fill a semi. The temperature had risen to sixty-eight, and the rainy black curtains had disappeared from the corner of the sky.

Shortly before one o'clock I pulled into the Winchester Wasteway Rest Area, aptly named for the terrain about its windswept, treeless mounds. Only five vehicles were in the parking lot. Incredibly, the few pavilions had no roofs—the wind would have ripped them right off. Instead, each little picnic area was a windbreak, with two sections of wire fencing anchored to squat pillars. Joined at right angles, the fences were interwoven with narrow slats for protection on the north and west sides.

I went straight to the information marker. *Water diverted from the Grand Coulee Dam irrigates croplands and hills, forming reservoirs, marshes, wetlands, pods, potholes, and puddles. The abundant water combines with complex landforms sculpted by past flooding. This creates habitats for numerous species that are not common to arid eastern Washington.*

As earlier, it all made perfect sense—I had been driving right through it all along, an Interstate geography lesson. But the notion of *arid* land farther east intrigued me.

Turning for the restrooms, I noticed two middle-aged women in windbreakers standing in the shelter of one of the pavilions. I went right over, and they greeted me warmly.

"There's too damn much traffic in Seattle," one began, as soon as I asked about the Interstates. "But it's nice over in this part of the state. Oregon's nice too. Of all the Interstates I've ever driven, by far the worst are in Louisiana. Did you see much of Louisiana?"

"More than I cared to," I said.

"When you go to these states," she continued, "you can immediately tell which are the most expensive to live in, because the tax money goes into the roads. My son is learning about the weather in junior high now, and now I understand why the weather is like it is in Seattle and the mountains. But when you drive out here you can literally *see* it. The autumn coloration, by the way, is just beginning. In a few weeks, the Interstates all through Washington will be gorgeous. It's a shame you'll miss it."

As she was speaking, a large tangle of brush—big enough to fill a wheelbarrow—flew across the parking lot and lodged in the fence at the first pavilion.

"Tumbleweed," the other woman said nonchalantly. But when she saw my astonishment, she elaborated. "Tumbleweed is nothing but dried sagebrush. In the summer it bounces along the highway and blows across it in little whirlwinds of dust. It can get caught in the grille of your car. Technically, I think it's some sort of thistle, a scratchy yellow-gray weed. Tumbleweeds are like giant bird nests, and when they dry out they begin to roll and bounce everywhere. They can be a nuisance and they can be very dangerous."

"A more interesting phenomenon," the other woman said, "is Mt. St. Helens. When it blew its top, there was ash all along the highway. Ellensburg back there got blacked out. For years you could see the ash piled up along the highway. It looked like dirty snow. These highway fences are for tumbleweed, not for snow. By the way, did you see the wild horses' monument back there? That pack of wrought-iron horses running across the landscape?"

Unfortunately, I had missed it. "I saw some *real* horses," I said. "And I have a bag of dust from Mt. St. Helens back home in Ohio."

The women seemed unimpressed—they'd had their fill of dust from Mt. St. Helens for years—so I excused myself, growing cold in the wind. The temperature had fooled me. I had left my jacket in the 'Vette and the wind was chilling me. But I retreated to the 'Vette greatly satisfied. I had seen—at last—my first tumbleweed.

* * *

Back on the road, I soon grew disappointed. Power lines began to crop up, strung across three short poles followed by a taller fourth one, a distinct and boring pattern. I had been taking their absence for granted— I preferred my Interstates open and wireless—and now I was paying for my ingratitude.

A sign for *Hiawatha Road* seemed out of whack. What was Hiawatha doing in Washington, away from the shores of Gitche Gumee? Hiawatha belonged in upstate New York—a leader of the Onandagas in the sixteenth century, when he had helped organize the Iroquois confederacy. *Moses Lake,* up next, I could understand—I was in a desert that people had wandered in search of a home. The little community was tree-lined, with lovely houses on both sides of the highway. And suddenly I wondered if the trees would continue all the way to Spokane.

Pothole State Park brought a new thought. Certainly the potholes had nothing to do with I-90. The road surface was A+ through here.

The park must have been named for the pockmarked features of the landscape, the potholes formed by scouring glaciers. But the same glaciers had made the territory flat and tedious, a tedium occasionally redeemed by rolling mounds through wide-rimmed bowls. The temperature had reached seventy-two, but an overcast sky subdued the sun. And just when I thought the rest of the way to Spokane would be nothing but dull, the entire smooth surface of the earth opened before me.

Suddenly the Interstate became a perfect black ribbon through angelhair terrain—from the curvature of the horizon ahead of me to the curvature of the horizon behind. There were no jagged edges anywhere, just flowing contours worn smooth by the ages. Here and there dark crevices stood out starkly. And then, miles ahead, large green rectangles loomed strangely in three dimensions, some sort of turf farm, perhaps. But the shapes eventually resolved themselves as bales of hay, cut—for some reason—while still green.

At a sign for *Ritzville* (pop. 1725) I made a mental note. I wanted to see just how ritzy Ritzville was. But all you can see of Ritzville from I-90 is a water tower, above an oasis of trees in a golden plain. It's a clean agricultural community of seed company farmers. Signs at the exit indicate a few motels, plus the promise of local cooking at Jake's Café (open 24 hours). Ritzy enough, given the terrain.

A frightening moment followed. A large tumbleweed flew in front of me, striking the bumper then whipping across the sunroof, leaving my heart thumping for miles down the highway. Fortunately, there were no other vehicles in sight—I might have swerved and lost control. But my Corvette karma was still very much intact.

Beyond Ritzville, slivers of dark rock begin to mark the landscape—smooth onyx-like outcroppings across rolling golden hills—so distinctive and pretty. Wire fencing flanked the highway again, for tumbleweed or cattle, with occasional white-topped silos as fat and wide as oil tanks. A lone windmill was churning away like mad atop a triangular frame, a relic of an earlier era, with wind enough to spare.

I was less than an hour from Spokane now, where I-90 skirts Sprague Lake for several miles. Driven by the wind, choppy whitecaps raced along the narrow body of water. Nearby, a grove of trees sheltered motor homes and campers. Railroad tracks lay to the south, a long gray freight train chugging on by, the first I'd seen in days. Then I pulled into a rest area at the eastern end of Sprague Lake. It was two o'clock. The temperature had slipped to sixty-three.

Situated on a slight hill overlooking the choppy water, the facility was but another windswept oasis, with picnic tables but no windbreaks. It was completely deserted except for a flock of seagulls, another Interstate surprise. Apparently the large, noisy birds were a nuisance. *Do Not Feed The Seagulls!* a sign implored. I watched the flock circle in the wind, screeching loudly, skimming the whitecaps and sweeping close enough to look me in the eye. Where had those gulls come from? Had they been blown across the Cascades from the Pacific? Whatever their fate, they seemed to rely on friendly tourists for food.

But not this tourist. They were still circling in disappointment as I pulled out.

I began to wonder how Spokane would emerge from the landscape now. It wouldn't be long—first city since Seattle.

A few ranches soon appeared on the right, with red houses and picturesque red barns. And then the terrain changed yet again. Butte-like outcroppings arose, with isolated mounds and flat-topped ridges, the smoothness giving way to rugged contours. Then, quite suddenly, beyond a sign for a place called *Fishtrap*, the pine trees returned—not in forests but in scraggly clumps and groves. Much shorter than their western Washington cousins, the pines were back nonetheless.

Farther ahead, the pines thickened, lining the median, and thirty miles from Spokane the groves blended into a forest. The change quickened my sensibilities, helping me to realize something that I should have realized much earlier—all signs for state routes intersecting the highway bore the familiar silhouette of George Washington with his haired pulled back. My Seattle musing had been correct. The state of Washington is named for the father of our country, the very land I was lapping on the Interstates, and the realization came just in time. Idaho is but twenty miles beyond Spokane. I could reflect on George Washington before leaving Washington behind.

Nearing Spokane, I began to look about the landscape for traces of urbanization, but roadside pines block the view. Then the highway funnels through a stretch of bronze outcroppings that had been blasted through a series of rolling crests. Golden mountains appeared on the far left and right, leaving me wondering if they'd been there all along. Then came *Four Lakes,* each lake but a large pond with whitecaps, and a few modest homes along the shore. More highways were merging with I-90 now, the afternoon traffic increasing from light to moderate.

Traces of industry followed, interspersed with ranch houses, bungalows, and trailers—by no means *garbage in*. Geiger Field, a small airport, sat just off the shoulder. Then came B. F. Goodrich, and more light industry on both sides of the highway. I was descending a long incline into a populated valley, a horizon of hills beyond. Then Spokane itself appeared (pop. 362,000), the road still two-laned but with a concrete divider. Middle-class neighborhoods flanked the way, packed in more densely at the very bottom of the slope.

Spokane has no skyline to speak of. A few modern structures stick out, but nothing brand new or glassy. Some buildings are reddish, some tan. Others are white. North of I-90, the Spokane River flows through the city—there are signs for Riverfront Park—but the highway doesn't span the river. It crosses instead a tributary called *Hangman River*, a hint of a violent past. Then you're downtown, ducking beneath a series of overpassses, while the skyline defines itself more clearly overhead. A building on the left sports breast-like domes. There's a small church with a prominent steeple, and a stretch of businesses. Gonzaga University and Whitworth College perch on a hill in the city center, near a castle-like Presbyterian church. Farther downtown, Spokane is like Akron—industrial, a mixture of old and new, from the Metropolitan Financial Center to rows of Archie Bunker housing. Then a high retaining wall escorts you out, the slopes above newly planted with trees.

Leaving the city, I expected suburbs, but they don't exist. There's just a brief stretch of *garbage out*. Then all traffic slowed for construction near my exit, where a huge white hemisphere announces GOLF in large block letters. It was a Friday-afternoon Interstate idle and my day was ending just as it had begun. I could see the sign for Motel Find-Me-Not but couldn't get to the premises. I had come three hundred miles only to be blocked by a maze of orange barrels and dusty improvised lanes.

Then it began to rain—as if to remind me of Seattle—and all that dust turned to mud. Traffic was jammed along new lengths of steaming asphalt, where I left wide muddy tracks when it was my turn to crawl through. I drove carefully. Manhole covers lurked like land mines in open stretches still waiting to be paved.

Half an hour later—in heavier rain—I negotiated one last minefield into Motel Find-Me-Not, the 'Vette's flanks spanked with mud and oily grit. As I sprinted inside to register, I found myself thinking—*the rain in Spokane falls mainly in the plain.*

But Ann had pronounced it *Spo-KAN.*

246

15

Idaho to Bozeman, Montana, a distance of four hundred miles.

The morning temperature—only forty degrees—surprised me, the lowest to date. But there was a beautiful blue sky as I left the Spokane Valley, sputtering along through the last of the construction until the traffic finally cruised at eighty.

Patches of pine and angelhair meadows marked the hilly terrain, with dark mountains circling the horizon. Between the hilltops, white mists lingered above blocks of orange, red, and yellow. Then I-90 rose from the Spokane Valley into pine-filled mountains. And old fears returned. In the higher elevations, the overnight temperature would have dropped to near freezing.

Idaho State Line. Welcome Center 8 Miles. But the "welcome" meant only billboards, and slower traffic, and a sign that now seemed all too much in season. *Bridge May Be Icy.* But I would be in Idaho for only an hour or so, just long enough to cross the northern neck, a stretch of about eighty miles.

Coeur d'Alene (pop. 25,000) appeared first, a place with a curious French name. *Coeur* means *heart,* but *alene* means *awl.* Was the name a bad pun—*in the heart of it awl?* Or maybe it was just some woman's name. At any rate, Coeur d'Alene sits *above* I-90 so you can't really see it, in a notch where the highway sneaks into the mountains.

The pines seemed more ragged now, more conical, as I began winding my way upward, leaving the foothills. A few attractive houses overlooked the chicanes, the morning sun reflecting off their dark picture windows as it crested the mountains. Soon, high above the wandering waters of Lake Coeur d'Alene, I crossed a flat and very clean concrete bridge—the Veterans Memorial Centennial Bridge. The chicanery continued beyond, weaving higher into the mountains as the highway crossed the lake again and again.

Dark pines filled steep hillsides right down to the water's edge, the constant green spattered with yellow from the deciduous trees. Angelhair grasses laced the median and filled the shoulders in browns and tans. This was the Lake Coeur d'Alene Scenic Byway, and it was living up to its name— an Interstate surprise as stunning as Lake Shasta. But large dark clouds soon swallowed the rising sun, checking the idyllometer's sudden surge.

Signs for *The Yellowstone Trail* and *Wolf Lodge Bay* conjured tantalizing images.

Then came a sign I feared. *Chain Up Area Half Mile.* The road was still climbing, steeply, with a warning in flashing yellow lights. *Watch For Ice Next 8 Miles.* Then something I hadn't considered. *Watch For Ice In Shaded Areas.* And there was plenty of shade, the sun moving in and out of thick dark clouds, not strong enough to warm the black surface. Or melt the overnight ice.

Rock ledges now rose vertically above me, steep ravines dropping away below. And still the mountains kept rising, in pyramid-like steps to which the pines were clinging desperately. I passed two dump trucks hauling sand up the mountain—not a good sign. Then a 'Vette exactly like mine came *down* the mountain in a hurry, without so much as a salute or a beep of the horn. Another bad sign. I fully expected to slide into oblivion at the very next curve.

The lengthy ascent finally crested at 3,069 feet. But the immediate descent brought no relief, dropping sharply at a five-point-five grade through rock ledges and pine. The posted speed dropped to fifty-five, the chicanes twisting like a corkscrew all the way to the bottom. Had the sun been out, the view would have been spectacular. As it was, deep shadows made it sinister. I focused on the dark spots, waiting for ice.

And then I was down—*Chain Removal Half Mile*—my heart knocking at my ribs in celebration. But the posted speed immediately returned to seventy-five, despite more chicanes and a series of narrow bridges. I was in Silver Valley, reminiscent of the Roanoke Valley on I-81. But there is nothing *silver* at all about Silver Valley. The silver must have been underground, I decided, and a sign for *Smelterville* (pop. 464) confirmed the notion.

Signs for *Cataldo Mission* and *Mission State Park* sparked new thoughts. What incredible hardships the missionaries must have faced in these rugged wilds! Where white mists curl upward like Indian smoke signals. Where another road sign—of indigenous sympathy?—proclaimed *Shoshone.*

Moments later the sun washed across the valley ahead of me, sweeping like the shadow of an airplane, brightening the yellow and burnt umber and deepening the purple and green. As if inspired by the landscape, a lone billboard cried out unabashedly, *Connie, I Love You! Will You Marry Me?* Amidst such beauty, how could Connie refuse?

Big Creek followed the highway near Exit 54. There were railroad tracks, too, tucked into the trees. What a chore it must have been to clear the way for them through the cracks and crevices of these mountains. Pockets of civilization revealed themselves as well—a cabin here, a trailer home there. *Lookout Pass 12 Miles*. I was hoping for a rest area at Lookout Pass and I'd have to watch for it closely—I was too busy gearing down for the flying chicanes.

This was definitely mining territory—Gold Creek, Silver Mountain, and Copper Street telling the story. But one mountain brought a large *M*, limed into a steep escarpment. *M* for *Montana*? This was Idaho, not Montana. Maybe the *M* stood for *mining*. Whatever it meant, it had to have been etched there by mountain climbers, rappelling down to risk their lives for the sake of a capital letter.

Another *Chain Up Area* caught me off guard. We were suddenly climbing again, my fear of ice returning as the posted speed dropped to fifty, the highway ascending to Lookout Pass in the Coeur d'Alene National Forest. As it twisted upward, the road surface worsened, the 'Vette proceeding cautiously in second gear. Then I passed through a chute of trees and the ascent abruptly ended—on the very edge of the earth—Lookout Pass at the Montana state line. *Elevation 4860*. The most stunning Interstate entrance to any state in America.

Overwhelmed by the sudden view, I slowed to a crawl. White mists floated straight down below me, across deep fissures in the valleys, where patches of gold laced the dark green pines. I was on the edge of a sheer precipice—like a roller coaster's first drop—then I was driving right down it, staring into the throat of colossal gorges. Lookout Pass, I realized immediately, is woefully misnamed. It ought to be called *Lookdown Pass*. Because that's all you can do—look straight down if you dare. Because straight down is exactly where you're going.

* * *

Here's an Interstate Item from the web site of the Lookout Pass Ski Area, which bills itself as *the #1 Powder Place* in northern Idaho:

Imagine a ski area of pristine beauty, exceptional snow quality, and a four-lane expressway right to the parking lot. At Lookout Pass, we're committed to providing you and your family with a great skiing experience. The snow comes early. It snows regularly. And our climate results in snow that tends to be light and fun to ski.

And getting here is easy and fast. We are located right alongside Interstate 90 at the Idaho/Montana border, midway between major airports in Spokane and Missoula. You can be on the snow in as little time as it takes to put on your equipment.

I just hoped that all of that early, regular, light, and fun-to-ski snow would hold off until I got to the bottom of the mountain, lest the 'Vette turn into a red snowboard.

* * *

Dark clouds blocked the sun. The temperature had dropped to forty, and just beyond the pass it began to drizzle. It was nine-thirty. Or ten-thirty. A sign at the crest had announced Mountain Standard Time. And *time* was exactly what I needed now—Mountain Standard or otherwise—to recover from the shock of Lookout Pass.

I began to search for a rest area, and there it was—a green shack with a roof of wooden shingles, on a dark quarter acre of immense pines.

Three large garbage cans sat beside the old structure. The pines had dropped brown needles all over it, forming a thick mat on the shingled roof where a furry green moss was growing, not quite the same green as the shack. Two pavilions nearby had matching shake-shingle roofs, their picnic tables weather-beaten to a pulpy gray. This must be Montana, I told myself, where we don't stand on ceremony. As if to prove it, a glass case displayed a wrinkled map of the state, held in place at the corners by black electrical tape.

The only other vehicle in the small parking lot was a gray minivan, and as I was studying the map, a middle-aged couple and their college-aged son stepped from the shack and headed towards it. I intercepted them on the sidewalk and we stood around in the rain, discussing the Interstates.

"We're going to Missoula for the big game," the father said. "Montana versus Cal State Northridge. It's two hundred miles, but we can make it in less than three and a half hours, thanks to I-90."

His wife was more blunt. "Life would suck without the Interstates," she said. "We couldn't go to the game today, for one thing. I think the Interstates are great. You can quote me on that."

"These are the foothills to the Rockies," her husband explained. "We're in the Bitterroot Range. All those yellow cone-shaped trees you've been seeing are *tamaracks*, a kind of pine that actually turns color—first yellow, then red. Nature's tricked it into believing it has leaves. The tamarack is related to the larch tree."

Their son, who had wandered over to inspect the 'Vette, soon rejoined us.

"You've got the right car for these winding roads!" he said. "You'll need it down below. It gets even more winding."

I couldn't believe it. The chicanes I'd just driven had been the most challenging I'd seen. "I thought Montana was supposed to be *flat*," I said. "I was hoping to let the 'Vette open up."

"Oh, it'll get flat all right," the student's father said, "over in the eastern part of the state. As people who know Montana always say, *it's miles and miles of nothing but miles and miles.*"

I caught up with the family in the minivan a short while later, zipping by them with a beep of the horn in a severe chicane. The rain had abated—a fluke of Lookout Pass—but despite sharp curves and deer warnings and ice warnings, the speed was still posted at seventy-five.

Incredibly, no median now divided the east–west lanes. Nothing separated the traffic but a few yards of flat concrete and a thin yellow line. The absence of a divider came as a shock—something I'd seen nowhere else in America.

On full alert, I spiraled farther down into Montana, past the St. Regis River and Camel Hump Road, into the crotch of mountains that rose straight up from the guardrail to my right. Then came the warning the student had mentioned. *Attention Truckers! Sharp Curve Advisory Next Few Miles.* And suddenly all curves were posted at forty-five—the slowest I'd seen, still no problem for the 'Vette. I slipped through the turns easily in fourth gear.

The St. Regis River soon appeared again—on the left, then the right—shallow and winding and about fifty yards wide. Occasionally, it funneled cut logs. Brown mountains rose above me, totally barren of pines, white mists curling up their steep slopes. And always a river followed the contours of the highway.

251

Clark Fork—named for Lewis and Clark—soon replaced the St. Regis, running black in the trees. Broadening, then narrowing, it burbled its way beneath a series of flat bridges, where trailer homes and double-wides housed the local population. A few billboards advertised casinos and exotic dancing. Otherwise, the isolation was total.

Alone on the road, I began hunting for the next rest area. It appeared at ten-twenty, larger than the last and less rustic, among high pines with sparse branches at the very top. The main building was concrete, with an eight-sided metal roof. Nearby, three pavilions were divided into quadrangles, each sheltering cement tables and benches. A few vehicles sat at intervals along the length of the parking lot, but their passengers were keeping to themselves. I contented myself with the historical information.

The Iron Mountain Mine, one of the largest successful quartz mines in western Montana, was located about 12 miles north of here. L. P. Jones, a former Northern Pacific Railroad brakeman, discovered the ore body in 1888. The discovery, the marker explained, had resulted in the formation of the Iron Mountain Company. Here were two more minerals to add to the local catalogue. But if they had mined quartz, why wasn't this called *Quartz* Mountain?

Back on the highway, I became intrigued by a new look to the landscape—mountains rising straight up from both shoulders of the road. Sheer gravel escarpments scarred their pine faces, a menacing sight beneath an overcast sky. I tried the radio for company but found only static. Soon, far below me, a freight train with colorful boxcars was making its way along the tracks beside a river, ducking in and out of the trees. Brown sandbars lined the shallow waterway. Then, thirty miles from Missoula, small farms with red barns began to appear in brief clearings. With always a river in the bottomlands and valleys.

A River Runs Through It. This was it, I suddenly realized. I was entering the very territory described in the book by Norman F. Maclean, his account of trout fishing on the Big Blackfoot River. Trout fishing as a religion. In God's country.

And like a biblical revelation, the sun suddenly blazed forth, sending the idyllometer all the way to one hundred. I was in the center of a valley surrounded by undulating mountains, the highway stretching straight ahead like an airport runway. Here was the chance I'd been waiting for.

Slipping Eric Clapton into the CD chamber, I took the 'Vette to a hundred and ten with *Layla!* screaming in my ears. But the sun vanished just as suddenly as it had burst forth, curbing my attempt at a double one hundred.

I flew into Flathead Lake Glacier National Park, where rolling mountains completely circled the valley. And a wry billboard confirmed my earlier notion. *A Creek Runs Through It.* The locals were enjoying a measure of fame brought by the film based on MacLean's book. Or maybe the billboard was a sardonic comment on the lingering drought.

More billboards preceded Missoula (pop. 79,000), where the University of Montana football team was preparing for Cal State Northridge. It was *garbage in* to the left—a succession of house trailers and junkyards. But some attractive ranch homes were scattered about the hills to the right.

Then Missoula itself appeared—at the far end of the valley—a few square miles of trees cradled by brown mountains. The place grew prettier on approach, a quaint college town, where another large white capital *M* had been blazed into the hillside. A white-domed bell tower rose above the foliage—the town hall, perhaps. There was a pointy church steeple, and small houses on neat tree-lined streets, their leaves shining in soft reds and yellows.

From I-90, Missoula is a utopia. You can see the entire community from a distance—all the boundaries that define people's lives. *Here* is the valley and *there* are the mountains. And below the mountains lies

Missoula, the university in its midst. After the rugged passage through Lookout Pass, I found the sight humbling—so unpretentious and pleasant. Here was the promise of life as it could be lived within a few square miles.

And I could see it all from the Interstate.

On the far side of Missoula, I-90 rises again into steep mountains, dipping occasionally but always ascending toward a notch at the outer rim of the world. Rivers come and go through hills and valleys—the *Blackfoot*, the *Rattlesnake*, the ubiquitous *Clark Fork*. All were lined with orange and yellow foliage, amidst a thick pelt of pine.

Signs now reflected the rural terrain—*Deer Lodge, Chalet Bearmouth, Beavertail Hill State Park, Granite County*. Small herds of cattle grazed in fields across the valleys, where some of the yellow trees, close by the shoulder, proved to be birch. It was fifty degrees at twelve-thirty as I crossed the Clark Fork yet again, converting the 'Vette's digital clock to Mountain Standard Time.

At one o'clock I stopped for a history lesson at the Bear Mouth Rest Area.

About one quarter mile east of here, a lone marker explained, *was a trading point for the placer camps of Beartown, Garnet, and Coloma, located in the hills to the north. The River, officially known as the Clark Fork of the Columbia, and so named for Captain William Clark of the Lewis and Clark Expedition, has many local names. Its source is the Silver Bow Creek, then it becomes the Deer Lodge River, then Hellgate River, then the Missoula, and ends as Clark Fork. It also has one other name, the Intrepid. In 1841 Jesuit Priest Pierre Jean de Smet called it the St. Ignatius River as he established a mission for the Flathead Indians.*

A glass case nearby presented information on trout fishing, ghost towns, and rockhounding. *In Montana*, it proudly concluded, *the west is a way of life that is rooted in history and hopeful for the future. It defines Montana both as a place and as people. We invite you to take the journey of a lifetime, a journey of time and space in Big Sky Country.*

Time and space and sky. Those are the keys to Montana, and they become more evident as you continue eastward—along stretches of I-90 that have been blasted through granite glaciers, bald now except for the tufts of yellow trees.

The sun had come out, but it was raining nonetheless. Dark curtains of a sun shower hung across the valley. Even so, the Big Sky extended to the perimeter of the planet. I was alone on the road again, the Saturday traffic nonexistent. Only the telephone poles hinted of people. And irrigation contraptions like the Wright brothers' plane. Gradually, the hills became more brown than green. A large capital C had been etched into one escarpment, a capital *D* in another. Cattle grazed on small farms through the bottomlands. And the pale sky stretched on forever.

As for time and space, a simple sign said it all. *Next Rest Area 212 Miles.*

But Butte (pop. 34,000) would come first, where I planned to have lunch. The road was deteriorating, *B-* since the last rest area, no better than *C* farther on. I was in high plains country, where brown mountains rise as foothills to taller mountains, and green pines fringe the edge of the earth. The meadows held horses now as well as cows, in monotonous regularity. The only distinctive landmark for miles around sat beyond the Warm Springs Wildlife Management Area, in the midst of a wide stretch of gravel on the right—a high smokestack, like those in England among the ruins of Phoenician tin mines.

I passed a sign for *Opportunity* and laughed out loud. The name had to be someone's idea of a joke. The rest area had touted Montana's *future.* But in all these empty spaces, Montana's future seemed synonymous with its past.

Suddenly, on the outskirts of Butte, I saw more police cars than I'd seen in days—half a dozen, each by a vehicle pulled over on the shoulder. A harvest of zealous football fans, perhaps. The sparse traffic was cruising at eighty-five, and had the sun been out I would have been trying for a double-hundred. Which would have put me on the shoulder with a Montana state trooper.

Farther ahead, Butte lay shrouded in clouds and dark curtains of rain. Like Missoula, the city is nestled beneath a protective landform, a massive butte in this case—a sheer brown trapezoid. And like Missoula, the entire community can be seen in a glance across the barren terrain, another humbling Interstate perspective. Happily, Butte has few billboards. Bungalows line its straight streets, where the trees—now orange and yellow—give way to green pine at the city's far edge, right where that big brown wall rises straight into the sky.

Exiting into a Saturday-afternoon Interstate ambush, I fought the traffic around several blocks to a local restaurant. But I was the only one in a hurry. And the realization was chastening.

The feeling continued inside, where the waitress—a teenage girl—seemed to have all the time in Montana on her hands. There were only two other customers, another high school girl and her boyfriend, lingering over Cokes in a booth across the way. I ordered spaghetti, the first thing I saw on the menu, anxious to get back on the road. But the lunch hour crunch was over. There was nothing to do but stare out the window at the dark clouds above the butte, while the waitress made her way back to the kitchen, her every movement saying, *That butte ain't goin' nowhere, mister. So what's yer hurry?*

And had she asked, I wouldn't have known how to answer.

After lunch, it was only eighty-two miles to Bozeman, but first I had to negotiate that big butte. Initially, it looks like I-90 wants to avoid the issue, proceeding to the base of the wall, then suddenly turning right as if to outflank the enemy. But it turned left again just as suddenly, cutting up into the mountains—toward distant blue sky beyond the overhead clouds.

By now I was used to the mountain signs—*Chain Up Area*—and could predict what lay head. Still, the geography was puzzling. I had always associated *plains* with *sea level*, but that's not the case in Montana. Butte lies in a plain surrounded by elevations higher than Denver, and the altitude may have been the reason for the rough road surface, making the ascent as difficult and unpredictable as the buffeting winds.

I pushed the 'Vette up and up, through brown mountainsides of sparse pine and bent yellow trees. Then the warning signs began. *Icy Spots Next 10 Miles.* The temperature was only forty-five, warm enough, I hoped, to see me through. Yet the climb seemed endless, until I remembered that young waitress at the restaurant—with the palpable patience—and the thought of her slow pace sustained me to the very top. Where an Interstate surprise lay in wait.

Continental Divide. Elevation 6393. And suddenly there was nothing but Big Sky above me all the way across Montana. Nothing but Montana and its big blue sunny sky.

* * *

The road grew rougher on the descent, a perilous six percent grade, the posted truck speeds dropping steadily—*45, 35, 25.* Incredibly, the few cars ahead of me were racing down at seventy-five, despite steep ravines with rocky cliffs and pine-filled slopes. I was in the northwest extension of the Rocky Mountains, where enormous piles of gray boulders line the shoulders and medians, where white cliffs jut into the sky. And in a moment of Interstate clarity that suddenly seemed laughable, I finally understood how this mountain chain had earned its name.

Cresting a butte, I found myself alone on the road once more, facing a line of cliffs striated in pink, gray, and salmon. Striking them at an angle, the sun added an array of reds and golds, shooting the idyllometer immediately to one hundred. The road was straight and clear ahead of me for miles—another perfect opportunity—and I eased the 'Vette to a hundred and fifteen. But once again the sun betrayed me, ducking behind a shelf of high white clouds, thwarting another attempt at a double-hundred.

But my time would come. I was certain of that now. All I needed was a little more patience.

Coming down out of the mountains by Pipestone, near Exit 241, the road grew much smoother. Then a sign announced the Rocky Mountains Museum. But why go *inside* to see the Rocky Mountains? It seemed absurd, especially *here*—in a big valley surrounded by golden plains, brown foothills, and jagged peaks, where a band of pines met the wide blue sky. Then blue sagebrush laced the terrain through the Tobacco Root Mountains, the view extending in all directions for hundreds of miles. Impossible to believe, Montana's Big Sky was growing bigger by the minute.

Yellowstone National Park Next Right. But as with the museum, there was no need to exit. I was in a national park of my own on the Interstate, traversing a mountain desert outlined by rugged peaks. And there seemed no end to the warnings. *Chain Up Area One Mile.*

I crossed the Boulder River, into brown mountains bearded with green. Farmland here had been tilled a darker brown, and above the golden meadows beyond, the turning leaves added bursts of orange and yellow. And still a river ran through it—the Jefferson now—with quiet herds of cattle along its banks. Then came the Missouri Headwaters State Park. *Headwaters*—where it all begins. That's Montana, I decided. Headwaters-to-the-world. To which a new image soon presented itself. *Addison County Buffalo Jump.* I was driving through territory right out of *Dances with Wolves.*

Thousands of acres of open rangeland spread before me, filled with cattle in big valleys beneath the mountains. But the approach to Bozeman (pop. 23,000) broke the spell. Like Missoula, Bozeman is situated beneath a mountain range, but the city is more spread out, its approach oppressively flat. There are too many billboards, and the city has a helter-skelter look. Homes, businesses, gas stations, and motels are strewn about with no obvious plan or center.

Arriving at three-fifteen, I made my way to Motel Find-Me-Not, where two skinny teenage girls, hardly fourteen, were tending the desk for their parents. Wide-eyed and giggling, they were only too eager to tell me about the Interstates. I told them I was from out of town and was worried about the weather ahead.

"Well, you know," the older sister said, "between here and Livingston? Once you get through Bozeman Pass? In winter? The wind's so strong it blows down all the signs! It even blows the semis and trailers right off the road! So they'll close it, you know? Not for snow but high winds?"

The younger sister, elbowing for position at the desk, saw her chance. "Other than that," she said proudly, "the Interstate is always open. *Always*. And you know what? It snows here in *October*. We could get snow any day now!"

"Have some fruit," her sister added, as if it were anything but a non sequitur. She pointed behind me to a small table with a large basket of apples and oranges—the only such Motel Find-Me-Not offering in all of America—large red juicy apples and navel oranges, a Montana handout. I took one of each as the girls showed me to my room.

Then I went straight outside to wash the 'Vette. I had several warm hours before the sun would drop beneath the mountains, and I would need every minute of it. I hadn't washed the car since arriving in Seattle. It was streaked with oil and grit from all the construction areas, and I didn't want to give the gunk a chance to harden. So I got right to it, lying flat on my back beneath the car in the parking lot, scrubbing away at the rear flanks and wheel wells.

Then I heard a voice and looked up. A middle-aged man in khakis and a sweater was standing above me.

"I've been admiring your technique," he said earnestly. He had just checked in and was returning to the parking lot to fetch some things from his van. The large vehicle, bearing Illinois plates, was rugged and dirty and solidly packed to the roof.

I asked the man about the Interstates and soon wished that I hadn't. He was a zealot, unlike anyone else I'd talked to around the country.

"It's simply amazing," he began, "absolutely amazing, how the Interstates have opened up this nation. I'm in the education business, and there are opportunities for educators all over this country. But how do you get there? How do you *get to* all those opportunities? On the Interstates, of course!"

I told him I had passed a place called *Opportunity* back down the road, trying to make a joke about looking for a job. But the man would have none of it. He didn't seem to be listening.

"How else could America have developed," he said proudly, "if not for the Interstates? And you say you're celebrating that very fact?" Like the older sister inside at the desk, he had a penchant for speaking in questions.

I wish I could have heard the conversation when he checked in.

* * *

In the morning, for the first time on my Interstate odyssey, I woke to frost on the 'Vette—a snowflake-like coating as fine as Russian lace. Thin sheets of ice glazed the windshield. The sun was up, the temperature thirty-eight, and the Weather Channel was forecasting snow for parts of the state I'd driven through yesterday.

More Corvette karma. I had missed the treacherous conditions in the mountains by twenty-four hours.

In the meantime, the brilliant Sunday morning was a revelation, drastically changing my opinion of Bozeman. Cresting the mountains to the east, the sun was blazing in a deep blue sky so wide that little Bozeman seemed to be lost in outer space, looking back at the earth. If this was how the sun came up in Bozeman, I wanted to move here. I wanted to run into Motel Find-Me-Not, wake the owner of the van from Illinois, and shout—*I too have seen the light, and it is the light of the Interstates!*

Instead, I readied myself for the more practical problem of ascending through the mountains to Bozeman Pass.

After an early breakfast, I headed out and drove directly into the glare of the rising sun, climbing steadily into the kind of gorgeous blue-domed day that had not quite materialized yesterday. Mountains to the east stood out in sharp silhouettes, the trees bejeweled in fall colors. This was Canyon Road, curling up and up as the temperature slipped down and down. It was twenty-nine degrees now, below freezing, the frost gleaming on the mountain slopes, the granite crags glistening.

Whenever the sun ducked behind a mountain peak, the early morning turned gloomy. Deep shadows obscured the highway through slick curves. If there had been ice on my windshield down below, there had to be ice on the road up above. Or snow. Then came that fearsome sign—*Chain Up Area*—and it took all my courage to gear down and keep climbing.

Cattle and horses grazed in frosted valleys below, as chicanes kept winding up toward Bozeman Pass—to an elevation of nearly five thousand feet—where the idyllometer suddenly reached a perfect hundred. And stayed there. And as at Lookout Pass, the entire earth suddenly gleamed far below me. Then the road turned smooth, and I began the swift descent.

Two vans ahead of me each trailed a dory, the kind of open boats from which whales were once harpooned, boats made for rough going in choppy waters. Appropriately, one was named the *Pequod*. The other bore only an unpoetic brand name—*Drift Boat*. It was easy to imagine Lewis and Clark in such boats, fighting the currents in the rivers of Montana. But for the moment I was fighting gusty crosswinds of the sort the giggling girls in Bozeman had warned about. The *Pequod* swerved and recovered—the *Drift Boat* in turn—and then the sudden wind shear shook the 'Vette.

In the median, the reddish grass seemed aflame. Black lava-like outcroppings split the golden hills. Near Livingston (pop. 6701) the sun seemed pure white overhead. And then I crossed the Yellowstone

River for the first time. It had been wandering through the valley to my left—low, wide, rocky and shallow. Now its dark water glistened like sapphires in the early sun.

Directly ahead, smooth new blacktop continued eastward with a wide view of the Rockies. Having passed the two boats, I ran on alone, my excitement as high as Montana's Big Sky. I could sense something special in the making—I felt certain I'd bag my double-hundred. It was not yet nine o'clock, and I had the entire glorious day before me.

Several modern windmills, like three-pronged airplane propellers, twirled idly in the valley plain beyond Livingston, the winds less strong in the lower elevations. Yellow trees lined the Yellowstone, where a few houses and farms had the Rockies for their back yard. A jagged mountain range ran high to the left, its sheer face extending to a high butte directly ahead. Then the butte gave way to smooth hills, which dwindled in turn to flat plains, on the very circumference of Montana's Big Sky.

Cattle grazed on the hillsides near White Sulphur Springs as the Yellowstone continued by my side—alternately pebbly, stony, and gravelly—in a shallow riverbed lined with golden trees. There were no vehicles ahead of me for miles. I checked the mirror. No vehicles behind. The time had come. Montana had given me the time, the space, and the Big Sky. The rest was up to me.

Cruising at eighty-five, I floored the 'Vette to one-twenty, easing up minutes later in the teeth of a buffeting headwind. But I had achieved it at last, a goal I'd set in the Southwest—a double one hundred!—one hundred on the idyllometer and more than one hundred on the speedometer. It was Sunday, October 10, 1999, the most beautiful day of my grand lap of America. And my most beautiful day on the Interstates, ever.

But I instantly felt sad, as in Texas when the idyllometer finally hit one hunded. It had been all too easy, thanks to Montana and I-90. There was still half a continent to cross. But I doubted I'd see such perfect weather again, or an absence of traffic in such wide-open spaces.

Which left me but one option. To see what top speed I could reach as the day progressed.

* * *

Like a faithful old dog, the Yellowstone River follows I-90 for hundreds of miles through Montana. No wider than a football field now, its banks were lined with a ribbon of golden trees, a band of angelhair meadows beyond. Rocky shoals and sandbars split the center, its black water flowing rapid and smooth.

Farther along, green fields spread across the landscape, irrigated by long pipes on wheels. Occasionally, craggy buttes rose right from the banks of the Yellowstone, and I began to wonder how the river had gotten its name. Had it ever held gold? I could imagine its tranquil shores crowded with prospectors' tents, its shallows lined with men—elbow to elbow—working their pans. Gold or no, it was yellow enough with the surrounding autumn foliage.

Coming over the top of a rise, I discovered a father and daughter on twin white horses, trotting along in the grass just off the shoulder of the highway. The girl, no older than the giggling ones back in Bozeman, was wearing a bike helmet. Her father was the Marlboro Man. They ignored the 'Vette, and suddenly I felt foolish with all that horsepower beneath me. A single horse is all you need in Montana.

I soon entered a valley by Crazy Mountain, where a ranch called the Crazy-D brought a new idea. Maybe you had to be crazy to live out here. Or maybe everyone else was crazy for *not*. The red barns and white outbuildings of the Crazy-D were surrounded by golden plains that spread away to distant mesas. Then came the foothills to the ever-present Rockies. Add to this picture some cattle and sheep, the rippling Yellowstone, and the Montana Big Sky, and you find yourself questioning your own mortality. And suddenly Montana seemed a good place in which to die—in places like *Big Timber*, *Greycliff*, or *Sweet Grass County*. Even *Prairie Dog Town State Park*.

Needing a break from all the beauty, I stopped at ten o'clock at the Captain William Clark Rest Area, an open spot on the crest of a hill surrounded by a stand of tall pines. The small parking lot was empty, but another history lesson waited by the sidewalk.

You are now following the historical trail of the Lewis and Clark Expedition. On their return from the Pacific in July of 1806, Captain Clark camped for five days about forty miles downstream near Park City. The expedition had been looking for timber suitable for building canoes, ever since striking the river near Livingston. They found a couple of large cottonwoods here that would serve. They fitted their axes with handles made from chokecherry and went to work making two canoes. When finished, they faced them together with a deck of buffalo hides. Among seven men, Sacajawea and her child went curving downriver on this makeshift yacht, arriving at the mouth of the Yellowstone on August 3rd. Captain Lewis split off north on the return trip and explored the Marias River and returned via the Missouri, joining them on August 12th.

No doubt the landscape had changed little since Lewis and Clark had explored it. It seemed entirely possible to recreate their expedition now—running the Yellowstone by lashing the *Pequod* to the *Drift Boat*, shoving off from shore to drift through eddies and whirlpools and rapids. Or you could simply follow the river on I-90 in a swift red Corvette. Which thought attracted me to an innocuous poster:

Yes, Mario, there is a speed limit. It's called the Basic Rule, and they've never heard of it at the Indy 500. It means driving in a "reasonable and prudent" manner, based on weather, road, vehicle, and traffic conditions. You be the judge. If you don't take responsibility, the Highway Patrol will. Fines ranging from $75 to $500 will appear on your record. Basic Rule. It's more than a rule. It's the law.

The warning seemed outdated. Maybe *Mario* was an allusion to the Mario Brothers video game. But there was nothing very Italian about Montana, despite my spaghetti in Butte. A number of people had told me that speed limits didn't exist in Montana, yet I-90 was clearly posted at seventy-five. Which meant cruising at eighty-five. But I had already hit one-twenty and was primed to go higher. And according to the *Basic Rule*, that wouldn't be a problem—the weather was perfect, the road was grade A, I was driving a racecar, and the traffic was non-existent. So what was to prevent me from doing one-fifty? It was a nice round figure. A decent warm-up for the Indy 500.

Then it struck me. They must have meant *Mario Andretti*.

Beyond the rest area, in a stretch of highway lined with deer warnings, a large brown deer with a big white belly lay on the shoulder, as if napping in the sun. This was Stillwater County now, where the Yellowstone at times seems dead still, and where the landscape begins to change. The wide-sky horizons were steadily narrowing, until woods on both sides of the highway limited the view to several miles.

But still a river ran through it—I crossed the Yellowstone yet again, shallow, rocky, glinting—as white mists rose in deep valleys ahead of me. When the river lay to my right, it was star-spangled. When it ran on my left, it was quiet and blue. Everything depended on the angle of the sun.

I ascended through a valley of smoky mists, where sawtoothed pines lined the horizon beyond, constant foreground to the big blue sky. The idyllometer was holding steady at one hundred, and I began to look for the perfect stretch to cut the 'Vette loose.

Gleaming like bars of gold bullion, bales of hay lay scattered in distant fields. Then I ran a long ridge, mists curling above and below me like stray ghosts. Before long, far to the right, snowcapped mountains boldly raised their heads—for the first time in Montana. Small white clouds were floating above them in a royal blue sky. It was all I needed of church on this Sunday morning.

Then came the Beartooth Mountain Range near Columbus (pop. 1573), a community of doublewide homes. It was ten-thirty and the temperature had risen to forty-five. Reddish heather joined the purple sage on the rocky hillsides. And suddenly there was something in the

261

sky up ahead, floating above a blaze of orange trees. It looked like a spinnaker—a bright green and white sail—and beneath it a man lay prone on what looked like an ironing board.

I shook my head in disbelief. What a view that guy must have, floating in heaven on Sunday morning! He was seeing Montana in his own way, on his own terms. Like the Marlboro Man and his daughter on horseback. Like me in my 'Vette. I was no longer ashamed of all the horsepower beneath me. I was excited and proud, and I leaned on the horn as I flew beneath the flimsy airship.

But twenty miles from Billings the idyllometer began to slip. The terrain leveled out, and the Yellowstone ran the base of a craggy cliff. A kind of sandstone desert followed, with brown buttes and mesas, and telephone poles returned at the side of the road. Then the landscape turned downright flat and ugly. Industrial smokestacks spewed white chemicals. Near Exit 434, entire neighborhoods appeared out of nowhere—double-wide trailers and ranch homes, working class at best. Then came Billings' *garbage in*—a barrage of billboards, car dealerships, John Deere equipment, industrial parks, and an oil refinery as ugly as any on the New Jersey Turnpike. And as if to hide from the ugliness, the loyal Yellowstone disappeared. But I could still catch glimpses of distant mountains.

Billings (pop. 81,000) is an insult to Montana. An unaccustomed eyesore. On approach, a lone building defines its skyline, the rectangular dark Sheraton. Like Missoula and Bozeman, the city lies on the western side of the mountains, but it's a smaller mountain range that trails off to the south. Duplexes, double-wides, ranch homes, and split-levels form the suburbs, along the base of an outlying bluff. Then comes the downtown, drab and forgettable. Immediately beyond, by a sign for *Chief Plenty-Coups Cavern*, the Yellowstone returns, running beneath the highway, only to disappear amidst the smokestacks of Billings' *garbage out*.

This time, I was glad to see the river go. It had pained me to see it in such undeserving company.

As if to redeem itself for taking you through Billings, the Interstate soon rises into the mountains with a world-rim view—a panorama of brown hills laced with pine. A flock of Canada geese skimmed the yellow foliage in a far corner of the sky. Next came a sign for the Little Bighorn Battlefield. I was approaching an important fork in the road, where I-94 heads northeast for North Dakota and I-90 turns southeast for Wyoming.

As I veered left on I-94, Montana immediately acquired a new look—eroded terrain in a variety of shapes and contours, with rocky outcroppings jutting into the sky. Before long, I descended into a valley, then the land leveled out, heading straight for the horizon through a wavy mirage. And suddenly it seemed like Montana might get tedious. Was this where it began—the *miles and miles of nothing but miles and miles?*

I could see forever in all directions, only small and desolate buttes to catch the eye. It was a hundred and eighty miles to Glendive, my day's destination—just short of the North Dakota border—and I began to fear that I'd seen the last of the Yellowstone. Montana was growing smoother before my eyes, brown plains rolling away to my right, with flatter plains, then gray cliffs, to the left. Gusts of winds rattled the 'Vette. I saw a sign for *Pompey's Pillar*, but the landmark—named for the Roman general and politician murdered by Caesar—can't be seen from the Interstate.

To the left, the unsightly gray cliffs persisted, like the excavated walls of a gravel pit. Then the highway began to wind and dip and roll, and when it finally straightened out there was a river to the left, working its way along the foot of a rocky ledge. It was the Yellowstone—my old friend!—a white sandbar down the middle, drift-wood on it shores.

Montana was majestic again. The river made all the difference. The idyllometer agreed, rushing straight to one hundred, and in response I put my foot to the floor, hitting one twenty-five before the wind forced me to back off.

But that was nothing. I knew I could go faster.

16

AS SOON AS MY SABBATICAL HAD BEEN APPROVED BY THE UNIVERSITY WHERE I teach, I went in search of a Corvette for my Interstate odyssey. I was short on cash, but I had the *I Ching* on my side.

A creative approach was needed and someone suggested a sponsor. It was worth a try. I began with the local Chevy dealership where I'd purchased a '91 Caprice and a '96 Geo. Incredibly, the day after I mailed my proposal, the owner of the place was sent to jail on a variety of charges, making front-page news and leaving me wondering about my Caprice and Geo, let alone a Corvette. My letter went unanswered, so I sent the same proposal to the largest Corvette dealership in Ohio. Without a response.

Undaunted, I wrote to Zora Arkus-Duntov, the Belgian engineer known as the "Father of the Corvette." This time a response *was* forthcoming—I was politely informed that Mr. Zora Arkus-Duntov had retired.

So I tried the Corvette assembly plant in Bowling Green, Kentucky, receiving in return a lovely handwritten note from a woman in Public Information. She praised my proposal but referred me to General Motors headquarters in Detroit, *where all such decisions are made.*

So I went straight to the top, writing to Robert Stempel, CEO of GM. (*Dear Bob.*) But Bob never replied. And it became clear that nobody wanted to give me a Corvette, or let me borrow one, or arrange a deal of any kind.

But the *I Ching* was behind me and I was adamant. I wanted a Corvette for lapping America. No other car would do, despite a warning in *Newsweek*: *Corvettes certainly do have style and nostalgia. But beware: They verge on the cliché.*

All the better. In a *post*-postmodern society, irony is as important as ethos.

* * *

The Mt. Vista Rest Area was just ahead, and the timing was perfect. I needed a respite from the morning's exhilaration. It was eleven-thirty, and the name of the rest area promised a view of the landscape, including the Yellowstone.

Mt. Vista, nothing more than a small butte, appeared to be high enough for a commanding perspective of the surrounding plain. Only one truck and a car were in the small parking lot, just two pavilions in the grassy area by the comfort station. But it was the small sign out front that snagged my attention. *Rattlesnakes Have Been Observed. Please Stay On The Sidewalks.*

I took the clean white sidewalk to the next sign, a historical marker, *Junction Of The Bighorn And Yellowstone Rivers:*

The area which surrounds the mouth of the Bighorn River as it enters the Yellowstone 13 miles east of here is one of the most significant areas in the early history of Montana. The Yellowstone was known universally to the Indians as Elk River. Early French explorers called it Rivière Jaune. The Bighorn was called Le Corne. Captain William Clark of the Lewis and Clark Expedition, on his return from the Pacific Ocean, camped on the east fork of the Bighorn River. In 1878, during the Sioux and Cheyenne Indian campaign of that year, General Terry and Colonel Gibbon marched up the Bighorn to the site of Custer's defeat at the battle of the Little Bighorn. They arrived two days after the battle. The steamer Far West, *carrying supplies, plied the waters of both rivers and brought the wounded from that encounter back to Fort Abraham Lincoln in the Dakota Territory.*

Excited by the images, I followed the sidewalk to the end of the parking lot where a dirt path wound its way up through tall grasses, doubling back to the crest of the butte. The short climb winded me. Or maybe it was the excitement of history.

A pile of large boulders were clustered up top, deposited like ancient marbles by a passing glacier. A few sparse piñons laced the air with pine perfume. And in a V-shaped notch between the boulders, the promised vista opened up—the Yellowstone River curling across the terrain like a silver ribbon in the sun. Yellow and orange foliage lined its shores, then brown prairie spread away to distant green fields. Beyond the cultivated areas, dark pines dotted the landscape haphazardly. And arching over all was the big Montana sky.

I leaned against one of the smooth boulders, absorbing its warmth, staring at the timeless Yellowstone for timeless minutes. A cement picnic table sat in a brief clearing nearby, and when I grew tired of standing I stretched out flat on my back, staring straight into the sky, the bright sun on my face. The temperature was no more than fifty, the still air carrying a chill—a delicious combination of competing sensations.

I closed my eyes and soaked in the silence, gradually becoming aware of a general hum in the tall grass about me, a subtle soundtrack to the scenes I was imagining—Lewis and Clark floating along down below, the defeat of Custer across the prairie just to the east. It was history more vivid than in any classroom. American history as taught by I-94.

But a new sound abruptly ended the lesson, just as I was about to doze off—a distinct dry rattling a few feet from the picnic table, the proverbial snake in the grass, a Montana rattler. I studied the sound until I was certain of its location, then swung myself off the opposite end of the table, keeping to the exact center of the dirt path as I hustled back down.

A few miles beyond the rest area I passed Custer (pop. 280), the Little Bighorn battlefield to the far right. The Little Bighorn itself is a branch of the Yellowstone, and like its parent it was lined with yellow trees. Sparse pines grew in clumps across the brown landscape behind it, where erosion had left a variety of rocky outcroppings.

Before long, the highway began to rise again—into a perfect blue dome of a sky. Reddish scrub now laced the purple sage and orange heather, the prairie painted in autumn colors of its own. Then sandstone cliffs lined the way to distant mountains, and when I finally crossed those mountains, similar vistas were repeated beyond—more prairies, more mountains, more sky.

Ranch Access Half Mile. The sign was encouraging. All this land was under someone's control, although too vast for any boundaries to be seen. Dusty gravel roads, running parallel, provided access to the local interior from the Interstate. Occasionally, pickup trucks barreled along them, streaming dust. Old-fashioned windmills appeared occasionally as well—many-bladed, with tails like giant arrows.

Better Bred Red Angus Cattle. I was in Rosebud County now—Marlboro Country—and as if on cue two cowboys crested a hill on horseback, with a small herd of cattle. Which raised a question. How, in years gone by, had cattle ever been herded across these immense spaces without pickup trucks? It seemed utterly impossible.

The remnants of a frame house and weathered shack stood just off the shoulder, the home a dark shell with broken windows. But the blacktop beneath me was brand new, the idyllometer stuck on one hundred, so I floored the accelerator and left the cowboys to their cattle, setting a new double-hundred record with a speed of one-thirty.

These straight-ahead speed trials lasted only a minute or two, but they thrilled me as much as the mountain chicanes. Cruising at eighty-five, the 'Vette would slip ahead as if to pass another car, then keep accelerating until the steering wheel was vibrating in my hands, the only sound the noisy rush of the resisting air. Then the readout would hit triple digits—99 yielding to an even 100—and I'd keep my foot down until I'd increased my record by another five miles per hour.

Backing off was always a letdown. The 'Vette seemed to be crawling, the only residue of the attempt my thumping heart.

A rocky castle-like crag soon appeared off to the left, the only distinguishing feature on the landscape for miles. Then the highway crossed a ridge and the Yellowstone returned. I had lost it for a while, but now I was convinced the narrow river was eternal, that it would follow me all the way home to Ohio.

The Rosebud Recreation Area followed, where rocky ledges come right to the roadside and the distant mountains are contoured like knuckles. Then open farmland brought earth-rim views—with white cliffs and brown cliffs—and always the blue Yellowstone through the heart of the plain. On the left beyond Rosebud (pop. 10,505), the landscape turned lunar, while the Interstate ran straight ahead through grassy prairie. There was absolutely no traffic anywhere. Montana was mine for a leisurely Sunday drive.

White sandbars now split the Yellowstone like miniature beaches, its shores still banded by yellow trees. Then the highway ascended through a stretch of ragged buttes, only to curve around and down to catch the river again. There was no traffic in Custer County, either. Just brown cliffs and scattered gold trees. And blue skies with high white clouds.

A sign for *Moon Road* confirmed the nature of the landscape—absolutely lunar now in all directions. It was time for another go at the record, and a new sign spurred me on. *Range Rider Museum*. Like those cowboys back there, I was riding the range myself in my trusty red 'Vette, hoping to increase my speed record by another five miles per hour. But the highway rose slightly as I hit the accelerator, the slope creating headwinds that forced me to back off.

Hungry now despite my excitement, I stopped for lunch at a small restaurant in Miles City (pop. 8461)—amidst golden plains, tufted buttes, and yellow-treed groves, where the Tongue River flows south and jagged peaks line the horizon. It was early afternoon, and as I waited for my pizza to arrive, there was nothing to do but study the other customers in amazement.

Across the way, a family of seven had pulled two tables together and was sitting quietly over their spaghetti and meatballs—staid parents, three girls and two boys, the kids ranging in age from about eighteen to five. All of them were eating slowly, utterly devoid of anything that might be called *stress*. They talked in turn—unhurriedly, respectfully, the older kids assisting the younger as they ate—all ingenuous but by no means naive. Here was a family at peace with itself and the world. An obvious product of a peaceful and humbling landscape.

The young waitress exuded the same unhurried air, while a teenage boy and his girlfriend huddled contentedly in a corner booth. The young couple was in blue jeans and identical orange T-shirts bearing a message in bold block letters. TAKE YOUR BEST SHOT, the shirts said across the chest. WELL HUNT YOU DOWN, the shirt backs concluded. Ever the English professor, I couldn't help but notice the missing apostrophe in WELL. The boy, at least, had added one to his shirt with magic marker.

I wondered about the message. Did it have to do with the gun laws? The kids didn't seem at all like political activists. Maybe the T-shirts were simply linked to high school sports. I wanted to inquire, but any question—about guns or the Interstates—would be an intrusion, an affront to personal intimacy on a quiet Sunday afternoon.

So I sat there in silence.

Waiting for my pizza.

Trying to absorb the tranquility of the local population.

* * *

By the time I got back on the road, the temperature had climbed to sixty-five. It was only seventy miles to Glendive, my destination for the day.

Horses joined cattle across the tan moonscape now, but a spate of telephone poles dropped the idyllometer to ninety, annoying me greatly. The Weather Channel was calling for less brilliant weather on Monday. I was running out of chances to better my record—as Richard Petty or Mario Andretti.

Valley Access, a sign announced. Earlier it had been *Ranch Access*. Occasionally, it was *Local Access*. Yet *all* access was the same—by dusty dirt or gravel roads, running perpendicular or parallel to the highway. But it wasn't clear how you got there from here. There were few intersections. I was certain of only one thing. To access *America* you need the Interstates.

Rough Road Next 2 Miles. The sign dimmed my spirits. I needed smooth sailing for my speed trials. Now the road was not only bumpy but curvy, redeemed from time to time by a view of the Yellowstone— a blue ribbon along a line of sandstone cliffs, at times so close it looked like you could fish from the westbound lanes.

Except for vast green rectangles of irrigated farmland, the landscape was the color of hay, the tufted buttes striated in an array of colors—purple, gold, khaki, mauve, pink. Like the sky, the prairie seemed to be growing wider, the landforms ever-changing—from buttes and cliffs to mounds and valleys, with cattle grazing at will.

Then the telephone poles disappeared and I saw my chance. The idyllometer returned to one hundred again, the road suddenly smooth. No traffic anywhere. Close overhead, a redtailed hawk hugged the highway as if pacing the 'Vette, as vivid as any Audubon illustration. I took it as a challenge—the redtailed hawk versus my trusty red steed. Straddling the broken white line for safety, I accelerated to one thirty-five, the highest speed I would attain on my Interstate odyssey, the fastest I've ever moved except in an airplane.

Then the wind rebuffed me and I resumed cruising at eighty-five.

I passed *Powder River Road* and crossed the Powder River itself, which flows south from the Yellowstone with bright white sandbars. Colored by calcium or a similar mineral, the sand seemed a natural advertisement—*Got Milk?* Salmon-colored buttes near the river sported crew cuts of green pine, eroded below their crests to pink and gray. Then the road began to rise and fall through the Powder River Valley, a lovely agricultural region plowed in rich dark furrows.

Reddish cliffs soon joined the Yellowstone on the far left, a new color among the gray ledges. To the right, white powder lined the banks of the O'Fallon, another tributary of the Yellowstone. Farther right, the rim of the earth seemed to rise as it cut northward, forming a barrier across the horizon directly ahead. But the highway went right up into it—and right up into each horizon that followed—always re-orienting itself along the banks of the Yellowstone.

Like the cliffs, cattle appeared in all colors now—black, brown, red, gray—and there was an open farm truck ahead, with slatted sides, carrying what looked like a mountain of steer horns. Powder horns from the cattle of Powder River Valley? I passed an identical truck entering Dawson County, about twenty miles from Glendive, and this time I got a closer look. Those things weren't powder horns. They looked like some kind of turnip. And suddenly it irked me that I couldn't tell a steer horn from a turnip. Montana had reduced me to an Interstate dude.

Bad Boot Road increased the negative feeling. Then the telephone poles returned—high-tension wires this time—increasing my own tension. The terrain grew flat, with nothing but shimmering mirages ahead. Soon the Yellowstone disappeared, my old friend. An Arabian horse farm momentarily filled the void—then a gorgeous palomino grazing in a sagebrush draw—but *Cracker Box Road* continued the bad vibes, offering a perfect description of the few visible homes. *Whoopup Circle Road* came next, suggesting rowdy cowboys cutting up on Saturday nights. But this was Sunday, I had to remind myself. A day of rest, for all those mild-mannered folks I'd seen in the restaurant.

A truck ahead of me had another load of those turnip things. But now they resembled giant brown molars. It was two-thirty and I was on the outskirts of Glendive (pop. 4802), where I crossed the Yellowstone River for what would be the last time.

269

But I hardly noticed. The highway had begun to descend, the 'Vette on cruise control at eighty-five. I was searching for Exit 215, but the exits, I suddenly realized, weren't numbered consecutively. I didn't want to miss Glendive and have to turn around.

Hunched over the wheel, I bent my neck for a better view of the overhead signs, and when I looked in the mirror all I saw were flashing lights.

* * *

The trooper had come out of nowhere. I feared he was going to arrest me for doing one thirty-five earlier, sixty miles per hour above the posted speed. But how could he have known? Maybe he was working in tandem with that guy in the ironing board airship.

"May I see your license and registration," he said. "And proof of insurance."

The nameplate on his uniform read *R. Canen*, and according to the patch on his pocket he was deputy sheriff of Dawson County. A clean-cut young man in his midtwenties. But where the hell had he come from? There had been no one behind me. I had been searching for my exit, then he was there on my tail. It seemed a conspiracy to put an end to my Corvette karma.

I rummaged for my papers in the console at my right elbow, then handed them out the window and the deputy returned to his car, its electric red, white, and blue lights still sparking. I watched him in my rearview mirror methodically going about his business. He was on the radio now, speaking into a handheld microphone, while I prepared my *Basic Rule* defense. *The weather is perfect*, I would argue. *The road is grade A, I'm driving a sports car, and the traffic's nonexistent.*

A few minutes later the deputy put down the microphone, came back to my window, and returned my papers.

"Did you know that your insurance is about to expire, Mr. Smith?"

I'm the one who's about to expire, I wanted to say. Instead, I heard a dry voice reply, "We pay our car insurance every six months. It's due at the end of October."

"Just thought I'd let you know."

The deputy had a thick pad in his hand—flimsy sheets in various colors with carbon paper in between—and he was beginning to write me a ticket. *But for what?* That was the question that had my heart knocking at my ribs.

"I clocked you going eighty-six, back there, Mr. Smith. The speed limit is seventy-five."

I tried to swallow my joy. "The cruise control's set at eighty-five," I said finally. "You can see for yourself if you take the car for a spin."

The deputy shook his head. "That won't be necessary. You were clocked at eighty-six."

Gears shifted in my head, and I fished in the console for a press release about my grand lap of America.

"Look," I said politely, handing the release out the window. "I've come nine thousand miles around the country so far. Wherever the speed's posted at seventy-five, everybody cruises at eighty-five."

The deputy returned the news release, unimpressed. "I'll give you eighty-five, Mr. Smith. You're right about that. But not eighty-six."

So we were arguing over a lousy mile per hour.

But *one* was far better than *sixty*, I realized, albeit an injustice. And suddenly I clearly understood what had happened. As the road dipped into Glendive, the cruise control had kicked up a notch. Which is precisely why Deputy Sheriff R. Canen was concealed in the vicinity. To fill the Dawson County coffers.

"What about the *Basic Rule*?" I said. "I thought there weren't any speed limits out here anyway."

I was feeling more confident by the minute, having escaped a major financial disaster—loss of license, insurability, impoundment of my 'Vette, and whatever else Dawson County might have up its sleeve for outsiders caught racing on the Interstate.

"The law changed last spring, Mr. Smith—in May of '99—after a challenge by a professional race car driver. But let me tell you something. We often catch people out here doing one ten, one fifteen." He paused, as if to let the figures sink in.

Is that all? I wanted to say.

"It was a big case in the courts," he continued. "We stood to lose federal funding unless we came up with a speed limit. We picked seventy-five."

So all those people who had told me about Montana had been right. There *had* been no speed limit—until six months earlier.

"In this car," Deputy Sheriff R. Canen admitted, running his eyes up and down the 'Vette, "you would have had a case."

A Pyrrhic victory, nonetheless. "So what happens now?"

"I'm going to write you a ticket and assign you a court date."

My voice grew weak again. "*For when?*"

"End of the month."

"But there's no way I can make it back here, sir." I held up the press release again.

"Well," the deputy said, "tomorrow's Monday. You can call the judge at the Dawson County Courthouse and explain your situation. His name's Walter McKeen. It's in the phone book. He's the Justice of the Peace."

It was obvious that Deputy Sheriff R. Canen had no sympathy for my tight schedule—*If this is Monday, this must be Montana.* He had heard all such excuses before and wasn't about to budge.

"Tomorrow's Columbus Day," he added blankly. "It'd have to be Tuesday."

The irony made me smile. I had already celebrated Columbus Day in my own way—by discovering Montana. Now I never wanted to see the damn state again.

"Can't do it," I said just as blankly. "What do you suggest?" My voice was penitent this time, and the deputy's solution, I suddenly realized, was as routine as lying in wait on the outskirts of Glendive.

"You can pay me forty dollars, then forfeit your bond. That'll serve as your fine. It wouldn't be cost effective for us to come after you."

"That's *it*?" I said.

"I'll give you a receipt. Official notice will be sent to Ohio." (And it was).

I hit a button on the console and the hatchback popped open. "My money's in the back," I said.

Sliding out of the 'Vette, I walked to the rear of the car and slid open the black privacy shade above the luggage space. Then I removed two twenties from my suitcase and handed them over. Meanwhile, there was a story problem revolving in my head: *Class, if Mr. Smith is fined forty bucks for going one mile per hour over the legal speed limit, what would it cost him for going sixty over?*

I peered up into the big blue Montana sky. There was no ironing board airship. It could have been worse. My Corvette karma was intact. So I turned to Deputy Sheriff R. Canen. Why not interview him about the Interstates?

He seemed flattered, and his tone turned friendly.

"Well, Mr. Smith," he said, "I've been six years on the force. And let me tell you, it can get lonely out here. But you meet a lot of interesting people. One night my buddy pulled over our state senator. He tried to talk himself out of a ticket, same as you. But my buddy wrote him up. Then he shook his hand and complimented him for his record on the gun laws."

Ah, yes. The gun laws. TAKE YOUR BEST SHOT. WELL HUNT YOU DOWN. And in Dawson County they certainly will.

* * *

Here's an Interstate Item from the wire services that I encountered early in the new millennium, three months after returning home. It's the kind of thought that never occurred to me while crossing the wide-open spaces of Montana, where I rarely saw another car, and never witnessed an accident:

Highway fatalities fall in 1999.

Highway deaths declined last year, with the fatality rate hitting a record low, Transportation Secretary Rodney Slater announced.

There were 41,375 people killed on American highways in 1999, down from 41,471 the year before. That marked an all-time low rate of 1.5 deaths per million vehicle-miles driven, down from 1.6 a year earlier. According to Slater, 1999 was the third consecutive year of decline.

By comparison, the highway death rate was 5.5 per 100 million vehicle miles in 1966.

As for Montana, according to the National Motorists Association, when fixed speed limits were reinstated on Memorial Day weekend of 1999, fatal accidents began to rise again, whereas from January to May of 1999, after several years of no numerical or posted daytime speed limits, Montana had recorded its lowest fatality rate. Despite the irony—which officials are at a loss to explain—the Interstates remain the safest component of our national transportation system.

* * *

Monday was Columbus Day, but you couldn't tell in Montana. Monday was just like Sunday—same unhurried pace, same wide sky. Only the sky was more white now than blue, the temperature only forty-seven when I went to check out of Motel Find-Me-Not.

It was nine-thirty, and a man in the lobby was carrying a rifle in a long leather case as if it were just another piece of luggage. When he left the desk, I asked the clerk about the Interstates.

"I like the Interstates through Montana," she mused as she processed my credit card. "Glendive used to be an oil town, but now the railroad sustains it. Before the Interstate was built out here everybody used Highway 10, an old dirt-and-gravel road across from our family land. People would stop in for the night, but Glendive is as far as they get anymore. I've driven the Interstates over to Butte, then down I-15 into Utah. It's great down in Utah, all those mountains and trees. But it's too flat around here. We got a whole lotta road for a whole lotta distance."

She laughed, then turned reflective. "It gets real green here in the spring and summer. That's always pretty. But a month ago it all turned brown. Winters are cold and brittle. Snowdrifts always block the highway between here and Miles City. Year before last we had fifteen hundred trucks stuck in the Kmart parking lot. Nine hundred the year before. The only way you could get on the Interstates without being pulled off by the police was to be in an ambulance. Drivers were giving away their produce over to the Kmart. They were going to lose it, anyway. Didn't want a truckload of mush."

"What's it like in North Dakota?" I asked.

The woman laughed again. "You'll know when you get to North Dakota because the highway's so bad. Even the shoulders are pitted. And it's even flatter than here. The wind blows something terrible all the time. But every state has its own beauty, I guess. Like I said, I like the trees and mountains in Utah. But we got great hunting and fishing right here in Montana. I been to Minnesota once—nothin' but lakes and cattails. North Dakota has some pretty spots. I'm just partial to Montana."

She smiled and shook her head, as if she had never given the Interstates much thought. "You'll be changing to Central Time in North Dakota," she added finally, "right over the line near Medora."

Another time change. Something I hadn't considered. I was making progress across the continent, on my way home.

There was a telephone in the lobby, and I thought about calling the Dawson County justice of the peace before I left. To complain of entrapment. But he wouldn't be working on Columbus Day. I fancied catching him in bed, surprising him just as I had been surprised by Deputy Sheriff R. Canen. I wanted to make sure the deputy had forked over my forty bucks. But it was less than half an hour to the North Dakota border and I was worried about the road conditions there. I was headed to Fargo, four hundred miles to the east, and it could be a long day if the roads were as bad as the desk clerk said.

On I-94 outside of Glendive the attractive moonscape resumed, but it was marred by a stretch of telephone poles. And the pale sky itself was marred—by a series of jet trails crisscrossing high overhead. I hadn't seen any such blemishes in the Big Sky as I came across the state, which made me realize just how vast Montana is. So vast and isolated that no one flies over it.

How wonderful it would be to see this lunar landscape all in green—the mounds, the buttes, the ledges, the cliffs—the wiry sagebrush growing at will. But the terrain before me was all brown now. It looked like the windswept golf courses where the British Open is played.

On a rise to the right stood a lone dark horse, its head held high to sniff the wind. Beyond it the land ran right to the horizon. And on the rim of the earth was a flock of Canada geese, their black V-formation spreading wide, then closing ranks, then spreading wide again. As on Sunday, traffic was nonexistent. I could gaze where I wanted. But two large furry lumps drew my attention back to the highway. More unidentifiable roadkill. Prairie dogs? Coyotes? A mating pair? Certainly nothing I'd ever see in my own backyard.

I passed into North Dakota without fanfare by a place called *Beach* (pop. 1205), a place that's apparently misnamed, given the absence of sand or water. As predicted, the highway deteriorated immediately. The landscape seemed to deteriorate too, suddenly flat and devoid of all contours. Hundreds of miles to the right, the terrain was dotted with those Tootsie Roll hay bales, but at such a distance they looked like enormous goose turds—like the droppings of pterodactyls, ancient relatives of the geese I'd just seen.

A car was ripping along beside me on a parallel access road, in a cloud of dust so thick I couldn't tell the make of the vehicle. *North Dakota Tourist Information 2 Miles*. But so far there'd been nothing of interest to any tourist, except a distant butte, a welcome relief to the eye.

And suddenly, despite my speeding ticket, I missed Montana.

The posted speed dropped to seventy, a concession to the condition of the road surface, *C-* at best, the steady thumping reminiscent of Louisiana. But before long North Dakota began to redeem itself. Cresting that distant butte, I could see for thousands of miles in all directions, with a larger butte to the right amidst a knuckled landscape. The buttes had names through here—*Sentinel Butte* and *Flat Top Butte*—some of them rising to nearly thirty-five hundred feet. Unfortunately, power stations, antennas, and satellite dishes cluttered half a dozen of the largest.

From an escarpment to the left came a message in white rock— *Home On The Range*. And the range was the moon, with rolling mounds and breast-shaped hills, then a lovely stretch of green, like winter wheat. A large cross maintained a lonely vigil on one of the nearer buttes, less offensive than the towers and antennas, but still an eyesore.

Tootsie Roll bales of hay were strewn about for miles now, followed by the first rest area in North Dakota—an empty quarter-acre at the roadside, with half a dozen trees plus a playground and swings for children, the only nice touch. But it was too early to stop. I was barely underway.

Then, except for the mottled road surface, the state became more interesting by the minute, the terrain constantly changing. Large mounds rolled away from the shoulder, the highway cradled between them, leaving a view of soft contours and sky. I turned a corner and the land spread out to an array of distant buttes. I kept watching for the change to Central Time, but Medora—to which the desk clerk had alerted me—came and went without any such sign.

The National Grasslands followed, where dry creek beds cut between grassy mounds like clefts made by earthquakes, where a sign for *Buffalo Gap* put imagined bison before me, humped and grazing.

Farthest off, long cliffs lined the horizon, streaked in variations of red and white and pink and salmon. The unexpected beauty excited me, and I wasn't the only one to notice.

Scenic View One Mile. It was the Theodore Roosevelt National Park, with a canyon-like vista to the north and south. High red cliffs, striated horizontally, ran above a sandy band, with pastel streaks lower down. The perspective was humbling. It was like looking at cliffs from the Colorado River, only the river was the Interstate.

I crossed the scenic Little Missouri River, where yellow deciduous trees reappeared. Then came Painted Canyon, perfectly named for the roseate striations across its cliffs and buttes and outcroppings, to which sparse pines clung in defiance of gravity. I was driving the rim of a canyon now, the pale sunlight deepening the reddish tints, casting shadows from the buttes and mounds into the shallow swales. Had the sun been brighter, the sky bluer, the highway smoother, the idyllometer would have soared. As it was, it was stuck at eighty-five, making me glad I had achieved my double-hundred in Montana while I had the chance.

Then rolling mounds swallowed the highway and all I could see was pale sky. Soon the 'Vette crossed a butte and a wide vista opened up—across canyon land to the edge of the earth. It was ten-thirty and I was approaching Dickinson (pop. 16,097), about sixty miles into the state. And the name made me wonder. Had Dickinson, a college town, been named for the famous poet? *I like to see it lap the miles . . .* and lick the canyons up! Emily Dickinson had spent her life in her Amherst backyard. But on the Interstates, her backyard would have been America.

Beyond the canyons the terrain leveled out considerably. Then the road grew rougher, *D+* at best. This was Stark County, aptly named, where the only item of interest is a single oil derrick of the grasshopper variety. Thoroughly rusted, it was nonetheless working, bobbing for oil. Then came another, painted yellow and tan, but sitting idle.

A spate of fat silos followed, shaped like the hat of the Tin Man. This was agricultural territory, the land smooth but plowed—acres and acres of dark brown furrows interspersed with rectangles of dark green and tan. Along the shoulder bales of hay waited for pickup. Farther off, cattle grazed beneath telephone wires and power lines. It was sixty degrees now, the sky still pale, North Dakota all but deserted on this Columbus Day.

I checked the radio. Skies were overcast ahead of me, with rain and snow showers in the plains behind me. To make matters worse, local forecasters had issued a high wind warning. I was a day ahead of the bad weather and hoped to keep it that way.

Presidential candidate George W. Bush, the radio announced next, would be in Fargo later in the month. And later in the day I'd see Fargo for myself. But that was near the eastern edge of the state. I was still in the western part, entering Dickinson through a phalanx of billboards, one of which touts the Dakota Dinosaur Museum, proof of the ancient territory I'd just passed through.

Seen from the Interstate, Dickinson—home of Dickinson State University—is a flat, square mile of deciduous trees and dark pine. It has a lovely water tower, flat-roofed apartments, and groves of small homes. But the billboards detract, the only *garbage in* and *garbage out*. They passed quickly, and as I left the place behind, the radio mentioned that students in North Carolina were heading back to school, three weeks after the devastating floodwaters. While I was still playing hooky.

Unhappily, beyond Dickinson the road grew even worse, a dismal D. *Pa-dump, pa-dump, pa-dump.* But a silver half-moon of a geodesic dome distracted me. It sat on a distant butte, amidst a clutter of antennas and satellite dishes. I didn't like the trend—too many buttes were littered with scientific equipment, whereas elsewhere they sat stark and untouched. High above them, jets continued to mark the gray sky with great white *X*'s.

Off to the left now a pair of sleek windmills was turning slowly, like twin airplane propellers about to come to a stop—three blades each, atop tall white shafts. The slow revolutions of the blades raised a question. Given the stiff wind, why weren't they whirling in a blur? The wind was certainly buffeting the 'Vette. Maybe the speed of windmills is a function of wind direction.

In Richardton (pop. 625), twin towers rise from a lovely brick church in a grove of trees. A pert cross tops each spire. The structure reminded me of a miniature Notre Dame, the sight attractive enough to put tiny Richardton on the map, especially with its grove in autumn color. Dull reds now joined the earlier oranges and yellows. And the picturesque moment included a pretty sight up ahead—a smooth black ribbon of asphalt, as the bumpy pavement came to an end.

Farther along, by Exit 90, there's just a sign. *Exit 90.* Nothing else. Just a sign for where you can get off the Interstate, with nothing but a number to distinguish it. No place names, no services. Just bleak land beyond. I couldn't recall such a phenomenon anywhere else in America. In North Dakota, I was learning, you can exit the Interstate on the edge of nowhere. Just by getting off.

Then a new phenomenon presented itself—rows and rows of trees for a mile or so, perpendicular to the highway and planted like orchards—so hypnotic in their singularity that I had to avert my eyes.

Just beyond them, a dead bird lay on the shoulder, maybe a pheasant, a bright red band around its neck. I figured the geese I'd seen earlier had been migrating, but here was proof that other birds actually lived out here. An encouraging thought in such a stark and lonely landscape.

I blew by Hebron (pop. 888), a small brick settlement virtually devoid of trees, named for the city near Jerusalem where the biblical Abraham and Sarah were buried. No doubt the desert-like terrain here had provided the inspiration.

And after Hebron the moonscape returned, with horses and cattle among the weathered buttes, and stretches of highway under much-needed reconstruction. Softer contours dominated, with vast brown acres of a crop that looked like sunflowers. Knee-high and wrinkled, the drooping plants had heads the size of saucers—either a bad crop or one ready for harvest. But don't sunflowers grow as tall as corn?

Beyond the brown acres sat a desolate house with wooden shingles, like the house in *Christina's World* by Andrew Wyeth, as brittle in its own way as the withered sunflowers. The similarity deepened the lonely atmosphere. I couldn't imagine the stark life of whoever had lived there.

As I passed Exit 117—another no-name exit—the radio was predicting snow for parts of the state behind me. I was keeping just ahead of the kind of weather that could seriously delay me. It was one o'clock and a strange rest area was approaching, with a main building that looks like a Howard Johnson's, a curious brick structure with a curved half-roof, topped by an observatory within a widow's walk. Maybe it's supposed to be a tugboat. But the image doesn't fit the terrain.

The pavilions bore similar shapes, with slanted half-roofs, and a glass information case held a clue to the curious motif. Centuries earlier, the Mandan Indians had inhabited the Missouri River Valley of North Dakota, adapting their life and culture to the terrain. Maybe the local decor reflected their hogan-like homes.

The history of the Upper Great Plains, the display reads, *comes to life from the Ice Age to modern day, a natural playground of mastadons and Mandans. The majestic Missouri River flows through the Mandan-Bismarck area with Native American attractions such as Fort Berthod, Standing Rock, and Turtle Mountain.*

The rest area was empty except for two men in cowboy hats, conversing in low tones by one of the pavilions, so I hit the men's room and returned to the road.

The city of Mandan (pop. 15,177) lay less than an hour farther east, just short of Bismarck. But before you get there you encounter an enormous black-and-white cow, ten times normal size, on the crest of a hill.

It isn't a sculpture—I couldn't tell what it's made of—it's just an enormous black-and-white cow. Then a billboard owned up to it. *The World's Largest Holstein Cow.*

A few months earlier, the city of Chicago had displayed a herd of artistic cows in unexpected locations, in celebration of its own cow heritage. Here was North Dakota doing the same, in a single statement. But what a statement! The cow stands near Exit 127, which takes you to the Knife River Indian Villages, further homage to the historical landscape.

Off to the left by Sweetbriar Lake, the wilted sunflower-like crop appeared again. Could it be tobacco? I wondered. But there was no time for wondering. The road had turned rough again—*pa-dump, pa-dump, pa-dump*—a monotonous stretch straight ahead to the horizon. Unsightly telephone poles led the way to Crown Butte. Then I reentered the Central Time Zone outside of Mandan, near a community of ranch houses and doublewide trailer homes. Apparently the desk clerk had confused Medora with Mandan. But at least she had got the *M* right.

By Fort Lincoln State Park a billboard offered an interesting product—a concoction of St.-John's-wort and ginseng "to keep your spirits up." It sounded like a tonic sold by gypsies. Maybe it had been whipped up by a Mandan medicine man. Given the North Dakota landscape, you can understand the need to boost one's spirits.

Signs for *Custer House* and *Mandan Village* followed. Then, across a hillside on the outskirts of Mandan, a development of upscale modern homes shocked me back to the twentieth century. But the feeling didn't last long. *Scenic View One Mile.* The earlier scenic view had been spectacular, and this one didn't disappoint either. I crested a mound to a world-rim vista—horizon to horizon—across the length of a forested valley. Mandan lay ahead, with more homes among the trees, and then an onslaught of unsightly billboards.

Roadside flags rippled stiffly in the wind. *Lewis & Clark Riverboat On The Missouri River Three Miles.* Then I crossed the Missouri itself—on a black, three-sectioned Erector Set bridge—and the wide panorama gave way to a sandy shoreline, meandering cattails, and tree-topped bluffs.

On the far side of the river I-94 ascends the bluffs into Bismarck (pop. 50,000), the capital of North Dakota and easily its wealthiest community, judging by the array of large two-story homes. There were trees here I hadn't seen on the plains, their gray trunks and silvery leaves bending in the wind. A single brown building towered above the foliage to the right, the only hint of a skyline. Then the speed limit dropped to fifty-five through an industrial stretch—not quite *garbage in*, despite billboards, power lines, and telephone poles.

Bismarck has no downtown that defines it from the Interstate. The Capitol and Civic Center lie unseen to the south. But attractive suburban neighborhoods are nestled in hills to the left and right. Even the duplexes and apartment buildings have a modest appeal, and the last community of doublewides—beyond the billboards on the way out—looks refreshingly clean among the trees.

Then I was right back in the Upper Great Plains, where bales of hay waited to be picked up along the highway. And a billboard brought the smiling face of Lawrence Welk, an advertisement for his birthplace—Strasburg, North Dakota (pop. 553), an hour south. As a kid I had watched the *Lawrence Welk Show* with my family every week. As an adult I've often wondered what the attraction was. But driving through North Dakota helps you understand the plain appeal of Lawrence Welk, although I was yet to encounter anyone who spoke like him. Or people who spoke like the folks in the movie *Fargo*, people I'd be with at the end of the day.

Beyond Bismarck there was very little traffic, across the flattest landscape I'd encountered since heading east. Telephone poles paralleled the highway to the right, dwindling from sight hundreds of miles straight ahead. The grass in the median and along the highway was greener now than in any part of the state, yet the distant horizons remained brown and tan.

The next rest area was closed for renovation, a modern and stylish facility painted to match the landscape. Had it been open I would definitely have stopped. It looked as impressive as the new travel plaza I'd seen in Ohio. But I only got a quick glimpse, for suddenly, just beyond it, scudding tumbleweed came at me like a giant piece of broccoli. Basically harmless, it thoroughly startled me, and I hit the brakes, swerving wildly, before I knew what I'd done.

A short while later, as if to provide a preview of Minnesota, brief marshes with waving cattails lined both sides of the road. It was two o'clock and sixty-four degrees, the day still overcast, the wind pushing at the 'Vette in strong gusts. Then, for miles ahead, the marshes gave way to bales of Tootsie Roll hay along the shoulder. To the left and right, cows grazed in tall grass behind an endless wire fence.

But something was odd with this picture. The hay sat in the right-of-way of the Interstate, *outside* the wire fences. Had it been *inside*, the cows might have got into it.

No matter. Hay and cattle were soon gone, as the prairie became flat and monotonous, the gray sky scored by power lines. Occasionally, small bodies of water, whipped into whitecaps by the wind, came right to the edge of the highway—drainage areas several acres in size. This was Kidder County now, as in *Are you kidding me? Can this get any more tedious?*

And the answer is *yes*.

At two-thirty I stopped for gas in Steele (pop. 2420) where, right next door to the local service station, another enormous North Dakota figure rises into the sky. It has to be the world's largest marsh bird—some sort of giant crane—with long thin legs and a long pointed beak, a cartoonish creation. Made of sheet metal, it's thirty-eight and one-half feet high and weighs four and one-half tons. I could understand the world's largest Holstein earlier, but a *crane?* I thought the water I'd been seeing was only Interstate drainage. All I could think of were the pterodactyls I had imagined earlier.

As I pulled into the service station, a guy in a cowboy hat and blaze-orange vest was cleaning the windshield of his pickup, a shotgun racked across his rear window. I wanted to ask him about the big crane—maybe he was going crane hunting on Columbus Day—but he pulled out quickly.

I put a different question to an elderly man at the pumps.

"That brown crop?" he said. "No, that ain't tobacco. It's *sorghum*, a grain thet's cultivated for forage. They even use it in syrup."

But I wasn't so sure. What about all those sunflower-like heads?

I asked again inside, where a husky woman in a Scandinavian sweater was tending the counter. She had light blue eyes and a voice like a xylophone.

"Yah, dose are sunflowers. Sorghum is a kind of grass, altogether different."

I was going to ask her about the crane, but I needed the men's room, where I got distracted by a message scrawled on the wall. *Jesus said you must beleive in him and help the needy or you will surely burn in hell forever.*

I could always help the needy of North Dakota with their spelling.

17

AS SOON AS I GOT BACK ON THE ROAD, A NEW PHENOMENON CONVINCED ME that the small roadside ponds I'd been passing were simply catch basins for runoff water. Wire fences now ran right through the middle of them. Who'd put a fence through a pond?

There were new irrigation devices as well—not the Wright brothers type or the pipes on wheels, but like long windshield wipers without the rubber blades.

Camp Grassick. The sign made me laugh. I was getting pretty sick of all the grass myself. Across the flat prairies of North Dakota, you can't see the horizon for the grass.

Before long I passed again a brown crop that resembled tobacco, without the sunflower heads. Apparently everyone had been telling me the truth—I'd been seeing both sunflowers *and* sorghum. But it was too late now to ask about the giant crane. No matter. Another kind of bird demanded attention. Starlings were sweeping across the road in large dark flocks, occasionally settling into groves of trees, in a mostly treeless land.

The wind was strong from the south, blowing tumbleweed right to left. I was near Crystal Springs, where an abandoned church with a weather-beaten steeple sits beside an old schoolhouse. Both structures had their windows boarded up, a depressing sight.

In Stutsman County, where the flat terrain begins to swell a bit, marshy areas increased along the roadside, their surfaces chopped by whitecaps. One small pond forced me to rethink the watery fences I'd seen earlier. Neatly divided by a jetty-like rock wall, half the water was dark blue, half light green, as if it had been treated with two different chemicals. Beyond such ponds, extra-long Tootsie Roll bales of hay lined the fields in neat rows. Given the stiff wind, the rolled hay seemed logical. Maybe farmers had borrowed the idea from the tumbleweed.

Now cement barriers divided several roadside ponds, like holding tanks for fish. I hadn't seen so much water along the Interstate since the ponds in Ohio. But I preferred this Central Plains type, with their naturally irregular shorelines. The thought of Ohio brought a sign for *Cleveland*, near groves of dead birches, all slender gray trunks and withered leaves. A sign for *Prairie Oasis* followed, lending an appropriate image—an island respite for the prairie schooners of old. Then a sign for *Gackle* left me laughing. Maybe the starlings I'd seen were really *gackles*. Or *grackles*. Or *cackles*. Like those strange birds way back in Florida.

An abandoned brick schoolhouse sat on the left now, a two-story building with twin chimneys on each end and a cupola in the middle of the roof. The old chimneys conjured images of long winter school-days, when the same wind now buffeting the 'Vette must have chilled the bones of the students at their desks. Farther along, a farmer was gathering hay along the highway, arranging the long bales in a pyramid of logs on the flatbed truck behind his tractor. The farmer wore a cowboy hat, and it suddenly occurred to me that I'd seen more cowboy hats in North Dakota than in Texas.

As the tractor disappeared in my rearview mirror, a train appeared beside me trailing a hundred or more identical hoppers—all the same silver color, with blue trim. It was following the Interstate at exactly my speed, mesmerizing me, until nothing seemed to be moving whatso-ever. Time had stopped. The 'Vette had stopped. And the train seemed a solid gray wall—a found art object, a North Dakota masterpiece by Cristo. Add the bleached blacktop, the white sky and gray landscape, and you have a recipe for paralysis.

I blinked, averted my eyes, and all motion resumed, the train now a kinetic work of art racing across the prairies of America.

Every so often in North Dakota the highway ascends towards an eternal horizon and you can see for thousands of miles in all direc-tions. Which always raises a question—what will you see when you get to the horizon? And each time the answer is the same. A flat highway running straight to oblivion.

Occasionally a local gravel road ran parallel, with pickup trucks raising thick dust clouds that forced me to close the 'Vette's air vents. Then came more sunflowers, the same curious knee-high crop I'd seen elsewhere. And soon it was North Dakota déjà vu—another enormous animal in a distant pasture, a big buffalo of stone or papier-mâché. A herd of animals grazed beside it, maybe real buffalo, too far away to say for certain.

It was three-thirty now, with a dismal disk of a sun behind me and nothing but dark gray clouds straight ahead. Across the median, the few westbound cars had their headlights burning, a sure sign of rain farther east. Despite the lack of sun, I'd been wearing sunglasses, but I switched to regular glasses in an attempt to lighten the world—just in time for a puzzling sign. *Continental Divide. Elevation 1490.*

I thought I had passed the Continental Divide days ago. Could there be more than one? Who was divvying up the continent, anyway? I couldn't believe the elevation. Nearly fifteen hundred feet. The terrain had been flat and smooth, with no relief to the eye—sea level for sure. But I was wrong.

Smoke was blowing across the highway ahead, from a grass fire miles away. I had to shut the vents again, then slow my speed through a series of curves in the face of stiff wind. Before long I passed the source of the fire—a few blackened acres smoldering at roadside, a brush fire outside of Valley City (pop. 7163), sixty-eight miles from Fargo.

By a brief stretch of water near Valley City the wind was so strong that small waves were rippling across the highway. Afraid of hydroplaning, I killed the cruise control and splashed on through. The sign for *Valley City* puzzled me. *What* valley? Then the highway descended slightly—into the *valley?*—and a large billboard brought a political message. *Protect What's Right. Hunting Fishing Trapping.* Here was North Dakota's answer to Montana's bright orange T-shirts.

Shortly before four a few school buses joined the light traffic, struggling through the gray and windy afternoon. The sight of school buses on the Interstates intrigued me. In my own experience, that always meant field trips. But I could tell by the bored faces of the students in the windows that they were merely on their way home for the day, putting in miles on a dreary landscape just as they had put in a dreary day at school. As I overtook the buses I realized how lucky I was to be playing hooky—despite the gray day and the weed-studded shoulders that make I-94 an eyesore in eastern North Dakota.

Signs for *Tower City* and *Buffalo* flew by, but neither towers nor buffalo materialized. A place called *Alice* reminded me of the town in Australia. Was there a connection in the desolate landscapes? Signs for *Wheatland* and *Chaffee* seemed like bad puns. Maybe the one place had been named for the other. Chaff of the wheat.

High above, a flock of Canada geese seemed impervious to the wind that was punishing the 'Vette. I wondered if those geese were aware of the subtle change in the landscape below. The stretches of tilled earth—formerly brown—were now absolutely black. Richer soil?

School buses were trundling the access roads now as well, kicking up dust, a small light sparking atop each as on an airplane's wingtip. There were parallel railroad tracks too, with signs for the *Red River Valley & Western Railroad.* And suddenly I broke into song: *Come and SIT by my side if you love me. Do not hasten to BID me adieu. . . .* Dooby do do *the Red River VALLey . . .* and the cowboy that loves you so true?

Twenty miles from Fargo, I-94 runs straight ahead with ambling fencerows, dipping gently, and I wondered if this was where they had filmed the opening scene of the movie *Fargo.* But successive barrages of billboards took the movie from my mind. Then the road became the roughest of the day. Annoyed by the pounding, and fearing an Interstate idle in the Fargo rush hour, I exited early, to spend the night in West Fargo.

It was a mistake and I knew it instantly, because West Fargo is truly ugly—*garbage throughout*—a flat stretch of granaries and fairgrounds and agri-businesses, all cluttered beneath neon signs and wires. Like the rest of the nation, there's a Frontage Road, with a succession of traffic lights, fast-food joints, and service stations. Yet the gas, to my surprise, was only a buck forty. And the clerk at Motel Find-Me-Not, a portly man about my own age, was friendly and amusing.

"There's no such thing as a rush hour in Fargo," he said. "You coulda gone right on through. And people here don't talk like they do in that damn movie. You might find a few in northern Minnesota, though."

I told him the Interstate was one of the worst in the nation, but he didn't seem offended.

"It's thirty-something years old," he said. "It's even worse in Nebraska."

Then I asked about the winter and he laughed again.

"*Winter?* It's so windy here in winter that the winter blows right on through!"

Now *I* was laughing, and it felt good after a long day on the road.

"What about those things in the slatted trucks?" I asked. "Like cow horns."

"Sugar beets," he replied. "That's how we get our crystal sugar. A few miles east of here you'll cross the Red River. The Red River Valley has some of the richest farmers in the world. They all grow sugar beets. They get rich on sugar beets."

"And those sunflowers?" Despite what I'd been told, I still wasn't sure about the sunflowers.

"Those are sunflowers, all right. They start out tall, then shrink up like little people."

"What about all that water along the highway?"

"Those are sloughs." He pronounced it *slahffs* but I didn't pursue it. I had given up on *sloughs* back in Seattle.

"I used to live in Bakersfield, California," the clerk went on, "and I thought it was windy *out there!*" He laughed yet again. "There's nothing like the North Dakota wind. But without the Interstates," he concluded thoughtfully, "I would never have moved here."

And I could tell by the expression on his face that he felt it'd been worth it.

285

* * *

Six o'clock Tuesday morning, in total darkness, I crossed the parking lot to eat breakfast at a local restaurant, and when I asked the waitress about the rush hour in Fargo, she laughed in my face.

"You mean cars all jammed up and such? No. There'll be a few people, but the traffic will move quickly."

Back at the motel, CNN was reporting that the six billionth person in the world had just been born in Sarajevo. In a worried tone, the commentator detailed the problems of overpopulation. But I had traveled four hundred miles on Monday and seen but a handful of people. Overpopulation is not a problem in North Dakota. So I switched to the Weather Channel—six inches of snow in the Rockies. Wet weather ahead.

I left West Fargo, still in darkness, at ten to seven. It was fifty-three degrees, the sky inky and starless, the traffic light to nonexistent. Moments later I passed through Fargo, which is no prettier than West Fargo—a neon strip in the dawn—where the only distinctive Interstate feature is a pedestrian bridge shaped like an eyebrow. Other than that, Fargo is *garbage in* and *garbage out*.

A few miles later I crossed the Red River, unable to judge its width in the blackness below. The occasion inspired a raucous reprise of yesterday's song: *Come and SIT by my side if you love me. Do not hasten to BID me adieu. Something-something Red River VALLey, and dooby dooby dooby dooby-do.* It was early, but I was excited about getting out of North Dakota. Today was a two-state day—three hundred and thirty miles through Minnesota into Wisconsin. Destination, Eau Claire.

The Red River separates Fargo from Moorhead, another natural Interstate boundary, and on the far shore Minnesota welcomed me. I had applied for a job in Moorhead once, imagining the place to be like the moors in England. But I was wrong. Moorhead is a strip mall, with a water tower that looks like an alien—a narrow stalk with a red bubble on top. Had we moved there, I now realized, *I* would have been the alien.

But there was one good thing—beyond the Red River the highway improved immediately. It was two hundred and twenty miles to Minneapolis, the traffic cruising at eighty. Yet not even Minnesota could help the landscape, which remained oppressively flat. The rising sun was struggling to break through, but it looked like another long gray day ahead. Then the new blacktop disappeared. So much for Minnesota's welcome.

Before long I crossed the narrow Buffalo River into the flattest terrain I've ever seen. There was a sign for a place called *Downer*, obviously named for the landscape. Searching for something to cling to, my eyes settled on a few scattered trees. Oddly enough, for the first time in a long time, the median grass was green. Rich black earth followed, tilled in neat furrows, through hills with scattered horses, cows, and hay.

Soon a sign for Pelican Rapids inspired a recitation—*The Pelican*, a poem by Henry Gibson, an old joke from TV's *Laugh In: A marvelous bird is the pelican. Its beak holds more than its belly can.* I think Henry Gibson had been poking fun at Henrik Ibsen. But what could a pelican do in Pelican Rapids? Get a bellyful of water? This was Ottertail County. Maybe the otters knew.

Mercifully, the terrain soon began to roll a bit—hills and dales and mounds and green fields, with scattered groves of trees among them. Then someone flipped a switch and the morning turned picturesque. Small farms slipped by, neat and attractive, with red barns, matching outbuildings, and white two-story farmhouses. Black-and-white cows grazed in sloping pastures, and the dim morning light turned the wheat fields dull gold.

Neat is the operative word in Minnesota. And *wheat* is the operative crop. Golden rectangles alternated with green among dark stretches of furrowed soil. In the intermittent groves, many trees had already lost their leaves, the few oaks all brown. Others wore subdued colors, waiting for the sun to make them shine. There were pine trees as well, through gently rolling countryside. Minnesota, I was beginning to realize, has idyllometer potential.

In the Chippewa Valley I stopped at the Iveson Lake Rest Area, as neat as the area farms. Brown brick pavilions matched the brick rest facilities, flower gardens sat behind the benches, and the grassy areas were newly mown. Lake Iveson itself was tucked away behind a large grove of colorful trees. Only the sun was needed for a perfect autumn picture, despite a brisk wind and a temperature of forty-three.

The parking lot was empty as I stepped to the information board. *Minnesota. The Land of 10,000 Lakes:*

Tourists have come to Minnesota since the mid-1830s to enjoy the climate, the diverse scenery, fishing, and other sporting activities. Prior to the Civil War easterners and southerners took "the fashionable tour," a steamboat excursion on the upper Mississippi River to St. Anthony Falls and Fort Snelling. Following the war, newly constructed railroads encouraged people in the east and south to visit "cool Minnesota" where Lake Minnetonka was prized as "the queen of resorts." In the late 1800s fishing attracted sportsmen to northern Minnesota. In many instances homesteaders provided lodging for guests and the region's resort industry was born. It was the automobile, however, that triggered Minnesota's rapid development as a vacation playground. The automobile opened the north woods to recreational development and popularized travel among the middle class.

Add the Interstates, I was thinking, and the rest is history.

Clean sidewalks wound away behind the comfort facility through a grove of tall oaks. Beyond the trees I could see Lake Iveson, about two miles in circumference. Tall marsh grasses fringed the coves along its banks. I crunched through the leaves, startling a duck at the edge of the woods, then a gray squirrel scurried along in front of me.

Across the lake, another duck was floating like a hunter's decoy, while swept-winged white birds wheeled high overhead. Farther along, I discovered white birches with yellow leaves. Some trees had bright red leaves. Others stood denuded or in forlorn brown. And in a valley beyond the lake sat a farmhouse and barn. You could come to this rest area for a serene picnic. And do your fishing right out back.

Back on I-94, I noticed more and more evergreens in the median strip, obviously planted for relief to the eye. Plowed fields and newly harvested fields filled the hillsides, their pretty patterns contrasting with the green and gold. Occasional billboards were advertising scenic leaf tours, but in Minnesota it's the lakes that catch your eye, lakes that seem to be named for their shapes—*Elbow Lake* and *Pomme de Terre*. The land of ten thousand lakes. Minnesota earns its motto along the Interstate.

Bodies of water came in all shapes and sizes now. By eight-fifteen I had counted more than fifty, losing myself in images of the ancient glaciers that had created them. Lakes lined the highway like a gauntlet, ringed by a variety of cattails, bullrushes, and marsh grass. Larger than the North Dakota sloughs, they were slate gray on this dim Tuesday, their surfaces wrinkled by small waves and occasional whitecaps.

One lake up ahead came right to the edge of the highway. A seagull stood on the shoulder there, picking at a roadkill. A quaint change, I was thinking, from crows and vultures. But when I got closer, the gull was frightening, so much larger than you'd expect.

The road was curving now continually, veering left and right through rolling hills, and I wondered if the great monotonous straight stretches of America lay behind me forever. Flocks of Canada geese were on the move, Morse code against the gray sky. In a distant black field thousands of birds had congregated—all white—the stark contrast like a Chinese painting. Occasionally, attractive homes appeared in protected glens, lovely ranch types or stately Cape Cods. Maybe the trailers and doublewides were behind me as well. A sign for *Lake Lakota* spoke of the Indian past. Did Minnesota have a counterpart to General Custer?

One thing about Minnesota—there are few earth-rim views. The state has a cozier feeling than North Dakota. I was sixty miles from St. Cloud, wondering why a saint had been named for the weather. But St. Cloud was the perfect name for today. Patron saint of dull grayness.

The small farms now had curious silos—cinderblock cylinders with domed tops like red and white beanies. There were grain hoppers as well, and black-and-white cows. Then a billboard for *Gopher Prairie Motel* fixed my position on that giant relief map in my mind. My little Corvette was still in the prairies. With the gulls and the gophers.

I passed *Saulk Center*, the famous medical research center, then *Sinclair Lewis Avenue*. In my teens I had read Lewis' *Main Street* and *Babbitt*, too young to understand what he was saying about American middle-class life—the kind of life led in the neat middle-class homes I was now passing near Saulk River.

In middle-class suburbs created by the Interstates.

* * *

Short of St. Cloud, I-94 straightens out for a while and the terrain becomes flat, just when I had grown used to its dip and sway. Pig farms and chicken farms came and went, and for the third time I crossed the Saulk River—a meandering stream about twenty yards wide, its banks thick with marsh grass. Then New Munich put Minnesota in a new context. German immigrants. But in my imagination there was no room for Germans in Minnesota. I'd been corrupted by Garrison Keillor's stories of Norwegian bachelor farmers on *A Prairie Home Companion*.

And what was *this*? A church in the median? It certainly seemed so. Miles ahead, near the crest of a hill, the dark cone-shaped steeple of an old church rose above the Interstate, topped by a small cross. It sat there quietly, as if it had refused to budge when the Interstate was built. But it proved an optical illusion, the highway curving at the last moment to put the church in its rightful place off to the left.

Then came Freeport (pop. 556), where the water tower, which looks like a Chinese skyrocket, has a smiley face. There's a little old church as well, brown sandstone with a modest steeple, and—a kind of miracle—a working clock!

Beyond the church, off to the left, a stretch of woods held more reddish leaves than I'd seen to date—autumn reds that matched the local barns and outbuildings, leaving the bright white for the homes. And once again I was struck by the Nordic neatness. Minnesota is nothing if not *neat*.

Near Albany (pop. 1548) the road deteriorated, *pa-dump pa-dump* once again. But there was an attractive local golf course, a college campus on a hill, and some lovely upscale homes in a new development on the left—by far the largest housing development I'd seen since Seattle. A few miles later, on a stretch reminiscent of Connecticut's Merritt Parkway, I pulled into the Big Spunk Rest Area, curious about the name.

289

I went to the historical marker first, but it said nothing about Big Spunk. It focused instead on the Germans, *The Benedictines in Minnesota*.

Between 1854 and 1857 many Catholics came to the United States from Germany and settled in Central Minnesota. At St. Cloud and in the Saulk Valley their religious and educational needs were met by the Benedictines. . . . The Benedictines of Minnesota have established high respect through their many services to humanity for nearly a century and a half. They created important academies, schools of higher education, hospitals, orphanages, homes for the aged and missions which extend beyond Minnesota to distant parts of the country and the world. In addition, they are pioneers in establishing public radio, the liturgical and ecumenical movements, pastoral work, educational publishing, arts and crafts, and the development of a world-renowned library.

Interesting. But I wanted to know about *Big Spunk*. And there was no one to ask. It was nine-thirty, fifty-four degrees, and I had the rest area all to myself, a facility as neat and clean as the earlier one, with shingled pavilions and clean sidewalks through the grassy mounds and trees.

As I was about to leave, a tractor-trailer pulled in, the driver waving me over as he jumped from his cab. Maybe he would know the history of *Big Spunk*. But why was he calling me? He was dressed in jeans and a T-shirt and, despite the gray day, wore Batman-like sunglasses. Unlike many truckers I'd met, he was small and slim, without a potbelly. Thick veins bulged from his wiry arms.

"You the professor?" he said.

"How'd ya know?"

"They've been talking about you on the CB. I was hoping I'd catch up."

"And why is that?"

"Because I used to be a professor too. Publish or perish, right?" He spit on the sidewalk. "I did both. But I suppose you're tenured, if you're still a professor."

I didn't know how to respond. The guy seemed to have an agenda, to be nursing a grudge. He sounded as if he'd rehearsed his words as he trailed me east.

"Where did you teach?" I said finally.

He named a prestigious East Coast university.

"When they gave me the pink slip, I turned to trucking. I've been trucking for twenty years all over the Interstates, in all forty-eight states. You've been asking folks about the Interstates, isn't that right? Well, there isn't any better way to see America. But have you ever seen any heavier women than in the Midwest? What incedible porkers!" He spit on the sidewalk again.

"Well," I said, "I'd better be on my way."

"What's your hurry?"

"I'm going to Eau Claire, Wisconsin. I want to get through the Twin Cities before noon. As my father used to say, 'I gotta see a man about a horse.'"

The trucker-professor spit yet again as I headed for the 'Vette.

Disconcerted by the encounter, I had forgotten to ask about the etymology of *Big Spunk*. But a few minutes later, back on the highway, I solved the puzzle on my own. A small sign announced *Middle Spunk Creek*. No doubt a relative of *Big Spunk*.

Suburban communities flanked the way now, including some tidy tract housing and industry. The sudden density was startling. Was this where the midwestern suburbs begin for good? Right *here*, en route to Minneapolis–St. Paul?

More lakes followed, and then a spate of universities—St. John's, St. Joseph's, and the College of St. Benedict, their spires rising above the red and orange foliage as the sun struggled to break through. Then, bypassing St. Cloud to the south, I-94 crossed the Saulk River yet again, and soon a construction area brought a brief stretch of smooth blacktop. I was seventy miles west of Minneapolis and the lakes were relentless—*Clear Lake*, *Maple Lake*, *Silver Creek*, and *Locke Lake*—a body of dark water surrounded by gorgeous upscale homes. Had Locke Lake been named for the philosopher John Locke? I liked to think so. Perhaps a Benedictine influence.

Views to the left and right were minimal now, the terrain blocked by groves of trees that merged like a forest. The median was greener than ever, complementing the red, orange, and yellow leaves. If only the sun would come out! But the only source of light was a strange lighthouse that suddenly appeared on the left, a cone-shaped cement tower. About three feet wide at the base, the structure rises to a point that is topped by a tiny house. But if it housed a light, that light wasn't shining. I was beginning to fear the dull weather would escort me all the way home.

I flew by *Hasty*, taking the sign at its word. Then Monticello (pop. 4941), a Minnesota Star City. But Monticello has more billboards than stars, an interstate strip of *garbage throughout*, its signs stacked high above the highway, rudely competing for attention. If Monticello had been named for Thomas Jefferson, he would have rejected the honor. I've seen *the* Monticello, and the one in Minnesota is an insult.

Glorious new blacktop pointed the way to Minneapolis. But the billboard barrage continued, as ugly and disappointing as in the worst stretches down South. Suburban developments multiplied as the traffic thickened, pressing ahead beyond Elk River in three lanes, where the *garbage-in* of the Twin Cities begins in earnest.

Of all the cities in America on my Interstate odyssey, I had looked forward the most to Minneapolis–St. Paul. As with Seattle, I'd never heard a bad word about these Siamese twin municipalities that are joined at the hip by the Mississippi River. Culture, entertainment, good food, genuine people—Minneapolis–St. Paul is said to have everything. But as seen from the Interstate, no place in America disappointed me more.

Inside the Minneapolis beltway, where I-94 enters Brooklyn Park, a big old brown structure rises with green epaulets, about six stories high. *It's a grammar school*, I was thinking, *or a hospital perhaps*. But I was wrong on both counts. It's the Northland Inn.

The traffic increased, moderate to heavy, escorted by a wall of horizontal planks. But at least the trees were in color, among some lovely ponds and lakes.

Soon a tan urban wall took over, its bricks the size of cinderblocks, and a ragged median divided the traffic. On the horizon to the left I recognized the Hilton, old and brown, its name in white letters across the top. Then the highway swept to the right, heading due south for the city center, where the speed drops to fifty-five and a fourth lane is added. But there was still no view of the city—just twin smokestacks, one shorter than the other.

In Minneapolis proper, a dull skyline emerged through a gray haze to the right, all structures with familiar designs—a flat-topped building with a fly roof, another like the Empire State Building, and yet another like the United Nations Building. And that was it for my first glimpse of Minneapolis, an old brown city of nearly four hundred thousand people. Which left me wondering what all the shouting was about.

Closer in, you begin to realize that Minneapolis is a *long* city, its buildings low and spread out. On the right, above an ornate church, sits a dome with a spire and cross. Modern buildings follow, but older ones set the tone in a melange of dark brick. It was eleven o'clock, the traffic moving steadily beneath a series of viaducts, the highway curving left and right through downtown.

Another spire popped up on a domed pillar, a wedding-cake affair among green copper roofs, the architecture reminiscent of Notre Dame or London's St. Paul. Then I entered a tunnel like the one in Baltimore and the speed dropped to thirty-five, the highway curving toward a distant patch of light. At the very end of the tunnel the light brightened—the sun had broken through at last, albeit weakly, reflecting off a stretch of gaudy apartment buildings beyond.

Before the good people of Minneapolis get on my case, here's an appropriate Interstate Item:

On page 476 of *America's Highways: 1776–1976*, there is a photograph of a bicycle path that has been built within the right-of-way of I-94 in Minneapolis. According to the caption, it *extends for over half a mile and safely connects two neighborhoods.* I missed it, however, concentrating as I was on the traffic and the skyline. Or perhaps I missed it because it is so very close to the highway. But it's comforting to know that one sort of traffic doesn't preclude another, and that safety is always considered where the Interstates are concerned.

In two days' time I would miss something else that is featured in *America's Highways: 1776–1976.* On page 470 is a photograph of a rest area on I-94 near New Buffalo, Michigan, in the extreme southwest corner of the state, just a few miles from the Indiana line. I didn't stop there because I had stopped earlier, and didn't notice it in passing. The caption of that photograph reads: *This attractive rest area and information center on I-94 near New Buffalo, Mich., is the result of a combined effort of architects, landscapers, and design engineers to preserve mature trees and to provide grassy picnic areas. The pond was purposely created from a 4-acre borrow-pit.*

Compare that testimonial to the one on page 472, beneath an attractive photograph of I-70 in Colorado: *Gently curving I-70 in the Eagle River Valley of Colorado provides the motorist with new vistas of the countryside with each turn. The weathering-steel guardrail blends with its surroundings. Flat slopes, designed for safety, are quickly regaining vegetation because of the topsoil salvaged during early stages of construction.* Although I've never seen that particular spot, I have seen similar vistas, driving I-70 west out of Denver into the ski resorts. The Interstates were directly responsible for Colorado's booming ski industry.

Finally, on page 479 of *America's Highways: 1776–1976,* there's a photograph of another place I've driven through. The caption reads: *The plants and vegetation used along I-64 in Greenbrier County, W. Va., were selected to blend with the natural vegetation on the rolling hills of the Greenbrier River Valley.*

The theme here is evident—ecological, environmental, and safety concerns are integral to the planning and the aesthetic appeal of the Interstates. But photographs are poor substitutes for hitting the road and experiencing the real thing.

When I crossed the Mississippi River into St. Paul, I thought I was back in Bridgeport, Connecticut. Smaller than Minneapolis, with fewer

293

than three hundred thousand people, St. Paul is an industrial cityscape with underpasses, overpasses, and high concrete walls—brick, brick, and more brick. A Rapunzel-like tower rose on the right, capped by a witch's hat above a kind of belfry. Beyond it, the Mississippi River ran parallel, lined by trees splashed with autumn color. A sign for *Cretin Avenue* made me wonder—did it take a *cretin* to appreciate such an unattractive, nondescript place? St. Paul is a city of smokestacks and brick, its population crammed into Archie Bunker houses.

But things get better downtown, where tall buildings suddenly form a compact skyline. There's one like an electric shaver, one like a trapezoid, and one like a glass pyramid with a truncated top. The state capitol sits beyond, just off the right shoulder—a greenish wedding-cake with column-like candles, above a bronze trapezoidal base. Then I-94 curves beneath glass walkways, evidence of Minnesota winters, with two unenclosed overpasses for the brave. Soon plank retaining walls line turn-of-the-century neighborhoods. Then the strip malls take over, *garbage-out* all the way to the beltway.

The Twin Cities take up fifty miles of the Interstate, and it took me less than an hour to pass through. The pace was moderate and civilized, there was no Interstate idle, and I found St. Paul a bit more attractive than its counterpart, which isn't saying much.

At Keats Avenue—I hoped it was named for the poet—the speed returned to sixty-five, and soon new residential communities ushered a return to the countryside. Despite a sign for *Alps Ski Area*, the terrain was level. Then the highway descended slightly to the Mississippi, where a sign thanked me for having visited Minnesota.

* * *

Crossing the Mississippi River on I-94 is like crossing the Hudson. Ample autumn foliage colored the far shore. I had lost count of the states that have rivers as natural boundaries, but North Dakota–Minnesota—and now Minnesota-Wisconsin—had to be added to the list.

On the far bank Wisconsin welcomed me with three proud words—*Industry, Recreation, Agriculture.* To which the license plates added, *America's Dairyland.*

Beyond the river, lovely grassy hills rolled on towards Eau Claire, just sixty miles distant. Red autumn colors began to dominate, although the sun was still weak. And despite the order of the official words of welcome, Wisconsin's agricultural area came first—pine valleys and woodlands with fields of wheat, grazing cows, and red barns. *Top Shelf Genetics,* a lone billboard proudly touted. *Here's a Farm For You.* It was not yet noon and I was back in the country, a welcome respite from the megalopolis I'd just traversed, and those waiting farther east to swallow me whole.

The return of pine trees took me by surprise. Pines spread away in vast stands to the left and right, filling hillsides and valleys, too uniform to have occurred naturally. Then my ears popped as I descended into a lovely valley, the highway split by a long median, the westbound lanes high above me on the left. Surprisingly, gentle mountains ringed the green horizon, a wide perspective I thought I'd lost forever. I was on the Laura Ingalls Wilder Historic Highway, where echoes of *Little House on the Prairie* replaced *A Prairie Home Companion*. Half Pint, Mary, and Pa.

A short while later I stopped at the Menomonie Rest Area, the first in Wisconsin and one of the very few in the nation with decent playground equipment for children. Its pavilions are unique as well, each flat green roof supported by six pillars. The historic information concerned Chippewa Valley white pine:

Here and northeast of here lies the vast Chippewa Valley. At the start of lumbering in Wisconsin it held one sixth of the nation's white pine. Surveyors estimated the total pine stand in the state at 136 billion board feet. Lumbermen considered the supply inexhaustible. Chippewa Valley White Pine helped build the homes and cities of the Corn Belt, the Great Plains, and Chicago after its fire. This valley made strong men, record log jams, tall tales and prosperous cities all while wasting 60 percent of its pine in stumps, slashings, culls, sawdust slabs and fires. The harvest here that began in 1830 with five foot diameter trunks 160 feet high, ended 80 years later taking five inch logs. Today the Chippewa Valley is green again with farms and pines. Reforestation began in 1920. Early plantings are now merchantable timber. In time the Chippewa Valley will again stand with mature pine.

The marker confirmed what I'd guessed about all the pines I was seeing. But there wasn't a word about the Chippewas, who'd been removed from Wisconsin as systematically as the pines. Given the recent groundbreaking for the Native American Museum in Washington, D.C., it was a glaring omission. The roadside message— posted in 1973—needs a politically correct update.

Fish Wisconsin, another display said, listing all the fish you can catch in Wisconsin—muskelunge, walleye, northern pike, yellow perch, smallmouth bass, largemouth bass, white bass, black crappie, pumpkinseed, bluegill, rainbow trout, brown trout, lake trout, brook trout, coho salmon, and black bullhead. Nothing you can't catch in Ohio, except for the salmon.

Wisconsin had celebrated its sesquicentennial in 1998, and the result was a stack of helpful brochures alerting travelers to the wonders of Wisconsin, as well as highway work zones ahead. Recycling bins for aluminum, glass, and plastic stood about the sidewalks, as if to reinforce the state's commitment to conservation and tidiness. I stretched my legs, hit the men's room, then got back on the road, anxious to get to Eau Claire and give the 'Vette a much-needed bath. In such a tidy state as Wisconsin you have to look your best.

Farther along I crossed the Red Cedar River, pretty and wide, with dark tree-lined shores. Cows grazed in the farmland beyond, identified by signs as *Priceland Jerseys*. There were roadside marshy areas too, a lingering touch of Minnesota. Then the day warmed a bit, the humidity rising too, and by mid-afternoon I was in Eau Claire, washing the 'Vette in dull sunshine outside Motel Find-Me-Not.

The chore took me two hours, working with my squirt bottle, squeegee, and paper towels. For some reason I couldn't get the trucking professor out of my mind. He was right about one thing, though. The women in the Midwest are incredibly large. All I had to do was look about me, as they waddled in and out of Motel Find-Me-Not.

Later, in the lobby, I discovered a clerk at the desk who sounded exactly like Marge in the movie *Fargo*.

"*Oooh kay*," she said, "you want to know aboot the Interstates. Well, I drive 'em every day but I never think aboot 'em. They just get me to where I'm going quicker. I drive 'em *to* work, *for* work, and *after* work. It's usually pretty busy out there."

She paused when I laughed. "And what's so funny aboot *that?*"

Compared with other parts of the country, I told her, Wisconsin has very little traffic.

"*Oooh kay*," she said, raising her eyebrows. "If you say so."

While we were speaking, one of the motel maids squeezed in behind the desk to check a computer screen. She seemed to be eavesdropping, so I told her what I was up to and asked her about the Interstates.

"I don't wanna be in no book," she said flatly, leaving the desk in a huff.

Oooh kay, I said to myself. *I won't put you in.*

18

BUT I WAS GOING TO TELL YOU HOW I FINALLY GOT MY 'VETTE.

In June of 1999, three months before my scheduled departure, I searched the Midwest for any six-speed hardtop with "lumbar" sports seats. Those were my only requirements. I didn't care about the color, the interior, the fancy options.

To my surprise, the vast majority of available 'Vettes were automatics, like our family cars, the Caprice and Geo. And therefore no fun to drive. Only two met my specifications—a green '96 in Michigan with 27,000 miles on it, and the red one I bought in Ohio, a virginal '96, only 5000 miles old. The latter was at Bud's Chevrolet, less than an hour away, and since *Bud* is my nickname, I felt my first twinge of Corvette karma.

But the car was more than I could afford.

"What about the boys' college fund?" my wife Elaine suggested finally.

That's what I was thinking too. But I wanted her to say it first. We had been squirreling away money for our sons' education since the day they were born. And we had an ace in the hole. As long as they studied at the university where I teach, they could study tuition-free, an enormous savings at today's exorbitant college prices. Our older son was already on campus. The younger would begin in the fall. So there was a large sum of money just sitting in the bank.

"I'll just take enough for a down payment," I compromised. "Then we'll see what happens."

What happened was that I bought the 'Vette at Bud's, Elaine and I took a "shakedown" cruise to visit relatives in Illinois, then—at the end of July—I had a repeat operation for a herniated disk in my back, part of the game plan all along.

Six weeks after surgery, I began my Interstate odyssey.

* * *

Eight-thirty Wednesday morning I left Eau Claire for the Chicago area. The day was dark and overcast, only forty-five degrees, with a bruising wind out of the north.

Of course, it had rained during the night, true to Murphy's Interstate Law—*If you wash it, it will come.* But I had slept solidly for eleven hours, so even the inky morning sky couldn't depress me. I was getting closer to home and the 'Vette seemed to sense it, its own red flash complemented by the duller reds of the autumn trees.

On the outskirts of Eau Claire (pop. 85,000), I flew by a series of middle-class housing developments, duplexes, and apartments. The main signs were for Madison now. Then brand-new blacktop began, causing the idyllometer to take notice. But there wasn't enough sun for a substantial reading, despite lovely rural valleys of golden wheat. And groves of colorful trees among the pines.

On one hillside, a local farmer had mowed a message into the landscape, a simple question like a message to the gods—*Y2K?* It made me glad I'd be home well before the millennium. Given all the doomsday forecasts, the highway might not be the safest place to be.

I crossed the Chippewa River on a pretty two-lane bridge, the westbound traffic on its own section to the left. The speed limit was posted at sixty-five now, and I wondered if I'd ever see it at seventy again.

The morning news on the radio was not encouraging. In Pleasanton, Texas, just south of the Interstate near San Antonio, a sniper had killed two deputies overnight. And basketball great Wilt Chamberlain had died. On the plus side, according to NPR, today's children in America have a good chance of living to one hundred, whereas in Russia the life expectancy is only half that. But the black-and-white cows to my left seemed unimpressed with this news, contentedly chewing their collective cuds in lovely pastures. Amidst red barns, golden wheat, and autumn groves.

298

An hour east of Eau Claire I passed a car with a driver holding a hot-water bottle to her cheek, no doubt en route to the dentist. Then I crossed the Black River, which is lined with majestic pines, and the terrain flattened out for a bit. But before long it began to roll again, by a sign for Spring Green (pop. 1287), site of Frank Lloyd Wright's *Taliesin*—the famous home in his Prairie School style. Given the pastoral terrain, it was easy to see the inspiration for Wright's natural architecture, his desire to fit his home to the landscape.

Hoping for information on the genius architect, I pulled into the very next rest area. But the historical notes dealt with sphagnum moss: *Wisconsin's Invisible Industry.*

Marshy sections of Jackson, Monroe, Wood and Clark counties produce large quantities of sphagnum moss, providing a major but little known state resource. The ability of sphagnum to hold 20 times its weight in water makes it invaluable for keeping plants and nursery stock alive in shipment. It is also used in hydroponic gardening, for air shipment of flowers, and because it is sterile it is used in surgical dressings and seed germination to prevent fungus attack in seeds. Sphagnum replaces itself in the central wetland marshes after harvest and is ready to be pulled again every three years. Harvest season runs from spring until marshes freeze in the fall. No other state produces sphagnum commercially.

Well, before long it would be sphagnum-pulling season. In the meantime it had begun to drizzle, and after a visit to the men's room I had to sprint to the 'Vette to keep from getting soaked. I had no sphagnum to hold above my head.

The rain increased as I continued towards Madison, rinsing the windshield at a rate out of sync with my wipers. Distances were stated in kilometers now as well as miles, a concession to Canada. A sign for *Mill Bluff State Park* conjured a pleasant image. Then a striking natural rock formation appeared on the left, the sort I'd seen in the desert Southwest—twin rock towers like a pair of old faces. But a sign identified them less poetically as *Castle Rock*.

A short while later Wisconsin became a state of billboards, all flaunting its most famous local product—cheese. Cheese, cheese, and more cheese. Cheese factories, cheese outlets, cheese shops, cheese boutiques. Bring your camera to Wisconsin, America! There's enough cheese to make everybody smile.

Halfway between Eau Claire and Madison, I-94 joins I-90 again for the first time since Montana. And suddenly it seemed that the great strands of my journey were beginning to wrap themselves up. I could sense a psychological wrapping up as well. Once I got to Chicago I'd be in familiar territory, a thought that increased my excitement of returning home.

I zipped through a stretch called *The Wisp Dells Parkway*—such a charming name! The area reminded me of Connecticut, with rocky ledges and outcroppings along the rolling terrain. Then white pines surrounded Mirror Lake and the darker water of Devils Lake. And a puzzling billboard followed—*Ho-Chun Casino*. It sounded Chinese. I thought Native Americans had cornered that market.

Traffic was increasing steadily now, police cars tucked in the median at regular intervals. I winced each time I saw one. But I had set the cruise control at seventy-four, taking no chances of a repeat arrest. Now signs for places beyond Madison were beginning to crop up—*Milwaukee 100, Chicago 180*.

The rain fell more sharply. Bales of green hay lay everywhere, absorbing the showers like blocks of sphagnum moss. I crossed the lovely tree-lined Wisconsin River on a flat, open bridge and pulled into the rest area beyond, where an interesting marker addresses the history of Wisconsin rest stops.

I read it hastily, standing in the rain.

Early roadside rest areas were rural schoolgrounds and country churchyards with their two little houses in back. In Wisconsin by 1920 curves were built to eliminate sharp road corners. Local garden clubs with the American Legion auxiliaries began to beautify many of the resulting triangles with

299

flowers and shrubs. Motorists used these places to relax and picnic. In 1931 the Wisconsin legislature authorized highway beautification for the familiar waysides—small roadside parks at first and for many years without water and sanitation. In 1940 garden and women's clubs, the Legion, the Friends of Our Native Landscape, and others organized the Wisconsin Roadside Council, joined by the Council Highway and County Boards Association, to aid the State Highway Commission in roadside development and increasing and improving waysides. Through such initiative Wisconsin gained the experience to become one of the very first states to provide these modern full-facility rest areas you are now enjoying approximately every 50 miles.

Well, it was a lovely rest area, green and clean, but I couldn't enjoy it in the rain. The day had turned miserable—wet and cold—leaving travelers scurrying to their vehicles, in no mood to chat.

I returned to the highway at eleven o'clock, heading for Madison in three lanes of moderate traffic, among more trucks than I'd seen in many days. Still, the road ran by rural pastures, wheat fields, and red barns. And then the countryside disappeared, giving way to attractive middle-class housing developments. There were apartments and condos and suburban business strips and banks—not quite Madison's *garbage in.* Then I-90 branched south for Chicago, taking most of the truck traffic with it, while I kept to I-94 toward Milwaukee, skirting Madison to the north.

300

Soon the road surface deteriorated, the worst in days, with rumbling bumps every three or four seconds. But delightful place names provided a diversion—*Lake Mills, Sun Prairie, Glacial Drumlin State Trail.* A *drumlin* is a streamlined hill, a ridge of glacial drift, an image that added an ancient air to the local geography. I crossed Rock River into rolling terrain marked by tree-lined dark meadows. And despite the dreary wet day, children were running about excitedly outside a local elementary school, making the most of their noon recess.

Give Yourself A Hug, a sign urged. *Buckle up.* How did that old football fight song go? *Buckle up, Wisconsin, buckle up!* Or is it *Knuckle down, Wisconsin?* I'm not enough of a Big Ten fan to know the difference.

On the approach to Milwaukee a helpful scoreboard sign was flashing above the Interstate—*Travel Time to Downtown: 17 Minutes.* It proved amazingly accurate. The traffic moved steadily at sixty by a string of modern corporate headquarters. Then it thickened closer in, and as I passed beneath a huge arch that spans I-94, a car cut in front of me without signaling. But it was easy to see why. Steering with one hand, the black-suited businessman held a cell phone in the other. So how could he signal? He'd have to miss his conversation. For such drivers, time is money. My life doesn't matter.

Milwaukee traffic has the same moderate midwestern pace as Minneapolis–St. Paul, but with one negative distinction—trucks run continuously in the left-hand lane. Despite their mudguards, they generated a constant spray from the wet surface. Then dull plank retaining walls lined the way into town, with more overhead wires than any Interstate city in America.

Milwaukee's another Bridgeport, only uglier—an industrial valley to the right, then a forgettable skyline marred by high-tension wires. You pass County Stadium, the circular home of the Milwaukee Brewers, then cramped Archie Bunker neighborhoods. Once again a Hilton dominates. Right beside it is an attractive pink and brown building with an angular roof, amidst a few spires and a rocket-like structure. Marquette University sits off to the left, then I-94 swings to the right—high into the air for Chicago, arching above a flat industrial stretch of old brick and smokestacks.

Because Milwaukee's a port city, I-94 leaves downtown on a long stretch of high bridges, Lake Michigan brimming wide to the left. More Archie Bunker neighborhoods follow, dotted with old church steeples and the spires of Woodland School. One old building looks like a state capitol, but it's a church, its large dome topped by a smaller one, plus a ball-and-cross belfry.

I had no expectations for Milwaukee, so it didn't disappoint me. Like too many American cities, it's a functioning relic of an industrial past. I liked best the brand-new blacktop on its outskirts that sped me south toward Chicago.

And ever closer to home.

* * *

The rain let up at the Illinois line, where—according to the signs—the people of Illinois welcomed me and the Tri-State Tollway began.

But *tri-state* was confusing. Wisconsin was above me and Illinois below. Who else was claiming a share of my toll? Not that I was complaining. With the Illinois line comes a brief respite of country terrain. Then the tract housing and strip malls begin again for good—*garbage in* all the way to Chicago. Among the clutter is a Six Flags amusement park, where an orange-and-white roller coaster rises into the sky in a contorted mass of twisting tracks.

The speed was posted at fifty-five but the big trucks were doing seventy-five. Occasional communities of large homes surrounded artificial lakes. At one point a congested rest area served both north and southbound traffic—a rare Interstate phenomenon—with an overhead walkway spanning all lanes. Had I continued, I would have hit Chicago just in time for the afternoon rush, a massive Interstate idle I knew I'd be facing in the morning. But I had planned my day to avoid it, exiting north of downtown on Route 22 West, to spend the night in Cary at the home of my sister-in-law's brother.

Jay and Penny live in a secluded country neighborhood thick with tall trees. Although I had seen Jay recently, I hadn't seen Penny in more than a decade. No one was home when I arrived at four o'clock, so I set to work in the driveway washing the 'Vette again. The dashboard trip monitor read 9,929. In leaving Chicago in the morning I would hit an even ten thousand miles—a grand lap milestone.

Penny returned at five with the news that Jay had been called to Nassau on business that very morning. She had two friends with her who had come to see her new carpet, and as soon as they left she put two steaks on the grill.

During dinner we talked of family, then the Interstates.

"I grew up in Dayton," Penny said, "but we moved to Elyria near Cleveland. In those days that drive took forever! We went from Dayton to Cleveland often, always traveling at night to avoid the traffic. All the little towns would be lighted up at night. My brothers and I used to call them *fairy towns*, because that's exactly how they looked strung out in the darkness. My grandparents were still in Dayton, and when they came to visit us in Cleveland they'd stay for several weeks, simply because it took so long to get there. Today, you can make the same trip on the Interstates in three and a half hours."

After dinner Jay phoned from Nassau, full of apologies. But I was happy he called. When in Cary he commutes to Chicago. I was anxious for his opinion of the daily grind. He'd lived in the area for two decades, and I wanted to know what I'd be facing in the morning.

"To get into the city in an hour," he said, "I gotta leave by five forty-five. If I leave at six, it takes an hour and a half. But one good thing about Chicago—the express lanes work. From six to nine it's bad, but by nine the rush is all over."

I made a mental note of the three-hour window as Jay continued like a salesman.

"There's plenty of money in the metropolitan area to keep the roads in good shape, so there's always construction, but they do it at night. The train system lightens the load. You can set your watch to the trains right to the minute. I used to drive into the city, and I've taken a limo several times, but now I rely on the train. But let me tell you something about Chicago. I've been caught in the Los Angeles rush hour several times. It's absolutely the biggest logjam in the world. In L.A. the people live out their road rage. You won't find any of that in Chicago."

"Can I quote you on that?" I laughed.

"Chicago's not so easy," Penny said when Jay hung up. "When I was single I once drove with a friend from Colorado to Cleveland. There are so many expressways in the Chicago area that it's easy to get confused. We passed through Chicago late at night and got totally lost. Because of that trip I still get in a panic when I'm on the Interstates. There's no worse feeling." She started to get up. "Another beer?"

I waved her off, and so she continued.

"When I first moved to Chicago I took the train to work, because it took two hours each way just to drive forty miles. But the main problem with the Interstates is that you can't get off if something happens. There are no alternatives. I was in Indiana once when a gasoline truck wrecked, spilling gas all over the place. Traffic was backed up for two hours. We had to shut the engine off and wait. You know how maddening that gets?"

I nodded. The old Interstate idle. But it had been a long day. I had had a few beers and a big steak and was feeling drowsy. The city of Chicago, my last Interstate hurdle, would have to wait until morning.

* * *

Had Jay been in Cary, we would have spent Thursday at his country club. Instead, I was free to leave a day earlier than anticipated, which would put me home in Ohio on Friday.

The impending end to my Interstate odyssey filled me with a sudden air of expectancy. But first I had some unfinished business up in Olivet, Michigan. Several years earlier I had given the eulogy at a colleague's funeral there. Ron had died of cancer not long after early retirement. I wanted to see his grave and visit his widow. But Florence was expecting me on Friday, not Thursday. So I telephoned ahead in the morning—Penny was off to a dance class—but got no answer.

As in Seattle, I lingered over breakfast until nine o'clock in order to escape the teeth of the morning rush. The TV news featured a woman in Tarbox, North Carolina, whose backyard, due to the earlier flooding, had become a breeding ground for tadpoles. Now thousands of frogs were hopping around out there. She feared they'd attract snakes. Worse yet, another hurricane was threatening Florida. Hurricane Irene, near Cuba, was expected to hit the Florida Keys with seventy-five-mile-per-hour winds. So my Interstate odyssey was ending as it had begun. In the face of a hurricane.

But it was a clear blue day and forty-five degrees when I left Cary, retracing my way along Route 22—a suburban country lane—to where I had exited I-94 South. Despite my intentional delay, the road was jammed from the morning rush. Nothing to do but edge my way in and creep along. Then I-94 merged with I-90 again and I saw a sign for Des Plaines—home of the original McDonald's, a dubious Illinois distinction.

Congestion ahead south of Dempster through Devon, a lighted sign warned. But since I knew neither Dempster nor Devon, it wasn't much help. It was nine-thirty and only one thing was clear—the Interstate idle was in full force, bumper to bumper through industrial, commercial, and suburban sprawl, three lanes on either side of a cement divider, the air choked with cars, trucks, and exhaust fumes.

At ten o'clock came another scoreboard message—*Congestion continues through Pratt.* How good of them to let me know. But where was *Pratt*? The road surface, despite what Jay had claimed, was all bumps and rumbles—grade *C* for *Chicago.*

Then the idyllometer hit absolute zero. A complete standstill. No movement whatsoever. The air rippling with grit for long minutes on end. Ultimately, however, the previous yellow warning proved prophetic. After Pratt, the speed picked up to thirty, and at the north branch of the Chicago River I swung into the express lanes.

My first view of the Chicago skyline consisted of twin tall buildings side by side, like the Empire State Building and the Chrysler Building. I had seen so many similar structures all around America that I was convinced that the New York originals were responsible for the archaic style. With blue sky and bright sun behind them, the buildings made an attractive pattern of light and shadow. But a hazy, polluted sky waited in the distance, and the express lanes suddenly dropped to five miles per hour. Overhead, Metro trains rattled into the city, the stations elevated to the left of the median.

Express Lanes to Indiana. The sign made me laugh. The Express Lanes were expressly going nowhere, as gray and gritty sky replaced the blue.

A greater skyline eventually materialized through the haze to my left. Then the speed picked up and I had to focus on my driving. Jay had been right about one thing—there isn't much road rage in Chicago, because you can't see the road for all the traffic. Local commuters looked to their cell phones, earphones, books, and laptops to defuse the ongoing frustration.

Farther along, large glassy buildings reflected dull sunlight as I slipped beneath tunnel-like underpasses. *Congestion continues through I-55 ramp,* a sign warned. Beyond the tunnels more skyline opened up, above an industrial stretch of dirty brick and tall apartments— Bridgeport again, to the *n*th power. By ten-forty I was passing yet another ugly stretch where I-90 heads east for Gary, Indiana. Then

I-57 branched south for Memphis. But such distant destinations seemed utterly impossible in the jaws of this Interstate idle. I couldn't imagine what the congestion had been like earlier.

Chicago, like Milwaukee, is a port city on Lake Michigan, with marshy *garbage out* to the east, through a grid of black iron bridges and overhead wires. I reached I-80/94 at eleven-thirty—two and a half hours to go but seventy miles. Had I had a cell phone myself I would have telephoned Jay in Nassau to give him a piece of my mind.

Then it was *Welcome To Indiana—Crossroads to America!* But those crossroads were clogged with trucks.

Trucks had taken over the two right-hand lanes, leaving just one for all other vehicles. But at least we were moving. Across the cement divider everything had stopped, with trucks strung out for miles. Fifteen minutes later the westbound traffic was still screeching to a halt, unaware of how far ahead of them the traffic was snarled. Eastbound, a black man was down on his knees beside a beat-up car on the shoulder, his hands cuffed behind him, several police officers hovering above him, their cars parked at all angles, lights flashing.

And suddenly I remembered my digital trip monitor. It now read 10,007. Dang! I had missed the big moment, but I pulled off anyway at the next exit to celebrate.

Never again, I swore on the spot, would I drive through Chicago. I had done it one last time and survived. Now I had to survive the Interstate ambush into which I had put myself, plus a maniacal Indiana service mart. But gas was only one twenty-eight for supreme, the lowest price of my entire grand lap. The Corvette karma was still with me.

I elbowed my way through a throng of noisy people inside, grabbed a bottle of orange juice and a donut, then retreated to the packed parking lot for a late-morning snack. The day had warmed considerably. I could scrape the humid grit from my face with my fingernails. Cars were careening in and out of the parking lot, while up on the Interstate the westbound lanes remained idle, the eastbound moving rapidly.

Moments later I rejoined the madness, through the industrial ugliness in the marshy woodlands of I-80/94, a highway flanked by billboards and divided by a concrete barrier. But there was hope. To the east the blue sky was beginning to return, albeit gradually—a lighter, strained blue.

The noon hour found me on I-94 proper, heading north, where Michigan soon welcomed me—*Great Lakes, Great Time!* I was on the eastern shore of Lake Michigan now, straight across from Chicago. A green V-shaped median had replaced the cement divider, and there were ragged cornfields, rolling meadows, sandy dunes, and small farms.

Then the speed returned to seventy and the traffic cruised at eighty, through soft woodlands of yellow, red, and orange. After a string of Chicago zeros, the idyllometer took notice. Yet the sensitive monitor couldn't exceed seventy-five. There were too many trucks, too many billboards, too many overhead wires.

I snapped on the radio and the antenna slipped into the air, just in time to catch a lilting Strauss waltz. And suddenly I was waltzing my way to Olivet on a warm October afternoon.

Waltzing—I realized suddenly—my way home.

* * *

Beyond Warren Dunes State Park, I-94 bends to the northeast. A '99 'Vette—red like my own but with a black ragtop—was heading southwest. I honked my horn and got a wave in response.

A short while later I crossed the St. Joseph River, winding and tree-lined but pea green in color. There was another 'Vette up ahead, cruising lazily in the right-hand lane, and the elderly gentleman driver, in a neat white shirt and bright tie, gave me the high sign as I sped by—a happy reminder of the Corvette salute on my first day out. Things were definitely coming full circle.

Soon I-196 turned north for Grand Rapids and I-94 continued east for Kalamazoo, fifty miles distant. Out of the Chicago wasteland now and in no hurry whatsoever, I stopped to stretch at a rustic rest area—an island of green grass and trees in gentle autumn colors, with picnic tables of solid stone.

A retired man and his wife were standing beside their station wagon as I pulled in. Their vehicle, crammed to the roof with suitcases and boxes, bore Wyoming plates. The man wore a cowboy hat, had a paunchy belly, and was fighting on a leash the ugliest creature I've ever seen, some sort of bulldog with a genetic mutation.

"Isn't Chicago just horrible?" the woman said when I introduced myself. "We came on I-80 all the way from Cheyenne, then picked up I-94 in Chicago. But it was no picnic through Chicago, let me tell you. The road was horrible in Iowa as well." She paused to dig in her purse for a camera. "Aren't these leaves simply lovely? All the yellows and reds?" Turning away, she began to snap away at the surrounding trees. Meanwhile, her husband was still struggling with their ugly dog.

"If you ask me," he said when he caught his breath, "I-80 is excellent in Nevada and tremendous in Wyoming. But in Wyoming they put it in the wrong place—right where there's the worst scenery and the worst weather. They shoulda put it about fifty miles north of where it is. But the decision was made in D.C., and you know how those folks are. I'm old enough to remember the arguments over where to put the darn thing. But what do *we* know? We only live there!"

Then the ugly dog yanked its master from the curb, pulling him all the way across the parking lot into a clearing beyond. Exasperated, the man finally gave up, anchoring the leash around a thick oak with a length of cable.

"Don't forget to adjust your watch, John!" his wife called after him. "We lost an hour leaving Chicago!" She turned to me. "And a few years of our lives, let me tell you!"

"Thanks for the reminder," I said, adjusting my own watch to two o'clock. Then I left the woman to her leaf photography.

En route to the men's room I stopped at an information display on *The Michigan State Capitol.*

When the United States Capitol in Washington added a new dome and wings in 1851–1863, it was without architectural precedent among major secular buildings. Following the Civil War, the Michigan capitol became one of the first statehouses to emulate the new design.

I made a mental note to watch for it in Kalamazoo.

Beyond the rest area, the road surface deteriorated significantly and the median grass stood uncut. How such simple things affect Interstate travel! Even the local vineyards—knee high—were dry and ragged, not the lush and pastoral acres of upstate New York. There were orchards too, and signs for winery tours, then a putrid country stench all but killed my afternoon waltz. The only pleasant sight was a yellow 'Vette—a vintage '73 banana—heading west with the top down.

On the approach to Kalamazoo, the median disappeared. A concrete barrier divided the four lanes, then a galvanized guardrail. Then a brown metal wall flanked the way until the billboards took over. Traffic was moderate, mostly trucks. But on the whole, Kalamazoo is neat and clean—not quite *garbage in* or *garbage out*—thanks to an abundance of tall pines that block the view. I looked for the capitol building and soon realized why I didn't see it. The capital of Michigan is Lansing, north of Battle Creek on I-69. I'd be taking I-69 from I-94 as far as Olivet.

A sign for *Climax* made me laugh. Sister city to *Intercourse,* Pennsylvania? Climax sits just south of the Interstate, its meager population (677) belying its name. By far, the greater population near Climax consisted of trucks. Trucks, trucks, and more trucks. According to my hasty count, nine out of ten vehicles were trucks— huge rumbling rigs pounding the pavement and emitting black smoke as they carried Michigan's goods to the rest of the nation from industrial hubs like Detroit.

Then came Battle Creek and Kellogg—clean like Kalamazoo—as the blue of the sky began to deepen above the stands of pines, above the brown sand and gravel of the highway shoulders. At ten past three I turned north on I-69, where all lanes were under construction, the going slow. New concrete was being poured over old blacktop, something I didn't think could be done. The wide median, all dirt and straw, had been freshly seeded.

The construction was tedious, but it was only a few miles to the tiny college town of Olivet (pop. 1604), where Florence was expecting me on Friday. And as I feared, she wasn't home. Nor was her car in the garage. So I left the 'Vette in the gravel driveway and hiked into town— all the way from Spruce Street to the old graveyard near campus—to pay my respects to Ron.

The afternoon was warm and dry, perfect for a stroll along old sidewalks lined with large trees. The graveyard was tree-lined as well, its hummocks lank with green grass, and it took me awhile to locate Ron's grave. A headstone had been added since the funeral. I had carried a flag around the nation to plant there—one for my father's grave in Connecticut as well—but I wanted both flags to make the entire grand lap with me, including tomorrow's short run home. After Friday I would mail a flag to Florence and another to my brother, so they could complete the ceremony on my behalf.

By the time I got back to Spruce Street, Florence was home, puzzling over the car in the driveway. She greeted me enthusiastically in a colorful print dress, her eyes flashing brightly as always. She explained that she had been out of town with friends. Now she was flustered. She had been reserving tomorrow to prepare her usual grand meals.

"This is El Gato," she gushed, introducing me to her new black cat. "He's a stray I took in. The other two are quite angry about that!"

El Gato had moved into the old white two-story home as if he owned the place, usurping a favorite chair of one of the resident cats and causing the other to hide away upstairs. Or perhaps my presence was responsible for the one upstairs.

It didn't matter. Florence and her cats took my mind off the Interstates. For the first time in weeks. She had been visiting art galleries and excitedly filled me in. She had been redoing the old home and showed me the changes.

My Interstate odyssey was all but over.

* * *

Friday morning—October 15, 1999—I headed to Ada, Ohio, a two-hundred-mile drive. The pleasant visit with Florence had reacquainted me with the familiar, and I was anxious for home. It was the thirty-third day of my grand lap of America. I had seen thirty-three states, plus the District of Columbia, in thirty-three days.

Departing Olivet at midmorning, I renegotiated the construction along I-69 South, then picked up I-80/90 in the northwest corner of Indiana. A short while later Ohio welcomed me back to *The Heart Of It All*, the cornfields and woodlots just as I'd left them. Only the corn was taller and the trees wore soft colors. Some fields were all stubble. Others had been plowed into rich brown furrows, emitting a lovely aroma of damp earth. The day was cool and breezy—sixty degrees as I crossed the state line—with a blue sky that I knew would never again be blue enough for me, never the deep blue of the great American West. Just the weak pale blue of the Rust Belt.

That was one casualty of my grand lap. I had lost the sky forever. And I had lost cities as well—Boston, Miami, L.A., Chicago. And entire states, Louisiana for sure. And North Dakota. And the greatest loss of all, my home state of Connecticut.

Police cars were camped in the median outside of Toledo, but it was a pleasantly wide median—no concrete barrier—and I cruised by them prudently at seventy-four. There was no hurry now, and the increasing traffic didn't bother me as I turned south on I-75 at high noon.

But one last Interstate idle awaited me, caused by the same construction below Bowling Green that I had encountered on my opening day. Yet I could see that progress had been made, as it was being made in all of the maintenance projects I had encountered nationwide. I was used to it now, even grateful. The Interstate System was intact, keeping the American economy intact, and keeping the vast majority of all travelers very satisfied. And so I powered down the windows and limped along in first gear, my mind a blank, waiting for revelations that never came. My Interstate odyssey had simply confirmed what I'd already suspected—that America is very big and very beautiful.

In the months to come, my grand lap would return to me in unexpected ways. Inspired by events in the news, I would cruise once again in my little Hot Wheels Corvette on that great relief map in my mind. A front-page story in the *Hartford Courant* would reveal that I-95 through Connecticut averages one death per mile annually, confirming my judgment of that stretch as the worst in the country. In Miami, Florida, just a few blocks from where I had planted my second Interstate flag, the world would follow the dramatic story of Elián Gonzalez. In drought-ridden San Diego County, a wildfire along I-8 would rain ash on San Diego itself, burning luxury homes and forcing families to evacuate. And as Ann and Ed would inform me from the state of Washington, the I-5 corridor through Seattle was eerily empty of traffic during the violent protests against the World Trade Organization.

Meanwhile, right here in Ohio, a campaign would get underway to beautify the overpasses along I-75, in the kind of colorful designs I had seen in the Desert Southwest. Later, to lessen traffic on local highways, the speed limit for trucks on I-80/I-90—the Ohio Turnpike—was raised from 55 mph to 65 mph, the same as for automobiles, increasing accidents involving all kinds of vehicles by twenty-seven percent.

Gasoline would exceed two dollars per gallon for *regular*, making the one-ninety I had paid for *supreme* in Sacramento seem like a bargain. And truckers nationwide would protest proposed federal regulations to cut their daily driving hours from fifteen to twelve. *Fifteen to twelve!* I was glad I hadn't known of the standard practice when I hit the highway.

But it was the little things that would stick with me most, like a photo in the local paper, the kind of AP filler I usually ignore. Taken along I-10 in Arizona, it showed a white-winged dove perched on a spiny saguaro cactus, a full white moon rising behind it, the same moon that had risen so often on the hood of my 'Vette.

Or a brief article about the Great Wall of China, a structure that—with the rediscovery of ancient earthen walls—would gain three hundred and ten miles in length for a grand total of 4,470 miles. Still, the Great Wall of China was but one-tenth the length of the Dwight D. Eisenhower System of Interstate and Defense Highways, the engineering wonder of the modern world.

And I would rely on that system to attend my mother's funeral in Connecticut, where she was laid to rest beside my father, an Interstate flag at the base of their headstone.

* * *

Before returning home to Ada, Ohio, here's a final Interstate Item:

In June of 2005 I telephoned Richard Weingroff, Interstate historian for the U.S. Department of Transportation, who had helped with my research in advance of my grand lap of America. I wanted to know what the Federal Highway Administration had in store for the golden anniversary of the Dwight D. Eisenhower System of Interstate and Defense Highways in 2006.

"The official date of the anniversary is June 29," he told me, "and the FHA is in the process of deciding what to do. It's been reaching out to the American Road and Transportation Builders Association (ARTBA) and the American Association of State Highways and Transportation Officials (AASHTO), both of which were instrumental in the building of the System. Back in 1996, for the fortieth anniversary, one of our administrators retraced Eisenhower's 1919 drive in reverse, driving from San Francisco to the Ellipse here in D.C. Upon arrival, he was met by Vice President Gore with tokens of appreciation. But fifty years is a much more significant number, and so we'll be reaching out to all the media."

"What's on the drawing board?"

"Well, ARTBA is planning a dinner, or perhaps a luncheon, at the Reagan Building near the White House. But AASHTO's planning a commemorative tour like the one our administrator made in 1996, driving from San Francisco to the Ellipse so as to arrive on June 29. You can bet there'll be a lot of hoopla. The Eisenhower Institute here in D.C. is also involved, but it's planning a more serious seminar."

"Is the System complete now?"

"Not yet. There's still one last section to be built, a stretch of I-95 just north of Philadelphia that will connect the Pennsylvania Turnpike to the southern end of the New Jersey Turnpike. But that will be it for the System designated by the 1956 legislation. To tell you the truth, unless someone invents jet packs in the future so we can fly from here to there, the System will never be finished. Right now there are plans to extend I-69 from Indianapolis all the way to the Texas-Mexico border. I-66 will run through Kentucky to Illinois, and I-73 and I-74 will go through the Carolinas all the way to Michigan. But these stretches are not part of the original, designated System. They aren't covered by federal funds from 1956. The states will have to find other means of funding."

When I asked Mr. Weingroff for his own Interstate anecdotes, his answer was ironic: "I'm not a traveler," he said. Then he gave me the name of a person to contact at ARTBA in D.C. so I could get in on the golden anniversary fun.

I began my grand lap of America on September 9, 1999, nearly two years to the day before the terrorist attacks of September 11, 2001. Over the Fourth of July weekend in 2005, as the United States celebrated its 229th birthday, the following piece by editorial page columnist Tom Lucente appeared in the conservative *Lima* (Ohio) *News*, which had carried several stories about my travels. Its concluding paragraphs offer a final—and ominous—Interstate Item:

Let's be clear, the war in Iraq had nothing to do with terrorism—at first. Today, however, Bush has created the world's largest terrorist training camp. Osama bin Laden would be proud.

Every low-level terrorist in the world is flocking to Iraq to engage the most powerful military on the planet—and learn from the experience. How long before the terrorists, thanks to the training Bush is giving them in Iraq, begin placing roadside bombs on America's interstates?

Think about that while driving to work this week.

* * *

In mid-afternoon I arrived in Ada to the familiar crunch of gravel in our driveway, our little green ranch house—just another Monopoly trinket along the Interstates—looking very much intact. I tooted the horn as I had done upon departure, and Elaine came out to greet me with a hug. Then she took my picture as I kissed the ground behind the 'Vette, the rear vanity plate in full view—LAP USA. A symbolic moment to mark the end of my Interstate odyssey. I would give those plates to my sons for Christmas gifts as a reminder to pursue dreams of their own.

Then Elaine helped me carry my things inside. And Saturday morning, right after breakfast, I made some telephone calls and sold the 'Vette.

Home at last.